LTE^{TM} Cellular Narrowband Internet of Things (NB-IoT)

LTE™ Cellular Narrowband Internet of Things (NB-IoT)

Practical Projects for the Cloud and Data Visualization

Dr. Hossam Fattah

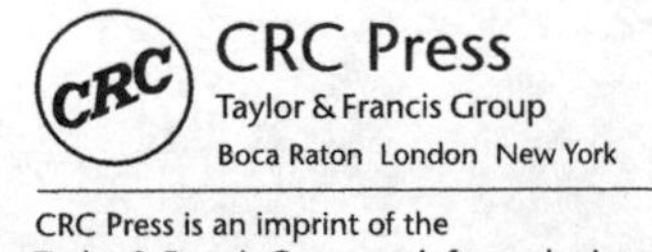

CRC Press is an imprint of the
Taylor & Francis Group, an **informa** business

First edition published 2021
by CRC Press
6000 Broken Sound Parkway NW, Suite 300, Boca Raton, FL 33487-2742

and by CRC Press
2 Park Square, Milton Park, Abingdon, Oxon, OX14 4RN

ISBN: 978-0-367-63629-6 (hbk)
ISBN: 978-1-003-12001-8 (ebk)
ISBN: 978-0-367-69014-4 (pbk)

Typeset in Times
by KnowledgeWorks Global Ltd.

Author Notices

The publisher and author of this book have used their best effort in preparing this book. These efforts include methods, products, instructions, information, or ideas contained in this book. The book includes open source and third-party software and libraries and URLs to web sites and servers. The publisher nor the author make no warranty of any kind, expressed or implied, with regard to the contents of this book nor the publisher nor the author make endorsement of any product or service of any kind expressed or implied. To the full extent of the law, neither the publisher nor the author, assistants, contributors, or editors assume any liability for any damage and/or injury to individuals or property as a matter of products negligence, liability, or otherwise, or from any use. The author and publisher have attempted to trace the copyright holders of all materials reproduced in this publication and apologizes to copyright holders if permissions to publish in this form has not been obtained. If any copyright material has not been acknowledged, please write and let us know so we may rectify in any future reprints.

Preface

Cellular communications and networks have evolved dramatically during the past few decades: WiFi, WiMax, ZigBee, Bluetooth, RFID, 2G/3G systems (GSM®, EDGE, GPRS), and finally 4G/5G systems (LTE™, LTE™ Advanced, LTE™ Advanced Pro, and New Radio). These cellular networks have become the de-facto standard in daily life and routine. They have been used by billions of users around the globe and their use grows every day. This is because most of the cellular technology transformed from a voice-centric technology to a technology that supports modern applications and features such as rich multimedia, Machine Learning (ML), Artificial Intelligence (AI), native cloud and virtualization support, big data, and smart applications.

5G cellular technology is the most recent broadband cellular technology aiming at increasing data rates and providing connected devices that can be used in different smart applications such as home appliances, smart transportation, smart building, and smart cities.

The Internet of Things is a network of connected devices where each device performs a specific function. IoT devices can be used in home automation which includes lighting, heating and air conditioning, media, and security systems. IoT devices used for elder care help elderly individuals, such as with sensors that monitor for medical emergencies such as falls or seizures. IoT devices used for smart transportation provide smart traffic control, smart parking, electronic toll collection systems, logistics and fleet management, vehicle control, safety, and road assistance. IoT devices used for smart farming measure temperature, rainfall, humidity, wind speed, pest infestation, and soil content and are used to automate farming techniques, make informed decisions to improve quality and quantity, minimize risk and waste, and reduce effort required to manage crops.

LTE technology offers a new cellular Internet of Things called NB-IoT. NB-IoT devices use a similar networking protocol to those used in normal LTE mobile and cellular phones and handhelds while at the same time keeping NB-IoT devices much simpler and cheaper than legacy LTE cellular devices. This means NB-IoT has the advantage of being able to coexist with existing 4G and 5G systems and speeds up its deployment and use cases. NB-IoT is the first IoT technology used for cellular communication. It provides the largest area coverage, in terms of square Km, and outdoor coverage compared with its IoT counterparts such as Bluetooth or WiFi IoT.

The NB-IoT technology presented in this book is based on 3GPP™ Release 13 technical specifications, which is the pre-5G technology. Release 13 is fundamentally the same LTE technology as in the 5G LTE technical specifications where the latter is released in Release 15. Pre-5G and 5G technical specifications for the cellular LTE NB-IoT are very similar and there are no fundamental differences between the two releases in terms of protocol stack layers and over-all operation. Yet,

5G LTE technical specifications in Release 15 introduce more improvement and higher speed for NB-IoT devices.

This book provides hands-on and practical experience of how to use the cellular NB-IoT for different applications, with the cloud, and visualize the data emitted from NB-IoT devices. The book provides many Arduino™ projects on how to connect an NB-IoT device to the cellular network and infrastructure; how to use networking protocols with the NB-IoT device and mobile operator; how to use sensors and actuators; how to connect the NB-IoT device to the cloud; and how data visualization is used to display data in graphical and colorful charts.

The book explains the cellular NB-IoT which is used for cellular connectivity to cellular networks. It starts by giving detailed instructions on how to configure and control the NB-IoT device through AT commands; followed by instructions on how to connect the device to the cloud platform; how to use the cloud for uploading and downloading data transmitted or received by the NB-IoT device; and how to use JSON-formatted text for communication between the device and the cloud.

Data visualization is the technique where the raw data from an NB-IoT device is rendered into insightful, graphical charts and dashboards. Data visualization is essential to be used with NB-IoT devices because a picture is worth a thousand words. It is easier for users to interpret data through charts rather than from raw numbers and data. Using Google Maps, a project is presented that explains how to plot the geo-location of the device on the map and how to use charts for plotting sensor data such as a temperature dataset.

Arduino projects are presented and explained for different application domains such as for networking, sensors, or actuators. Arduino projects are given in four parts. Part I explains the networking projects where it shows how to connect the device to the cellular and mobile operator network and performs communication through using different network protocols such as TCP, HTTP, SSL, or MQTT. Part II provides Arduino projects that are aimed at understanding the microcontroller unit and how to use it for basic and fundamental Arduino projects. Part III provides the sensors projects, while Part IV presents the actuators projects such as servo motor, DC motor, or relay.

Arduino projects are given in different chapters of this book. Chapter 3 explains how to install the Arduino software and IDE required to run and use the NB-IoT device and its projects. Chapter 4 provides an overview about the hardware board, which is used throughout this book, including both the microcontroller and the cellular NB-IoT modem units. Chapter 5 explains the AT commands to configure and operate the cellular NB-IoT modem. Chapter 6 and 7 explain the data serialization and deserialization, the cloud platform, and how to use them with a NB-IoT device to transmit or receive data between the cloud and the NB-IoT device. Chapter 8 explains data visualization and how to use datasets stored on the cloud and to visualize them

Arduino networking projects are included in Chapters 9 to 15 and they aim at explaining how to use the NB-IoT device to make a connection to the cellular network while running protocols such as TCP, SSL, MQTT, or HTTP. Networking projects include a project that shows how the device can be used for location and GPS application and another project to update the firmware of the NB-IoT device. Fundamental and essential Arduino projects for the microcontroller are given in Chapters 16 to 26 and they explain how to use the microcontroller with essential projects. Sensors projects are explained in Chapters 27 to 34. Sensor applications use the NB-IoT modem to upload data to the cloud. Actuator projects are given in Chapters 35 to 37 and they explain how to use the microcontroller to control actuators such as a motor or relay. Controlling an actuator can be done from the cloud and is demonstrated in the actuator projects.

Arduino projects presented in this book are using Arduino IDE and tools. Not only does the book present many projects about the LTE cellular NB-IoT, but it also aids developers with developing their own projects and using different hardware sensors and actuators to build new use cases and scenarios. The projects presented in this book are suitable for a wide range of ages and skills, from beginners, to intermediates, to professionals.

Bothell, WA, USA
August 2020

Dr. Hossam Fattah

Acknowledgements

LTE cellular NB-IoT technology is a new and challenging technology. It involved a long process until the final version of this technology became mature and published by the standard and authority body, 3GPP. The NB-IoT technical specifications and reports have been drafted, finalized, and released by many stakeholders and partners including professional individuals, working groups, companies, regulatory bodies, and researchers. We acknowledge their efforts and the final technical specifications that have been released. Without the effort of those stakeholders and their partnership, this book and this technology would not have come to light.

Finally, the author provides his gratitude to the publisher, assistants, and editors for their continuous effort and support in improving the materials and presentations of this book.

Contents

List of Listings

Chapter 1

About This Book

1.1 Organization of the Book

This book is a hands-on and practical guide for the new LTE cellular Internet of things known as Narrowband Internet of Things (NB-IoT). The book provides projects using Arduino, Google map, and Node.js for data visualization. Projects are used for cellular networking and protocols, sensing and measurements, controlling and actuating, plotting GPS geo-locations, and data visualization. The book is organized into the following chapters:

- Chapter 2: Provides an introduction about LTE and cellular NB-IoT. It covers an introduction about 5G and LTE systems, 3GPP NB-IoT protocol stack, NB-IoT core network, NB-IoT use cases, NB-IoT in the 5G new radio, and the use case for smart city. Readers are advised to refer to a companion book titled **"5G LTE Narrowband Internet of Things (NB-IoT)"** [1] if a deeper understanding of the full protocol stack of NB-IoT technology as released by 3GPP standardization body is needed.
- Chapter 3: Explains the Arduino software tools need to be installed and setup to run the Arduino projects for the NB-IoT.
- Chapter 4: Explains the NB-IoT hardware board for Arduino that is used throughput this book to run the different projects. It explains the microcontroller and the NB-IoT modem on the hardware board, board technical specifications, and pin definitions.
- Chapter 5: Explains the AT commands. It covers a set of AT commands used to configure and control the NB-IoT modem. AT commands covers commands for different protocols such as TCP/IP, SSL, MQTT, HTTP, GNSS, file, and firmware update commands. It also explains the configuration needed to connect with the mobile operator network.
- Chapter 6: Explains data format used for exchanging information between an NB-IoT device and the cloud. It covers the JSON and CBOR data formats. It explains two methods used with each data format; serialization and deserialization. It provides steps to install and run JSON and CBOR libraries and provides Arduino projects for serializing and deserializing JSON and CBOR data formats.

- Chapter 7: Explains the cloud and how to use it with the NB-IoT device. Amazon Web Services (AWS) is used as the cloud operator and is used through all Arduino projects. It explains how to setup cloud for receiving or transmitting data to the NB-IoT device and how to store NB-IoT data in the cloud. It also shows the cloud dashboard for real-time communication and testing the NB-IoT device.

- Chapter 8: Explains data visualization of the NB-IoT data through the use of Google map and charts to visualize data stored on the cloud by the NB-IoT device. This chapter explains how to use Google map APIs to plot GPS location of the NB-IoT device. It also explains how to use Chart.js, the JavaScript library, to visualize sensor dataset such as temperature.

- Chapter 9 to Chapter 15: Covers the cellular networking projects that can be used with the NB-IoT device. Lessons and Arduino projects provided show how to turn on the NB-IoT modem and how to use the modem to run different networking protocols such as TCP, SSL, MQTT, GPS, and HTTP. An Arduino project on how to update the NB-IoT firmware is also explained.

- Chapter 16 to Chapter 26: Covers different Arduino projects that explains the capability of the NB-IoT hardware board and how to use it for different lessons such as RGB LEDs, keyboard, buzzers, push buttons, joystick, clock, IR remote, RFID, and 7-segment display.

- Chapter 27 to Chapter 34: Covers sensors projects. It covers different Arduino projects used for sensing and measurements such as photocell, ultrasonic, tilt, temperature, humidity, water-level, thermometer, gyroscope, accelerometer sensors. All sensors projects show how to interface and upload sensing data to the cloud.

- Chapter 35 to Chapter 37: Covers actuators projects. It covers different Arduino projects used for actuating, and controlling devices such as stepper motor, servo motor, and relay. All actuator projects show how to interface and control the motors from the cloud.

- Chapter 38: Lists all hardware parts and components used throughout projects explained in this book.

1.1.1 How to Read This Book

This book presents the new LTE cellular NB-IoT technology as released by 3GPP in Release 13 which is the pre-5G technology. In this edition of the book, we provide practical guidance and lessons on how to use this NB-IoT for practical projects that can be used in everyone daily life and needs and for home, office, or industrial applications and use cases.

For the purpose of this book, an NB-IoT hardware board, based on Quectel BG96 chipset, is designed and manufactured to demo applications and use cases for the LTE cellular NB-IoT. The NB-IoT hardware board is compatible with Arduino software and tools. Arduino is an easy to use and open-source electronics and programming language platform that is suitable for wide spectrum of users and skills. Users who are beginners, intermediate, professional and whether they are teachers or students can thus exercise and prototype the NB-IoT applications and lessons presented in this book.

The book contains several and diverse lessons which use Arduino, Google map, and Node.js. They represent the most essential and fundamental lessons that are common lessons and practical lessons to use with the NB-IoT. More derived lessons can be extracted from the lessons presented in the book. As the NB-IoT hardware board is Arduino-compatible, users can independently build and prototype their own projects based on their specific needs.

Lessons includes hardware components required to run the project, schematic and breadboard diagrams, and Arduino sketches. Fritzing is an open-source software editor for drawing schematic and breadboard diagrams. Schematic and breadboard diagrams in this book are provided in Fritzing for easy understanding and implementation of the NB-IoT Arduino projects. The book contains a lot of illustrations and diagrams to help in digesting and implementing the NB-IoT use cases.

NB-IoT data is synonymous with data visualization as the latter is the technique used to visualize NB-IoT dataset in graphical format easy for interpretation and for quicker insights and decision making. The book covers data visualization through two main examples. Use of Google map to plot GPS locations and the use of charts for plotting raw data. Google map, when used with NB-IoT devices, facilitates wide range of geo-location applications such as tracker, navigation, and fleet management. Charts are rich graphical elements that can be used to plot many of sensors data such as humidity, proximity, or thermometer datasets.

Users interested in understanding the protocol stack and 3GPP technical specifications about 5G LTE NB-IoT can obtain the book **"5G LTE Narrowband Internet of Things (NB-IoT)"** available through CRC press at `https://www.routledge.com/` [1]. This book serves as a sequel book that provides practical experiments and lessons on how to use the NB-IoT technology.

This edition of the book is one of its kind in the area of practical uses of the NB-IoT technology and serves as a handbook for people who need to practice and exercise this technology or are looking for guidance about how to use this new technology. The book presents the most recent and up-to-date information and specifications about NB-IoT. The book is a valuable material for technical and non-technical readers who are willing to learn and find comprehensive information about the NB-IoT technology.

The book concludes after providing a comprehensive number of projects that use Arduino, Google maps, and Node.js. The projects are used with the cloud and their data are visualized. We wish the reader to enjoy the book, the practical projects, and the information provided, and keep the book among his(her) library of books for 5G and cellular technology.

1.1.2 Software and Hardware Tools Used in This Book

Software used in this book uses the following tools and can be downloaded at the following URLs:

- Arduino IDE: `https://www.arduino.cc/en/main/software`.
- The NB-IoT hardware board: `https://github.com/5ghub/NB-IoT`.
- Arduino board package, sketches, and library: `https://github.com/5ghub/NB-IoT`.

- Quectel BG96 modem driver for Windows: https://github.com/5ghub/NB-IoT
- Node.js: https://nodejs.org/en/.
- Amazon Web Services Software Development Kit (SDK) for Node.js: https://docs.aws.amazon.com/sdk-for-javascript/v2/developer-guide/installing-jssdk.html.
- Chart.js library: https://www.chartjs.org.
- Visual Studio Code: https://code.visualstudio.com/.

1.1.3 Conventions Used in the Book

The following are the typographical conventions used in this book:

loop(), bitSet(), int
Arduino function names and data types of the Arduino programming language are colored according to the Arduino IDE coloring scheme.

Bold Text
Functions names or variables used in Arduino sketch such as **Foo()** and **Bar()**. Bold text is also used for button name, menu item, file name, software class name, software object name, API, or HTML tags.

0b00011000
Binary numbers followed by eight bit of binary values.

0xFE189
Hexadecimal numbers followed by a number of digits in hexadecimal format.

1.1.4 Security Keys and Certificates

The book uses many API keys, public and private keys, and X.509 security certificates. All of them are long sequence of characters. Shorter sequences of characters are used instead to protect the security and integrity of web and cloud services involved and keep the Arduino sketches short and focused on how to use and utilize these security keys and certificates. However, with real communication scenarios with web server or clouds, these security keys and certificates are to be replaced by the real security keys and certificates.

1.1.5 Hardware Parts

LTE cellular NB-IoT technology is exercised and explained in this book through the use of many use cases and hardware parts for sensing, measuring, or actuating. The main lessons and projects presented in this book explain and guide the reader through different uses cases and scenarios, how to utilize and integrate NB-IoT with the cloud technology, and how to visualize NB-IoT data. The hardware parts used are widely available from different online stores and electronics suppliers. They are affordable in price and available in the market. However, projects presented can be extended to use other hardware parts that can have more functionalities or have other unique feature. Reader is encouraged to use and experiment with more use cases and new hardware parts and integrate them with cloud and visualize NB-IoT data using the guidelines presented in this book.

1.1.6 Feedback of the Book

When you get this book and read through it, please leave a feedback and review of the book on the same place where you purchased this book.

Chapter 2

LTE Cellular Narrowband Internet of Things (NB-IoT)

2.1 4G and 5G System

LTE is a known wireless and cellular network that provides cellular connectivity to mobile phones and users round the world. LTE marks the start of the cellular system known as 4G (fourth Generation) system. 4G system is released and published in a series of documents called Releases. The organization responsible for releasing these documents are 3GPP (3rd Generation Partnership Project) (`www.3gpp.org`) [2].

LTE or 4G cellular technology has been first introduced in 3GPP Release 8 in 2008 as a new broadband cellular technology. LTE saw its first commercial deployment in 2009. 4G comes with advanced capabilities and features such as higher peak data rates (300Mbps on DL and 75Mbps on UL), improved system capacity and coverage, better spectrum efficiency, low latency, reduced operating costs, and seamless integration with existing 2G/3G systems.

5G is the next and most released advanced version of the 4G system [3]. 5G wireless communication network is the next generation connectivity and technology for the next decade and beyond that is set up to exceed 4G systems in capability and features. 5G technical specifications start in 3GPP Release 15.

5G technology promises a large number of state-of-art devices called Narrowband Internet of Things (NB-IoT) for a connected world. 5G is delivering a rich number of features such as connected cars (Vehicle-to-Everything (V2X)), machine type communication, device-to-device communication, small cells, and relay networks.

In 5G technology, it introduces Machine Type Communication (MTC) and Narrowband Internet of Things NB-IoT. MTC is a technology that enables communication between devices and the underlying data transport infrastructure. The data communication can occur between an MTC device and a server, or directly between two MTC devices. MTC manifests itself in a wide range of applications and services. Those application can be found in different industries, such as healthcare, manufacturing, process automation, energy, and utilities. MTC devices support different network technologies such as point-to-point, multi-hop, ad-hoc networks, or mesh wireless networks.

NB-IoT is one realization of MTC. However, NB-IoT has lower complexity and simpler implementation. MTC and NB-IoT devices are communicating with each other and with servers and applications residing on the network. NB-IoT can be used for smart sensors, such as ambient lights, temperature, or humidity sensors. In addition, the number of these NB-IoT devices can be large; ranging from up to few per household to hundreds of thousands per square kilometer. NB-IoT devices are often battery-powered and without any other external power source. The number of devices is expected to be ultra-large with an estimated device density of 100,000 devices per square kilometer.

2.2 LTE Cellular Narrowband Internet of Things (NB-IoT)

3GPP introduced a new type of network called Narrowband IoT (NB-IoT). It has been introduced in Release 13 and has been extended in Release 15. NB-IoT continue to be adopted and enhanced in Release 16 and future releases. Release 13 is a pre-5G technology while Release 15 marks the start of the 5G technology. NB-IoT technology in Release 13 or Release 15 are fundamentally the same in terms of protocol stack layers, control-plane, and data-plane operations. Release 15 introduces new category, known as Cat-NB2, which provides higher speed than Cat-NB1 [4, 5]. In addition, Release 15 added more protocol stack enhancements and optimizations such as more frequency bands.

NB-IoT is designed to connect a large number of devices in a wide range of application domains forming so-called Internet of Things (IoT). Connected devices are to communicate through cellular infrastructure. NB-IoT devices supports data rate from 10s of bits per second (bps) up to few hundreds of Kbps. NB-IoT is also planned to introduce advanced features for massive IoT which are high numbers of NB-IoT per square Km estimated to be 1 million devices per square Km.

NB-IoT is a Low Power Wide Area Network (LPWAN) [6] solution that operates in licensed spectrum bands. 3GPP includes this technology as a part of LTE cellular networks to benefit from the big ecosystem offered by LTE technology and mobile operators.

Not only does NB-IoT enhance existing cellular uses cases, but it expands to a new era of use cases and scenarios; massive IoT, smart homes, smart cities, smart transportation, smart grids, smart utilities and meters, wearables and remote sensors, autonomous and self-driving vehicles, object tracking, mobile virtual reality, remote control and process automation for aviation and robotics, and mission-critical control. It is projected that, over the coming few years, there will be an explosion in the number of IoT connected devices. For example, by 2025, it is expected that more than 5 billion devices will be connected through NB-IoT.

2.3 NB-IoT Applications and Scenarios

Many of the NB-IoT deployment scenarios will be using sensors or actuators. Sensors and actuators are becoming the endpoints for NB-IoT networks, collecting increasing amount of context aware data and information (e.g, location, weather conditions) and injecting a large amount of structured and unstructured data into the networks, applications, and servers. Data generated by sensors are transported and delivered by NB-IoT devices which ultimately facilitate stakeholders and decision makers to analyze and apply insights in real-time. Big data, analytics, and predictions have thus become an apparent synonymous for NB-IoT. Those NB-IoT devices used as sensors can be used for the following applications:

- Measuring weather condition such as temperature, humidity, pressure, and ambient lights.
- Control and steer motors, gates and doors, lights, mechanical relays and switches, or home appliances.
- Detecting sounds, object location and orientation, asset tracking, fleet management, or object distances and proximity.

The following examples are now possible with the NB-IoT:

- Smart Home: Lighting systems, smart appliances, connected TV sets, gaming consoles, sound and theatre systems, smoke and alarm systems, wearables, and kids and pets tracking devices.
- Smart City: Monitoring highway traffic lights, and street intersections, monitoring and control of infrastructure grids such as electricity, gas, and sewage, public safety and disaster management, video surveillance, traffic violations, and law enforcement [7].
- Smart Transportation: Communicating between vehicles, pedestrians, or cyclists for traffic warning, collisions, and accident avoidance, traffic safety and traffic sign enforcement, public buses, trains, and underground transportation information and management, and public parking and parking meter communication.

NB-IoT devices can be sensors or actuators which form a large number of connected devices or connected things such as in smart buildings and sensors in a gas station.

2.3.1 NB-IoT Sensors

A sensor measures, determines, or senses a particular parameter of a system or environment. The sensor reports this parameter in a manner that can be compiled and understood by humans or other devices. Example of sensors are weather, ambient, or thermometer sensors which sense climate condition, light, or human body heat.

2.3.2 NB-IoT Actuators

An actuator is a special type of device that takes an action based on a system behavior. A sensor reports the status of a particular parameter of a system whereas an actuator can act to influence that parameter or other parts of the system. An example of an actuator is a pipeline motor that is used in a natural-gas or oil refinery plant where the motor controls the volume of gas or oil flow in the pipeline according to an internal pipeline pressure. A flow relay can also shut down the pipeline valve in case of emergency or other unnormal conditions.

2.4 NB-IoT Core Network

NB-IoT devices are connected to the mobile operator base station, known as eNodeB. The eNodeB is connected to the core network. Core network contains the mobile operator network servers such as the server that authenticate and authorize the device to use the core network and be able to transmit and receive data through the core network. Authorization and authentication of the device are done by exchanging the data stored on the USIM used by the device. The core network also contains an Access Point (AP) and the device has to specify the Access Point Name (APN) when establishing a connection with the eNodeB. AP provides the NB-IoT device with connectivity to the Internet. The APN is the name of this access point which provides internet connectivity to the NB-IoT device. The APN is a name which follows the same rules of DNS naming convention.

Figure 2.1 shows one application of NB-IoT in smart buildings and smart metering where NB-IoT devices are connected to the eNodeB and they collect a large amount of data and information and send them to a remote server for processing.

Devices can range from simple wearables, such as a smart watch or a set of sensors embedded in clothing, to more sophisticated wearable devices monitoring body vital statistics (e.g., heart rate, blood pressure). They can also be non-wearable devices that communicate in a Personal Area Network (PAN) such as a set of home appliances (e.g., smart thermostat and entry key), or electronic devices in an office setting (e.g., smart printers), or a smart flower pot that can be remotely activated

2.5 Message Queue Telemetry Transport (MQTT)

NB-IoT devices requires a special application-layer protocol suitable for efficient data-transfer to transmit and receive their data. The widely used application-layer protocol is the Message Queue Telemetry Transport (MQTT) [8].

MQTT is an application-layer transport protocol that runs on top of the TCP/IP protocols. MQTT is suitable for NB-IoT devices that have small memory and processing power, are battery-powered, or have scarce bandwidth. MQTT is lightweight and simple messaging protocol that is best suited for NB-IoT devices and MTC.

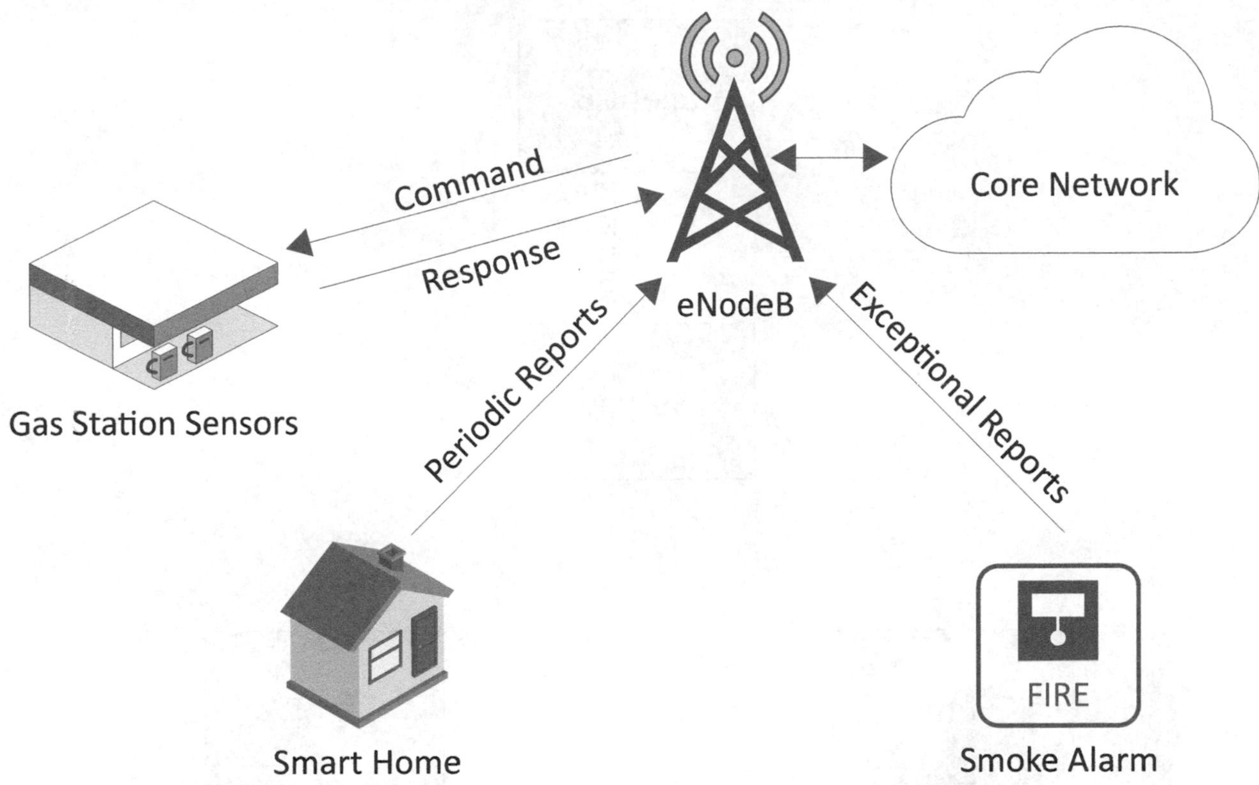

Figure 2.1: NB-IoT in Smart Building and Metering.

MQTT uses publish/subscribe model to communicate between a transmitter and receiver. In this model, one-to-many distribution is provided. Transmitting applications or devices do not need to know anything about the receiver, not even the destination address. Receiver, on the other hand, does not need to know about the transmitter as well. The publish/subscribe mode is illustrated in Figure 2.2. In the figure, a single device publishes its data to the server while other devices may subscribe to the server to receive such data from the publisher.

NB-IoT device publishes its messages, through the eNodeB, to the MQTT server (the MQTT server is also called a broker). Other MQTT clients, connected to an eNodeB, can subscribe to the MQTT server to receive the data they are interested in.

2.5.1 Publish/Subscribe Model

MQTT protocol is using a publish/subscribe model. The center piece of this mode is the use of what is called **topics**. MQTT devices are either a client or server. A client can publish messages to a topic. A client can also subscribe to a topic that pertains to it and thereby receives any message published to this topic by any other client that publishes to this topic.

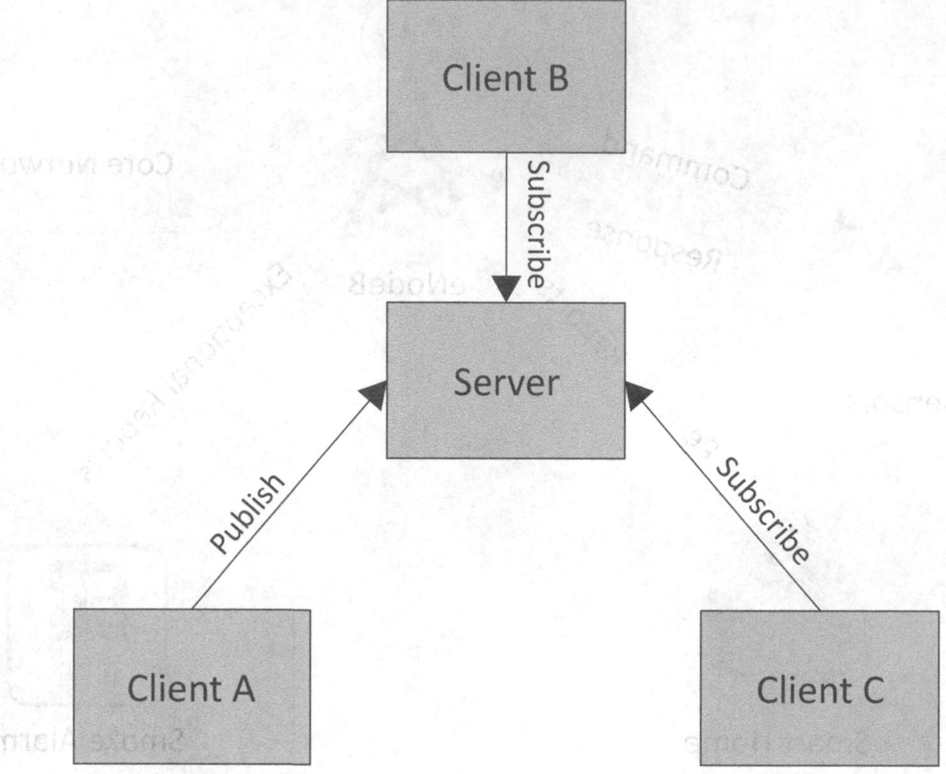

Figure 2.2: MQTT Client and Server.

2.5.2 Topic and Subscription

Client in MQTT publishes messages to a topic (or a number of topics). A topic is typically a representation of subject areas. Client can sign up to receive particular messages by subscribing to a topic. Subscriptions can be explicit which limits the messages that are received to the specific topic at hand. Subscriptions can also use wildcard designators, such as a number sign (#), to receive messages for a number of related topics.

2.5.3 Retained Messages

MQTT server can keep the message even after sending it to all subscribers. If a new subscription is submitted for the same topic, any retained messages are then sent to the new subscribing client.

2.5.4 Will

When a client connects to a server, it can inform the server that it has a will, or a message, that should be published to a specific topic or topics in the event of an unexpected disconnection. A will is particularly useful in alarm situation where a user must know immediately when a remote sensor has lost connection with the network.

2.5.5 Quality of Service Levels

MQTT supports three quality of service (QoS) levels for message delivery to the server. Each level designating a higher level of effort by the server to ensure that the message gets delivered to clients. QoS is symmetric which means that the same QoS level is guaranteed both from client to server and from server to other clients. Higher QoS levels ensure higher reliability for message delivery but can consume more network bandwidth or subject the message to delays due to retransmissions. MQTT supports three level of message delivery as follows:

- QoS Level 0: At most once: This is a one-way handshake. Sender publishes the message only once. Server can receive the message only once or not at all. No retry is performed by the sender and no response is sent by the server. Message can be lost between sender and server.
- QoS Level 1: At least once: This is a two-way handshake. Sender publishes the message and receives an ACK from the server. If an ACK is not received, the sender publishes the message again. Server receives the message and sends an ACK. If the sender does not receive an ACK from the server, it retransmits the message again until an ACK is received. Message can be duplicated between sender and server.
- QoS Level 2: Exactly once: This is a four-way handshake. Sender publishes the message and receives an ACK from server. If an ACK is not received, the sender publishes the message again. When the sender receives an ACK, it sends a RELEASE message to the server. The sender expects to receive an ACK for the RELEASE message and if not, it retransmits the RELEASE message. If the server receives a duplicate message, it responds by an ACK and never send the duplicate message again to others.

QoS level 0 is lowest and loosest QoS while QoS level 2 is the highest and stringent QoS level. NB-IoT device can choose the QoS that is most appropriate to the application.

Figure 2.3 shows an example if using MQTT for smart application that collects meter readings and uploads it to an MQTT server hosted on a cloud. Data processing and insights are provided on a real-time dashboard where a supervisor or user can interpret the data and generate usage statistics. The cloud can be used to host the MQTT server. In this book, we used Amazon Web Services (AWS) for NB-IoT as the cloud to demo how NB-IoT can connect with it and upload data to this cloud or receive data from it.

2.6 5G New Radio (NR)

5G New Radio (NR) is a new Radio Access Technology (RAT) currently being developed by 3GPP that is designed and aimed at being the global standard for the air interface of 5G cellular networks.

5G LTE and 5G NR are different technical specifications and they are specified by 3GPP in different releases. 5G LTE is defined in series 36 while 5G NR are defined in series 37 and series 38 [9]. 5G NR is built upon 5G LTE specifications with the addition of major features, improvements, and more frequency band. 5G NR initial phase of development and technical specifications

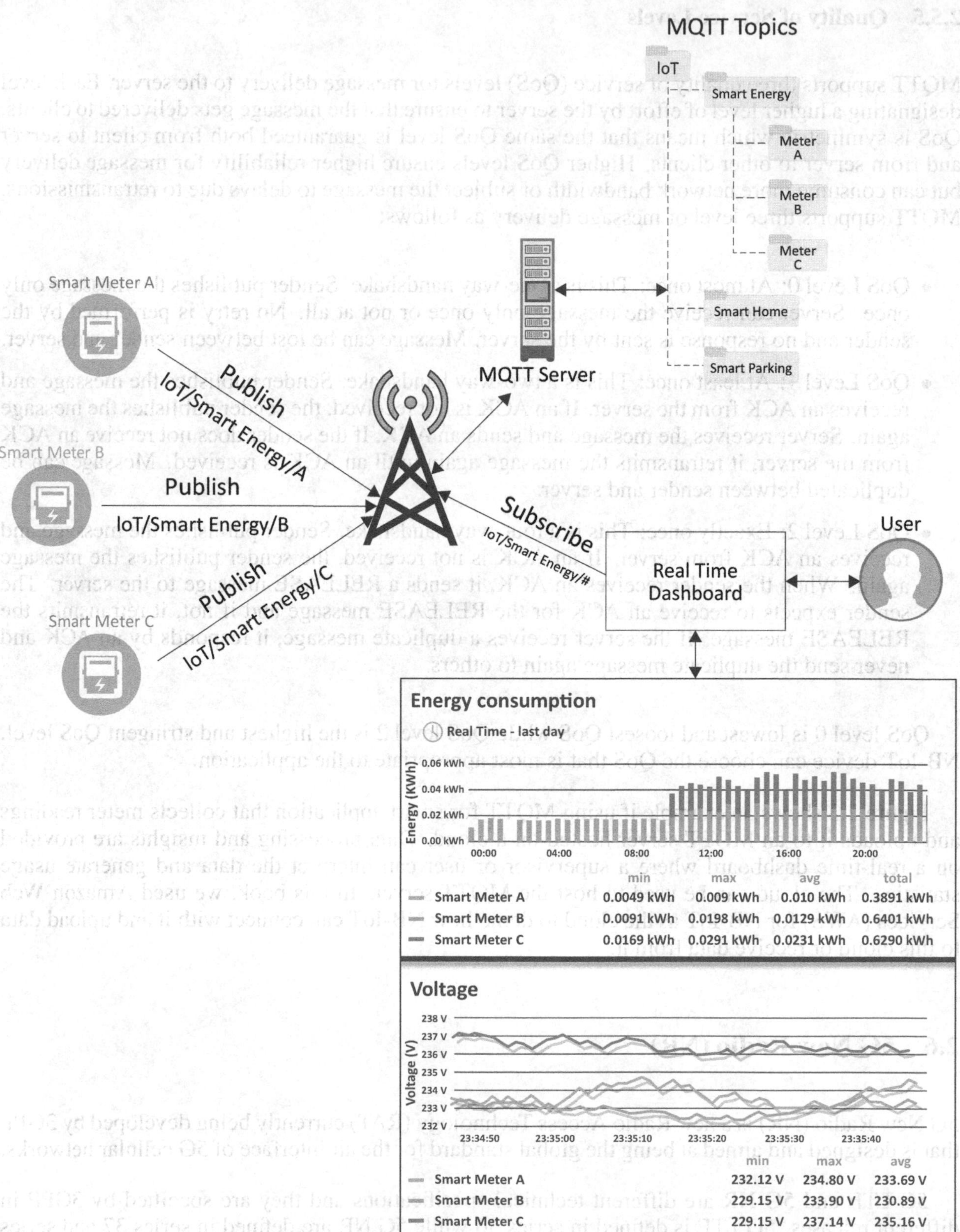

Figure 2.3: MQTT with the Cloud and Analytic.

has been completed in Release 15 and Release 16, and is currently under development in Release 17 and beyond. In addition, 5G NR network depends on 5G LTE network and infrastructure for initial deployment and commercialization by mobile operators around the world.

5G, whether LTE or NR, are providing higher speeds that benefits the users and enable much more applications that were not possible under previous technology. 5G usage scenarios focus on the following three distinct areas:

- Massive Internet of Things and Machine Type Communications (mIoT & mMTC): These are the types of devices and applications that do require connectivity to everything and everywhere. These connected "things" can be smart phones, sensors, actuators, cameras, vehicles, etc., ranging from low-complexity devices to highly complex and advanced devices. A significant number of connected devices are expected to use the cellular 5G system.
- Enhanced Mobile Broadband (eMBB) applications: These are the type of services that require super-fast multi-gigabit speeds to support fast downloading, high-quality UHD video streaming, 3D videos, etc. These high speeds can be achieved by the use of higher frequencies, especially in the millimeter-wave region. This way, large channel bandwidths can be used, and together with advanced spectrum efficient techniques such as carrier aggregation, MIMO, and high modulation schemes will support super-fast data rates.
- Ultra-reliable, Low-latency Communications (URLLC): This is the 5G area that will provide services with the most demanding requirements on very low latency and very high reliability. 5G systems should be able to provide end-to-end latency as low as 1 *ms* for applications that require ultra-low response times and ultra-high reliability such as e-Health, remote surgery, tactile Internet, autonomous driving, real-time traffic control optimization, emergency and disaster response, smart grid, or efficient industrial communications.

NB-IoT is a LPWA and will continue to serve LPWA 5G NR use cases and coexist alongside other components of 5G NR which meet the various 5G NR use cases. Mobile operators deploy different components and features of 5G NR, will also deploy NB-IoT to leverage their investment and secure more streams of revenue and income to their mobile networks.

Current proposals for future 3GPP releases such as Release 16 and Release 17 is that NB-IoT continues to be the LPWA solution and serves the 5G NR LPWA use cases and scenarios. Potential enhancements to the already coexistence between NR and LTE-NB-IoT in Release 15 may be studied and additional improvement can be standardized if useful and not adversely affecting legacy NB-IoT devices.

2.7 Case Study for Smart City: City of Coral Gables, Florida

The city of Coral Gables, located in Florida, USA, became the leading city in the USA for promoting the development of a smart city ecosystem that fosters IoT innovation [10]. The smart city engineering framework features IoT sensors and actuators platform and smart connected devices for numerous applications. The city IoT network relies on a transport layer of high-speed resilient communications with wireless infrastructure that covers the city most critical arteries, facilities, smart districts in Downtown as well as university campus and residential areas. The city IoT systems rely on a cloud platform and data visualization. Realtime IoT data is visualized and presented to the public and all stakeholders for consumption and collaboration via the Coral Gables **Smart City Hub** public platform.

The smart city solution implements a **Smart City Hub** as shown in Figure 2.4 [10] and available at `www.coralgables.com/smartcity`. The smart city hub is a public collaboration and open data platform that supports a beautiful and smart city. It aggregates in one place many elements: a data marketplace, an application store, transparency portals, citizen engagement tools, enterprise systems and eGovernment city services, IoT sensors and actuators data and dashboards, crime intelligence center, data platforms, GIS applications and open data, APIs and developer tools, and many more features and services. Together these interconnected and interoperable elements foster transparency, value creation, open data and analytics, actionable information, efficiencies, citizen engagement, mobility, accessibility, crowdsourcing, inclusion, and collaboration.

Some of the city use cases and applications include environmental sensors (temperature and humidity, water levels, air quality, voice and noise detectors); smart parking sensors (available/occupied spots detection), a street network of actuators for smart lighting controllers, drones, fleet management systems using geo-locations and GPS data, RF sensors (traffic behavioral patterns and identification), traffic sensors (pedestrians, vehicles, bicycles, visitors), public safety sensors (CCTV, cameras, smart policing and street safety devices), smart city digital interactive kiosks, smart building structural health monitoring sensors, telemetry sensors and actuators, connected vehicles, among other uses.

For the city, IoT sensor data is strategic and actionable information for traffic engineers, public safety units, urban planners, city management, first responders, academia, businesses, technologists, the public, and citizen. The smart city hub collects different IoT sensor and actuators data and information. Data at the smart city hub is aggregated and analyzed. Smart city hub is used to help Coral Gables engineers designing safer roads, crosswalks, curbs, and multimodal mobility infrastructure, and help urban planners and city officials measuring development impact and effectiveness of city infrastructure projects and government initiatives. Smart city hub also helps local businesses improve sales and marketing strategies, helps academic researchers conduct studies (environmental, crime, urban, traffic, technology), and helps developers, builders and real estate agencies with tools and actionable information for development and construction. Smart city hub can be used by public safety, emergency management officers and first responders with situational awareness and high visibility.

The smart city hub implements a model called "Horizontal Integration" model as shown in Figure 2.5 [11]. This model implements a system engineering topology and architecture which is data centric for smart city interoperability. In this design, a centralized city dashboard provides city leaders and staff comprehensive and robust visibility over enterprise functions and environmental variables. The design includes key city metrics and performance indicators by location and by discipline, as well as the ability to retrieve geo-location, real-time IoT sensor data and information from multiple and diverse sources connected to the data marketplace through a central cloud and data bus and centralized API management.

Figure 2.4: Smart City Hub with IoT.

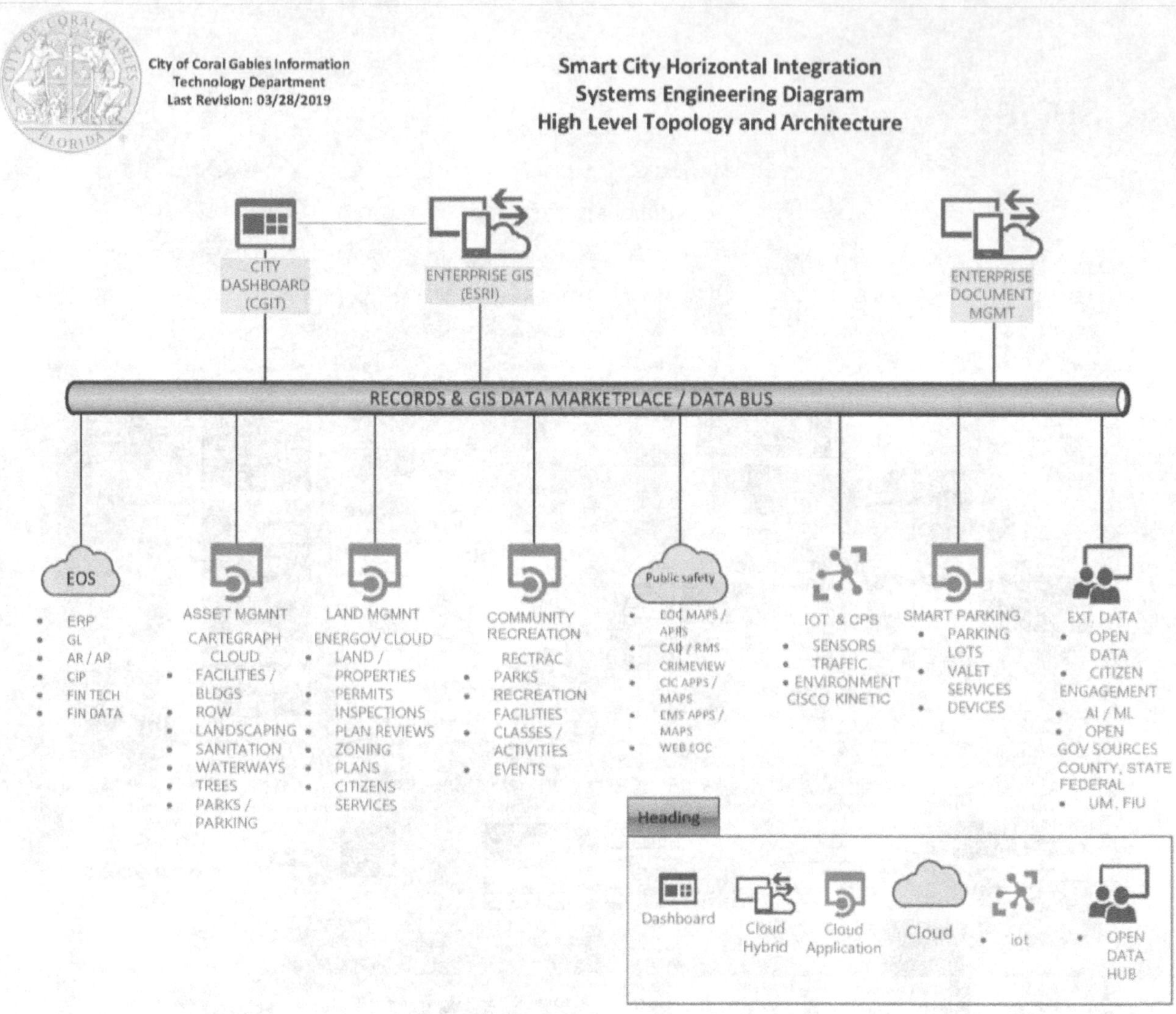

Figure 2.5: Smart City Horizontal Integration Model.

2.7.1 IoT Use Cases in the Smart City Hub

Smart city hub utilizes a lot of IoT sensors and actuators that are located and distributed throughout the city, its streets, buildings, public lands and parks, business centers, school and university, campuses, health and fitness centers, vehicles and fleets, residential areas, and other stationary or moving objects in the city. The IoT sensors and actuators are used for sensing, measuring, or controlling the following applications:

- Environmental sensors (water quality and flooding sensors, air quality, noise, carbon emissions (CO/CO2) and air pollutants).
- Smart lighting controllers and smart lights.
- Traffic sensors (vehicles, pedestrians, bicycles metrics).

- Smart building management and automation systems (HVAC, energy, lighting, smart grid energy system).
- Smart parking sensors in garage gates (realtime occupancy to the city parking lots, street parking smart devices).
- RF sensors for traffic pattern detection and behavioral analytics.
- Public safety sensors (geo-location, automated license plate readers, CCTV, speed and red-light enforcement devices, telemedicine technology and Electronic Patient Care (ePCR) mobile systems).
- Fleet management, connected mobility, transportation (trolley tracker, fleet route optimization).
- Telemetry sensors and actuators.
- Drones for public safety, first responders, and various emergency operations such as hurricane-impacted areas with restricted access due to flooding, fallen trees and other terrain hazards.
- Smart City interactive touch-screen Kiosks, with embedded environmental sensors and smart applications.
- Mobile workforce and engaged citizens with smart devices connected to the city enterprise systems and smart city hub mobile applications, open APIs and collaboration platforms.
- Structural Health Monitoring (SHM) and new public safety building smart technology design (servo-velocimeters and servo-accelerometers for wind-induced vibration, anemometers for wind profile, stress sensors, concrete health sensors, roof substrate moisture sensor, and others).

2.7.2 Smart City Hub IoT Dashboard

IoT dashboards are one of the most visited and used features of the Coral Gables smart city hub. The hub is a "digital supermarket", that brings in one place the city digital information that includes:

- IoT portals, dashboards and analytics: environmental sensors data and real-time pedestrian and vehicular traffic data dashboards.
- Data marketplace.
- Transparency portals.
- Community intelligence center.
- Open data platforms and GIS portals.
- Business intelligence dashboards with government KPI/KBI metrics.
- Application store.

- eGovernment enterprise systems and digital citizen services.
- Citizen engagement tools, portals and initiatives.

The smart city hub democratizes city data science and technologies. This platform is open to the public on the city's website at: `www.coralgables.com/smartcity`

2.8 Commercial NB-IoT Modems

NB-IoT is a cellular IoT that works only with mobile operator and cellular infrastructure like mobile phones and other cellular gadgets connected to the mobile operator network. In order to use NB-IoT technology, a hardware module or chipset that acts as the cellular NB-IoT modem is needed that connects to the mobile operator network and exchanges control and data messages.

There are multiple manufacturers in the market who manufacture such modems for the NB-IoT cellular technology. The following are the key manufacturers who provide NB-IoT modems:

- SIMCom (`https://www.simcom.com`)
- Quectel (`https://www.quectel.com`)
- Sierra Wireless (`https://www.sierrawireless.com`)
- u-blox (`https://www.u-blox.com`)
- Telit (`https://www.telit.com`)

NB-IoT modules offered by different companies are based on 3GPP technical specifications and releases and follow the 3GPP protocol stack for NB-IoT technology as explained in the Book **"5G LTE Narrowband Internet of Things (NB-IoT)"** [1]. These modems can support different Radio Frequency (RF) bands and thus become suitable for specific mobile operator network or geographical locations. Modems also pass regulatory and mobile operator certification and testing whereas the modem go through rigorous testing to guarantee its conforms to the 3GPP intended behavior and operation. The NB-IoT modems pass RF emission, health, and environmental tests to make sure the modem does not pose interferences to other wireless devices nor does it poses harm to human health and safety.

Table 2.1 summarizes the modems that are available from different companies. In the table, it shows the capability included in the modem and supported RF bands. Most of the modems supports additional LTE technology such as LTE-M for machine type communication and GNSS for satellite and geo-locations applications. In this book, we used the modem BG96 available from Quectel as it is a flagship modem widely available in the market and with abundant functionalities and features. More modems available from other manufacturers and can be found on GSMA website at[12].

Table 2.1: Samples of NB-IoT Modems in the Market.

Modem	Manufacturer	Capability	Supported RF Bands	Picture
SIMCom	SIM7070E	LTE-M, NB-IoT	1, 2, 3, 4, 5, 8, 12, 13, 18, 19,20, 25, 26, 28, 31, 66, B85	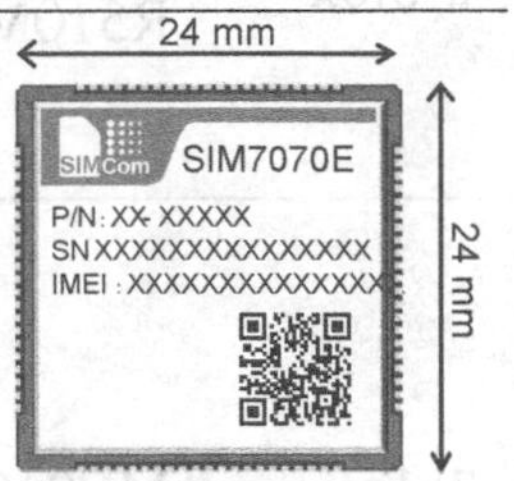
SIMCom	SIM7090G	LTE-M, NB-IoT, GNSS	1, 2, 3, 4, 5, 8, 12, 13, 18, 19, 20, 25, 26, 28, 66, 71, 85	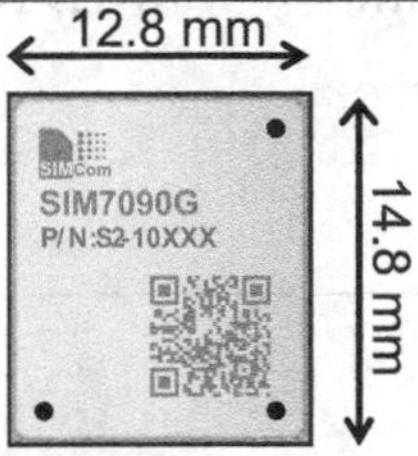
Quectel	BG96	LTE-M, NB-IoT, GNSS	1, 2, 3, 4, 5, 8, 12, 13, 18, 19, 20, 26, 28, (39 LTE-M only)	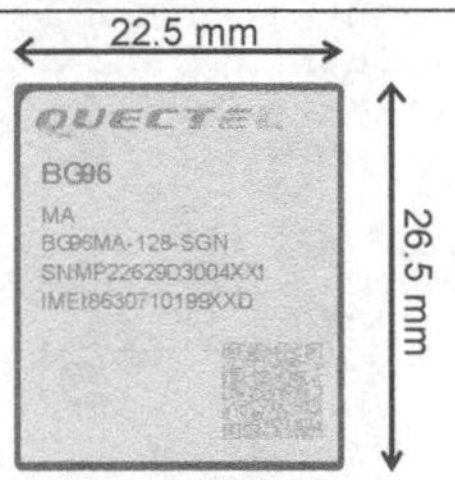
Quectel	BG77	LTE-M, NB-IoT, GNSS	1, 2, 3, 4, 5, 8, 12, 13, 18, 19, 20, 25, 28, 66, 71	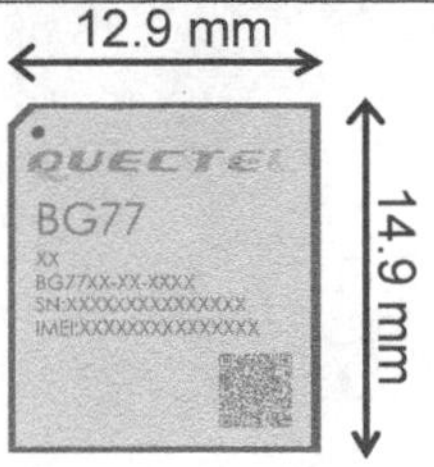
Sierra Wireless	HL7802	LTE-M, NB-IoT, GNSS	1, 2, 3, 4, 5, 8, 9, 10, 12, 13, 14, 17, 18, 19, 20, 25, 26, 27, 28, 66	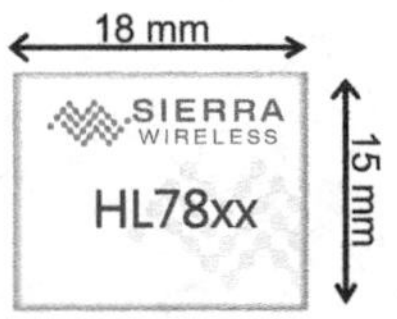
Sierra Wireless	AirPrime WP7700	LTE-M, NB-IoT, GNSS	1, 2, 3, 4, 5, 8, 12, 13, 17, 18, 19, 20, 26, 28	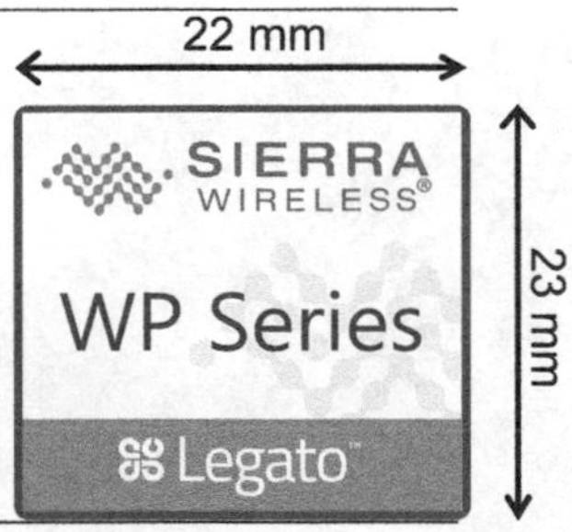

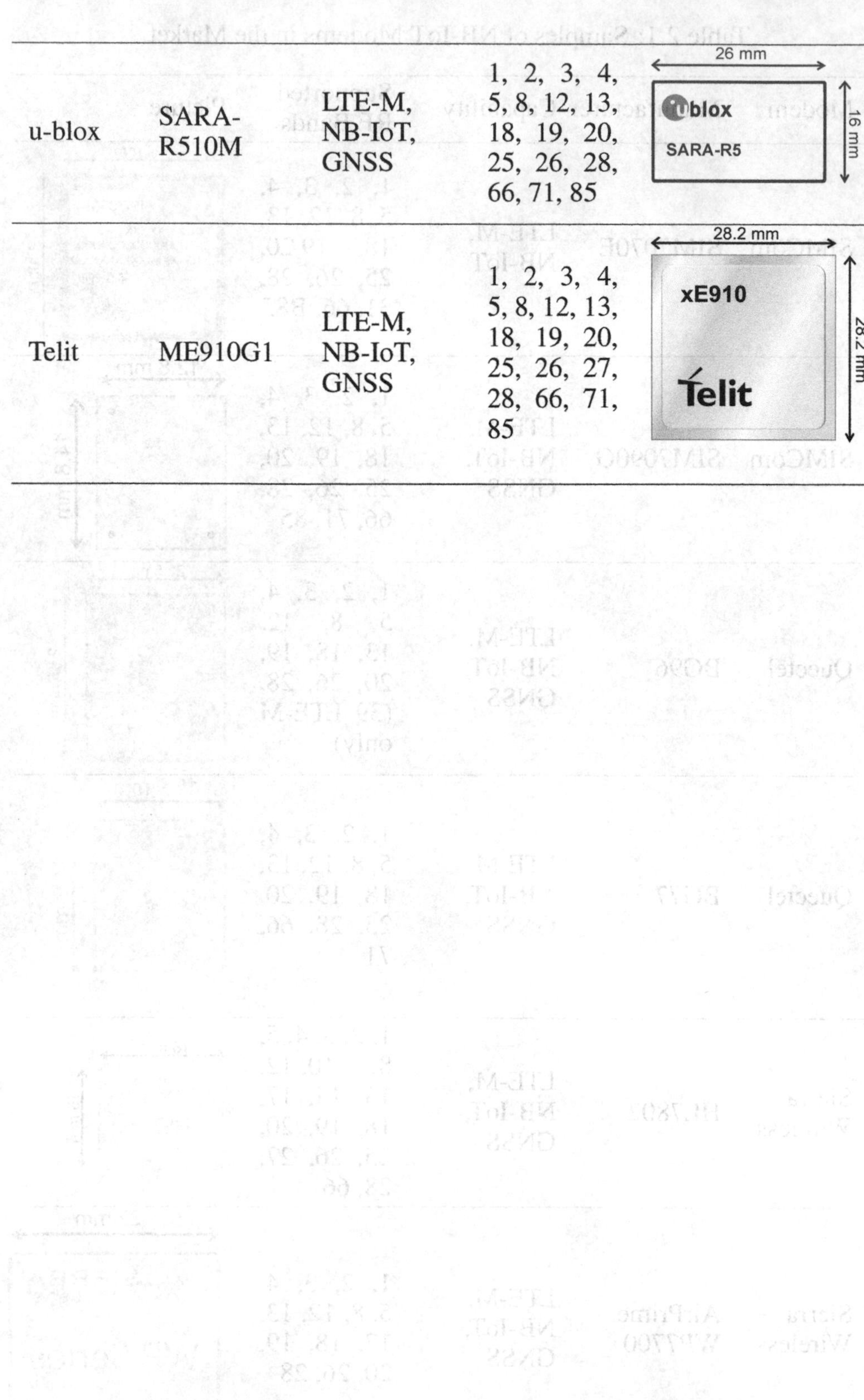

u-blox	SARA-R510M	LTE-M, NB-IoT, GNSS	1, 2, 3, 4, 5, 8, 12, 13, 18, 19, 20, 25, 26, 28, 66, 71, 85	
Telit	ME910G1	LTE-M, NB-IoT, GNSS	1, 2, 3, 4, 5, 8, 12, 13, 18, 19, 20, 25, 26, 27, 28, 66, 71, 85	

Chapter 3

Installing and Setting up Hardware and Software

3.1 NB-IoT Hardware Board and Software

To use the NB-IoT hardware board with Arduino IDE and starts running Arduino projects and sketches, install the following software:

1. Download and install the NB-IoT hardware board package.
2. Download and save the file **5G-NB-IoT_Arduino.zip**. This zip file contains the Arduino library and projects used in this book.
3. Download and install BG96 modem driver for Windows.

NOTE:
Through the book, we refer to the NB-IoT hardware board as NB board. Both terms can be used interchangeably

NOTE:
The software code written inside the Arduino IDE is called an Arduino sketch. The word sketch is a common term used by the Arduino community which means the Arduino software code. Arduino sketch, software, or lines of code presented in the book are meant to be uploaded to the NB board and provides executable instructions to the microcontroller or modem

3.2 Installing Arduino IDE and NB-IoT Hardware Board Package

Arduino Integrated Development Environment (IDE) is a popular software editor for writing software code that runs on Arduino-compatible hardware boards and kits. In this chapter, you will learn how to install and setup your computer to use Arduino IDE and to connect to the hardware board and run the different projects that follow.

Arduino IDE is available for Windows, Mac and Linux. The installation process is different for all three platforms. To install Arduino IDE, follow the following steps:

STEP 1: Go to `https://www.arduino.cc/en/Main/Software` and down the latest Arduino IDE. The version available at this website is the latest version, and the actual version may be newer than the version in the picture. Download and install the Arduino IDE compatible with Windows (You can install Arduino IDE for another operating system).

STEP 2: Launch Arduino IDE and configure it. In this step, you launch the Arduino IDE and configure it to work with the NB-IoT hardware board. Launch Arduino IDE and choose **File->Preferences**. In the Additional Boards Manager URLs, insert the following URL:
`https://raw.githubusercontent.com/5ghub/NB-IoT/master/package_5G-NB-IoT_index.json`

In Arduino IDE, choose **Tools->Board->Boards Manager,** select and install **5G-NB-IoT SAMD Board** (Figure 3.1). In the Arduino IDE, select **Tools->5G NB-IoT (Native USB Port)** (Figure 3.2).

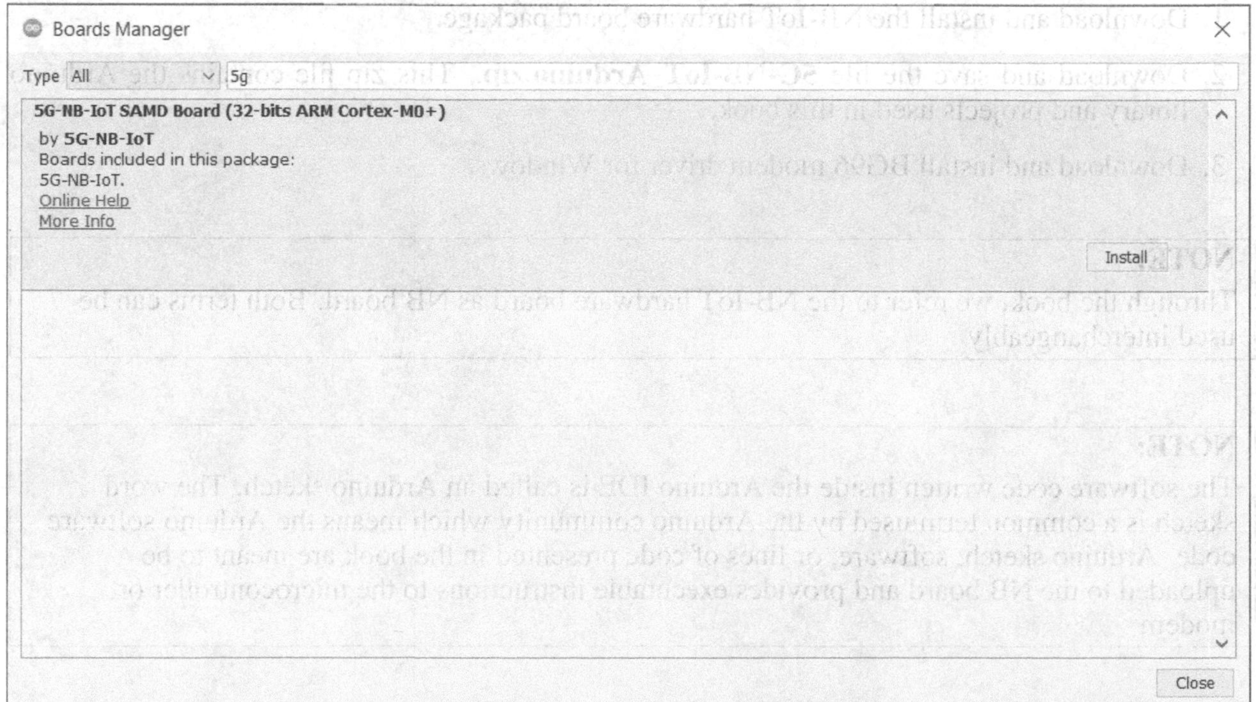

Figure 3.1: Arduino IDE Board Manager.

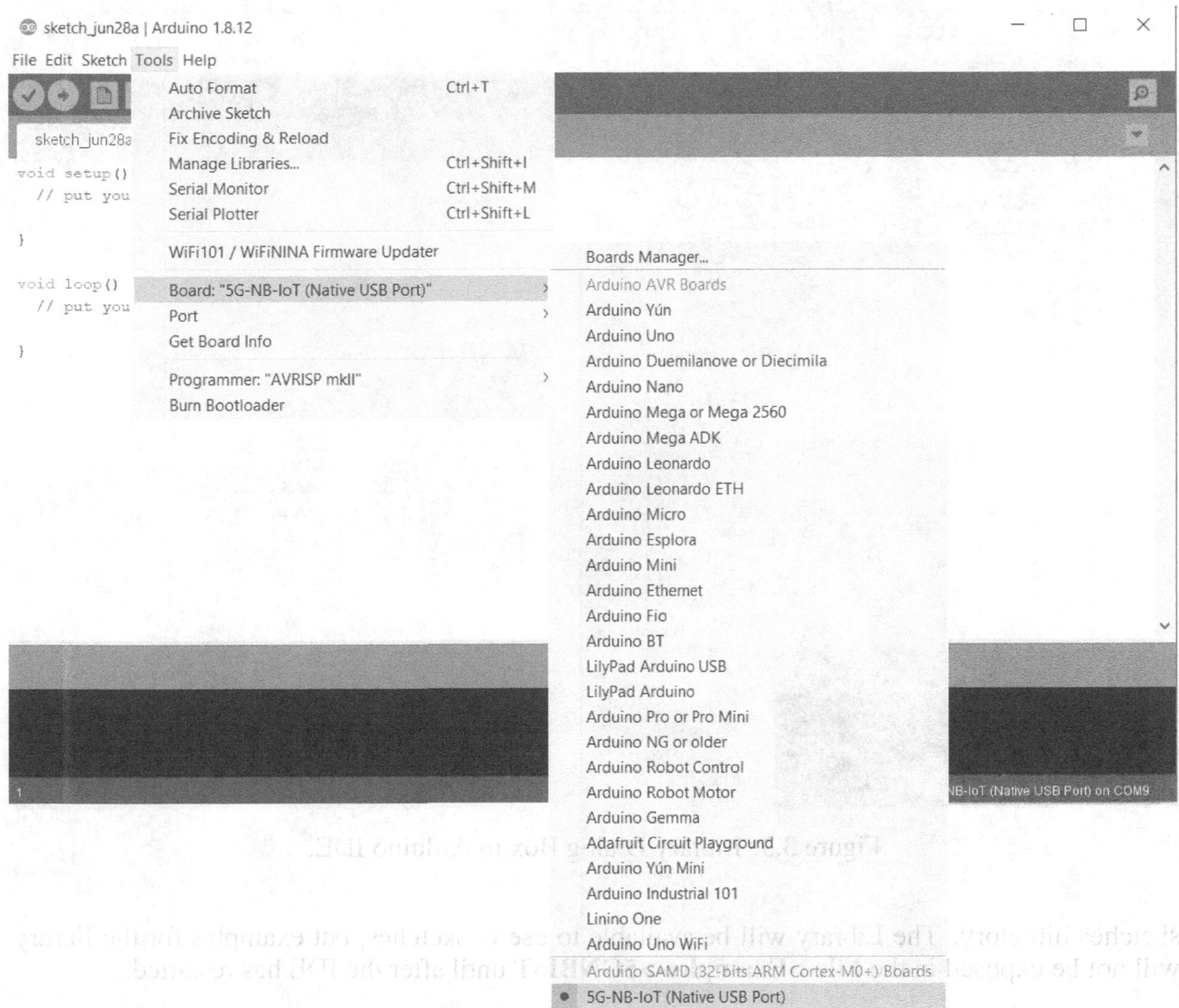

Figure 3.2: Board Selection in Arduino IDE.

3.3 Installing Library

Libraries are a collection of code that makes it easy to use other hardware peripherals such as sensors, motors, LCD, or have other example Arduino sketches. For example, the build-in Liquid Crystal library in the Arduino IDE makes it easy to talk to character LCD displays. There are hundreds of additional libraries available on the Internet for download. To use additional libraries, you need to install them. Libraries are often distributed as a ZIP file or folder.

Here, you will install the library for the NB-IoT hardware board. It includes Arduino sketches and API interfaces to the cellular and GNSS modem. To install the library, in the Arduino IDE, Choose **Sketch->Include Library->Add .Zip Library** and select the file **5G-NB-IoT_Arduino.zip**. You should now see the library at the bottom of the drop-down menu as in Figure 3.3. It is ready to be used in your sketch. The zip file will have been expanded in the libraries folder in your Arduino

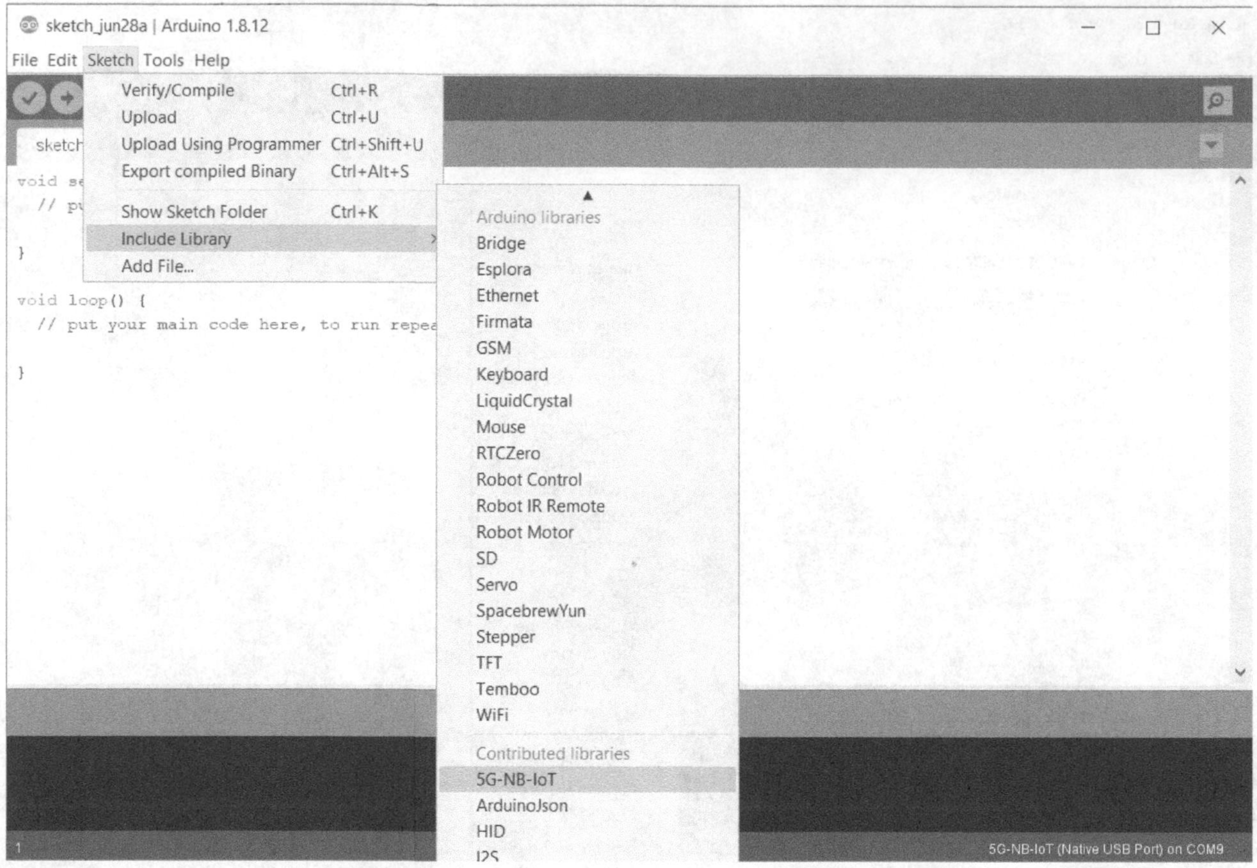

Figure 3.3: Library Dialog Box in Arduino IDE.

sketches directory. The Library will be available to use in sketches, but examples for the library will not be exposed in the **File->Examples->5GNBIoT** until after the IDE has restarted.

Several of Arduino projects described later need additional library to be able to compile and upload the sketch to the NB board. For example, stepper motor sketch, needs the stepper motor library. To install those additional libraries needed for a sketch, in the Arduino IDE, Choose **Sketch->Include Library->Add .Zip library** and select the library *.zip file located in the folder.

3.4 Setting up the NB-IoT Hardware Board

The NB board has two USB ports. The first USB port, which is connected directly to the MCU, can be connected to the computer using a micro-USB cable. This USB port powers on the board. Arduino IDE can detect and communicate with the board and can upload Arduino sketches through this MCU USB. After installing Arduino IDE, add the board package, and install the library for the NB board, you can connect the NB board, through a USB cable to the PC. Once the board is connected you are ready to start building your first Arduino sketch and upload it to the NB board to verify that it is functioning on the board. Once the NB board is connected to PC, you can verify that

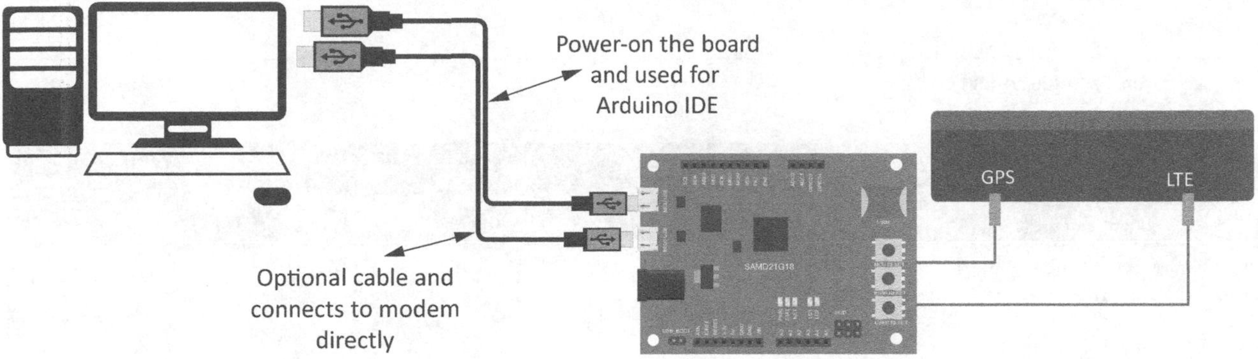

Figure 3.4: Connecting the NB Board to a Personal Computer.

the Arduino IDE is communicating with the NB board correctly by choosing **Tools->Get Board Info** and you shall see few information about the NB board.

Figure 3.4 shows how to connect the NB board to a PC. Detailed description and explanation of the NB board are provided in Chapter 4.

3.5 Arduino Serial Monitor

Arduino IDE is used to open, write, or compile a sketch and uploads it to the NB board. Most hardware board communicates through serial port or USB port. Because of this serial communication, using a serial-communication software (terminal) is an essential part of working with Arduino-compatible hardware boards and other microcontrollers. A serial terminal is included with the Arduino IDE software. Within the Arduino environment, this is called the "Serial Monitor". Serial Monitor comes integrated with the Arduino IDE. To open it, simply click the Serial Monitor icon as in Figure 3.5.

The Serial Monitor is a great quick and easy way to establish a serial connection with the NB board. There are many other Serial Monitor programs that can be used to show up data exchanged with the NB board. However, if you are using the Arduino IDE, it is enough to use the build-in Serial Monitor tool.

Selecting which port to open in the Serial Monitor is the same as selecting a port for uploading Arduino code. Once the NB board is connected to the PC, go to **Tools->Port** and select the correct port as in Figure 3.6. After selecting the correct port for the NB board, you shall be able to see it in **Tools** menu.

You can open the Serial Monitor and it will show the correct COM port where the NB board is connected to. The Serial Monitor has few numbers of settings that are enough to handle most of the serial communication needs. The first setting you can alter is the baud rate. Click on the baud rate drop-down menu to select the correct baud rate (115200 baud) that is to be used with the NB board. You can also set the Serial Monitor to do automatic scroll or display the timestamp with each serial communication with the NB board. Having the screen shoot in Figure 3.7 means that you have connected and communicating successfully with the NB board.

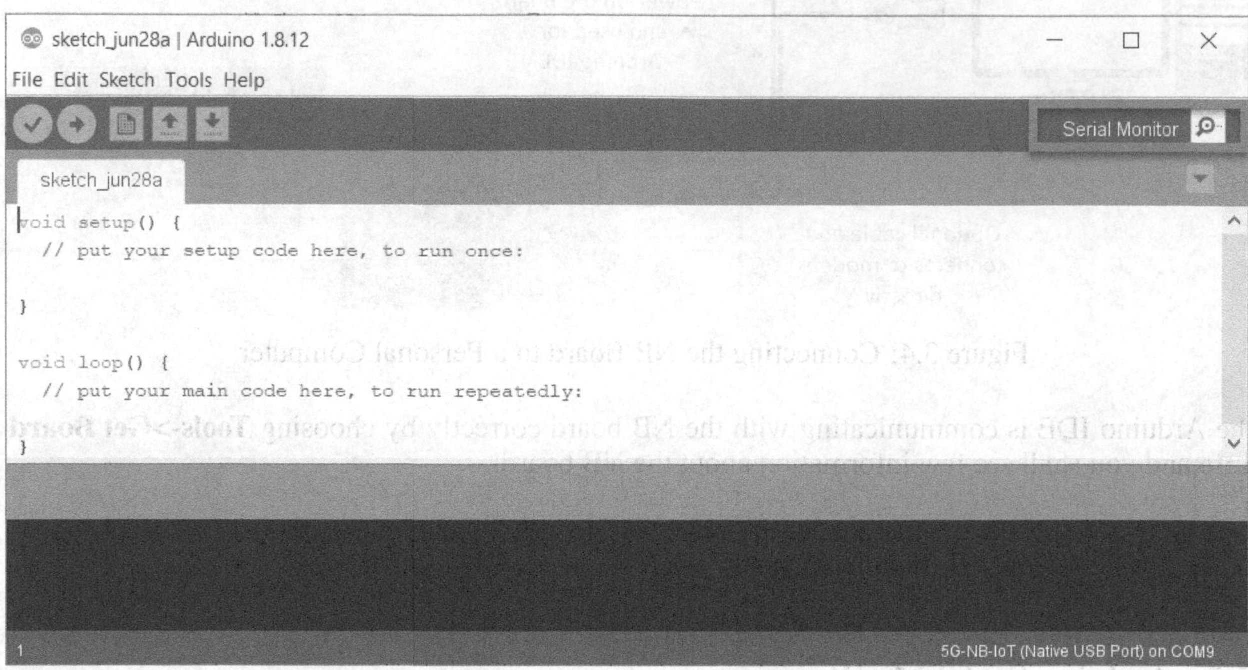

Figure 3.5: Launching Serial Monitor from Arduino IDE.

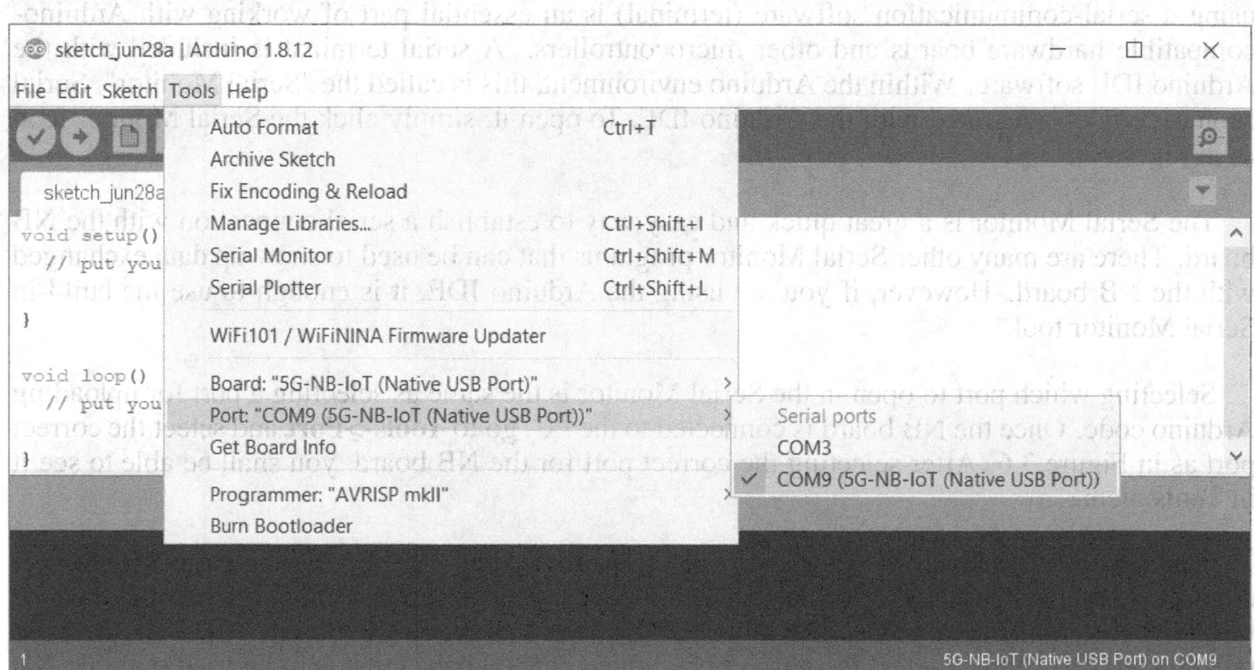

Figure 3.6: Selecting Port for NB Board.

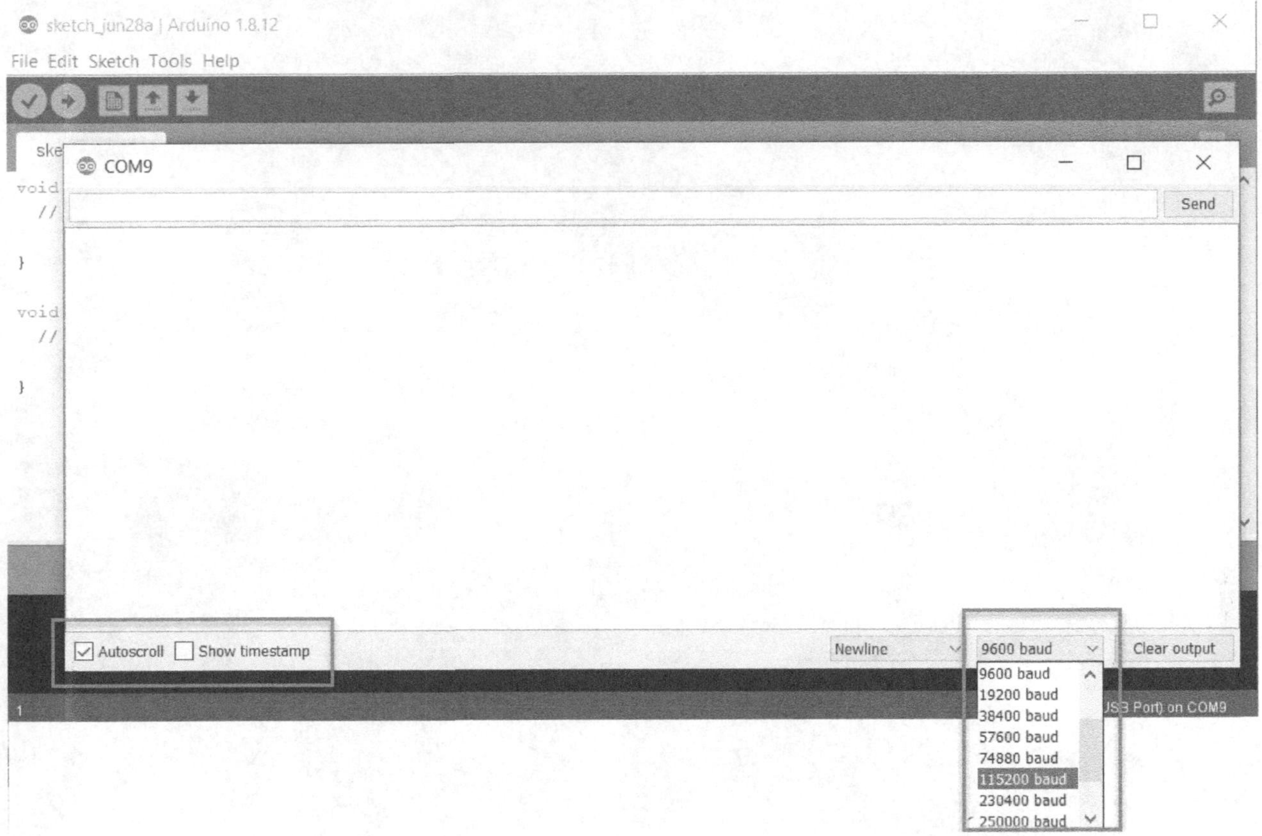

Figure 3.7: for Setting Baud Rate of the Serial Monitor.

Chapter 4

Microcontroller and NB-IoT Modem Units

In this chapter, you will go over the NB-IoT hardware board (Arduino-Compatible). The board is used in all projects and cloud applications presented in this book. The board uses a cellular NB-IoT modem to connect to the cloud and Internet. How to configure, program, and connect the board to the cellular mobile operator and infrastructure are explained.

The NB-IoT hardware board is a feature-rich board that features a microcontroller and cellular modem. The microcontroller is an Atmel's SAMD21G18A MCU which features a 32-bit ARM Cortex® M0+ core. The cellular modem is Quectel BG96 chipset which uses embedded cellular NB-IoT (LTE Cat-M1, LTE Cat-NB1 and EGPRS) technology. The modem is also equipped with Global Navigation Satellite system (GNSS) wireless module that adds location and positioning capability to the modem [13].

4.1 Microcontroller Unit (MCU)

The MCU is Microchip SAMD21G18 chipset. This MCU is a low-power, high-performance ARM® Cortex®-M0+ based flash microcontroller. The MCU is ideal for a wide range of smart applications, consumer, metering, and industrial applications. It features:

- Up to 48MHz operating frequency
- 256KB of flash and 32KB of SRAM
- Operating voltage is 3.3V
- Six serial communication modules (SERCOM) configurable as UART/USART, SPI or I^{2}C
- Up to five 16-bit timer/counters
- 32-bit Real-Time Clock(RTC) and calendar
- Watchdog Timer (WDT)

- CRC-32 generator
- 20 PWM channels
- One 12-bit ADC with 14-channel
- One 10-bit DAC
- 16 External interrupts and External Interrupt Controller (EIC)
- One non-maskable interrupt
- Two-pin Serial Wire Debug (SWD) for programming, test and debugging interface
- Idle and standby sleep modes
- 12-channel Direct Memory Access Controller (DMAC)
- One full-speed (12Mbps) Universal Serial Bus (USB) 2.0 interface

4.2 Quectel BG96 LTE Cellular NB-IoT Modem

BG96 modem is a cellular NB-IoT and wireless GNSS modem. It supports cellular LTE NB-IoT according to 3GPP technical specifications in Release 13. The NB-IoT supports global frequency band and ultra-low power consumption. It also provides a maximum data rate of 375Kbps downlink and 375Kbps uplink. It features ultra-low power consumption, provides data connectivity on LTE-TDD/LTE-FDD/GPRS/EDGE networks, and supports half-duplex operation in LTE networks. It also provides GNSS that provides high-precision location information.

4.3 Key Features of the NB-IoT Hardware Board for Arduino

The hardware board combines both the MCU and the NB-IoT modem. Both provide the following key features:

- Atmel ATSAMD21G18 MCU
- Quectel BG96 NB-IoT and GNSS modem
- External GPS antenna connector
- External LTE antenna connector
- Supports LTE NB-IoT and Machine Type Communications (MTC)
- Supports EGPRS
- Global Frequency Band B1/B2/B3/B4/B5/B8/B12/B13/B18/B19/B20/B26/B28/B39 (B39 for Cat-M1 only) for LTE and 850/900/1800/1900MHz for EGPRS

- Supports the protocols TCP/UDP/PPP/ SSL/ TLS/ FTP(S)/ HTTP(S)/ NITZ/ PING/ MQTT
- Supports SMS
- Supports GNSS technology (GPS, GLONASS, BeiDou/Compass, Galileo, QZSS)
- Compact board size of 58mm x 42mm
- Nano USIM card slot
- Arduino Compatible
- The board can operate on an external power supply of 3.8V to 5V. The recommended voltage is 5V.
- The board can be powered via the USB connector or with an external DC power supply. The power source is selected automatically.
- External DC power supply (non-USB) can be provided from an AC-to-DC adapter (such as a wall-wart) or battery, and can be connected using a 2.1mm center-positive plug connected to the board power jack, or directly to the GND and VIN pins.
- Each of the 14 General Purpose Input/Ouput (GPIOs) pins on the board can be used for digital input or digital output using pinMode(), digitalWrite(), and digitalRead() functions. Pins used for Pulse Width Modulation (PWM) can be using analogWrite() function. All pins operate at 3.3 volts. Each pin can source or sink a maximum of 10 mA and has an internal pull-up resistor (disconnected by default) of 20-60 KΩ.

The Table below summarizes the feature of the NB hardware board.

Table 4.1: Technical Specifications of the NB-IoT Hardware Board.

Technical Specification	
Microcontroller (MCU)	Atmel ATSAMD21G18, 32-bit ARM Cortex M0+
Clock Speed	48 MHz
Flash Memory	256 KB
SRAM	32 KB
Cellular NB-IoT modem	Quectel BG96
Dimension	42 mm (width) by 52 mm (length)
Weight	18
Power Supply	DC power supply (3.8-5V), USB (5V), VIN (3.8-5V), or battery
LED	LED1, LED2, Power LED, Status LED, Netlight LED
Voltage output	5V, 3.3V

Table 4.1 – Continued from Previous Page

Technical Specification	
RESET buttons	Two; one for MCU and one for BG96
User-defined Button	1 connected to MCU
General-purpose digital I/O (GPIO)	14 (A0-A5, PA6, PA7, SS, MOSI, MISO, SCK, SDA, SCL)
ADC	6 (8/10/12-bit ADC, 6-channels)
DAC	1 (10-bit DAC)
USB	2
I^2C	1
SPI	1
UART	1
External interrupts	14 (All GPIO pins)
Additional GPIO	2 connected to BG96
Additional ADC	2 connected to BG96
JTAG Debug	Cortex Debug Connector (Single Wire Debug)
USIM	Nano
GNSS	GPS, GLONASS, BeiDou/Compass, Galileo, QZSS
Antenna	1 main LTE antenna and 1 GPS antenna
Band	B1/B2/B3/B4/B5/B8/B12/B13/B18/ B19/B20/B26/B28LTE-TDD: B39 (for Cat-M1 only)

The following picture shows real pictures of the NB-IoT hardware board for both the top and bottom views.

The following table explains pins on the NB board shown in Figure 4.1.

Table 4.2: PIN Definitions of the NB-IoT Hardware Board.

PIN	Direction	Description
DC Power Jack	I	The board can be supplied with power either from the DC power jack (3.8V-5V), the USB connector (5V), or the VIN pin of the board (3.8V-5V)
LED (PWR)	O	LED is lighted on when the board is power on from the MCU USB port

Table 4.2 – Continued from Previous Page

PIN	Direction	Description
LED1 (USER)	O	LED which can be controlled from MCU (D25). When the pin is HIGH value, the LED is on, when the pin is LOW, it is off
LED2 (USER)	O	LED which can be controlled from MCU (D26). When the pin is HIGH value, the LED is on, when the pin is LOW, it is off
LED (NET)	O	Indicate the BG96 operation status
LED (STAT)	O	Indicate the BG96 network activity status
MCU RESET button	I	Reset the MCU
BG96 RESET button	I	Reset the BG96 module
User Button	I	Connected to digital pin, D0, of MCU and can be used for user-defined purposes
IOREF	O	Provides the voltage reference with which the MCU operates. A device can read the IOREF pin voltage and select the appropriate power source or enable voltage translators on the outputs for working with the 5V or 3.3V
3.3V	O	3.3V generated by the on-board regulator. Maximum current drawn is 300 mA. The regulator also provides power to the MCU and BG96
5V	O	5V generated from the board. The board can be supplied with power either from the DC power jack (3.8V - 5V), the USB connector (5V), or the VIN pin of the board (3.8-5V). Supplying voltage via the 5V or 3.3V pins bypasses the regulator and can damage the board if it is not sufficiently regulated (This is not recommended)
GND	IO	Ground
VIN	I	Input voltage to the board when it uses an external power source (as opposed to 5V from the USB connection or other regulated power source). You can supply voltage through this pin, or if supplying voltage via the power jack, access it through this pin

Table 4.2 – Continued from Previous Page

PIN	Direction	Description
SCL	IO	I^2C. The SCL (clock line). Can be used as GPIO
SDA	IO	I^2C. The SDA (data line). Can be used as GPIO
AREFA	I	Input reference voltage for the analog inputs used for either ADC or DAC
SCK	IO	SPI Interface. Can be used as GPIO
MISO	IO	SPI Interface. Can be used as GPIO
MOSI	IO	SPI Interface. Can be used as GPIO
SS	IO	SPI Interface. Can be used as GPIO
PA7	IO	GPIO. Can be used as GPIO
PA6	IO	GPIO. Can be used as GPIO
A0 A1 A2 A3 A4 A5	IO	Six analog inputs which can provide up to 12 bits of resolution (i.e. 4096 different values). Input ranges from ground to 3.3V. A0 can also be used as a 10-bit DAC output. A0-A5 can be used as GPIO
Cortex Debug Connector (SWD)	IO	Using Single Wire Debug to burn bootloader and debug the board
ADC0	I	Connected to BG96. General purpose analogue to digital converter
ADC1	I	Connected to BG96. General purpose analogue to digital converter
GPIO26	IO	Connected to BG96. General purpose IO
GPIO64	IO	Connected to BG96. General purpose IO
USIM	I	Used to insert a Nano USIM. Connected to BG96
USB Boot	I	Connected to BG96. Force the BG96 to enter emergency download mode
USB1	IO	Connected to MCU
USB2	IO	Connected to BG96

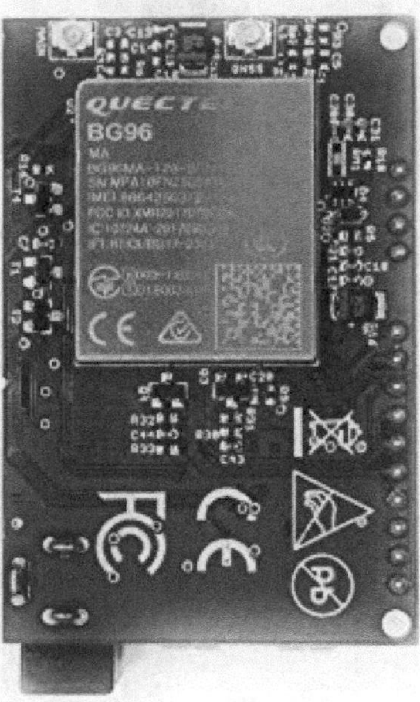

Figure 4.1: Top and Bottom Sides of the NB-IoT Hardware Board.

4.4 Inside NB-IoT Hardware Board for Arduino

The NB-IoT hardware board includes both the MCU and cellular modem. The board is compatible with the Arduino IDE and Arduino development toolsets (Arduino IDE, libraries, and many other open-sources sketches). The board provides rich sets of Internet protocols, industry-standard interfaces (USB/UART/I2C/Status Indicator) and abundant functionalities.

Arduino projects used in the following chapters are using Arduino IDE. Many Arduino projects for cloud and smart application are provided. These projects demo how to use NB-IoT for building smart applications and to connect to the cloud for rich data analytics and Insights.

The top and bottom sides of the NB board in shown in Figure 4.2. The top side contains the MCU, SAMD21G18, one power jack, an USB port connected to the MCU and a second USB port connected to the modem, USIM card slot, a reset button for the MCU, a reset button for the modem, and a reset button that can be used for user-defined purposes, and large number of pin connectors for different signals and functionalities such as analog pins (A0 to A5), digital input/output (PA6, PA7), I^2C interface (SDA, SCL), SPI interface (MOSI, MISO, SCK, SS).

On the bottom side of the board, there is the modem which is based on Quectel BG96 chipset. It also contains two antenna connectors: one for the main LTE antenna and the second antenna for the GNSS antenna.

The following figure explains the schematic diagram of the board and how hardware components such as the MCU and modem are connected.

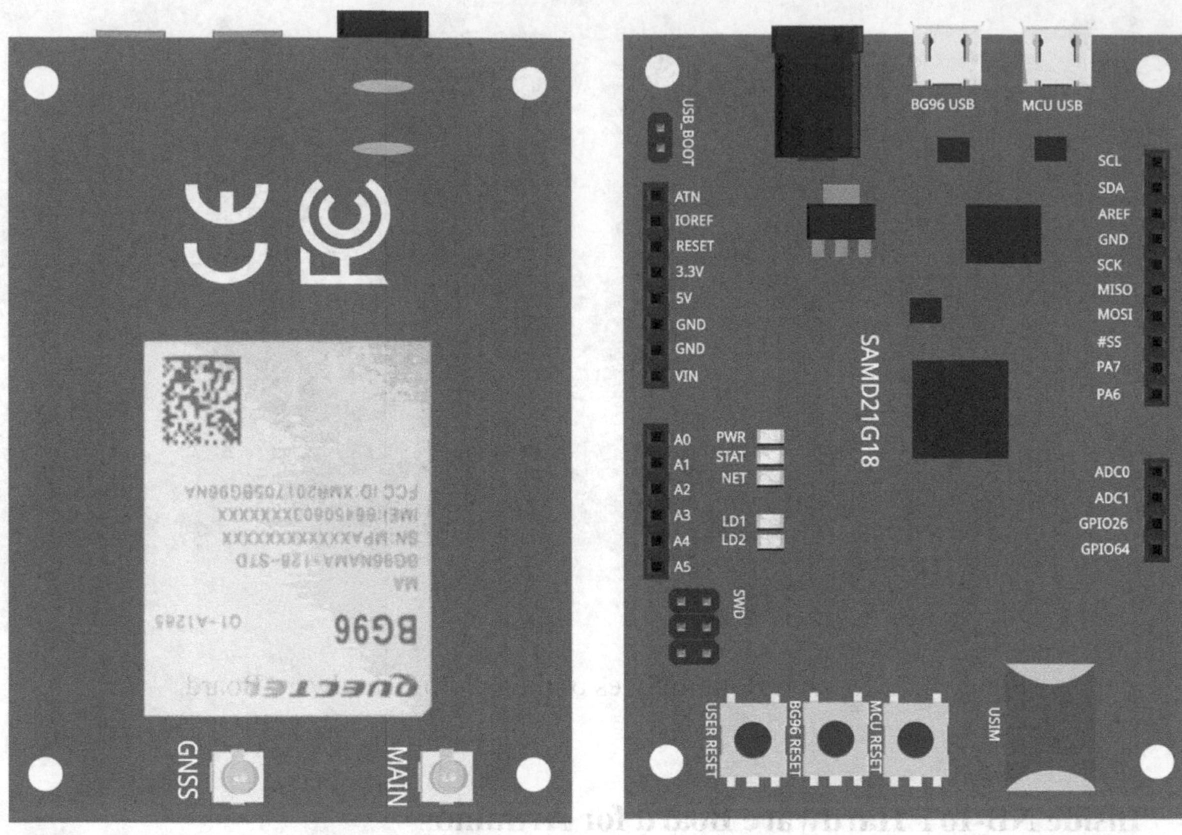

Figure 4.2: Top and Bottom Sketches of the NB Board.

There are two USB ports on the schematic. The first USB port is connected directly to the MCU. Through this USB, the board is powered on, Arduino IDE can detect and communicate with the board and can upload Arduino sketches through this MCU USB. The MCU drives, controls, and interfaces with the BG96 modem. Through Arduino sketches uploaded to the MCU, it can control the BG96 modem. The second USB port is connected directly to the BG96 modem and can be used to run any external software tool that communicates directly with the BG96 without the involvement of the MCU.

The board can be powered by connecting the MCU USB to a computer USB. The USB port provides 5V to the board and 5V for external uses. The board can be powered also through its power jack, from external DC power source through its VIN pin. Power provided through the power jack or through the VIN pin can range from 3.8V to 5V. The board internally provides 3.3V to the MCU. MCU pins thus can tolerate a maximum voltage of 3.3V.

The board has a nano USIM card slot. As the BG96 modem is a cellular NB-IoT modem, it needs to connect to the mobile operator eNodeB and network. The nano USIM is the smallest form factor and size for USIM card as shown Figure 4.4 for the different three USIM sizes available. The nano USIM need to be plugged into the USIM card slot before powering on the board.

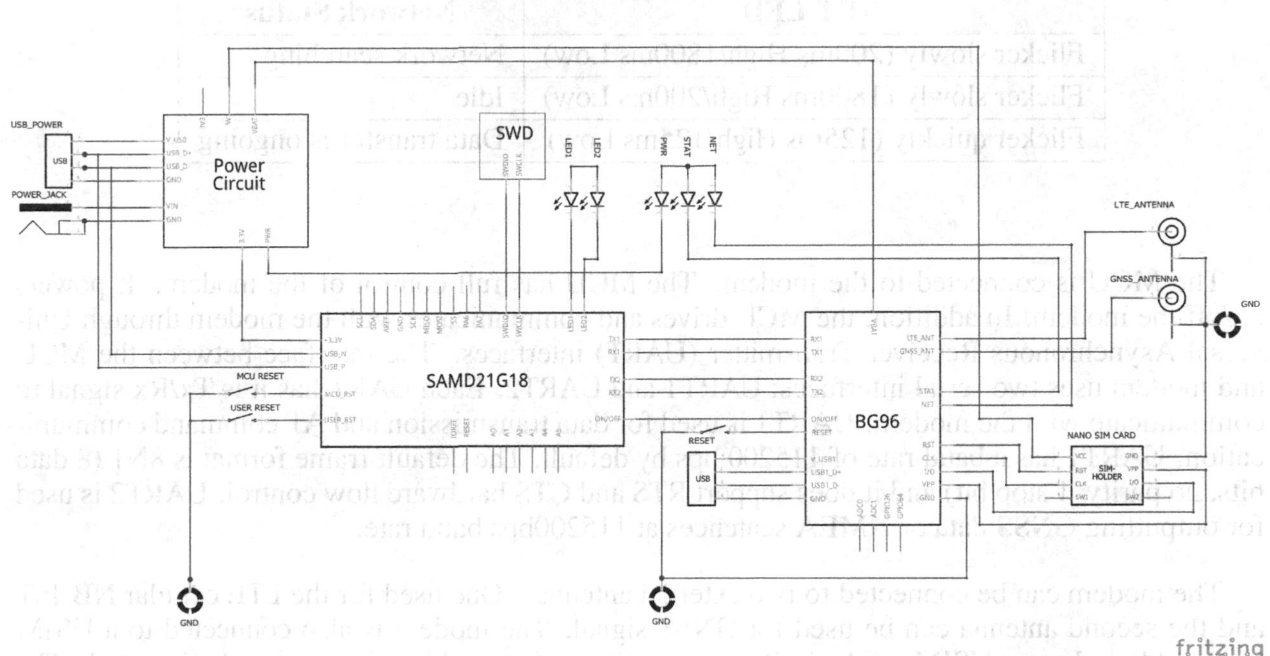

Figure 4.3: Schematic Diagram of the NB-IoT Hardware Arduino Board.

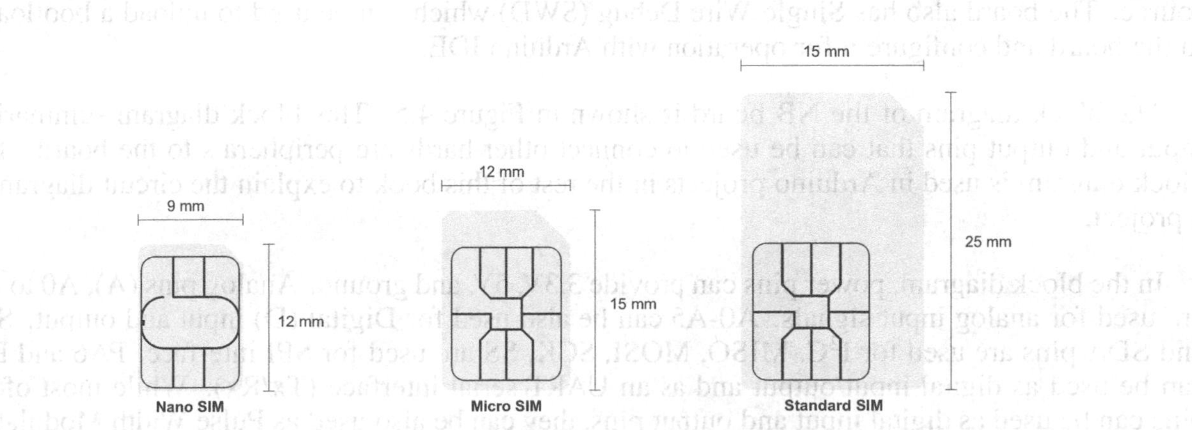

Figure 4.4: USIM Card sizes.

Table 4.3: NET LED Status Indication.

NET LED	Network Status
Flicker slowly (200ms High/1800ms Low)	Network searching
Flicker slowly (1800ms High/200ms Low)	Idle
Flicker quickly (125ms High/125ms Low)	Data transfer is ongoing

The MCU is connected to the modem. The MCU has full control of the modem. It powers on/off the modem. In addition, the MCU drives and communicates with the modem through Universal Asynchronous Receiver Transmitter (UART) interfaces. The interface between the MCU and modem uses two serial interfaces; UART1 and UART2. Each UART has it is Tx/Rx signal to communicate with the modem. UART1 is used for data transmission and AT command communication. UART1 has a baud rate of 115200 bps by default. The default frame format is 8N1 (8 data bits, no parity, 1 stop bit) and it does support RTS and CTS hardware flow control. UART2 is used for outputting GNSS data or NMEA sentences at 115200bps baud rate.

The modem can be connected to two external antennas. One used for the LTE cellular NB-IoT and the second antenna can be used for GNSS signal. The modem is also connected to a USIM card holder where a USIM card, similar to the one used in mobile phones, can be inserted. The USIM card slot size holds a nano-sized USIM card which is the smallest size of USIM card.

The MCU controls two LEDs which can be controlled by uploading an Arduino sketch that writes into the pins of these two LEDs. The modem controls two other LEDs; STAT, and NET. The STAT is always on when the modem is powered on. The NET LED indicates the status of the modem and whether it is searching for mobile operator, connected to mobile operator but no data transfer (Idle), or connected and there is data transfer. Table 4.3 summarizes the NET LED status.

There is another LED, PWR, which is turned on when powering on the board through its power source. The board also has Single Wire Debug (SWD) which can be used to upload a bootloader to the board and configure it for operation with Arduino IDE.

The block diagram of the NB board is shown in Figure 4.5. This block diagram summarizes input and output pins that can be used to connect other hardware peripherals to the board. This block diagram is used in Arduino projects in the rest of this book to explain the circuit diagram of a project.

In the block diagram, power pins can provide 3.3V, 5V, and ground. Analog pins (A), A0 to A5, are used for analog input signals. A0-A5 can be also used for Digital (D) input and output. SCL and SDA pins are used for I^2C. MISO, MOSI, SCK, SS are used for SPI interface. PA6 and PA7 can be used as digital input/output and as an UART serial interface (Tx/Rx). While most of the pins can be used as digital input and output pins, they can be also used as Pulse Width Modulation (PWM) output.

AREF is analog reference signal used as reference signal for analog signal used for either the ADC or the DAC. The block diagram includes RESET pins for resetting the MCU or the modem. There is also a user-defined button that can be used and read from Arduino sketches. The board

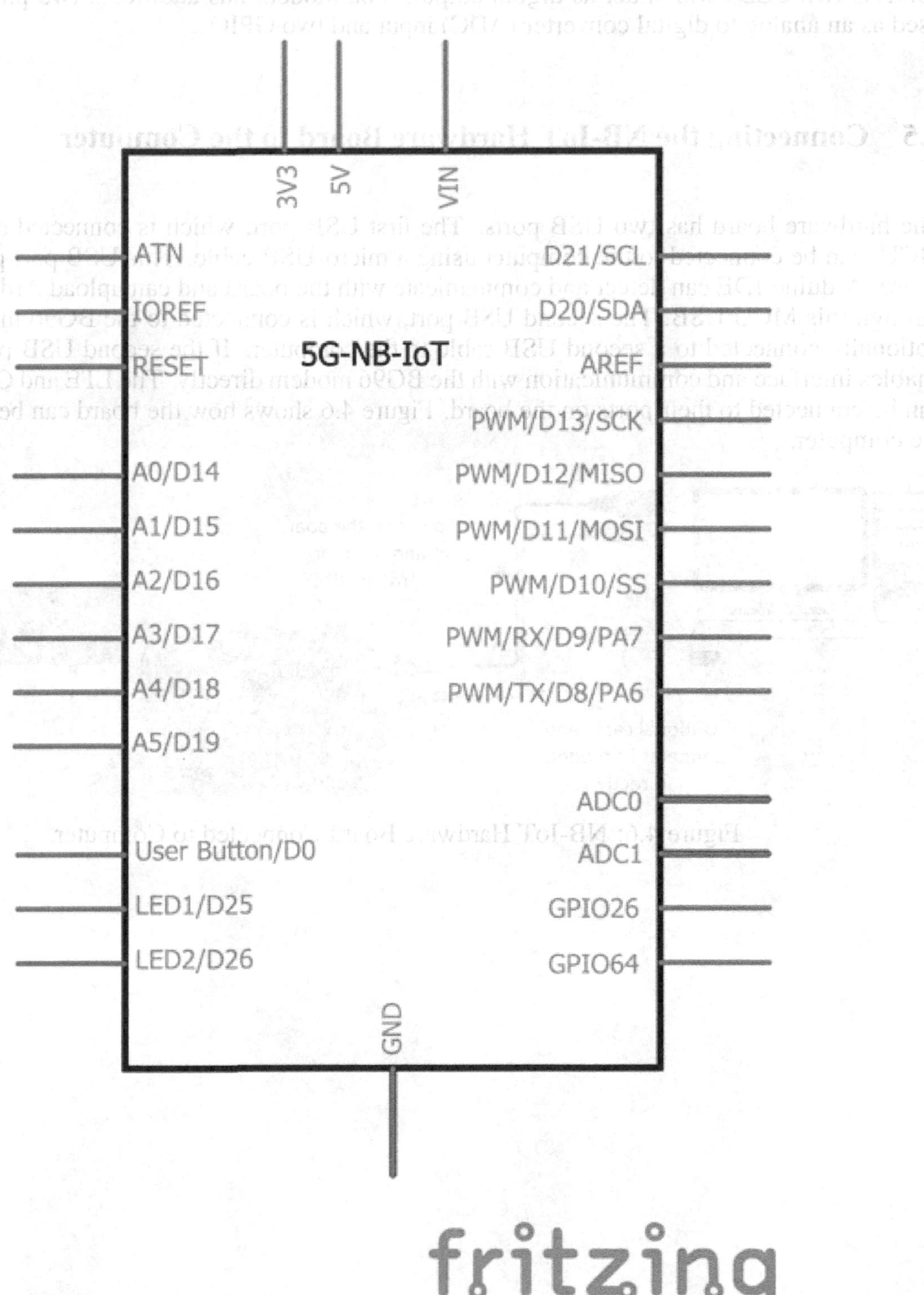

Figure 4.5: Block Diagram of the NB-IoT Hardware Board.

controls two LEDs which act as digital output. The modem has additional two pins that can be used as an analog to digital converter (ADC) input and two GPIOs.

4.5 Connecting the NB-IoT Hardware Board to the Computer

The hardware board has two USB ports. The first USB port, which is connected directly to the MCU, can be connected to the computer using a micro-USB cable. This USB port powers on the board, Arduino IDE can detect and communicate with the board and can upload Arduino sketches through this MCU USB. The second USB port, which is connected to the BG96 modem, can be optionally connected to a second USB cable to the computer. If the second USB port is used, it enables interface and communication with the BG96 modem directly. The LTE and GNSS antenna can be connected to their ports on the board. Figure 4.6 shows how the board can be connected to the computer.

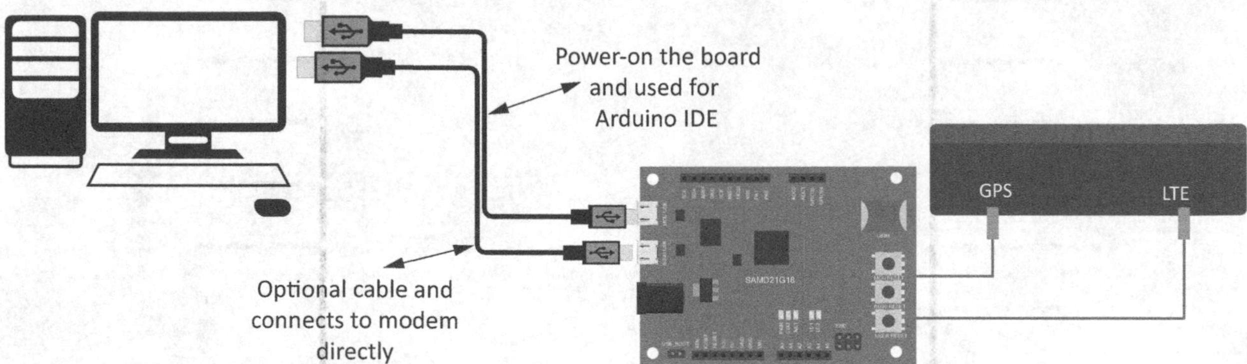

Figure 4.6: NB-IoT Hardware Board Connected to Computer.

Chapter 5

AT Commands

Attention commands formally known as AT commands are instructions used to configure, control, and interface with a modem. In AT commands, every command line starts with **AT** or **at**. The starting **AT** is a prefix that precedes the command. It is not part of the AT command name. For example, E is the actual AT command name in ATE<value> which sets the modem to echo mode (echo any AT command received by the modem) and <value> can be either 0 or 1 indicating to disable echo or enable it.

The following are a list of some examples of what AT commands can do:

- Get basic information about the mobile phone or modem. For example, name of the manufacturer (AT+CGMI), model number (AT+CGMM), IMEI number (International Mobile Equipment Identity) (AT+GSN), and the software version (AT+CGMR).

- Get the status of the mobile phone or modem. For example, mobile phone activity status (AT+CPAS), mobile network registration status (AT+CREG), radio signal strength (AT+CSQ), battery charge level, and battery charging status (AT+CBC).

- Configure the modem to connect to mobile operator network. For example, configure the network search order AT+QCFG="nwscanseq" to search sequence for LTE Cat-M1/Cat-NB1/GSM). AT+QCFG="nwscanmode" to configure the scanning mode (LTE only or GSM). AT+QCFG= "iotopmode" to search for network under LTE category such LTE Cat-M1 or LTE Cat-NB1 or both. AT+QCFG="band" to configure the radio frequency band (GSM or LTE band).

- Perform security-related tasks, such as opening or closing facility locks (AT+CLCK), checking whether a facility is locked (AT+CLCK), and changing passwords (AT+CPWD). (Facility lock examples: SIM lock (a password must be given to the SIM card every time the mobile phone is switched on) and PH-SIM lock (certain SIM card is associated with the mobile phone; to use other SIM cards with the mobile phone, a password must be entered).

- Control the presentation of result codes/error messages of AT commands. For example, you can control whether to enable certain error messages (AT+CMEE), and whether error messages should be displayed in numeric format or verbose format (AT+CMEE=1 or AT+CMEE=2).

- Get or change the configurations of the mobile phone or modem. For example, change the GSM network (AT+COPS).

5.1 AT Command Syntax

The **AT** or **at** prefix must be set at the beginning of each command line. To terminate a command line, a **<CR>** is entered. Commands are usually followed by a response that includes **<CR><LF><response><CR><LF>**. The **<CR><LF>** are typically omitted and not shown in the AT response [14].

The AT commands have the basic format of **AT<x><n>**, or **AT&<x><n>**, where **<x>** is the command, and <n> is/are the argument(s) for that command. An example of this is ATE<n>, which tells the modem whether the received characters should be echoed back to the computer according to the value of <n>. <n> is optional and a default will be used if it is missing.

AT commands can have also extended format. These extended commands can be operated in several modes, such as read or write mode. Read command mode take the form **AT+<x>?** while write command mode take the form **AT+<x>=<..>** [15].

In this section, we explain the different AT commands needed to configure and program the NB-IoT modem. All AT commands required to run projects in this book is presented and explained. The AT command follows the format in the table below.

AT Command
Explanation of the AT command
Format of the AT command
Return value after running the AT command
Argument(s) that can be used with the AT command or in the return value (Some AT commands will have their argument(s) first before the return value)
Example of the AT command

The following are AT commands that can be used with the modem. They are the most essential commands and are used in the Arduino projects. They are organized into general commands, status commands, networking commands, packet domain commands, TCP/IP commands, SSL commands, MQTT commands, HTTP commands, GNSS commands, file commands, and firmware update commands.

5.2 General Commands

General AT commands are used for general purposes such as querying the modem firmware version or displaying IMEI of the modem.

ATI
Display product identification
ATI
OK
ATI Quectel BG96 Revision: BG96MAR02A07M1G OK

AT+GSN
Request IMEI of the modem
AT+GSN
OK
AT+GSN 866425031237797 OK

AT+CPIN
Enter a password or query whether the modem requires a password before it can operate
AT+CPIN?
OK
AT+CPIN? +CPIN: READY OK

AT+QCCID
Retrieve the ICCID (Integrated Circuit Card Identifier) number of the (U)SIM card.
AT+QCCID
OK
AT+QCCID +QCCID: 89011703278342370742 OK

ATE
Set Echo Mode
ATE<value>
0 Echo mode OFF 1 Echo mode ON
OK
ATE0 OK

5.3 Status Control Commands

Status control commands are used to control the modem and sets modem configuration such as network scan order, frequency bands to be used for scanning, or type of network to register (NB-IoT or MTC network)

AT+CFUN
Control the functionality level
AT+CFUN=<fun>[,<rst>]
<fun> 0 (Minimum functionality), 1 (Full functionality (Default)) **<rst>** 0 (Does not reset the modem), 1 (Reset the modem)
OK
AT+CFUN=1 OK

AT+QCFG="nwscanseq"
Specify the search sequence of the radio access technology (LTE or GSM)
AT+QCFG="nwscanseq",<scanseq>
<scanseq> can be 00 Automatic (LTE Cat-M1 -> LTE Cat-NB1 -> GSM) 01 GSM 02 LTE Cat-M1 03 LTE Cat-NB1
OK
AT+QCFG="nwscanseq",030201 OK

AT+QCFG=”nwscanmode”
Specify the radio access technology (LTE or GSM) allowed to be searched
AT+QCFG=”nwscanmode”,<scanmode>
<scanmode> can be 0 Automatic 1 GSM only 3 LTE only
OK
AT+QCFG="nwscanmode",3 OK

AT+QCFG=”iotopmode”
Specify the network category to be searched under LTE
AT+QCFG=”iotopmode”,<mode>
<mode> can be 0 LTE Cat-M1 1 LTE Cat-NB1 2 LTE Cat-M1 and Cat-NB1
OK
AT+QCFG="iotopmode",1 OK

AT+QCFG=”band”
Specify the radio frequency bands to be searched
AT+QCFG=”band”,<gsmbandval>,<catm1bandval><catnb1bandval>
<gsmbandval> a value from 0 to F indicating GSM band **<catm1bandval>** a value from 1 to 400A0E189F indicating Cat-M1 band **<catnb1bandval>** can be 0x1 LTE B1 0x2 LTE B2 other values for LTE B3/B4/B5/B8/B12/B13/B18/B19/B20/B26/B28 0XA0E189F any frequency band
OK
AT+QCFG="band",F,400A0E189F,A0E189F OK

AT+QCFG="nccconf"
Configure features of the NB-IoT
AT+QCFG="nccconf",<cap_val>
<cap_val> Hexadecimal value. If one bit is set to 1, it means enable, otherwise it means disable. The specific meanings are as follows: Bit 0 Enable or disable the use of EMM_CP_CIOT Bit 1 Enable or disable the use of EMM_UP_CIOT Bit 2 Enable or disable the use of EMM_S1_U Bit 3 Enable or disable the use of EMM_ER_WITHOUT_PDN Bit 4 Enable or disable the use of EMM_HC_CP_CIOT Bit 5 Enable or disable the use of EMM_SMS_ONLY Bit 6 Enable or disable the use of EMM_PNB_CP_CIOT Bit 7 Enable or disable the use of EMM_PNB_UP_CIOT Bit 8 Enable or disable the use of EMM_EPCO_CIOT
OK
AT+QCFG="nccconf",5 OK

5.4 Network Commands

Network commands are used to query cellular network status such as checking if the modem registered on cellular network, the name of the network mobile operator, or RF signal quality indicators.

AT+CREG, AT+CGREG, AT+CEREG
Reads the registration status of the modem (CREG) or GSM registration status (CGREG) or LTE registration status (CEREG). Whether it is registered or not.
AT+CREG?
+CREG: <n>,<stat>
<n> can be 0 Disable network registration unsolicited result code 1 Enable network registration unsolicited result code **<stat>** can be 0 Not registered 1 Registered on home network 2 Not Registered but the modem is currently searching for a network 3 Registration denied 4 Unknown 5 Registered, roaming

+CREG: <n>,<stat>
AT+CEREG? +CEREG: 1,1

AT+COPS
Reads the current mobile operator whether the modem is registered or not
AT+COPS?
+COPS:<mode>[,<format>[,<oper>][,<Act>]]
<mode> 0 (Automatic mode), 1 (Manual mode), 4 (Manual/Automatic selection) **<format>** 0 (Long format alphanumeric), 1 (Short format alphanumeric) **<oper>** Operator name **<Act>** 0 (GSM access technology selected), 8 (LTE Cat-M1), 9 (LTE Cat-NB1)
AT+COPS? +COPS: 0,0,"AT&T",9

AT+CSQ
Reads the current received signal strength (RSSI) and channel bit error rate
AT+CSQ
+CSQ: <rssi>,<ber>
<rssi> rssi*2-113 dBm (for example, if rssi is 2, it means 2*2-113 = 109 dBm) **<ber>** Channel bit error rate (in percent)
AT+CSQ +CSQ: 31,7

AT+QNWINFO
Reads network information such as the access technology selected, the operator, and the band selected
AT+QNWINFO
+QNWINFO:<Act>,<oper>,<band>,<channel>
<Act> can be No Service, GSM, GPRS, EDGE, Cat-M1, Cat-NB1, **<oper>** Operator in numeric format. **<band>** can be GSM 850, GSM 900, GSM 1800, GSM 1900, LTE B1 to B43 **<channel>** Integer type. Channel ID.
AT+QNWINFO +QNWINFO: "CAT-NB1","310410","LTE BAND 12",5156

5.5 Packet Domain Commands

Packet domain commands are used to open a connection to the cellular (mobile operator) network. The packet data protocol (PDP) context is a connection between the modem and the cellular network. After the modem connects to the cellular network, it has to activate a PDP context to send and receive data. After the modem no longer needs to send or receive data, it can deactivate the PDP context.

AT+CGDCONT
Define PDP Context.
AT+CGDCONT=<cid>,<PDP_type>,<APN>
OK
<cid> A PDP context identifier in the range 1 to 15 **<PDP_type>** can be “IP”, “IPV6”, or “IPV4V6” **<APN>** Access point name.
AT+CGDCONT=1,"IP","m2mNB16.com.attz" OK

5.6 TCP/IP Commands

The modem has an embedded TCP/IP stack which enables the modem to connect to the cloud and to the Internet via AT commands. The modem provides socket services such as TCP client, UDP client, TCP server and UDP server [16].

The MCU can configure the modem to activate or deactivate a PDP context, start, or close a socket service, or send and receive data via socket service. The following are the TCP/IP AT commands.

AT+QICSGP
Configure an TCP/IP Context
AT+ QICSGP=<contextID>,<context_type>,<APN>
OK
<contextID> TCP/IP context ID to be configured **<context_type>** can be 1 for IPV4 or 2 for IPV6 **<APN>** String type. The access point name.
AT+QICSGP=1 +QICSGP: 1,"m2mNB16.com.attz","","",0

AT+QIACT, AT+QIDEACT

Activate or deactivate an TCP/IP Context

AT+ QIACT=<contextID>

OK

<contextID> TCP/IP context id to be activated

AT+QIACT=1
OK

AT+OPEN

Open an TCP/IP Socket

AT+QIOPEN=<contextID>,<connectID>,<service_type>,<IP_address>/ <domain_name>,<remote_port>

OK

<contextID> TCP/IP context ID. The range is 1-16.
<connectID> socket service index. The range is 0-11.
<service_type> can be:
"TCP" Start a TCP connection as a client
"UDP" Start a UDP connection as a client
"TCP LISTENER" Start a TCP server to listen to TCP connection
"UDP SERVICE" Start a UDP service
<IP_address> IP address of remote server, such as "220.180.239.212".
<domain_name> The domain name address of the remote server.
<remote_port> The port of the remote server. The range is 0-65535.

AT+QIOPEN=1,1,"UDP","www.5ghub.us",80
OK
+QIOPEN: 1,0

AT+QISEND

Send TCP/IP data

AT+QISEND=<connectID> followed by the data and then press CTRL+Z

OK

<connectID> socket service index. The range is 0-11.

AT+QISEND=1
> "Hello World!"
"Hello World!"
<CTRL+Z>
SEND OK

AT+QIRD
Read TCP/IP data received by the modem
AT+QIRD=<connectID>
OK
<connectID> socket service index. The range is 0-11.
AT+QIRD=1 +QIRD: 12 Hello World! OK

AT+QICLOSE
Close an TCP/IP Socket
AT+QICLOSE=<connectID>
OK
<connectID> socket service index. The range is 0-11.
AT+QICLOSE=1 OK

AT+QPING
Ping a destination host (to check if it is reachable)
AT+QPING=<contextID>,<host>
OK
< contextID> context index. The range is 1-16. **<host>** the host address
AT+QPING=1,"www.5ghub.us" OK +QPING: 0,"107.180.51.85",32,452,255 +QPING: 0,"107.180.51.85",32,443,255 +QPING: 0,"107.180.51.85",32,420,255 +QPING: 0,"107.180.51.85",32,420,255 +QPING: 0,4,4,0,420,452,433

5.7 SSL Commands

These are the AT commands used to setup and configure SSL (Secure Socket Layer) and TLS (Transport Layer Security) protocols which are the protocols used to communicate securely over the Internet [17].

AT+QSSLCFG="sslversion"
Configure the SSL version to be used
AT+QSSLCFG="sslversion",<sslctxID>,<sslversion>
OK
<sslctxID> SSL context ID. The range is 0-5. **<sslversion>** SSL Version (0 SSL3.0, 1 TLS1.0, 2 TLS1.1, 3 TLS1.2, 4 All)
AT+QSSLCFG="sslversion",1,3 OK

AT+QSSLCFG="ciphersuite"
Configure the SSL cipher suites
AT+QSSLCFG="ciphersuite",<sslctxID>,<ciphersuites>
OK
<sslctxID> SSL context ID. The range is 0-5. **<ciphersuites>** SSL cipher suites (0xFFFF supports all RSA and ECDHE).
AT+QSSLCFG="ciphersuite",1,0XFFFF OK

AT+QSSLCFG="seclevel"
Configure the security level
AT+QSSLCFG="seclevel",<sslctxID>,<seclevel>
OK
<sslctxID> SSL context ID. The range is 0-5. **<seclevel>** Authentication mode. (0 No authentication, 1 Manage server authentication, 2 Manage server and client authentication)
AT+QSSLCFG="seclevel",1,2 OK

AT+QSSLCFG="cacert"
Configure the Certificate Authority (CA)
AT+QSSLCFG="cacert",<sslctxID>,<cacertpath>
OK
<sslctxID> SSL context ID. The range is 0-5. **<cacertpath>** Path of trusted CA certificate
AT+QSSLCFG="cacert",1,"ca_cert.pem" OK

AT+QSSLCFG="clientcert"
Configure the client certificate
AT+QSSLCFG="clientcert",<sslctxID>,<client_cert_path> OK
<sslctxID> SSL context ID. The range is 0-5. **<client_cert_path>** Path of client certificate
AT+QSSLCFG="clientcert",1,"client_cert.pem” OK

AT+QSSLCFG="clientkey"
Configure the client key
AT+QSSLCFG="clientkey",<sslctxID>,<client_key_path>
OK
<sslctxID> SSL context ID. The range is 0-5. **<client_key_path>** Path of client key
AT+QSSLCFG="clientkey",1,"client_key.pem" OK

AT+QSSLCFG="ignorelocaltime"
Configure the expiry time of a certificate
AT+QSSLCFG="ignorelocaltime",<sslctxID>,<ignoreltime>
OK
<sslctxID> SSL context ID. The range is 0-5. **<ignoreltime>** How to deal with expired certificate. (0 cared about expiry time, ignore expiry time)
AT+QSSLCFG="ignorelocaltime",1 +QSSLCFG: "ignorelocaltime",1,1 OK

AT+QSSLOPEN
Open an SSL network connection for the device
AT+QSSLOPEN=<pdpctxID>,<sslctxID>,<clientID>,<serveraddr>,<server_port>, <access_mode>
OK

<pdpctxID> PDP context ID. The range is 1-16. **<sslctxID>** SSL context ID. The range is 0-5. **<clientID>** Socket index. The range is 0-11. **<serveraddr>** The address of remote server. **<server_port>** The listening port of remote server. **<access_mode>** The access mode of SSL connection. (0 Buffer access mode 1 Direct push mode, 2 Transparent mode)
AT+QSSLOPEN=1,1,1,"a3kjt69iibf2h0-ats.iot.us-west-2.amazonaws.com",8883,0 OK +QSSLOPEN: 1,0

AT+QSSLSEND
Send data through SSL connection
AT+QSSLSEND=<clientID> followed by the data and then press CTRL+Z
OK
<clientID> Socket index. The range is 0-11. **<sendlen>** The length of sending data in bytes. The range is 1-1500.
AT+QSSLSEND=1 > Hellow World! Hellow World! SEND OK

AT+QSSLRECV
Receive data through SSL connection
AT+QSSLRECV=<clientID><readlen>
OK
<clientID> Socket index. The range is 0-11. **<readlen>** Length of data to be read. Range is 1-1500.
AT+QSSLRECV=1,1500 +QSSLRECV: 12 Hello World! OK

AT+QSSLCLOSE
Close SSL connection
AT+QSSLCLOSE=<clientID>
OK
<clientID> Socket index. The range is 0-11.
AT+QSSLCLOSE=1 OK

5.8 MQTT Commands

MQTT AT commands are used to configure and establish an MQTT connection to an MQTT server, subscribe to a topic, publish or receive from/to a topic, or close an MQTT connection [18].

AT+QMTCFG="version"
Configure the MQTT version to be used
AT+QMTCFG="version",<tcpconnectID>,<vsn>
OK
<tcpconnectID> MQTT socket identifier. The range is 0-5. **<vsn>** MQTT protocol version 3 MQTT v3.1 4 MQTT v3.1.1
AT+QMTCFG="version",1,3 OK

AT+QMTCFG="pdpcid"
Configure the PDP context to be used by the MQTT device
AT+QMTCFG="pdpcid",<tcpconnectID>,<cid>
OK
<tcpconnectID> MQTT socket identifier. The range is 0-5. **<cid>** PDP contextID AT+QMTCFG="pdpcid",1,1 OK

AT+QMTCFG="timeout"
Configure the timeout of message delivery
AT+QMTCFG=" timeout",<tcpconnectID>,<pkt_timeout>,<retry_times>, <timeout_notice>
OK
<tcpconnectID> MQTT socket identifier. The range is 0-5. **<pkt_timeout>** timeout of a message delivery. Range is 1-60 **<retry_times>** number of a message retries. Range is 0-10 **<timeout_notice>** 0 (No report of timeout message), 1 (Report of timeout message)
AT+QMTCFG="timeout",1,20,3,0 OK

AT+QMTCFG="ssl"
Configure MQTT to use SSL
AT+QMTCFG="ssl",<tcpconnectID>,<sslenable>,<ctxindex>
OK
<tcpconnectID> MQTT socket identifier. The range is 0-5. **<sslenable>** timeout of a message delivery. Range is 1-60 **<ctxindex>** SSL context index. Range is 0-5
AT+QMTCFG="ssl",1,1,1 OK

AT+QMTOPEN
Open an MQTT network connection for the device
AT+QMTOPEN=<tcpconnectID>,"<host_name>",<port>
OK
<tcpconnectID> MQTT socket identifier. The range is 0-5 **<host_name>** name of the MQTT server **<port>** MQTT server port number
AT+QMTOPEN=1,"a3kjt69iibf2h0-ats.iot.us-west-2.amazonaws.com",8883 OK +QMTOPEN: 1,0

AT+QMTCONN
Request an MQTT network connection from the MQTT server
AT+QMTCONN=<tcpconnectID>,”<clientID>”
OK
<tcpconnectID> MQTT socket identifier. The range is 0-5 **<clinetID>** string represents the client Id of the MQTT server
AT+QMTCONN=1,"basicPubSub" OK +QMTCONN: 1,0

AT+QMTSUB
Subscribe the device to an MQTT topic
AT+QMTSUB=<tcpconnectID>,<msgID>,”<topic1>”,<qos1>
OK
<tcpconnectID> MQTT socket identifier. Range is 0-5 **<msgID>** Message identifier of packet. Range is 1-65535 **<topic>** Topic that the client wants to subscribe to **<qos>** The QoS level at which the client wants to publish the messages. 0 (At most once), 1 (At least once), 2 (Exactly once)
AT+QMTSUB =1,1, "basicPubSub",0 OK +QMTSUB: 1,1,0

AT+QMTPUB
Publish a message to an MQTT topic
AT+QMTPUB=<tcpconnectID>,<msgID>,<qos>,<retain>,”<topic>”
OK
<tcpconnectID> MQTT socket identifier. Range is 0-5 **<msgID>** Message identifier of packet. Range is 1-65535 **<qos>** The QoS level at which the client wants to publish the messages. 0 (At most once), 1 (At least once), 2 (Exactly once) **<retain>** Whether the server retains the received message or not after it has been delivered to the current subscribers. 0 (Server will not retain the message), 1 (server will retain the message) **<topic>** Topic that the client wants to publish to
AT+QMTPUB =1,1, 0,0,"Hello World!" OK +QMTPUB: 1,1,0

AT+QMTDISC
Disconnect an MQTT network connection from the MQTT server
AT+QMTDISC=<tcpconnectID>
OK
<tcpconnectID> MQTT socket identifier. The range is 0-5
AT+QMTDISC=1 OK +QMTDISC: 1,0

AT+QMTCLOSE
Close an MQTT network connection for the device
AT+QMCLOSE=<tcpconnectID>
OK
<tcpconnectID> MQTT socket identifier. The range is 0-5
AT+QMTCLOSE=1 OK +QMTCLOSE: 1,0

5.9 HTTP Commands

Hyper Text Transfer Protocol (HTTP) is the protocol used for World Wide Web (WWW) communication. This protocol has a secure version of it which is the HTTPS. The following are the AT commands use to configure and setup an HTTP(S) connection [19].

AT+QHTTPCFG
Configure the PDP context to be used for HTTP/HTTPS
AT+QHTTPCFG="contextid",<contextID>
OK
<contextID> PDP context ID. The range is 1-16.
AT+QHTTPCFG="contextid",1 OK

AT+QHTTPCFG
Customize the request header
AT+QHTTPCFG="requestheader",<request_header>
OK

<request_header> Disable or enable to customize HTTP(S) request header. 0 Disable 1 Enable
AT+QHTTPCFG="requestheader",0 OK

AT+QHTTPCFG
Customize the request header
AT+QHTTPCFG=”responseheader”,<response_header>
OK
<response_header> Disable or enable to output HTTP response header. 0 Disable 1 Enable
AT+QHTTPCFG="responseheader",0 OK

AT+QHTTPCFG
Configure the HTTP content type
AT+QHTTPCFG: "contenttype",<content_type>
OK
<content_type> Data type of HTTP(S) body. 0 application/x-www-form-urlencoded 1 text/plain 2 application/octet-stream 3 multipart/form-data
AT+QHTTPCFG="contenttype",0 OK

AT+QHTTPURL
Configure the HTTP URL to be accessed on the server
AT+QHTTPURL=<URL_length>
OK
<URL_length> The length of URL in bytes. The range is 1-700.
AT+QHTTPURL=21 CONNECT http://httpbin.org/ip OK

AT+QHTTPGET
Send an HTTP GET request to the server
AT+QHTTPGET=<rsptime>
OK
<rsptime> The range is 1-65535, and the default value is 60 seconds. It is used to configure the timeout for the HTTP(S) GET response.
AT+QHTTPGET=80 OK +QHTTPGET: 0,200,49

AT+QHTTPREAD
After sending HTTP GET/POST requests, device can retrieve HTTP response information from HTTP(S) server via UART/USB port by AT+QHTTPREAD command
AT+QHTTPREAD=<wait_time>
OK
<wait_time> The maximum interval time between receiving two packets of data. The range is 1-65535, and the default value is 60 seconds.

AT+QHTTPREAD=80
CONNECT
{
"origin": "12.153.230.170, 12.153.230.170"
}
OK
+QHTTPREAD: 0

5.10 File Commands

The modem has non-volatile storage called User File Storage directory (UFS). This storage about 4K bytes and used to store some information such as certificates and private keys used during secure socket connection and communication [20].

AT+QFLST
List all files on the UFS
AT+QFLST
OK

AT+QFLST +QFLST: "ca_cert.pem",1457 +QFLST: "client_cert.pem",1211 +QFLST: "client_key.pem",1662 OK

AT+QFDEL
Delete a file on the UFS
AT+QFDEL=<filename>
OK
<filename> Name of file to be deleted. If used "*", delete all files
AT+QFDEL="*" OK

AT+QFUPL
Upload or write a file on the UFS
AT+QFUPL=<filename>,<file_size>
OK
<filename> Name of the file to be uploaded **<file_size>** The file size to be uploaded AT+QFUPL="StarfieldClass2.crt",1490 CONNECT +QFUPL: 1490,4911 OK

AT+QFDWL
Download or read a file on the UFS
AT+QFDWL=<filename>
OK
<filename> Name of the file to be downloaded
AT+QFDWL="StarfieldClass2.crt" CONNECT QFDWL: 1457,6b3e OK

5.11 GNSS Commands

These are the AT commands used for the GNSS to configure the GNSS or get the location and positioning information [21].

AT+QGPSCFG
Configure NMEA Sentences Output Port
AT+QGPSCFG="outport",<outport>
OK
<outport> Configure the output port of NMEA sentences, and the configuration parameter will be automatically saved to NVRAM. "none" Close NMEA sentence output "usbnmea" Output via USB NMEA port "uartnmea" Output via UART3 port
AT+QGPSCFG="outport","uartnmea" OK

AT+QGPS
Turn on the GNSS
AT+QGPS=<gnssmode>
OK
<gnssmode> Turn on the GNSS in any of the following modes: 1 Stand-alone 2 MS-based 3 MS-assisted 4 Speed-optimal
AT+QGPS=1 OK

AT+QGPSLOC
Acquire positing information
AT+QGPSLOC=<mode>
OK
<mode> Latitude and longitude display format. 0 <latitude>,<longitude> format: ddmm.mmmm N/S,dddmm.mmmm E/W 1 <latitude>,<longitude> format: ddmm.mmmmmm N/S,dddmm.mmmmmm E/W 2 <latitude>,<longitude> format: (-)dd.ddddd,(-)ddd.ddddd

Response: **<UTC>,<latitude>,<longitude>,<hdop>,<altitude>,<fix>,<cog>,<spkm>,<spkn>, <date>,<nsat>** **<UTC>** UTC time **<latitude>** Latitude **<longitude>** Longitude **<hdop>** Horizontal precision **<altitude>** The altitude of the antenna away from the sea level in meter **<fix>** GNSS positioning mode **<cog>** Course Over Ground based on true north **<spkm>** Speed over ground in Km/h **<spkn>** Speed over ground in Knots **<date>** UTC time when fixing position **<nsat>** Number of satellites
AT+QGPSLOC=2 +QGPSLOC: 063729.0,47.82670,-122.20605,1.1,14.0,2,0.00,0.0,0.0,161119,06 OK

5.12 Firmware Update Commands

These are the AT commands used to update the modem firmware [22].

AT+QFOTADL
Enables automatic firmware upgrade for module via DFOTA
AT+QFOTADL=<httpURL>
OK
<httpURL> String format starts with "HTTP://" or "HTTPS://", for example: "HTTP://<http_server_URL>:<http_port>/<http_file_path>"
AT+QFOTADL="https://www.quectel.com:100/update.zip" OK +QIND: "FOTA","HTTPTART" +QIND: "FOTA","HTTPEND",0 //Finish downloading the package from HTTPS server. +QIND: "FOTA","START" +QIND: "FOTA","UPDATING", 1% +QIND: "FOTA","UPDATING", 2% ... +QIND: "FOTA","UPDATING", 100% +QIND: "FOTA","RESTORE", 1%

```
+QIND: "FOTA","RESTORE",2%
+QIND: "FOTA","RESTORE", 100%
+QIND: "FOTA","END",0 //Finish upgrading the firmware
```

5.13 Mobile Operator Configuration

The modem can be configured to connect to different mobile operators and cellular networks around the world. To connect the NB-IoT device to the mobile operator network, you need to get a USIM card and insert it into the USIM card slot on the NB board. USIM usually are bought from mobile operator stores or online.

Hologram is one virtual mobile operator which provides NB-IoT cellular coverage in many countries around the world. A USIM can be obtained from their online store at `https://hologram.io/`and used with the NB board.

In addition, many mobile operators in the USA now provide NB-IoT cellular services such as AT&T, T-Mobile, or Verizon network. However, after obtaining a USIM and inserting it into USIM card slot on the board, the modem needs to be configured in order to be able to connect to the mobile operator network and send and receive data.

Table 5.1: AT Commands for AT&T Network in the USA.

AT Command	Explanation
AT+QCFG="NWSCANSEQ",3	Search only for LTE NB-IoT network
AT+QCFG="NWSCANMODE",3	Target only LTE network
AT+ QCFG="IOTOPMODE",1	Target only NB-IoT network
AT+QCFG= "BAND", f,400a0e189f,a0e189f	Configure the RF frequency bands to be all bands
AT+CGDCONT=1,"IP", "m2mNB16.com.attz"	Set the APN name to m2mNB16.com.attz
AT+CEREG? +CEREG: 1,1	If the LTE registration status is queried, value of 1 means it is registered to AT&T network
AT+COPS? +COPS: 0,0,"AT&T",9	If current mobile operator is queried, it returns that the modem is connected to AT&T network and value of 9 means it is LTE Cat-NB1 network
AT+QCFG="NCCCONF",5	Configure the extended protocol configuration of the NB-IoT modem

The Arduino projects used in this book for connecting to the mobile operator networks configure the modem automatically as part of the Arduino sketch. However, the modem can be configured manually by sending AT commands to the modem. The following table summarizes the configuration setting used to configure the modem to work with AT&T network in the USA and connect to its cellular NB-IoT network.

5.14 Arduino Sketch

The following is an Arduino sketch that acts as an AT command interface for the modem. The code has two serial interfaces; one is the MCU USB port which is used for the connection between the hardware board and the computer and the second one is the serial port between the MCU and modem. The code reads the user input, passes to the modem, receive the response from modem, and displays the response on the Serial Monitor.

When you run this code, launch the Serial Monitor. Enter any AT command in the Serial Monitor edit box, press **Send** button and it will be send to the modem. The response to the AT command will be displayed on the Serial Monitor as well.

```
#include <board.h>

#define DSerial SerialUSB
#define ATSerial Serial1

_5G_NB_IoT_Common _5GNBIoT(ATSerial, DSerial);

void setup()
{
  DSerial.begin(115200);
  while (DSerial.read() >= 0);
  DSerial.println("This is the _5GNBIoT Debug Serial!");

  ATSerial.begin(115200);
  while (ATSerial.read() >= 0);
  delay(1000);

  _5GNBIoT.InitModule();
  DSerial.println("\r\n_5GNBIoT.InitModule() OK!");

  _5GNBIoT.SetDevCommandEcho(false);
}

void loop()
{
  if (ATSerial.available())
  {
    char at = ATSerial.read();
```

```
    DSerial.write(at);
  }

  if (DSerial.available())
  {
    char d = DSerial.read();
    ATSerial.write(d);
    DSerial.write(d);
  }
}
```

Listing 5.1: Arduino Sketch for AT Commands.

The output from the Serial Monitor is shown below. Before you start using it, set the values of line ending to **Carriage return** and **baud rate** to 115200. You can use any of the AT commands in previous sections to query, configure, open a socket, or send and receive data from a remote server.

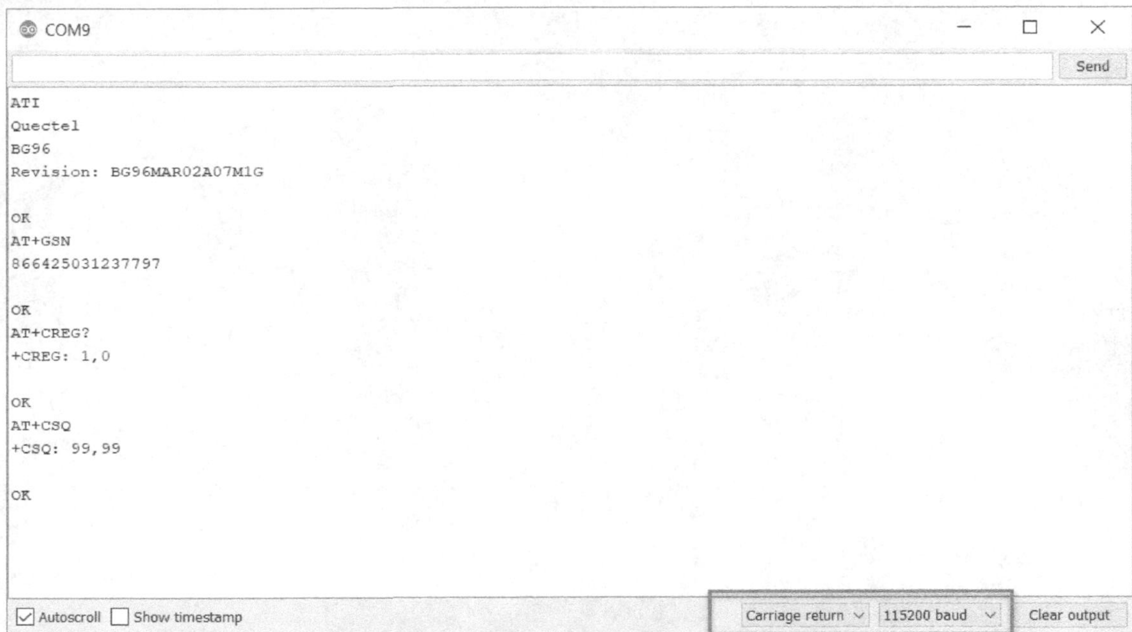

Figure 5.1: Serial Monitor Output for AT Commands.

Chapter 6

Data Serialization and Deserialization

6.1 JavaScript Object Notation (JSON) Format

JSON stands for JavaScript Object Notation. JSON is a human-readable and writable data format. It is easy for machines to parse and generate it. JSON is a text format that is language independent which means it can be used in a programming language like C/C++ or Java [23]. It also can be used with Arduino. These properties make JSON an ideal data-interchange language especially to the cloud and with web servers. JSON format is built using the following two structures:

- A collection of name/value pairs. In various languages, this is realized as an object, record, struct, dictionary, hash table, keyed list, or associative array.

- An ordered list of values. In most languages, this is realized as an array, vector, list, or sequence.

For example, the following is a JSON formatted text string that represents a reading from a GPS sensor. It has a name/value pair like "lat": 48.74801. The value of "lat" is a single value and can be an array of values.

When communicating with the cloud, the JSON data is sent to the cloud and when the data is received from the cloud, it is received using this JSON format.

```
{
  "sensor": "GPS",
  "lat": 48.74801,
  "lon": 120.1235,
  "cnt": 571
}
```

Listing 6.1: JSON Data for a GPS Sensor.

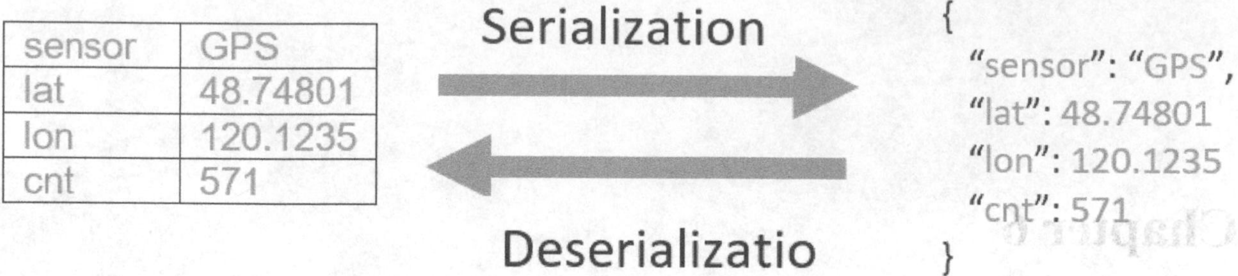

Figure 6.1: JSON Serialization and Deserialization.

6.2 JSON Serialization

Json serialization (or deserialization) is the process of translating a data structure or object into JSON formatted text or convert JSON formatted text back to a data structure or object. The following data structure when serialized, results in the JSON-formatted text. When deserialized, the JSON-formatted text results in the data structure.

6.3 JSON Library for Arduino

ArduinoJson is a JSON library for Arduino. To download it, launch Arduino IDE and select **Sketch->Include Library->Manage Libraries** and search for ArduinoJson and install it.

In ArduinoJson, the JSON-formatted text is called a document. ArduinoJson has many data types such as string, int, double. In the example above in Listing 6.1, the JSON text is composed of:

1. a string, named "sensor," with the value "GPS"

2. a double, named "lat" (for latitude) with the value 48.74801

3. a double, named "lon" (for longitude) with the value 120.1235

4. an int, named "cnt" (for a counter) with value 572

JSON ignores spaces and line breaks. JSON has become more popular than other formats, such as XML, because with XML, there is an opening and closing tag with each value which takes more size and is less human-readable.

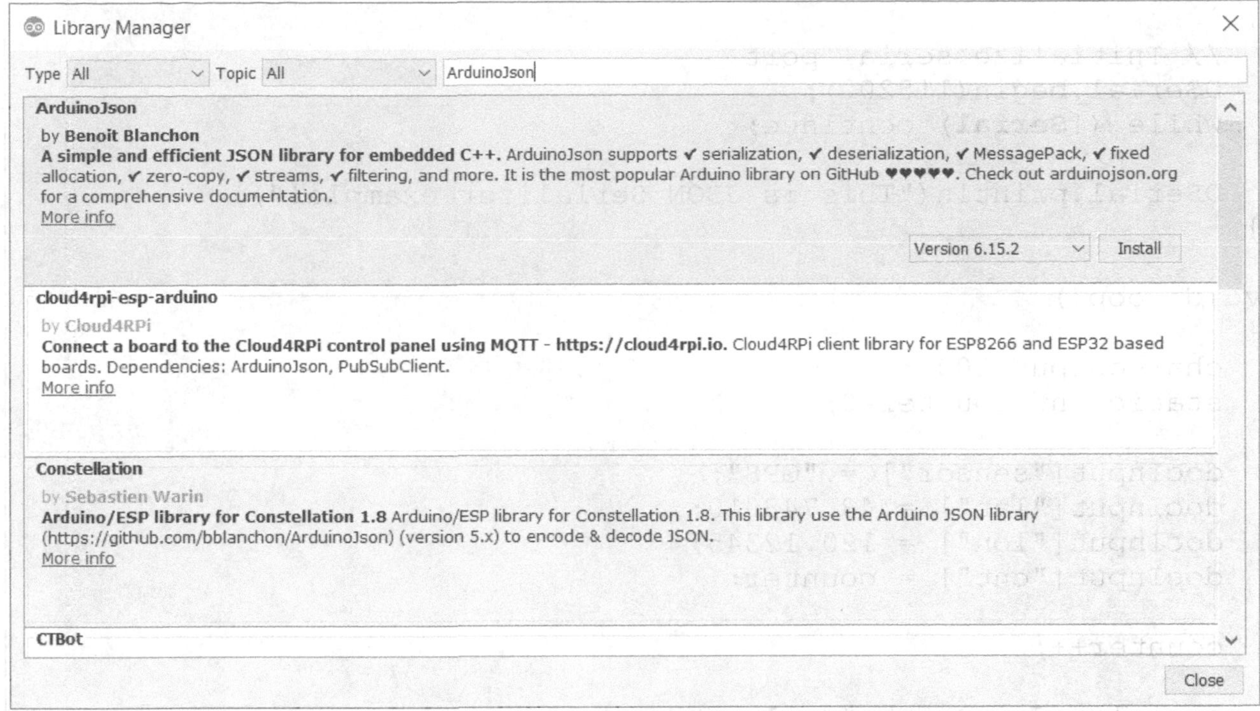

Figure 6.2: Installing ArduinoJason.

6.4 Arduino Sketch with JSON

The sample code in Listing 6.3 shows the basic of ArduinoJson and how to use it in an Arduino project and with MQTT.

It starts by including the header file, ArduinoJson.h, necessary to use the ArduinoJson APIs. Two documents are declared with a size of 500 bytes each with data type of **StaticJsonDocument**. **StaticJsonDocument** is a data type that is used to store and access the JSON object, its key, and values. Two documents are created; one to store the JSON text after serialization and a second document is created to store JSON object after deserializing a JSON text.

```
#include <ArduinoJson.h>

#define DSerial SerialUSB

// Allocate the JSON document used to serialize
// Inside the brackets, 500 is the capacity of the memory pool
// in bytes.

StaticJsonDocument<500> docInput;
StaticJsonDocument<500> docOutput;

void setup()
```

```
{
  // Initialize serial port
  DSerial.begin(115200);
  while (!Serial) continue;

  DSerial.println("This is JSON Serializer example!");
}

void loop()
{
  char output[500];
  static int counter=0;

  docInput["sensor"] = "GPS";
  docInput["lat"] = 48.748010;
  docInput["lon"] = 120.12345;
  docInput["cnt"] = counter;

  counter++;

  serializeJsonPretty(docInput, output);
  DSerial.println("Json format:\r\n");
  DSerial.println(output);

  DeserializationError error = deserializeJson(docOutput, output)
    ;

  if (error != DeserializationError::Ok)
  {
    DSerial.println("\r\n Error in Deserialization!");
    Serial.println(error.c_str());
    return;
  }
  DSerial.println(docOutput["sensor"].as<String>());

  if (docOutput["sensor"] == "GPS")
  {
    DSerial.println(docOutput["lat"].as<double>(), 6);
    DSerial.println(docOutput["lon"].as<double>(), 6);
    DSerial.println(docOutput["cnt"].as<int>());
  }

  delay(1000);
}
```

Listing 6.2: Arduino Sketch for JSON Serialization.

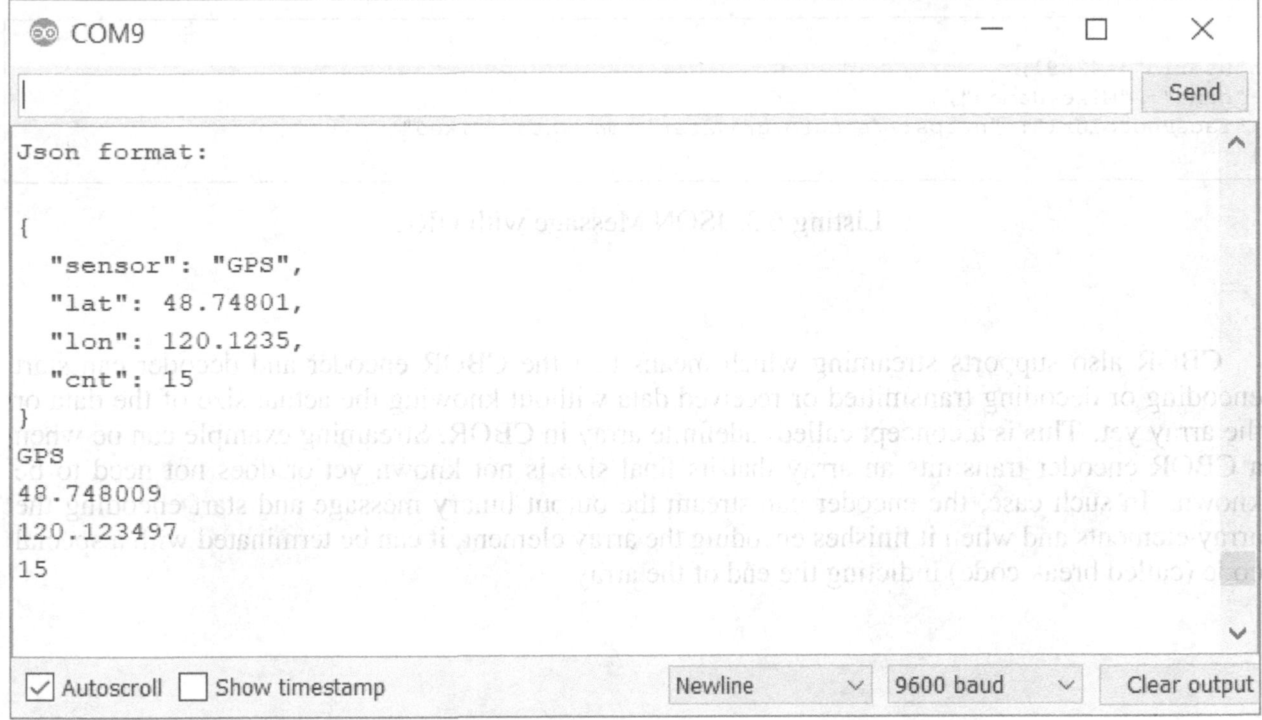

Figure 6.3: Serial Monitor for JSON Serialization and Deserialization.

The code performs serialization of the JSON object which contains the keys, sensor, **lat**, **long**, and **cnt** into JSON text. Then using the output from the serialization, it deserialize it back to the a JSON object which when parsed by the same keys yields the same values for the keys.

After serialization and deserialization, launch the Arduino IDE Serial Monitor, you can view the output after serialization and deserialization.

6.5 Concise Binary Object Representation (CBOR) Format

CBOR is a recent binary schema-less data serialization protocol similar to JSON. It introduces several novel concepts over JSON-formatted messages such as extremely small and compact message size, support for binary data, and explicit streaming support [24] [25].

CBOR support binary content. If an NB-IoT device is transmitting a CBOR message, it can transmit binary blobs. For example, if an NB-IoT device needs to transmit a picture or an image, it can transmit the following JSON-formatted message which requires the photo of the user through fetching it from the URL of the photo. The request of getting the photo from the URL can be avoided and reduces the overall communication time by embedding the binary content of the photo directly and thus saving unnecessary URL connection.

```
{
 "userId": 42891,
 "name": "Mike James",
 "facePhotolUrl": "https://secure.gravatar.com/avatar/MikeJ"
}
```


Listing 6.3: JSON Message with URL.

CBOR also supports streaming which means that the CBOR encoder and decoder can start encoding or decoding transmitted or received data without knowing the actual size of the data or the array yet. This is a concept called indefinite array in CBOR. Streaming example can be when a CBOR encoder transmits an array that its final size is not known yet or does not need to be known. In such case, the encoder can stream the output binary message and start encoding the array elements and when it finishes encoding the array element, it can be terminated with a special code (called break code) indicting the end of the array.

6.6 Data Item in CBOR

Unlink the name/value pair in JSON, CBOR refers to a semantic unit of data as **data item**. There are eight **major types** of data items. Data items of the same major type share the same **major type value**, which serves as a header used for determining the major type. Items of the same type have largely similar structures. The semantics of CBOR data items are defined in terms of bits and bytes, a byte being 8 bits. All well-formed items consist of 1 or more full bytes of data. The length of most data items can be determined from their headers.

A data item consists of a data item header and the data. The first byte of a data item (the major type byte) consists of 3 bits of information specifying the major type value. The remaining 5 bits are called **additional information** and are used to either store the item value, or to specify the size of the item to be stored in the following bytes.

The encoding of the data item can be either one of the two format as in Table 6.1 and Table 6.2. If the **information field** in the data item is used to store the item value, Table 6.1 is used, otherwise, if the value need more bytes, the data item uses the format in Table 6.2.

Table 6.1: Structure of Major Type Byte.

Byte	Data Item Header	
Field	Major type value	Additional information value
Bit	3 Bits	5 Bits

Table 6.2: Structure of Major Type Byte.

Byte	Data Item Header		
Field	Major type value	Additional information value	Variable
Bit	3 Bits	5 Bits	8 Bits x (Additional information value)

Table 6.3 shows the possible major type defined for CBOR. It includes, signed and unsigned integer, byte and text string, array, map (pair of name/values), and floating numbers. Major type value is 3-bit value and is represented in the binary format, 0xbXXX.

Table 6.3: CBOR Major Types.

Major Type	**Major type value (3 bits)**	**Addition Info**	**Additional Info Meaning**	**Data Item Size (Bytes)**
Unsigned integer	0 (0b000)	0 to 23	Use directly as data value	1
		24	Next byte is uint8_t	2
		25	Next byte is uint16_t	3
		26	Next byte is uint32_t	5
		27	Next byte is uint64_t	9
Signed integer	1 (0b001)	0 to 23	Use directly as data value	1
		24	Next byte is uint8_t	2
		25	Next byte is uint16_t	3
		26	Next byte is uint32_t	5
		27	Next byte is uint64_t	9
Byte string	2 (0b010)	0 to 23	0âĂŞ23 bytes follow	1 + up to 23
		24	Next byte is uint8_t	$2+2^8-1$
		25	Next byte is uint16_t	$2+2^{16}-1$

		26	Next byte is uint32_t	$2+2^{32}-1$
		27	Next byte is uint64_t	$2+2^{64}-1$
Text string	3 (0b011)	0 to 23	0âĂŞ23 bytes follow	1 + up to 23
		24	Next byte is uint8_t	$2+2^{8}-1$
		25	Next byte is uint16_t	$3+2^{16}-1$
		26	Next byte is uint32_t	$5+2^{32}-1$
		27	Next byte is uint64_t	$9+2^{64}-1$
Array	4 (0b100)	0 to 23	0âĂŞ23 items follow	1 + up to 23
		24	Next byte is uint8_t	$2+2^{8}-1$
		25	Next byte is uint16_t	$3+2^{16}-1$
		26	Next byte is uint32_t	$5+2^{32}-1$
		27	Next byte is uint64_t	$9+2^{64}-1$
Map	5 (0b101)	0 to 23	0âĂŞ23 pairs follow	1+size of 23 pairs
		24	Next byte is uint8_t	2+size of 2^{8} pairs
		25	Next byte is uint16_t	3+size of 2^{16} pairs
		26	Next byte is uint32_t	5+size of 2^{32} pairs
		27	Next byte is uint64_t	9+size of 2^{64} pairs
Float	7 (0b111)	0 to 23	Simple value 0 âĂŞ 23	1
		25	Next 2 Bytes uint16_t as IEEE 754 half-precision float	3

		26	Next 4 Bytes is uint32_t as IEEE 754 single-precision float	5
		27	Next 8 Bytes is uint64_t as IEEE 754 double-precision float	9

6.7 Major Type 0 (Unsigned Integer)

Data item of this type are used for unsigned integers in the range from 0 to $2^{64}-1$. Depending on the actual value, the 5-bit additional information has different meanings as defined in Table 6.1.

Small unsigned integers between 0 to 23 are encoded in the additional information 5 bits, which allows very compact encoding of small numbers. If the additional information has a value of 24, it means the following byte holds **uint8_t** value, and if additional information value is 25, it means that the following two bytes holds **uint16_t** value. If additional information value is 26, it means that the following four bytes holds **uint32_t** value. If additional information value is 27, it means that the following four bytes holds **uint64_t** value. Examples of this as below where a hexadecimal value of 02 means that it is major type 0 and additional information value is 2. The second example of the data item has hexadecimal value of 0x182A which means that major type is zero and additional information value is 24 indicating the next byte holds **uint8_t** value and has value of 42.

```
// 2
02 # unsigned(2)

// 42
182A # unsigned(42)
```

Listing 6.4: Major Type 0 (Unsigned Integer).

6.8 Major Type 1 (Signed Integer)

Data items of this type are used for negative integers in the range from -2^{64} to -1, in much the same way as unsigned integers.

```
// -2
22 # negative(2)

//-41
3829 # negative(41)
```

Listing 6.5: Major Type 1 (Signed Integer).

6.9 Major Type 2 (Byte Strings)

Data items of this type are used for storing sequences of zero or more bytes (octets). Byte strings have a fixed length (and can have indefinite length) specified in their headers. Additional information is used in a manner similar to that of previous types.

```
// # ""; empty byte string
40 # bytes(0)

// 416e792062797465732020d206576656e206e756c6c733a2 [...]
581B # bytes(27)
```

Listing 6.6: Major Type 2 (Byte Strings).

6.10 Major Type 3 (Text Strings)

Data items of this type are used for storing sequences of zero or more characters of UTF-8 encoded text. Text strings use the additional information in exactly the same way as byte strings do.

```
// # ""; empty text string
60 # text(0)

// 48656c6c6f20776f726c6421 # "Hello world!"
6C # text(12)
```

Listing 6.7: Major Type 3 (Text Strings).

6.11 Major Type 4 (Arrays)

Data item of this type are used for storing sequences of zero or more data items. Array length is encoded in much the same way as that of byte and text strings.

```
// [];empty array
80 # array(0)

// [1 2 3]
84 # array(4)
    01 # unsigned(1)
    02 # unsigned(2)
    03 # unsigned(3)
    63 # text(3)
        666f6f # "foo"
```

Listing 6.8: Major Type 4 (Arrays).

6.12 Major Type 5 (Maps)

Data items of this type are used for storing associative maps (a pair of name/value analogous to JSON). They are represented by a series of zero or more pairs of items. Length of maps is encoded using the same technique as for arrays.

```
// empty map
A0 # map(0)

/# {"foo": 42, "bar": []}
A2 # map(2)
    63 # text(3)
         666f6f # "foo"
    182A # unsigned(42)
    63 # text(3)
        626172 # "bar"
    80 # array(0)
```

Listing 6.9: Major Type 5 (Maps).

6.13 Major Type 7 (Floating-Point Number)

Data item of this type are used for storing floating-point numbers. The encoding defined by the IEEE 754 standard is used for the numbers, but only half-, single-, and double-precision floats are currently available. Additional information values from 0 to 23 refer to either true, false, null, and undefined value.

Simple values refer to true, false, null, and undefined value. As the standard contains no information about mapping of these values to the types of common programming languages, these values, especially undefined value, require extra attention when used.

```
//# true
F5 # primitive(21)

//# 3.141592653589793238462643383
FB 400921fb54442d18 # primitive(4614256656552045848)
```

Listing 6.10: Major Type 6 (Floating-Point Number).

6.14 CBOR Compact Data Size

The most important advantage of CBOR is that it has smaller and compact-sized message than JSON format. CBOR message has smaller footprint, and smaller size than JSON. Smaller size results in faster transmission speed and much less processing time. Memory consumption is also shown to be less with CBOR than JSON. Full comparison between CBOR and JSON can be found in this article [26].

To show how CBOR is more optimized for NB-IoT device, let us encode the following JSON-formatted text, in Listing 6.11, using JSON and CBOR encoding. Listing 6.11 shows a JSON data to be transmitted by an NB-IoT device. JSON are stored as hexadecimal values corresponding to the UTF-8 encoding of the name/value pair and the enclosing parentheses. The hexadecimal view of this JSON data is show in Table 6.4 and it occupies exactly 122 bytes on the desk space. This size of 122 bytes is what to be transmitted over the air from the NB-IoT device to a remote server.

```
{
  "DeviceID" = "123456789012345",
  "Timestamp" = 50406,
  "Device" = "Temperature Sensor",
  "OpCode" = "Read",
  "Temperature" = 30,
  "Unit" = "F"
}
```

Listing 6.11: JSON-Formatted Data from an NB-IoT Device.

Table 6.4: JSON Encoded Message in Hexadecimal.

00000000	7B 22 44 65 76 69 63 65 49 44 22 3A 22 31 32 33	{"DeviceID":"123
00000010	34 35 36 37 38 39 30 31 32 33 34 35 22 2C 22 54	456789012345","T
00000020	69 6D 65 73 74 61 6D 70 22 3A 35 30 34 30 36 2C	imestamp":50406,
00000030	22 44 65 76 69 63 65 22 3A 22 54 65 6D 70 65 72	"Device":"Temper
00000040	61 74 75 72 65 20 53 65 6E 73 6F 72 22 2C 22 4F	ature Sensor","O
00000050	70 43 6F 64 65 22 3A 22 52 65 61 64 22 2C 22 54	pCode":"Read","T
00000060	65 6D 70 65 72 61 74 75 72 65 22 3A 33 30 2C 22	emperature":30,"
00000070	55 6E 69 74 22 3A 22 46 22 7D	Unit":"F"}

For the same JSON data, it can be encoded using CBOR as shown in Listing 6.12. The CBOR encoded data in hexadecimal format is shown in Table 6.4 and occupies only 98 bytes. Compared to the JSON format which takes 122 bytes, this represents a reduction of about 19% in message size. The bigger the message, the more reduction can be obtained if CBOR encoding is used.

Listing 6.12 shows the CBOR encoded message which starts by the 0xA6 or 0b101_0110. This represents major type 5 (map) and number of name/value pair is 6. The following data item is the name "DeviceID" which is encoded as 0x68 or 0b011_01000. This represent major type 3 (byte string) a number of bytes of 8. All other data items are encoded as byte strings similarly except the value of temperature of 30 which is encoded as unsigned integer (major type 0).

```
A6                                                # map(6)
   68                                             # text(8)
      4465766963654944                            #"DeviceID"
   6F                                             # text(15)
      313233343536373839303132333435              # "123456789012345"
   69                                             # text(9)
      54696D657374616D70                          # "Timestamp"
   19 C4E6                                        #unsigned(50406)
   66                                             # text(6)
      446576696365                                # "Device"
   72                                             # text(18)
      54656D70657261747572652053656E736F72 # "Temperature Sensor"
   66                                             # text(6)
      4F70436F6465                                # "OpCode"
   64                                             # text(4)
      52656164                                    # "Read"
   6B                                             # text(11)
      54656D7065726174757265                      # "Temperature"
   18 1E                                          #unsigned(30)
   64                                             #text(4)
      556E6974                                    # "Unit"
   61                                             #text(1)
      46                                          # "F"
```

Listing 6.12: CBOR Encoded View of the JSON-Formatted Data.

6.15 Arduino Sketch with CBOR

The following Arduino sketch shows the CBOR encoder and decoder output for the JSON-formatted text in Listing 6.13. It uses and is based on an open source CBOR library known as YACL [27].The CBOR encoder encodes the JSON message and coverts it into a hexadecimal string as in Listing 6.12. Then the decoder takes the hexadecimal value generated by the encoder, decodes it, and results in the same JSON input message.

```
#include <board.h>
#include "YACL.h"

#define DSerial SerialUSB

void setup()
{
  DSerial.begin(115200);
  while (DSerial.read() >= 0);
  delay(3000);

  DSerial.println("{");
  DSerial.println("\t \"DeviceID\": \"123456789012345\",");
  DSerial.println("\t \"Timestamp\": 50406,");
  DSerial.println("\t \"Device\": \"Temperature Sensor\",");
  DSerial.println("\t \"OpCode\": \"Read\",");
  DSerial.println("\t \"Temperature\": 30,");
  DSerial.println("\t \"Unit\": \"F\"");
  DSerial.println("}");

  CBORPair data = CBORPair(100);
  data.append("DeviceID", "123456789012345");
  data.append("Timestamp", 50406);
  data.append("Device", "Temperature Sensor");
  data.append("OpCode", "Read");
  data.append("Temperature", 30);
  data.append("Unit", "F");

  DSerial.print("CBOR Encoded data size: ");
  DSerial.println(data.length(),DEC);

  DSerial.print("CBOR Encoded data: 0x");
  const uint8_t *cbor_encoded = data.to_CBOR();
  uint8_t cbor_data[256];
  for (size_t i = 0 ; i < data.length(); ++i)
    {
     if (cbor_encoded[i] < 0x10)
     {
      DSerial.print('0');
     }
     DSerial.print(cbor_encoded[i], HEX);
     cbor_data[i] = cbor_encoded[i];
   }

   DSerial.println("\nCBOR Decoded data:");

    // Import dictionary into a CBOR object
```

```
    CBOR data = CBOR(cbor_data, String((char*)cbor_data).length()
   , true);

    DSerial.println("{");
    DSerial.print("\t \"DeviceID\": ");
    char devid[32];
    data["DeviceID"].get_string(devid);
    DSerial.print(devid);
    DSerial.print(",\n");

    DSerial.print("\t \"Timestamp\": ");
    DSerial.print(uint32_t(data["Timestamp"]));
    DSerial.print(",\n");

    DSerial.print("\t \"Device\": ");
    char dev[32];
    data["Device"].get_string(dev);
    DSerial.print(dev);
    DSerial.print(",\n");

    DSerial.print("\t \"OpCode\": ");
    char opc[32];
    data["OpCode"].get_string(opc);
    DSerial.print(opc);
    DSerial.print(",\n");

    DSerial.print("\t \"Temperature\": ");
    DSerial.print(uint32_t(data["Temperature"]));
    DSerial.print(",\n");

    DSerial.print("\t \"Unit\": ");
    char un[32];
    data["Unit"].get_string(un);
    DSerial.print(un);
    DSerial.print("\n");

    DSerial.println("}");
}

void loop()
{
  delay(1000);
}
```

Listing 6.13: Arduino Sketch for CBOR Serialization.

The output message can be shown as below which shows the exact hexadecimal string as in Listing 6.12. The encoder generates hexadecimal string of length 98 as in Table 6.4

```
{
   "DeviceID": "123456789012345",
   "Timestamp": 50406,
   "Device": "Temperature Sensor",
   "OpCode": "Read",
   "Temperature": 30,
   "Unit": "F"
}

CBOR Encoded data size: 98
CBOR Encoded data: 0xA66844657669636549 4
                    46F3132333435363738
                    393031323334356954 6
                    96D657374616D7019C4
                    E666446576696365725
                    4656D70657261747572
                    652053656E736F72664
                    F70436F646564526561
                    646B54656D706572617
                    4757265181E64556E69
                    746146

CBOR Decoded data:
{
   "DeviceID": 123456789012345,
   "Timestamp": 50406,
   "Device": Temperature Sensor,
   "OpCode": Read,
   "Temperature": 30,
   "Unit": F
}
```


Listing 6.14: Arduino Sketch for CBOR Serialization.

6.16 JSON versus CBOR

Message size impacts network performance across the wire and wireless channel. It also impacts devices with memory and CPU constraints. JSON is a text-based format while CBOR is binary-based format. The binary-format is more compact than text-based format on the expense of less human-readability.

Binary formats require serialization and deserialization libraries. The payload cannot be read unless it is decoded. Use a binary format if you want to reduce wire footprint and transfer messages faster. This category of format is recommended in scenarios where storage or network bandwidth is a concern or if the device is truly constrained with memory and CPU.

The disadvantage is that binary-formatted payload is not human readable. Most binary formats use complex systems that can be costly to maintain. Also, they need specialized libraries to decode, which may not be supported if you want to retrieve archival data.

CBOR is recent and fairly new serialization protocol. JSON remains the widely popular and most used encoding scheme with NB-IoT device and with the cloud such as Amazon or Microsoft Azure. JSON has become more mature and has more support from different software (C/C++/C#), IDEs, libraries, open-source tools, and development.

CBOR is still not widely popular such as JSON. Till today, most of the cloud technology such as REST API, HTTP protocols, IoT hubs deployed in the cloud uses JSON while CBOR uses are limited. Thus, during the rest of this book, we use JSON format since it is widely supported by the technology industry, more human-readable, easy to understand, and has more support from Arduino community and tools. Users of this book can replace all Arduino sketches used throughout this book to use different serialization protocols as long as it is supported by Arduino tools, servers, or clouds.

Chapter 7

Amazon Web Services for IoT Devices (AWS IoT)

Amazon Web Services (AWS) is the cloud offered by Amazon. Amazon cloud is available world-wide and in different regions. AWS offers MQTT service where the MQTT server is hosted in AWS. NB-IoT device, acting as MQTT client, can communicate with the AWS.

The AWS for IoT is called AWS IoT and is available as a service offered by Amazon cloud. AWS IoT allows you to easily connect NB-IoT devices to the cloud. AWS IoT supports MQTT which is a lightweight communication protocol specifically designed to minimize the code foot-print on devices, reduce network bandwidth requirements, and is commonly used for IoT devices. You will use MQTT to connect NB-IoT devices to the cloud and make Arduino projects and sketches connect, upload, and download data to the cloud.

AWS IoT connects to IoT device by authenticating and providing end-to-end encryption to connected devices. Arduino sketches transmit and receive data to cloud after performing authenti-cation with the cloud and data is encrypted in both directions.

With AWS IoT, you can filter, transform, and act upon device data on the fly, based on rules that can be defined on the cloud. You can update your rules to implement new device and application features at any time. After a rule processes data received from devices, it can store these data for further visualization or processing such as storing it on the cloud database such as Amazon DynamoDB.

Figure 7.1 shows the setup of the NB board when connected to the cloud. The cellular modem communicates with the cellular base-station (eNodeB) and connects to the APN in the mobile operator core network. The APN acts as a router that connects the modem to the cloud and Internet.

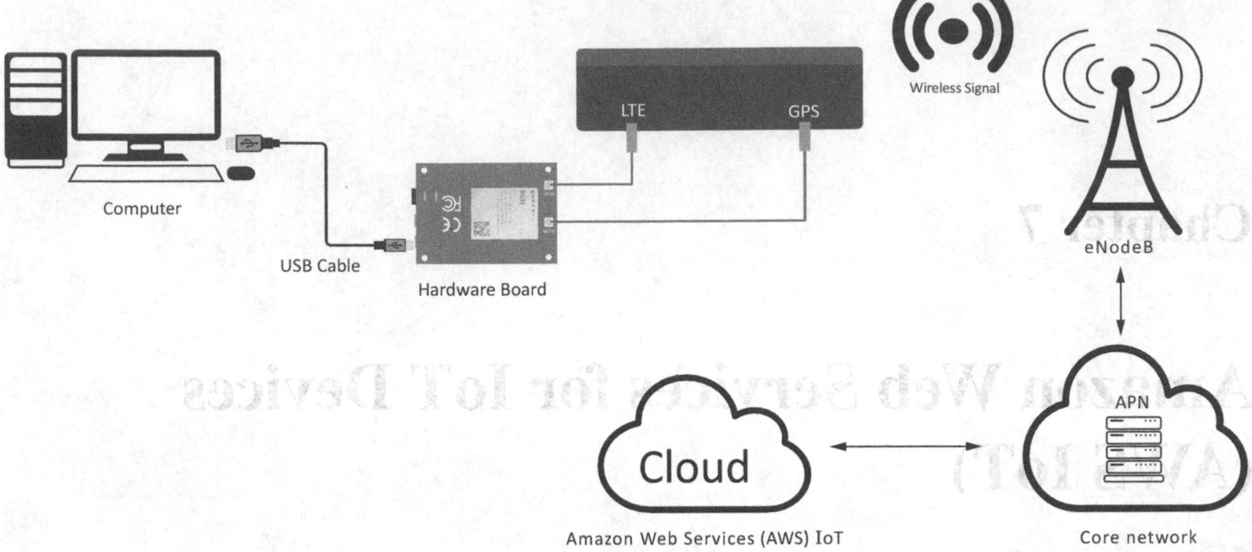

Figure 7.1: NB-IoT Hardware Board Connected to the Cloud.

7.1 AWS IoT Device Management and Configuration

The first step in connecting the NB-IoT device to cloud is to use AWS management console, as in Figure 7.2, which is used to access all AWS services including AWS IoT service. In AWS IoT, you can onboard new devices, create X.509 identity certificates, or create security policies. Then, you can configure the entire fleet of devices with this information with few clicks in the AWS IoT.

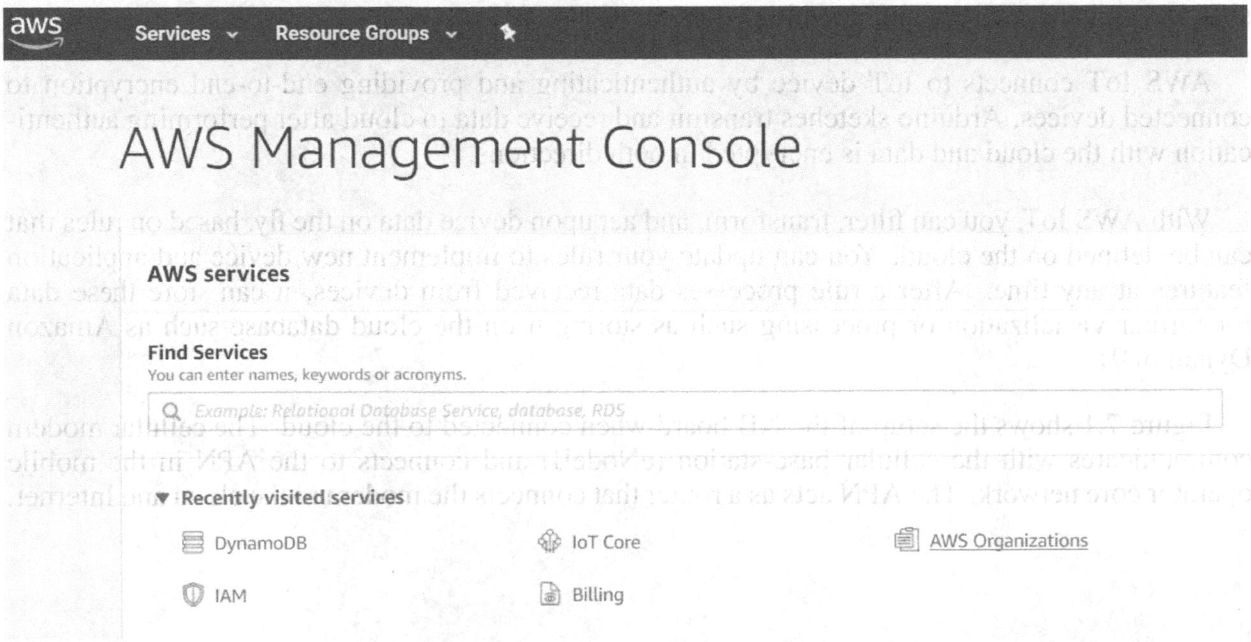

aws Services Resource Groups

AWS Management Console

AWS services

Find Services

You can enter names, keywords or acronyms.

Example: Relational Database Service, database, RDS

Recently visited services

DynamoDB IoT Core AWS Organizations

IAM Billing

Figure 7.2: AWS Management Console.

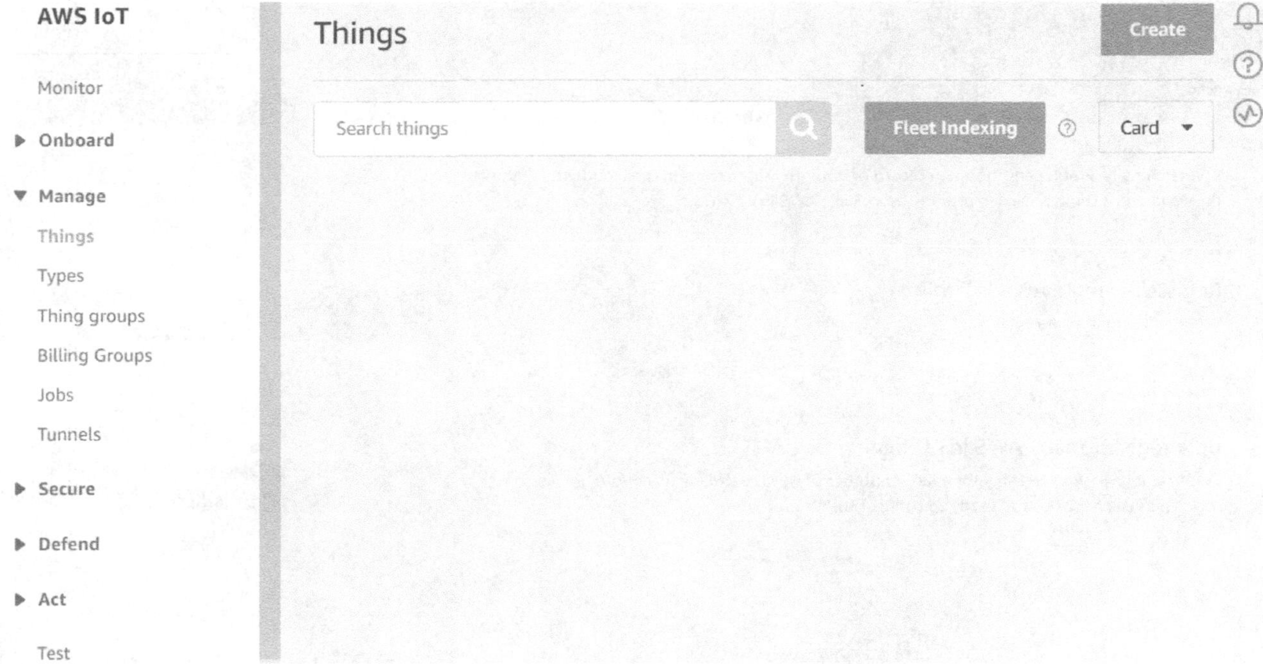

Figure 7.3: AWS IoT Dashboard.

7.2 Registering the Thing

When you go to AWS IoT, you can start adding new NB-IoT devices (called **Things**), creating new certificates and use them to authenticate the thing to the AWS IoT cloud, attach it to a policy and starts connecting the NB-IoT device using MQTT to transmit and receive messages and data.

In the left-hand side, there is a vertical menu bar. To start add NB-IoT device and connect to the AWS IoT, click **Manage->Things** and then click **Create**.

You will be prompted to register a new **thing**. Click **Create a single thing** to start registering your first NB-IoT device as in Figure 7.4.

In the first step of registration, enter the thing **Name**. Here, we choose to enter NB-IoT as the name of the new thing. You can enter additional optional information such as the **Type** of the thing (you can create any type as you would prefer) and **Create group** if you want to create different group for the NB-IoT device and you need to assign the new thing to a specific group. You can also add attributes for a thing such as color, manufacturer, or any other attribute of your choice.

7.3 Creating Security Certificates

AWS IoT uses asymmetric cryptography. Asymmetric cryptography uses a pair of keys, public and private keys, to enable messages to be securely transferred. A message can be encrypted using

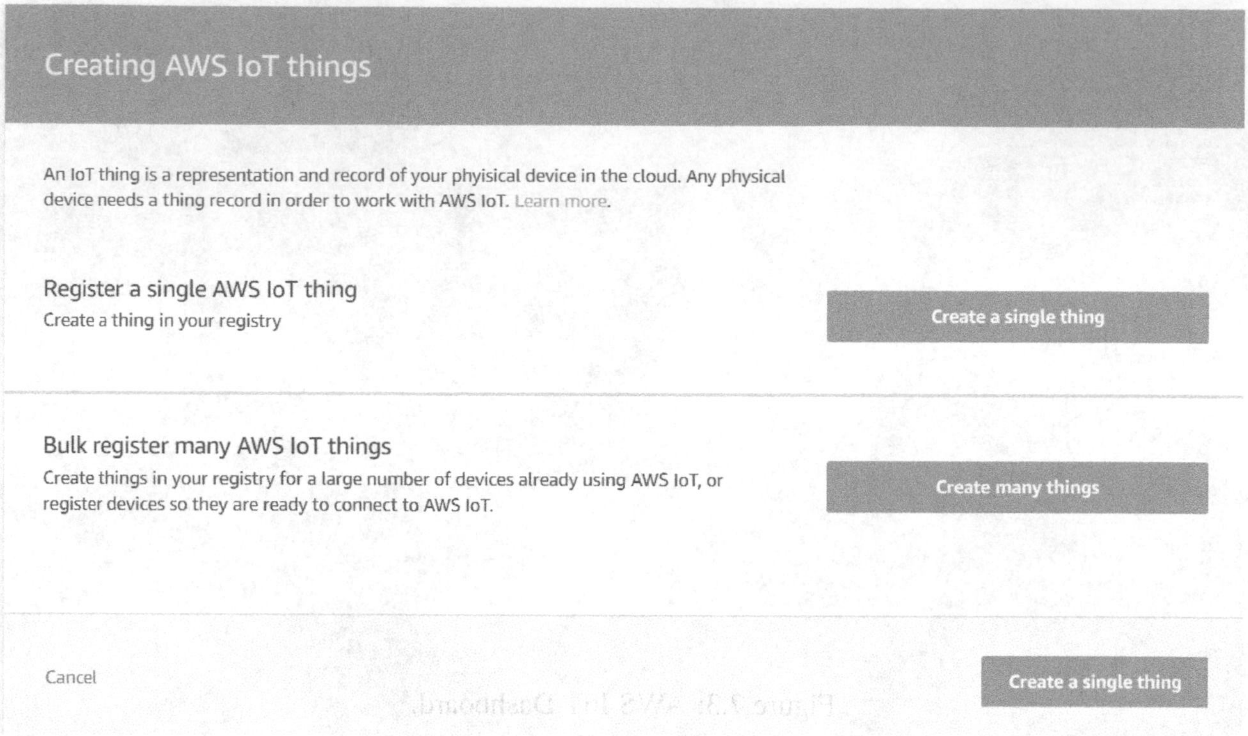

Creating AWS IoT things

An IoT thing is a representation and record of your phyisical device in the cloud. Any physical device needs a thing record in order to work with AWS IoT. Learn more.

Register a single AWS IoT thing
Create a thing in your registry

Create a single thing

Bulk register many AWS IoT things
Create things in your registry for a large number of devices already using AWS IoT, or register devices so they are ready to connect to AWS IoT.

Create many things

Cancel

Create a single thing

Figure 7.4: Creating AWS IoT Things.

a public key and the only way to decrypt it is to use the corresponding private key. Communication using public/private key is secure and can not be tampered with. Anyone with access to the public key can send an encrypted message that only the device, with private key, can decrypt and read it.

In addition, public and private keys also allow the device to sign a message. The private key can be used to add a digital signature to a message. Anyone with the public key can check the signature and know the original message has not been altered. The digital signature can be used to prove ownership of the private key. Anyone with the public key can verify the signature and be confident that when the message was signed, the signer was in possession of the private key.

In this step as in Figure 7.6, you will be prompted to add security for the thing. The security consists of creating a security certificate. The NB-IoT device need to use this certificate while opening a connection with the AWS IoT to authenticate each other. Click **Create certificate**. AWS IoT will create a public and private key and create a new device certificate signed by the AWS IoT CA private key.

The certificate will be created, and you will be prompted to download it to use it on the NB-IoT device. The certificate consists of a device certificate to be used by the thing, one public key, and one private key. Only the device certificate and private key are needed to be used by the NB-IoT device to connect to AWS IoT. You will also need to download a root certificate. The AWS IoT root certificate allows the NB-IoT device to verify that it is communicating with AWS IoT and not another server impersonating AWS IoT.

CREATE A THING

Add your device to the thing registry

STEP 1/3

This step creates an entry in the thing registry and a thing shadow for your device.

Name

NB-IoT

Apply a type to this thing

Using a thing type simplifies device management by providing consistent registry data for things that share a type. Types provide things with a common set of attributes, which describe the identity and capabilities of your device, and a description.

Thing Type

No type selected

Create a type

Add this thing to a group

Adding your thing to a group allows you to manage devices remotely using jobs.

Thing Group

Groups /

Create group Change

Set searchable thing attributes (optional)

Enter a value for one or more of these attributes so that you can search for your things in the registry.

Attribute key

Provide an attribute key, e.g. Manufacturer

Value

Provide an attribute value, e.g. Acme-Corporation

Clear

Show thing shadow

Cancel

Back

Next

Figure 7.5: Create a Thing in AWS IoT.

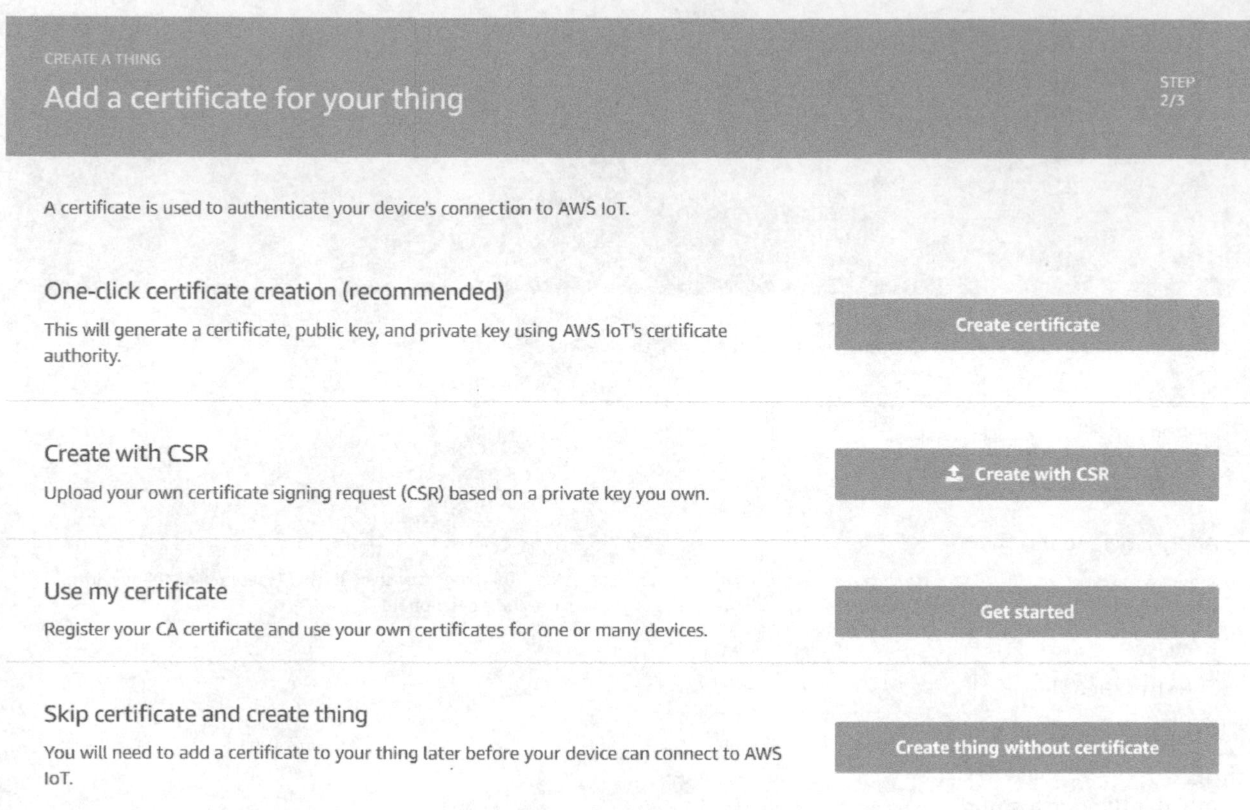

Figure 7.6: Create Certificates for the Thing in AWS IoT.

All three files, private key, device certificate, and AWS IoT root certificate, need to be stored on the NB-IoT device. After downloading certificate and keys, they need to be activated so just click **Activate** as in Figure 7.7 and Figure 7.8.

When the certificate and public/private keys are created, an TLS handshake is started between the device and AWS IoT, which will establish a secure communication channel between the device and AWS IoT. During the handshake, the device and AWS IoT agree on a shared secret, rather like a password, which will be used to encrypt all messages. A shared secret is preferred over using asymmetric keys as it less expensive in terms of computing power needed to encrypt messages, so the device can have better communication throughput. The TLS handshake contains details of the various cryptographic methods that the NB-IoT device is able to use. The AWS IoT picks the cryptographic method it wants to use to establish the shared secret and returns it to the NB-IoT device. Both the device and AWS IoT authenticate each other and start communicating using the shared secret.

When you return to the main menu item under **Manage->Things**, you will find the new thing has been created and appears in the dashboard under the name **NB-IoT** (Figure 7.9).

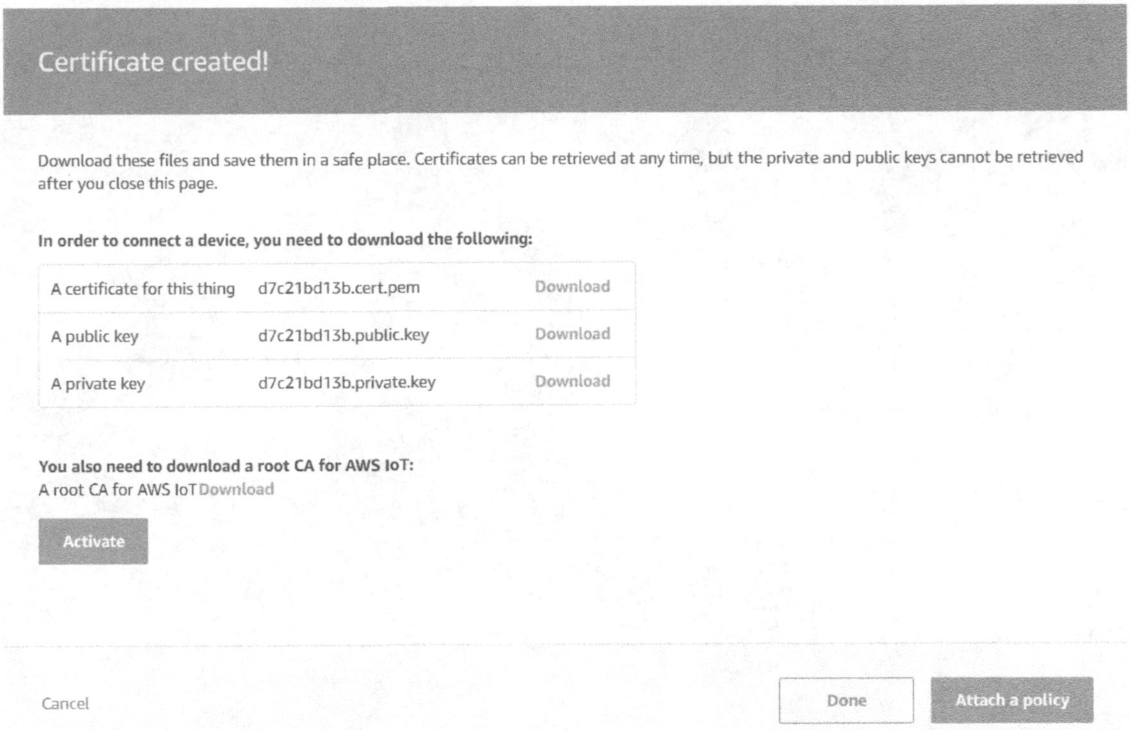

Certificate created!

Download these files and save them in a safe place. Certificates can be retrieved at any time, but the private and public keys cannot be retrieved after you close this page.

In order to connect a device, you need to download the following:

A certificate for this thing	d7c21bd13b.cert.pem	Download
A public key	d7c21bd13b.public.key	Download
A private key	d7c21bd13b.private.key	Download

You also need to download a root CA for AWS IoT:
A root CA for AWS IoT Download

Activate

Cancel Done Attach a policy

Figure 7.7: Successful Certificates Creation for the Thing in AWS IoT.

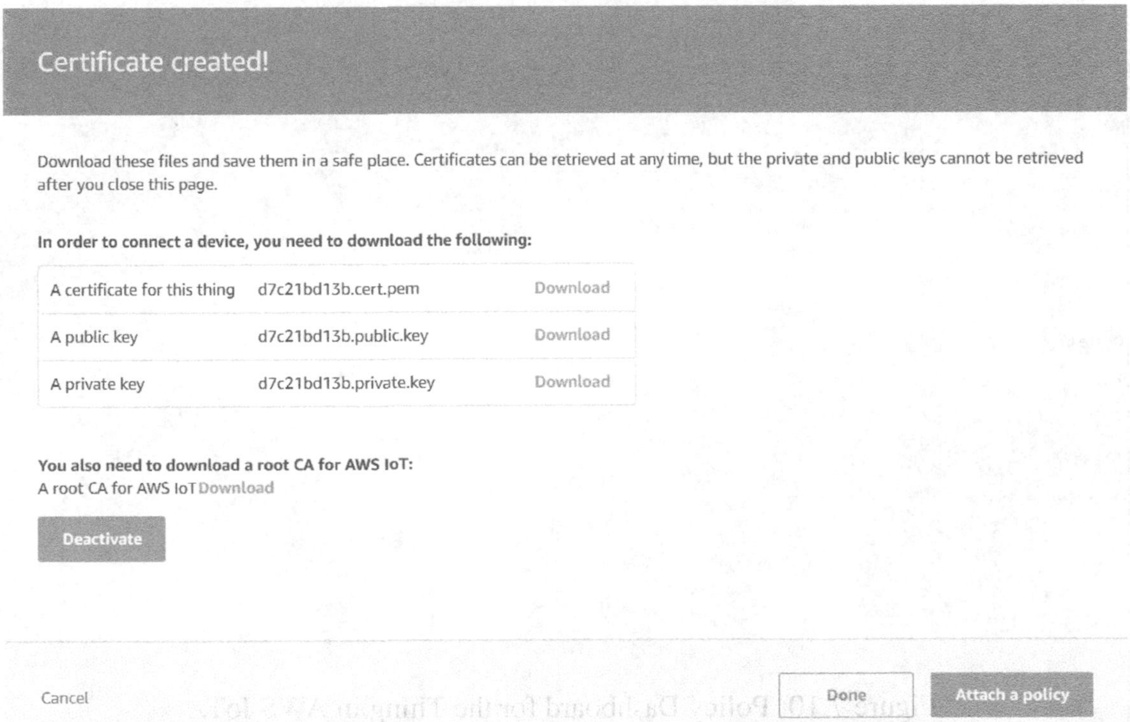

Certificate created!

Download these files and save them in a safe place. Certificates can be retrieved at any time, but the private and public keys cannot be retrieved after you close this page.

In order to connect a device, you need to download the following:

A certificate for this thing	d7c21bd13b.cert.pem	Download
A public key	d7c21bd13b.public.key	Download
A private key	d7c21bd13b.private.key	Download

You also need to download a root CA for AWS IoT:
A root CA for AWS IoT Download

Deactivate

Cancel Done Attach a policy

Figure 7.8: Activating Certificates for the Thing in AWS IoT.

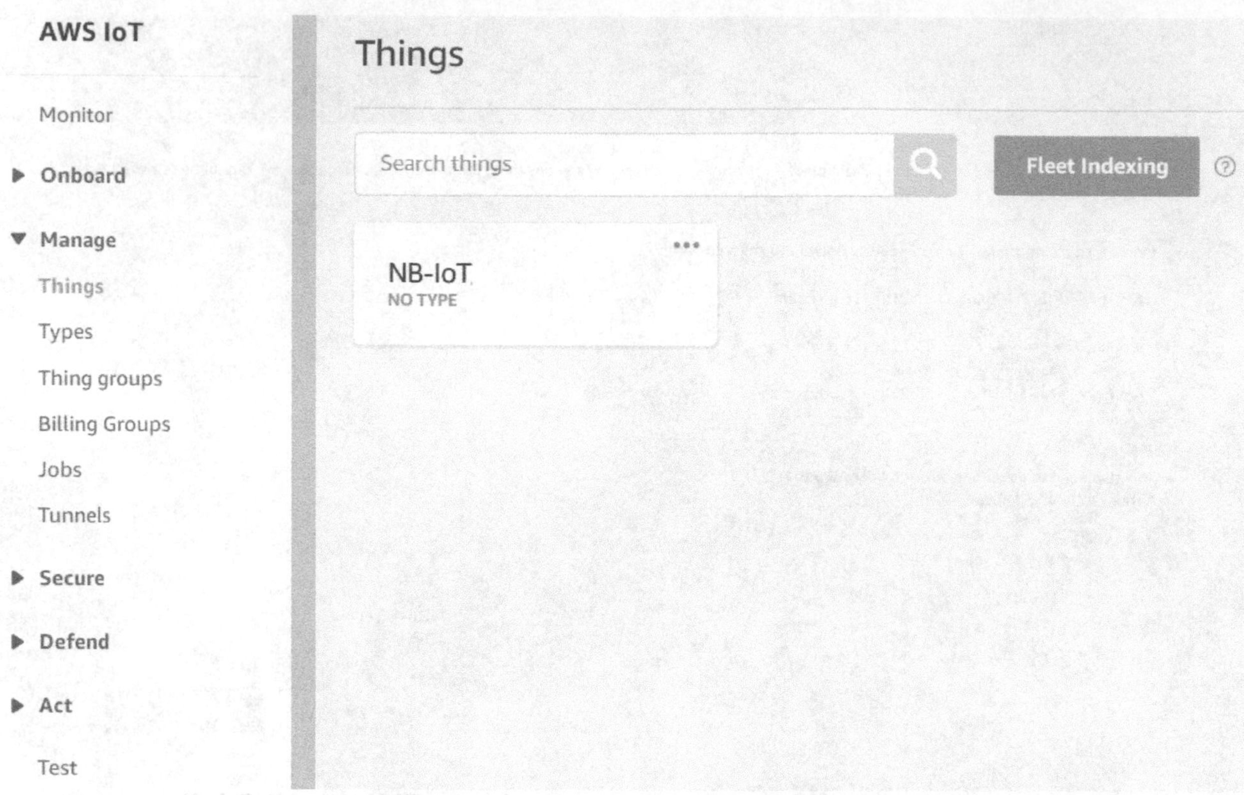

Figure 7.9: Successful Creation of the Thing in AWS IoT.

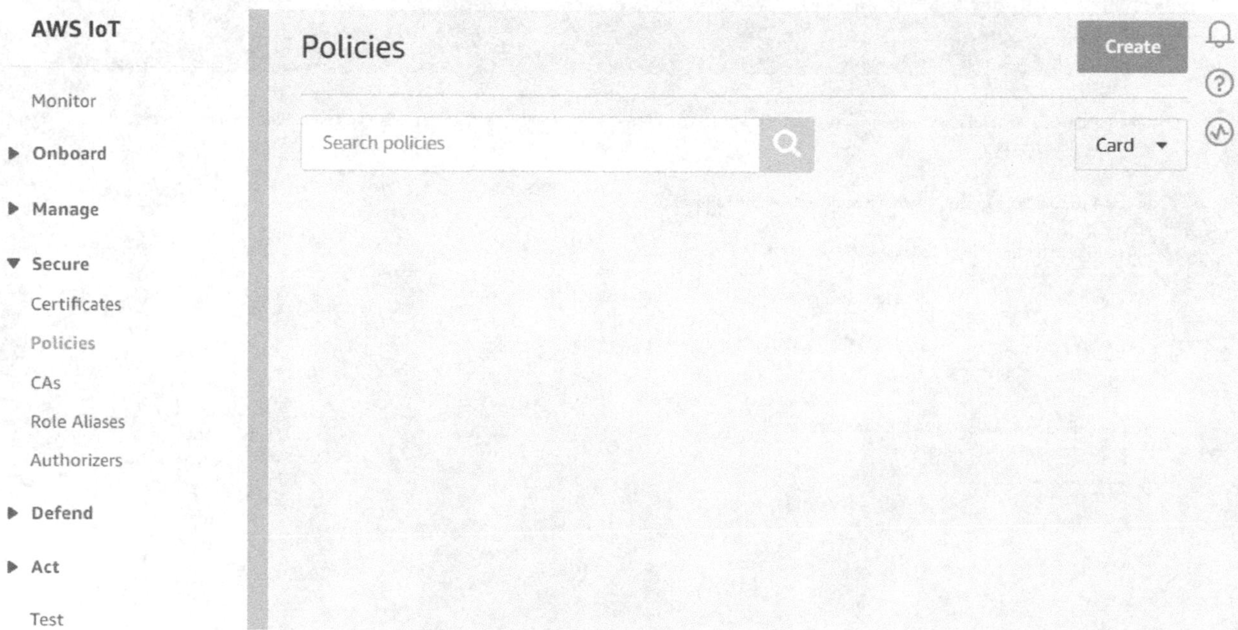

Figure 7.10: Policy Dashboard for the Thing in AWS IoT.

7.4 Creating Policy

You now need to attach a policy to the certificates created. A policy specifies what permissions or privileges the NB-IoT device can have such as publish, subscribe, connect, or receive from/to which topic. Go to the menu item **Secure->Policies**, and click **Create**

You are prompted to enter the actions that this policy allows or denies. In a typical scenario, a policy allows any NB-IoT device with the valid certificates to publish, subscribe, connect, and receive. Enter a **Name** for the policy and enter the permissions in the **Action** box. You can also check **Allow** to allow a device to do these actions. Then click **Create**. The new policy is created and shows up in the **Policies** dashboard as in Figure 7.12.

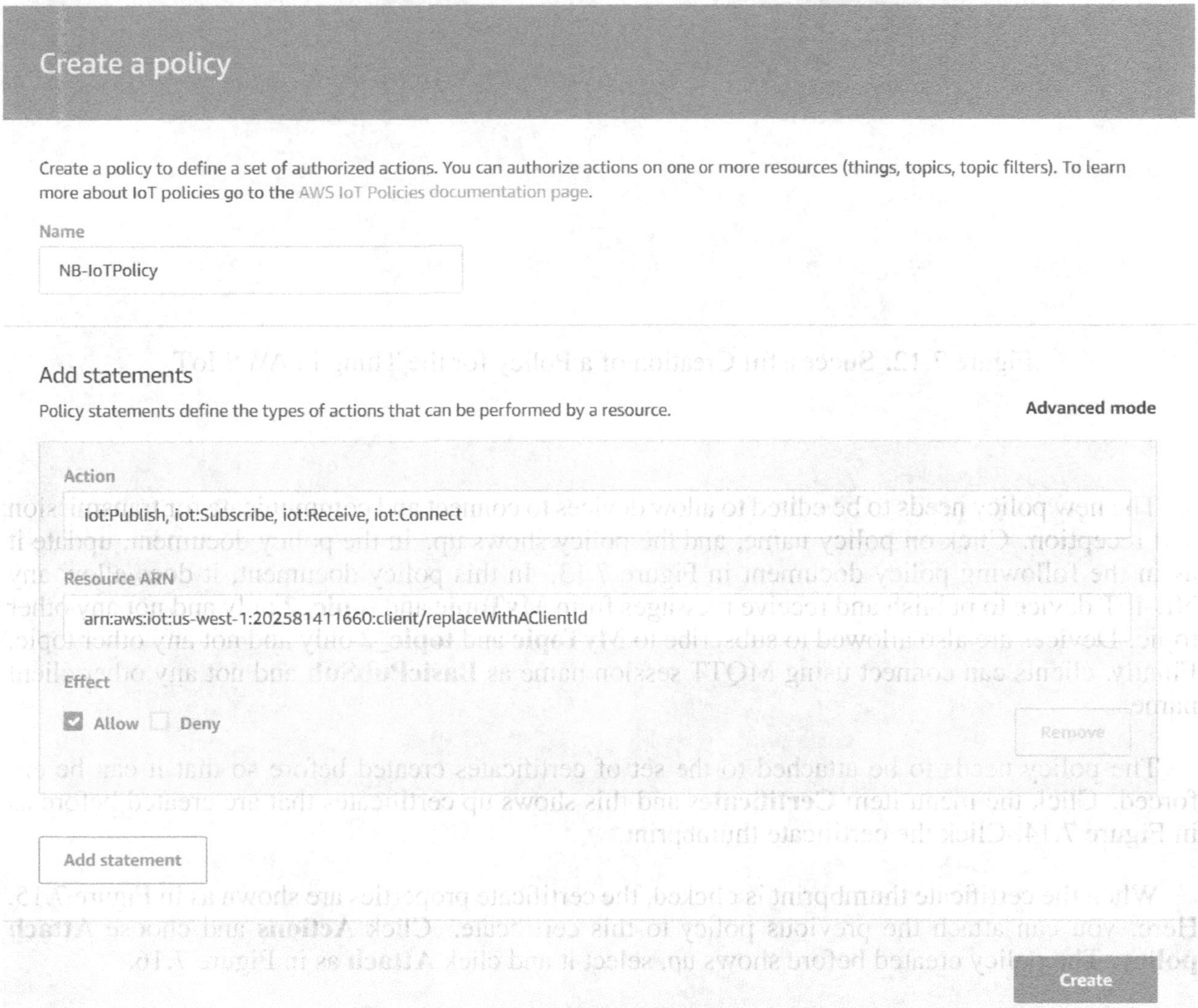

Figure 7.11: Creating a Policy for the Thing in AWS IoT.

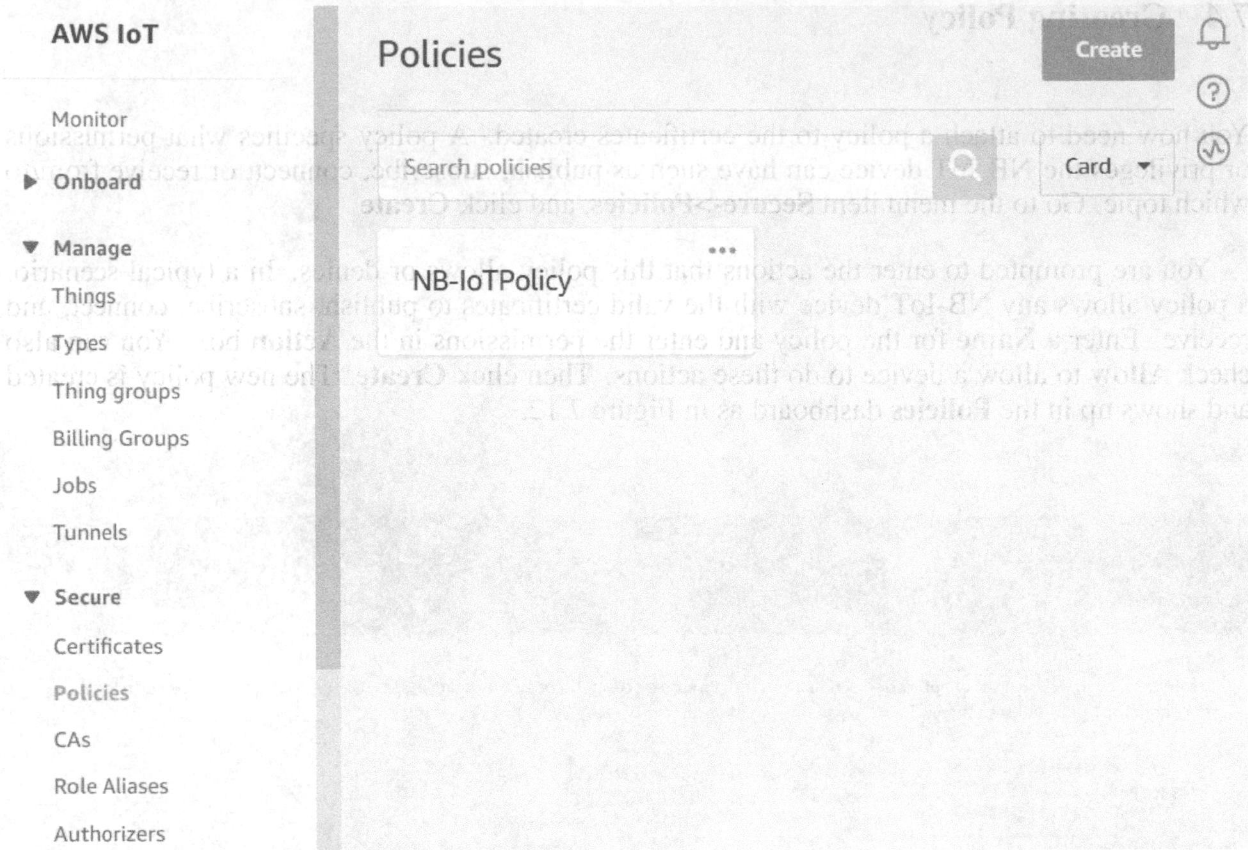

Figure 7.12: Successful Creation of a Policy for the Thing in AWS IoT.

The new policy needs to be edited to allow devices to connect and communicate for transmission and reception. Click on policy name, and the policy shows up. In the policy document, update it as in the following policy document in Figure 7.13. In this policy document, it does allow any NB-IoT device to publish and receive messages from **MyTopic** and **topic_2** only and not any other topic. Devices are also allowed to subscribe to **MyTopic** and **topic_2** only and not any other topic. Finally, clients can connect using MQTT session name as **BasicPubSub** and not any other client name.

The policy needs to be attached to the set of certificates created before so that it can be enforced. Click the menu item **Certificates** and this shows up certificates that are created before as in Figure 7.14. Click the certificate thumbprint.

When the certificate thumbprint is clicked, the certificate properties are shown as in Figure 7.15. Here, you can attach the previous policy to this certificate. Click **Actions** and choose **Attach policy**. The policy created before shows up, select it and click **Attach** as in Figure 7.16.

At this step, the first NB-IoT **Thing** has been created on AWS IoT, certificates have been created and downloaded, and a policy is attached to the certificates. You are ready to connect your first NB-IoT device to the AWS IoT cloud.

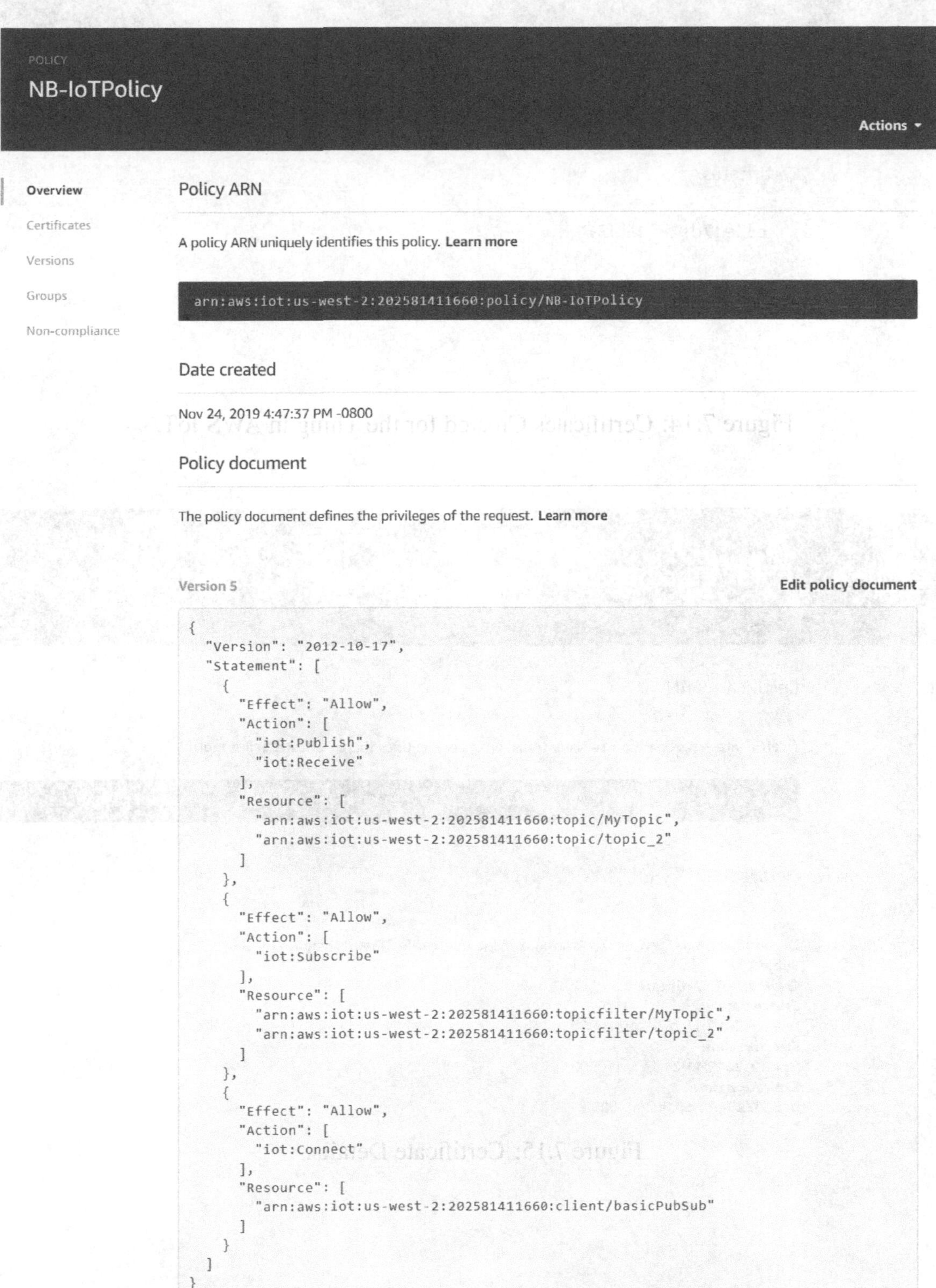

Figure 7.13: JSON Policy for the Thing in AWS IoT.

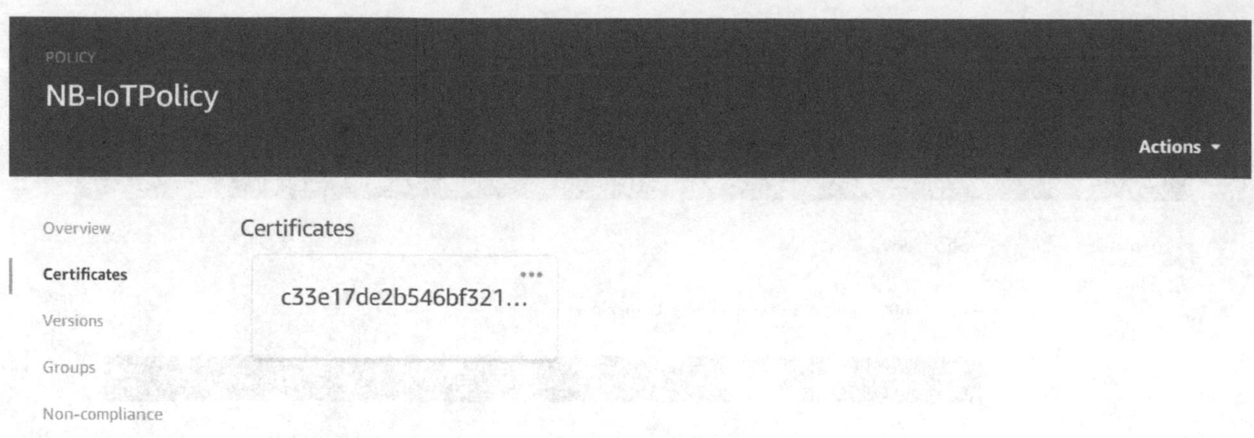

Figure 7.14: Certificates Created for the Thing in AWS IoT.

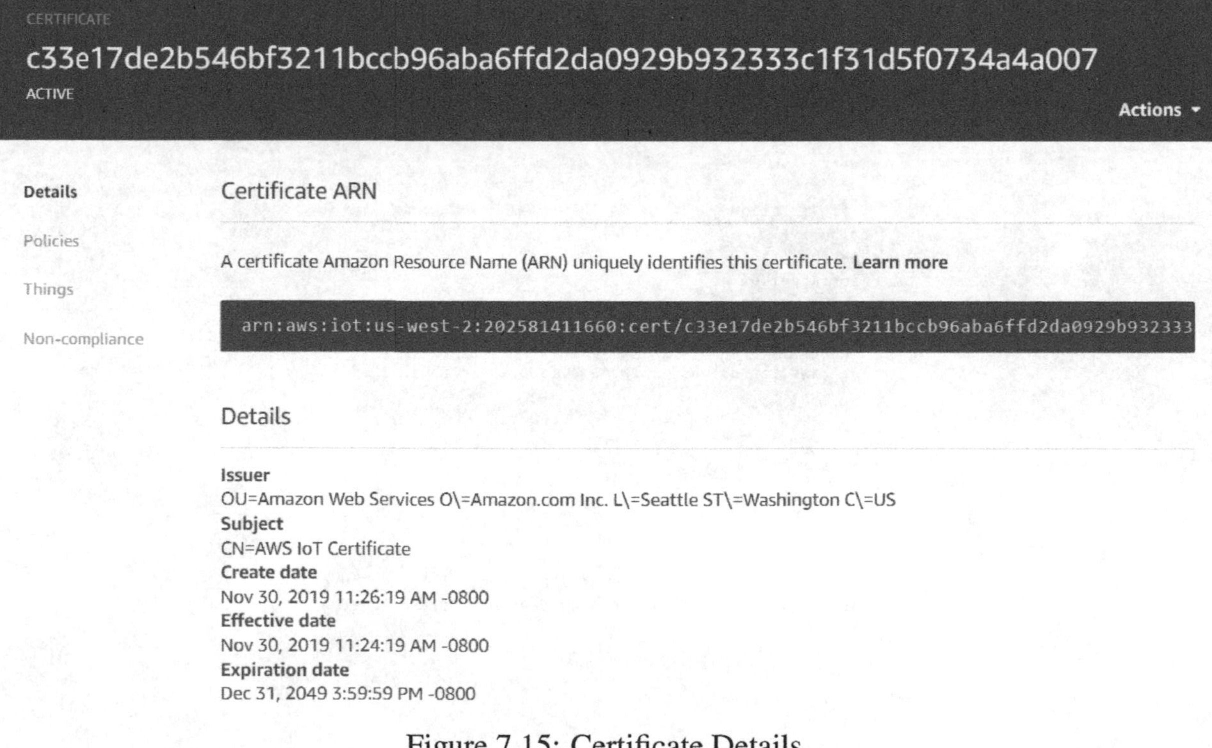

Figure 7.15: Certificate Details.

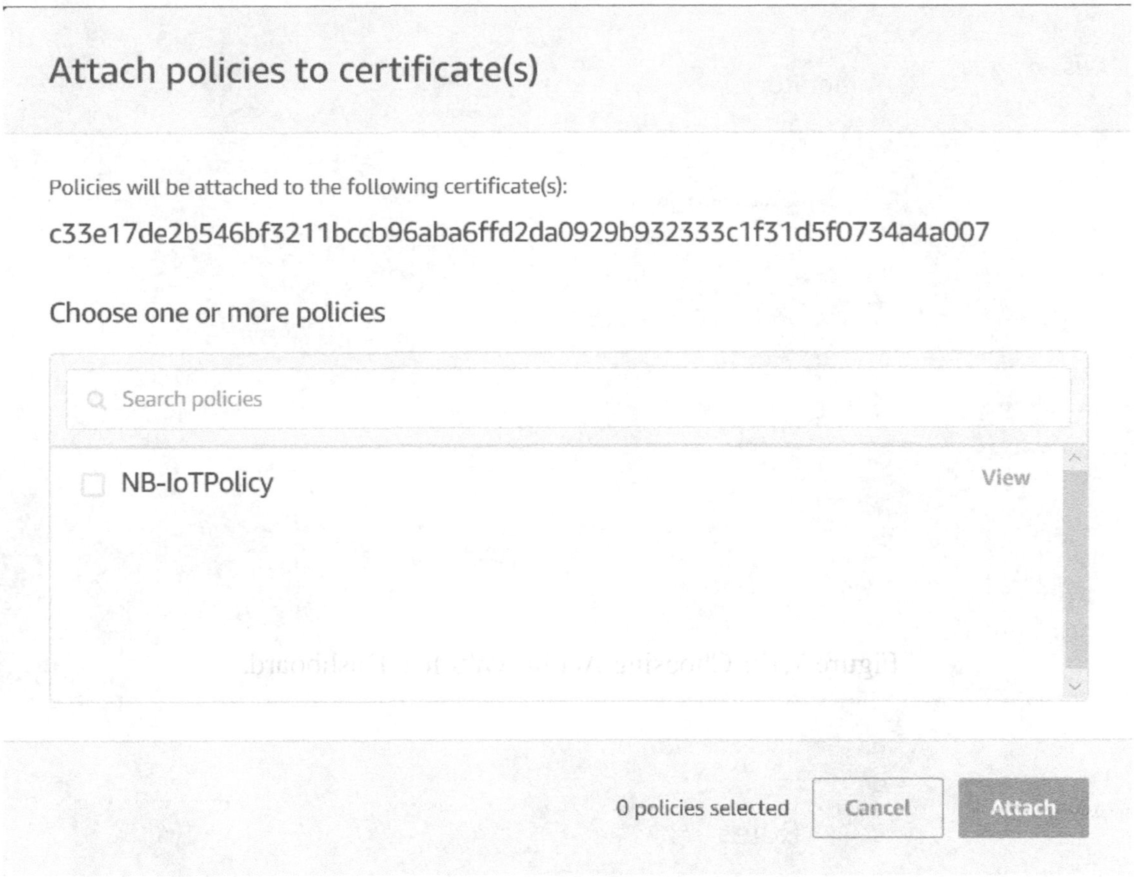

Attach policies to certificate(s)

Policies will be attached to the following certificate(s):

c33e17de2b546bf3211bccb96aba6ffd2da0929b932333c1f31d5f0734a4a007

Choose one or more policies

Search policies

NB-IoTPolicy View

0 policies selected Cancel Attach

Figure 7.16: Attaching a Policy to the Certificate.

7.5 Creating Rule

Defining a rule in AWS IoT, allow you to process, analyze, and store the messages sent or received from the NB-IoT devices. For example, you can setup a rule that reads a message from an NB-IoT device and extract the temperature reading transmitted in the message.

To create a new rule, in the AWS IoT console and in the navigation pane, choose **Act**. On the **Rules** page, choose **Create** as in Figures 7.17 and 7.18.

On the **Create a rule** page, enter a **Name** and **Description** for your rule. Under **Rule query statement**, choose the latest version from the **Using SQL version** list. For **Rule query statement**, enter **SELECT * FROM 'iottopic_2'**. This is shown in Figure 7.19.

This SQL query means that to read a message published to **MyTopic**. On **Select one or more action**, choose **Insert a message into a DynamoDB table**, and then choose **Configure action** as shown in Figure 7.20

The DynamoDB action is used to store MQTT message information into a DynamoDB table when a message is received from the device.

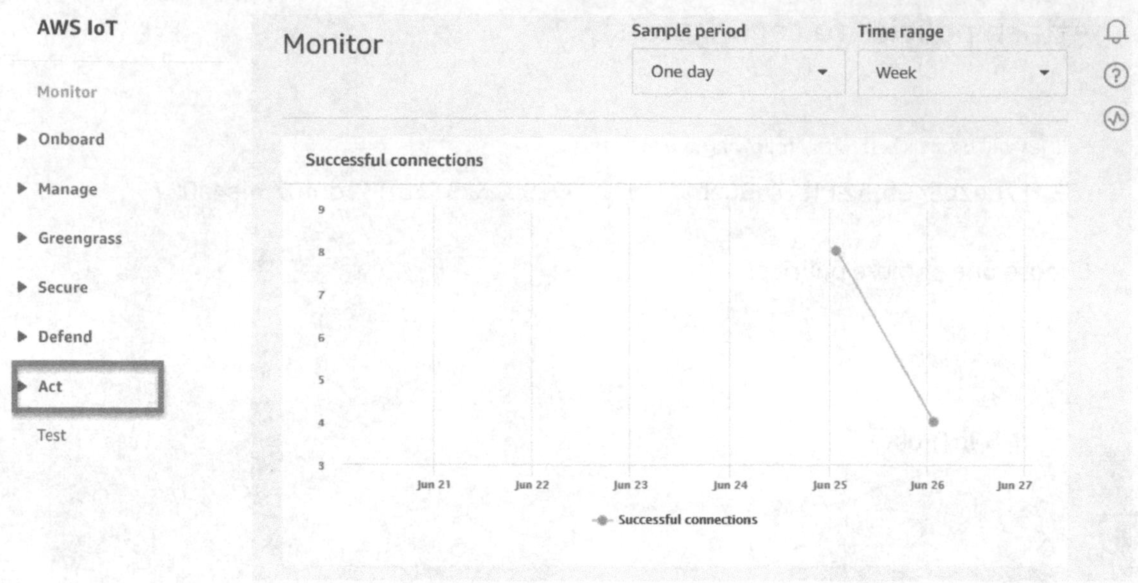

Figure 7.17: Choosing Act in AWS IoT Dashboard.

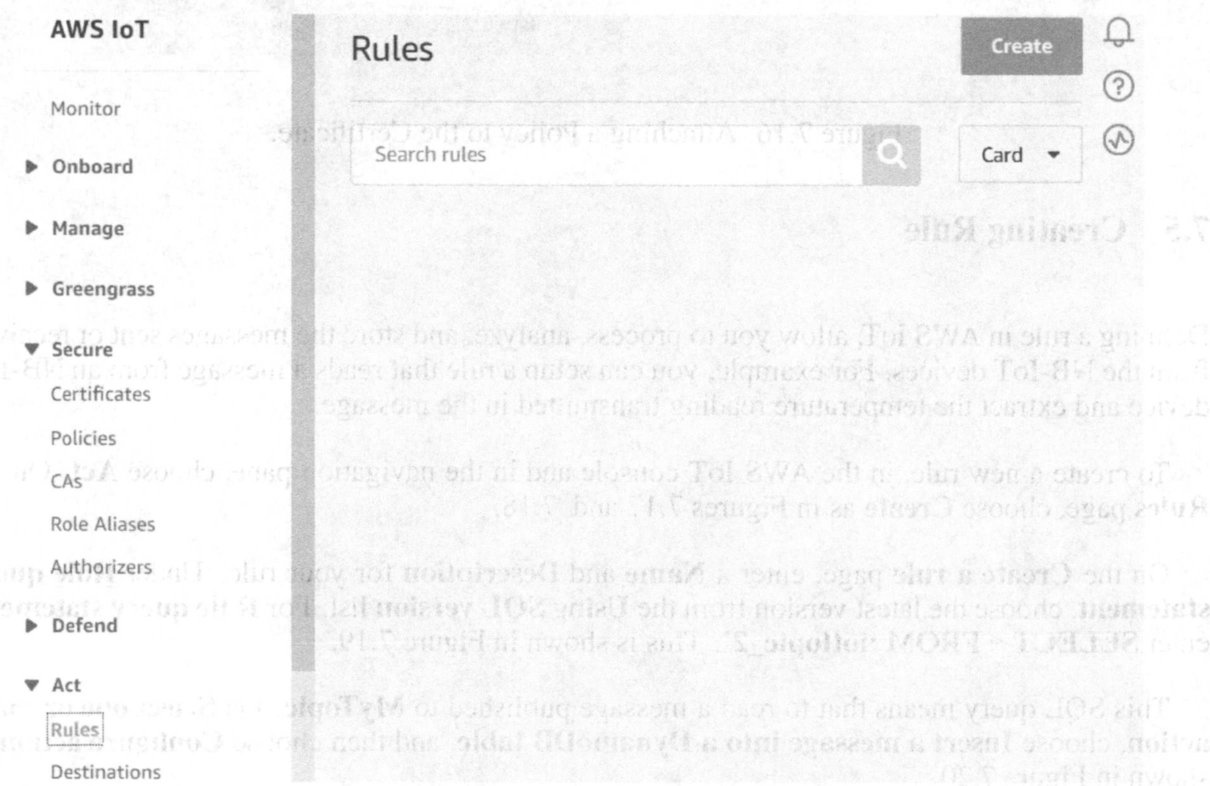

Figure 7.18: Adding a Rule in the Act Dashboard.

Create a rule

Create a rule to evaluate messages sent by your things and specify what to do when a message is received (for example, write data to a DynamoDB table or invoke a Lambda function).

Name

NBIoTRule

Description

Rule that extracts device ID, timestamp, and the payload of the message sent by the device into the DynamoDB

Rule query statement

Indicate the source of the messages you want to process with this rule.

Using SQL version

2016-03-23

Rule query statement

SELECT <Attribute> FROM <Topic Filter> WHERE <Condition>. For example: SELECT temperature FROM 'iot/topic' WHERE temperature > 50. To learn more, see AWS IoT SQL Reference.

```
1  SELECT * FROM 'iot/topic'
```

Set one or more actions

Select one or more actions to happen when the above rule is matched by an inbound message. Actions define additional activities that occur when messages arrive, like storing them in a database, invoking cloud functions, or sending notifications. (*.required)

Add action

Error action

Optionally set an action that will be executed when something goes wrong with processing your rule.

Add action

Tags

Apply tags to your resources to help organize and identify them. A tag consists of a case-sensitive key-value pair. Learn more about tagging your AWS resources.

Tag name	Value	
Provide a tag name, e.g. Manufacturer	Provide a tag value, e.g. Acme-Corporation	Clear

Add another

Cancel

Create rule

Figure 7.19: Create a Rule Dashboard.

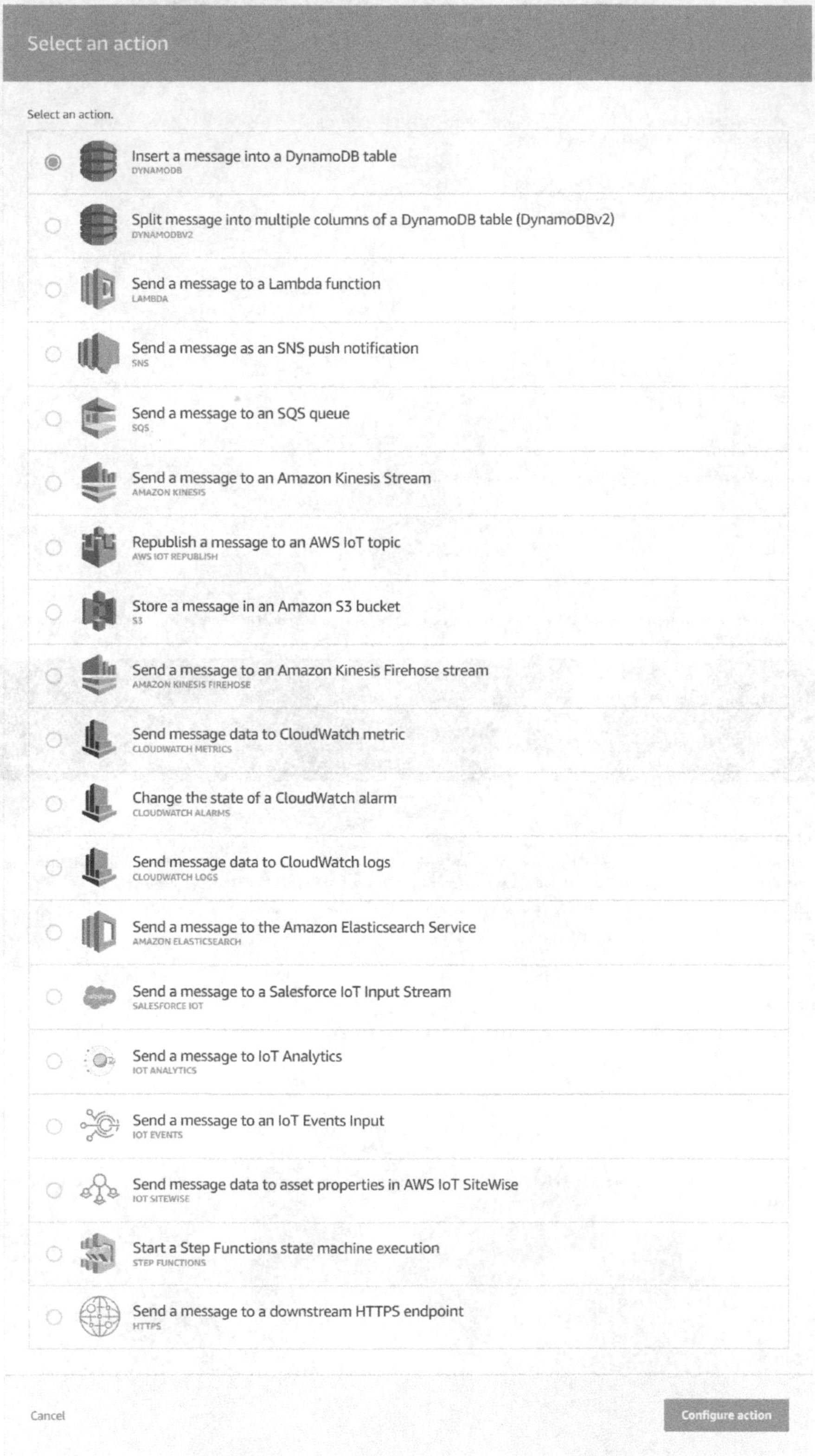

Select an action

Select an action.

Insert a message into a DynamoDB table
DYNAMODB

Split message into multiple columns of a DynamoDB table (DynamoDBv2)
DYNAMODBV2

Send a message to a Lambda function
LAMBDA

Send a message as an SNS push notification
SNS

Send a message to an SQS queue
SQS

Send a message to an Amazon Kinesis Stream
AMAZON KINESIS

Republish a message to an AWS IoT topic
AWS IOT REPUBLISH

Store a message in an Amazon S3 bucket
S3

Send a message to an Amazon Kinesis Firehose stream
AMAZON KINESIS FIREHOSE

Send message data to CloudWatch metric
CLOUDWATCH METRICS

Change the state of a CloudWatch alarm
CLOUDWATCH ALARMS

Send message data to CloudWatch logs
CLOUDWATCH LOGS

Send a message to the Amazon Elasticsearch Service
AMAZON ELASTICSEARCH

Send a message to a Salesforce IoT Input Stream
SALESFORCE IOT

Send a message to IoT Analytics
IOT ANALYTICS

Send a message to an IoT Events Input
IOT EVENTS

Send message data to asset properties in AWS IoT SiteWise
IOT SITEWISE

Start a Step Functions state machine execution
STEP FUNCTIONS

Send a message to a downstream HTTPS endpoint
HTTPS

Cancel

Configure action

Figure 7.20: Select an Action of a Rule.

7.6 Creating DynamoDB

DynamoDB is a database that is best suited for NB-IoT devices. DynamoDB is a key/value database which means that each record (or row) in the table consists of a key and value pairs. The DynamoDB is easier to setup and configure than traditional relational database, such as SQL database, because DynamoDB does not need a schema to create the table and each record consists only from a key and its value. The key used in the DynamoDB is the NB-IoT device ID which is better represented using its International Mobile Equipment Identifier (IMEI). IMEI is a unique identifier for any NB-IoT device. Along with the IMEI, a sort key is used which represents the timestamp of the message transmitted from the NB-IoT device. Both the IMEI and timestamp represents the key of a record in the table. Value of the record can be any data to be stored such as temperature reading or GPS location of the NB-IoT device.

To create the DynamoDB, after clicking **Configure action**, click **Create a new resource** as in Figure 7.21. You will create a new DynamoDB. On the Amazon DynamoDB page, click **Create table** as in Figure 7.22.

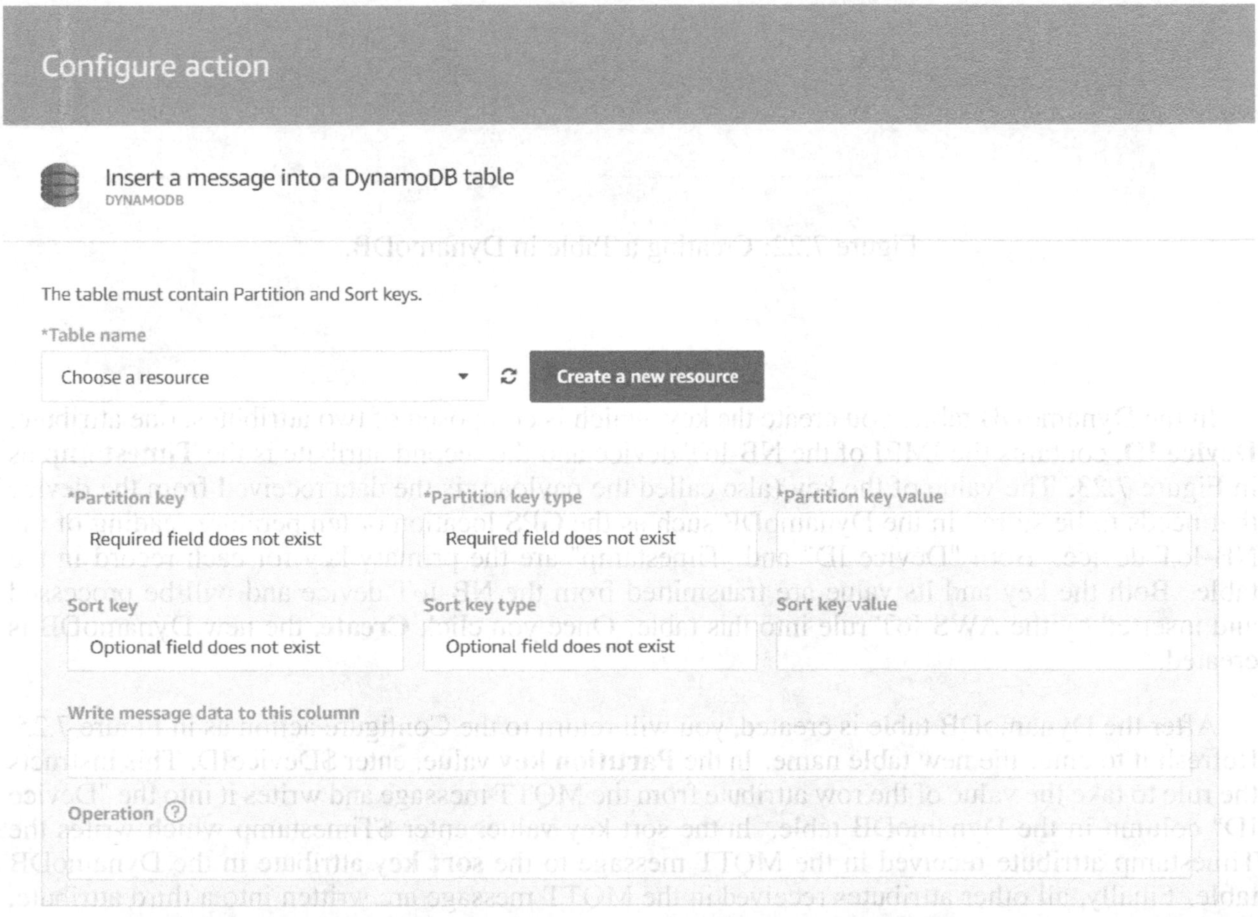

Figure 7.21: Setting Action on DynamoDB.

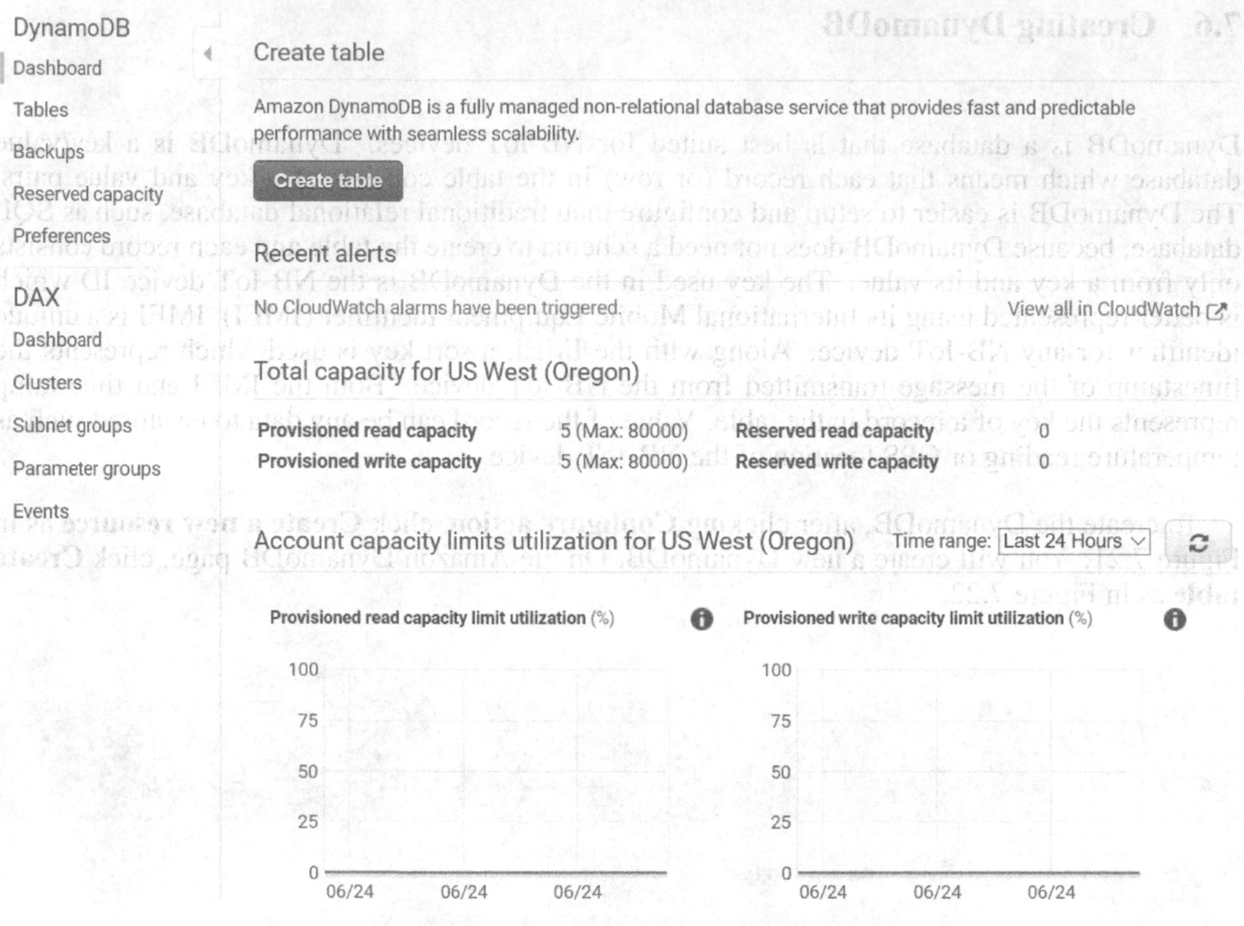

Figure 7.22: Creating a Table in DynamoDB.

In the DynamoDB table, you create the key, which is composed of two attributes, one attribute, **Device ID**, contains the IMEI of the NB-IoT device and the second attribute is the **Timestamp** as in Figure 7.23. The value of the key (also called the payload) is the data received from the device that needs to be stored in the DynamoDB such as the GPS location or temperature reading of the NB-IoT device. Both "Device ID" and "Timestamp" are the primary key for each record in the table. Both the key and its value are transmitted from the NB-IoT device and will be processed and inserted by the AWS IoT rule into this table. Once you click **Create**, the new DynamoDB is created.

After the DynamoDB table is created, you will return to the Configure action as in Figure 7.25. Refresh it to enter the new table name. In the **Partition key** value, enter $DeviceID. This instructs the rule to take the value of the row attribute from the MQTT message and writes it into the "Device ID" column in the DynamoDB table. In the sort key value, enter $Timestamp which writes the Timestamp attribute received in the MQTT message to the **sort key** attribute in the DynamoDB table. Finally, all other attributes received in the MQTT message are written into a third attribute, **payload**, in the DynamoDB which can contain any data to be stored such as temperature reading or GPS location.

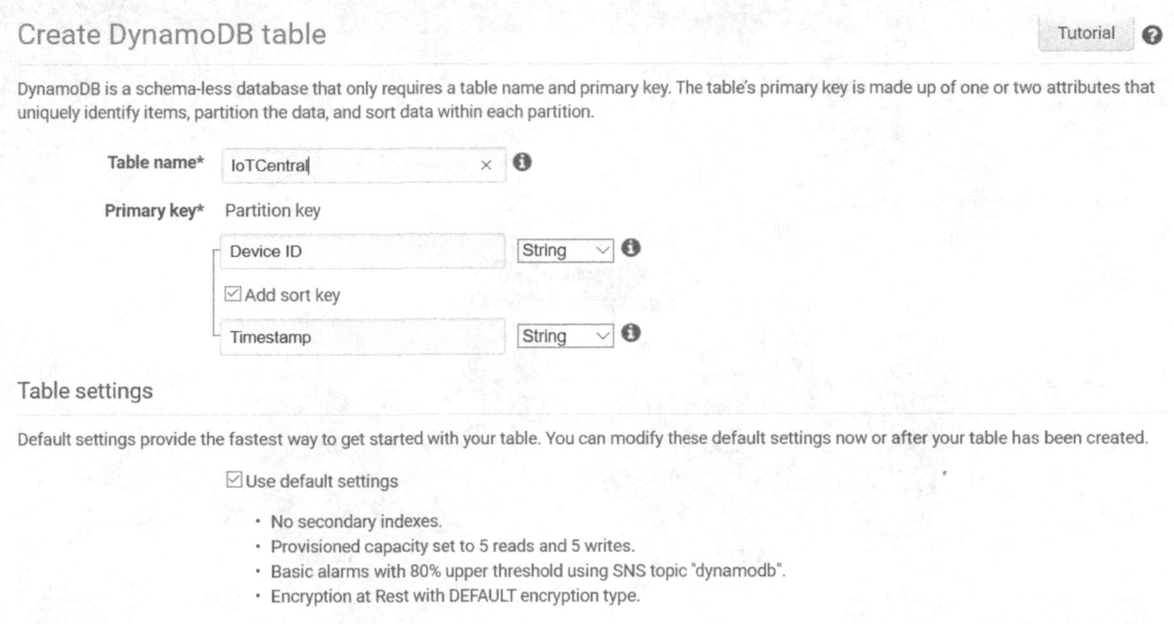

Figure 7.23: Adding Keys in the DynamoDB.

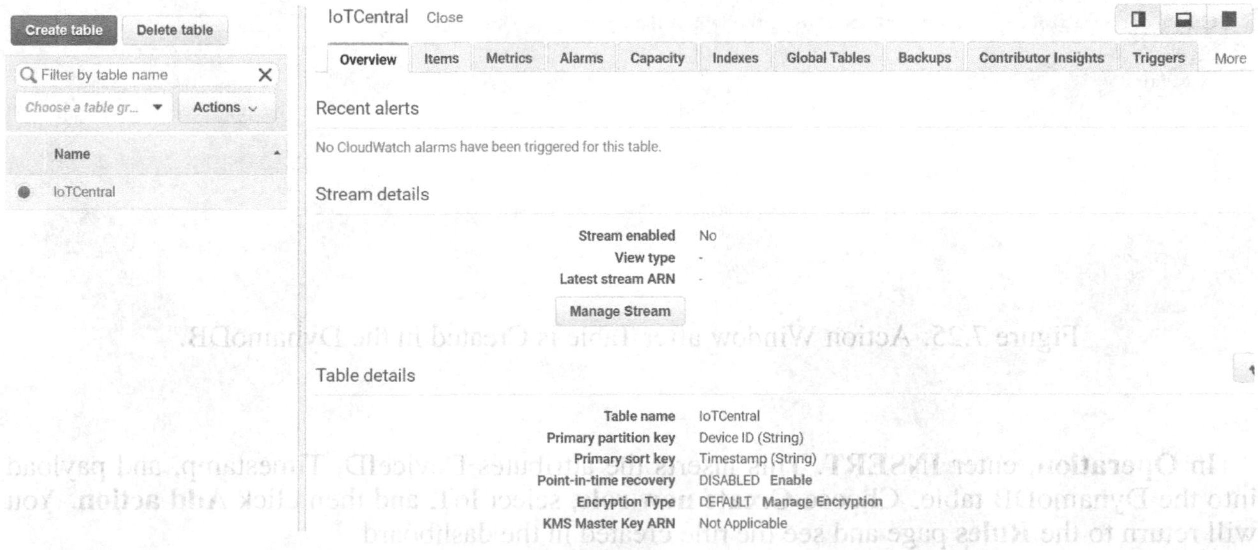

Figure 7.24: Table Details in the DynamoDB.

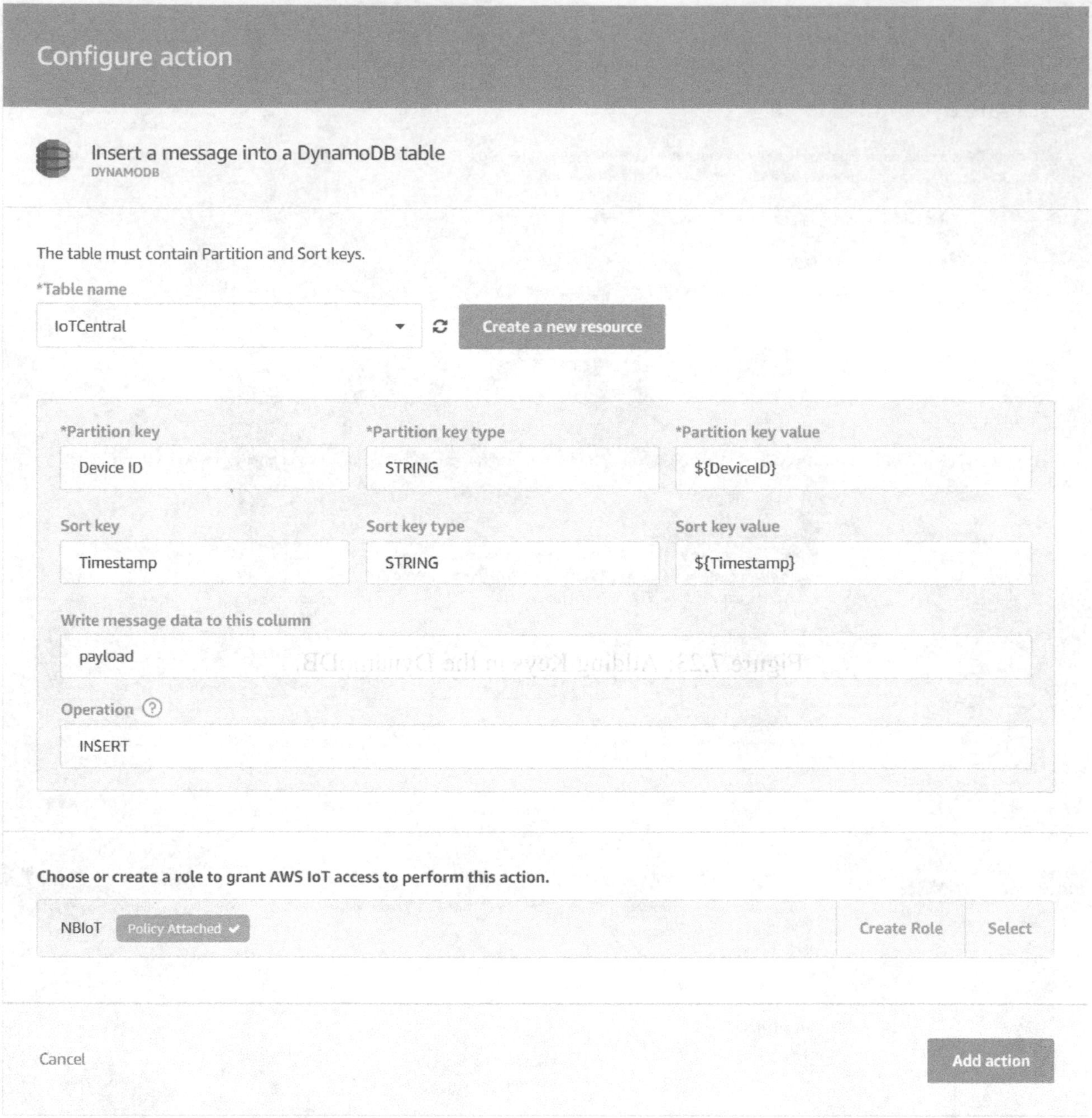

Configure action

Insert a message into a DynamoDB table
DYNAMODB

The table must contain Partition and Sort keys.

*Table name
IoTCentral
Create a new resource

*Partition key
Device ID
*Partition key type
STRING
*Partition key value
${DeviceID}
Sort key
Timestamp
Sort key type
STRING
Sort key value
${Timestamp}
Write message data to this column
payload
Operation
INSERT

Choose or create a role to grant AWS IoT access to perform this action.
NBIoT
Policy Attached
Create Role
Select

Cancel
Add action

Figure 7.25: Action Window after Table is Created in the DynamoDB.

In **Operation**, enter **INSERT**. This inserts the attributes DeviceID, Timestamp, and payload into the DynamoDB table. Choose **Create new role**, select IoT, and then click **Add action**. You will return to the **Rules** page and see the rule created in the dashboard.

You will see the new rule now appears in the rule dashboard. You are ready to connect your NB-IoT device, emits "Device ID", "Timestamp", and temperature reading. The key and its value are stored in the DynamoDB.

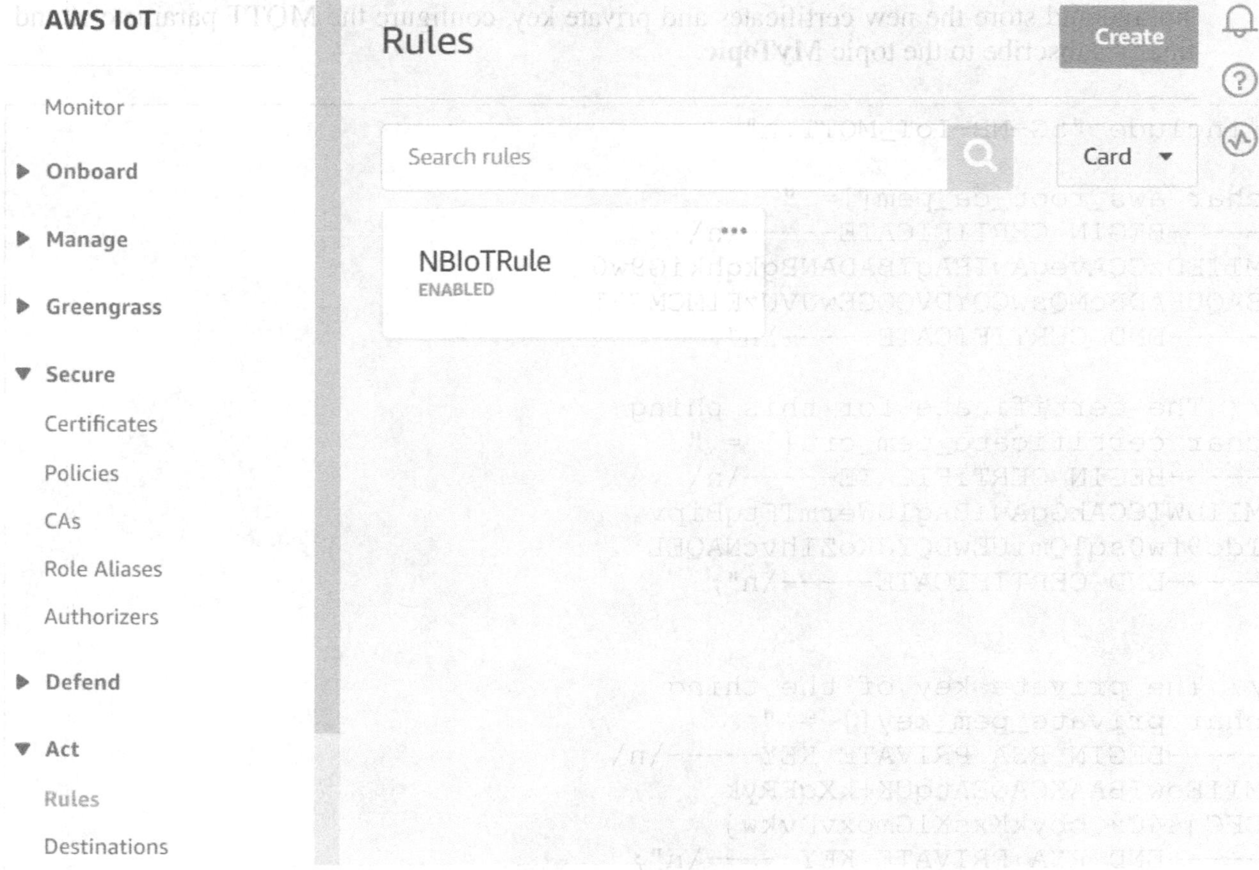

Figure 7.26: Rules Window after Table is Created in the DynamoDB.

7.7 Arduino Client Sketch with AWS IoT

Since you have setup the server side (AWS IoT) to be able to allow connections from the NB-IoT device. In this section, you will implement the Arduino sketch that runs on the device side, with JSON serialization, and connects to AWS IoT.

The Arduino sketch uses the header file in Listing 7.1. This file will be used in all coming sections to connect to the AWS IoT in the cloud using MQTT. Using this file, the device will be able to transmit and receive (publish and subscribe) to MQTT topics on AWS.

The file consists of the following:

1. It has two certificates and private keys. The first certificate is the root certificate to authenticate AWS IoT and the second certificate is to authenticate the thing and allows it to connect. The device also uses a private key which encrypts all communication with the cloud. The modem has internal file storage of 4K of bytes that allows to store the certificates and private key and use them for secure connection using SSL and MQTT.
2. The API, **InitModemMQTT(.)**, configures the cellular modem for cellular connection. It does several things such as retrieving the IMEI, set the APN, delete any old file in the modem

storage and store the new certificates and private key, configure the MQTT parameters, and finally subscribe to the topic **MyTopic**.

```
#include "5G-NB-IoT_MQTT.h"

char aws_root_ca_pem[]= "
-----BEGIN CERTIFICATE-----\n\
MIIEDzCCAvegAwIBAgIBADANBgkqhkiG9w0
BAQUFADBoMQswCQYDVQQGEwJVUzElMCMGA1
-----END CERTIFICATE-----\n";

// The certificate for this thing
char certificate_pem_crt[] = "
-----BEGIN CERTIFICATE-----\n\
MIIDWTCCAkGgAwIBAgIUWermTFtqBipv
Ido9fw0sqlQmiUEwDQYJKoZIhvcNAQEL
-----END CERTIFICATE-----\n";


// The private key of the thing
char private_pem_key[] = "
-----BEGIN RSA PRIVATE KEY-----\n\
MIIEowIBAAKCAQEAtqUK+kXqFRyk
CFCj44CxQbbykKxsKlGmpxvDvkwj
-----END RSA PRIVATE KEY-----\n";

bool InitModemMQTT(_5G_NB_IoT_MQTT  &AWSIoT,
                   Stream &DSerial,
                   char *APN,
                   char *LOGIN,
                   char *PASSWORD,
                   char *MQTTServer,
                   unsigned int MQTTPort,
                   char *MQTTClientId,
                   char *mqtt_topicName,
                   Mqtt_Qos_t MQTT_QoS = AT_MOST_ONCE,
                   unsigned int MQTTIndex = 3,
                   unsigned int PDPIndex = 1,
                   unsigned int SSLIndex = 2,
                   char *ModemIMEI = NULL)
{
  Mqtt_Version_t version = MQTT_V3;

  AWSIoT.InitModule();
  DSerial.println("\r\n InitModule() OK!");

  AWSIoT.SetDevCommandEcho(false);
```

```
  char inf[64];
  if (AWSIoT.GetDevInformation(inf))
  {
    DSerial.println(inf);
  }

  char imei_tmp[64];
  if (AWSIoT.GetDevIMEI(imei_tmp))
  {
    String s = String(imei_tmp);
    s.trim();
    s.toCharArray(ModemIMEI, 64);
    DSerial.println(ModemIMEI);
  }

  char apn_error[64];
  AWSIoT.InitAPN(PDPIndex, APN, LOGIN, PASSWORD, apn_error);
  DSerial.println(apn_error);
  char ssl_error[128];
  AWSIoT.InitSSL(SSLIndex, aws_root_ca_pem, certificate_pem_crt,
                 private_pem_key, ssl_error)
  DSerial.println(ssl_error);

  DSerial.println("\r\nStart Config the MQTT Parameter!");

  AWSIoT.SetMQTTConfigureParameters(MQTTIndex, PDPIndex,
      version, 150, SERVER_STORE_SUBSCRIPTIONS);
  DSerial.println("\r\nConfig the MQTT Parameter Success!");

  AWSIoT.SetMQTTEnableSSL(MQTTIndex, SSLIndex, true);
  DSerial.println("\r\SetMQTTEnableSSL the MQTT Parameter Success
   !");

  AWSIoT.OpenMQTTNetwork(MQTTIndex, MQTTServer, MQTTPort);
  DSerial.println("\r\nSet the MQTT Service Address Success!");

  AWSIoT.SetMQTTMessageTimeout(MQTTIndex, 10, 5, 1);
  DSerial.println("\r\nStart Create a MQTT Client!");

  AWSIoT.CreateMQTTClient(MQTTIndex, MQTTClientId, "", "");
  DSerial.println("\r\nCreate a MQTT Client Success!");

  DSerial.println("\r\nStart MQTT Subscribe Topic!");

  AWSIoT.MQTTSubscribeTopic(MQTTIndex, 1, mqtt_topicName,
   MQTT_QoS);
  DSerial.println("\r\nMQTT Subscribe Topic Success!");
```

```
  return true;
}
```

Listing 7.1: Header File to Initialize MQTT for AWS IoT.

Now, you come to the main part of the Arduino sketch. The setup() and loop() code are shown in Listing 7.2

The main part sets configuration values of the MQTT. This includes the AWS server name, port number, APN of AT&T network, client ID, topic to subscribe to, and the MQTT Quality of Service (QoS).

The setup() API mainly sets up the MCU USB and serial port of the modem and initializes the cellular modem using **InitModemMQTT(.)** API.

In the loop() API, **WaitCheckMQTTURCEvent(.)** API is called which waits until a payload is received by the client. If a payload is received, this API return MQTT_RECV_DATA_EVENT. Upon receiving a payload in JSON format, it is deserialized. The API also returns MQTT_STATUS_EVENT if any error is reported by the AWS IoT such as a closed or rejected session.

If a device is a temperature sensor and needs to report the temperature, it can do so by constructing a JSON-formatted text and publish it to the server. It constructs the JSON document using ArduinoJson, serialize it, and then publish it using **MQTTPublishMessages(.)** API. In Listing 7.2, the JSON part is enclosed in the code in Listing 7.3 and can be changed according to what need to be uploaded or downloaded from the AWS IoT or according to whether you are using different sensor or actuator. For example, you can modify the JSON part to upload GPS information or download command to move a stepper motor. Projects explained in Parts III and IV provide examples how to upload or download JSON messages from AWS IoT.

```
#include <board.h>
#include <ArduinoJson.h>

#define DSerial SerialUSB
#define ATSerial Serial1

char APN[] = "m2mNB16.com.attz";
char LOGIN[] = "";
char PASSWORD[] = "";

char mqtt_server[] = "a2h0-ats.iot.us-west-2.amazonaws.com";
unsigned int mqtt_port = 8883;
char mqtt_clientId[] = "basicPubSub";
char mqtt_topicName[] = "MyTopic";
unsigned int mqtt_index = 3;
Mqtt_Qos_t mqtt_qos = AT_MOST_ONCE;

StaticJsonDocument<200> docInput;
```

```
StaticJsonDocument<200> docOutput;

char IMEI[64];

_5G_NB_IoT_MQTT AWSIoT(ATSerial, DSerial);

void setup()
{
  DSerial.begin(115200);
  while (DSerial.read() >= 0);
  DSerial.println("This is the Debug Serial!");

  ATSerial.begin(115200);
  while (ATSerial.read() >= 0);
  delay(1000);

  InitModemMQTT(AWSIoT, DSerial, APN, LOGIN, PASSWORD,
                mqtt_server, mqtt_port,
                mqtt_clientId, mqtt_topicName,
                AT_MOST_ONCE, mqtt_index,
                1, 2, IMEI);
}

void loop()
{
  char payload[256];
  int res;
  DeserializationError error;

  Mqtt_URC_Event_t ret = AWSIoT.WaitCheckMQTTURCEvent(payload, 2)
   ;

  switch (ret)
  {
    case MQTT_RECV_DATA_EVENT:
        error = deserializeJson(docOutput, payload);

        if (error == DeserializationError::Ok)
        {
// This code from here is replaceable based on different sensors
   or actuators
         if (docOutput["Device"] == "Temperature Sensor")
         {
           DSerial.println("Device is a Temperature sensor!");

           DSerial.println(docOutput["DeviceID"].as<String>());
           DSerial.println(docOutput["Timestamp"].as<double>(),6)
   ;
```

```
            DSerial.println(docOutput["Device"].as<String>());
            DSerial.println(docOutput["OpCodes"].as<int>());
            DSerial.println(docOutput["Temperature"].as<int>());
            DSerial.println(docOutput["Unit"].as<String>());
          }
          else
          {
            DSerial.println("Device is not a Temperature sensor!"
    );
          }
// Until here
        }
        else
        {
          DSerial.println("\r\n Error in Deserialization!");
          Serial.println(error.c_str());
        }
      break;

    case MQTT_STATUS_EVENT:
        if (AWSIoT.CloseMQTTClient(mqtt_index))
        {
          DSerial.println("\r\nClose the MQTT Client Success!");
        }
      break;
  }

 // This code from here is replaceable based on different sensors
    or actuators
  docInput["DeviceID"] = IMEI;
  docInput["Timestamp"] = millis();
  docInput["Device"] = "Temperature Sensor";
  docInput["OpCode"] = "Read";
  docInput["Temperature"] = 30;
  docInput["Unit"] = "°F";
  serializeJsonPretty(docInput, payload);
 // Until here

  res = AWSIoT.MQTTPublishMessages(mqtt_index, 1, AT_LEAST_ONCE,
   mqtt_topicName, false, payload);

  if (res == PACKET_SEND_SUCCESS_AND_RECV_ACK ||
      res == PACKET_RETRANSMISSION)
  {
    DSerial.println("Publish Succeded!");
  }
  else
  {
```

```
    DSerial.println("Publish failed!");
  }

  delay(5000);    // publish to topic every 5 seconds
}
```

Listing 7.2: Arduino Sketch for MQTT with AWS IoT.

```
// This code from here is replaceable based on different sensors
   or actuators
...
// Until here
```

Listing 7.3: JSON Part in MQTT Arduino Sketch.

After running this Arduino sketch, you will see outputs on the Serial Monitor. You can see the device is publishing a message which is JSON-formatted to the topic **MyTopic**. And the same message published by the device is now received and appears on AWS IoT. This is shown in Figures 7.27 and 7.28.

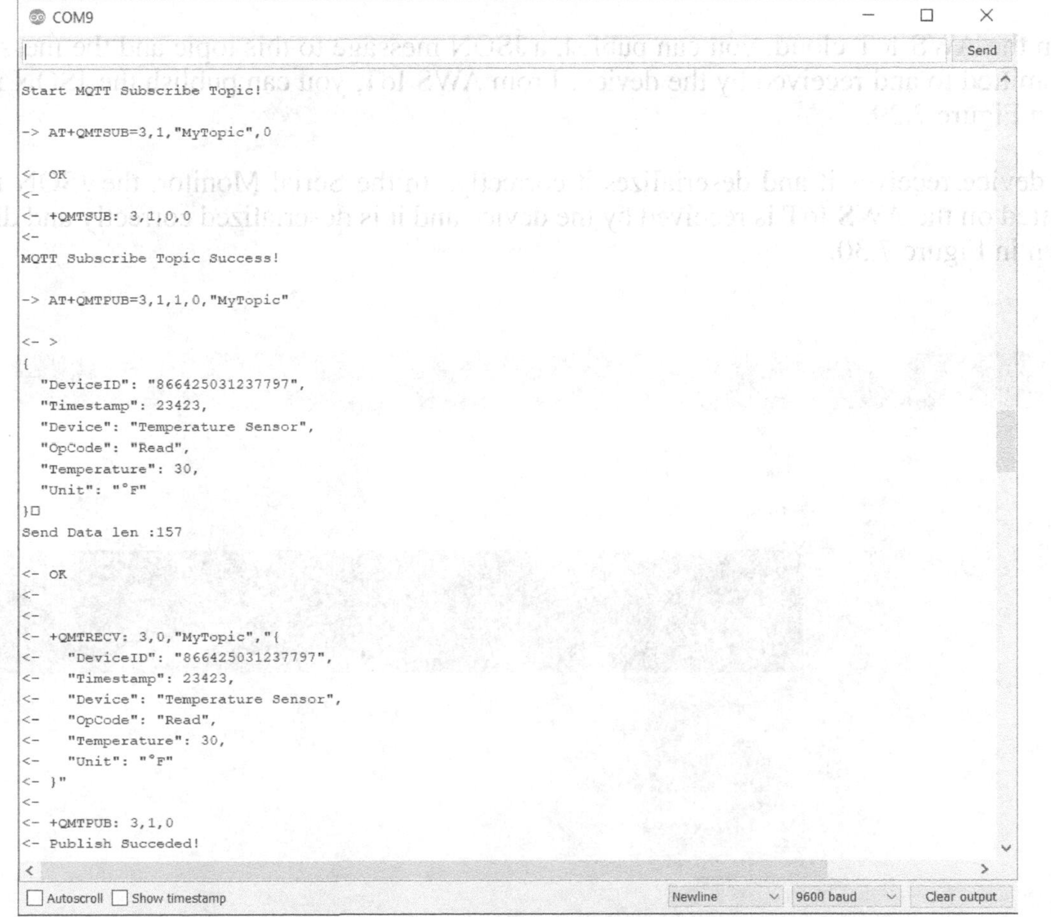

Figure 7.27: Serial Monitor Output for MQTT with AWS IoT.

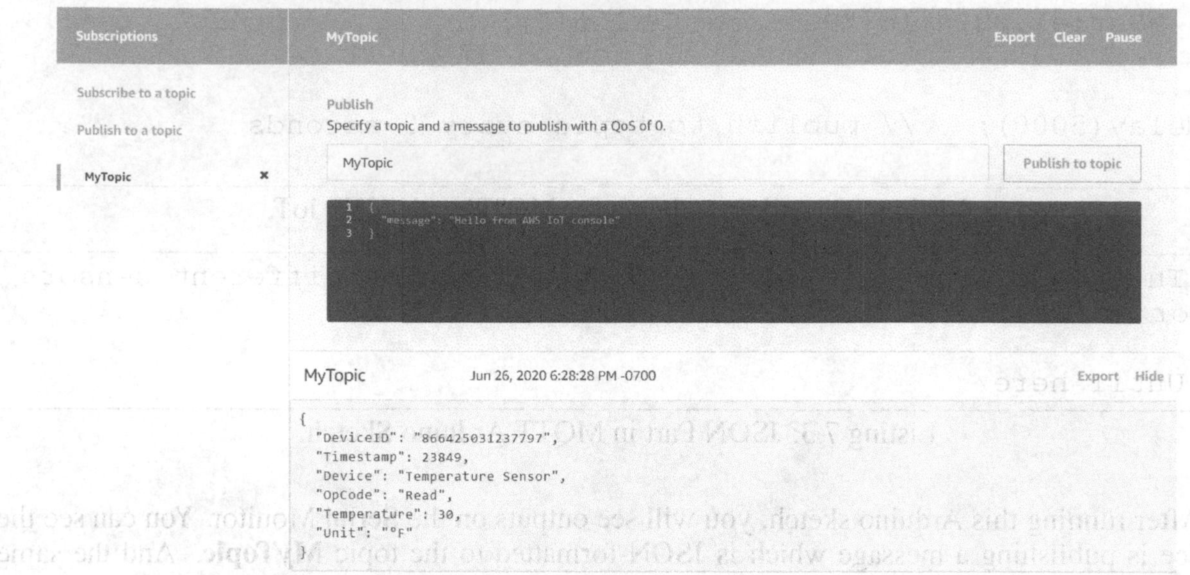

Figure 7.28: JSON Data on AWS IoT.

From the AWS IoT cloud, you can publish a JSON message to this topic and the message will be transmitted to and received by the device. From AWS IoT, you can publish the JSON message shown in Figure 7.29.

The device receives it and deserializes it correctly. In the Serial Monitor, the JSON message transmitted on the AWS IoT is received by the device and it is deserialized correctly and displayed as shown in Figure 7.30.

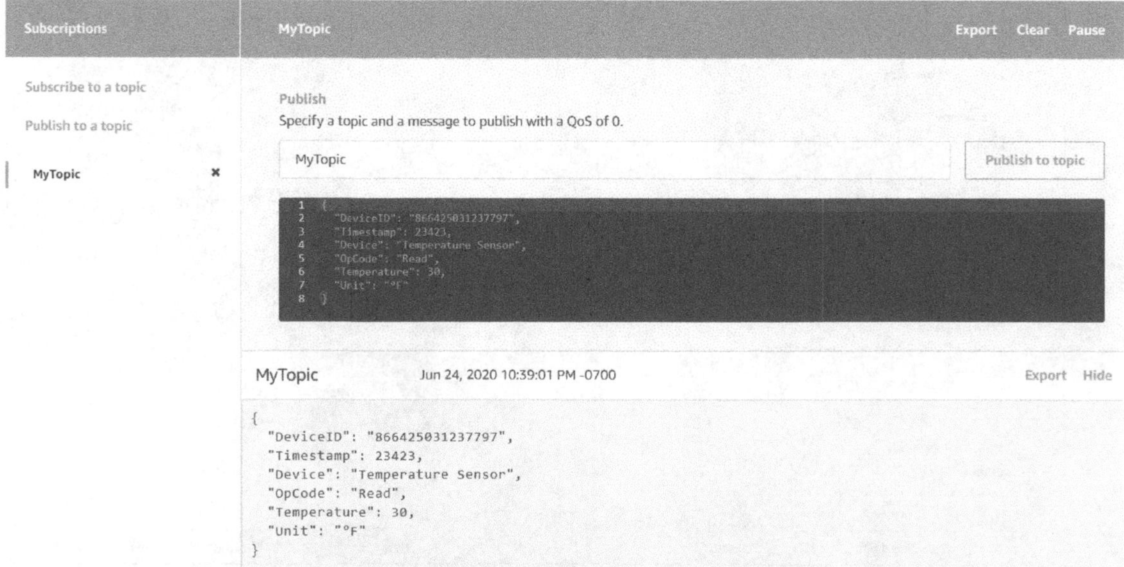

Figure 7.29: JSON Data Published from AWS IoT to the Device.

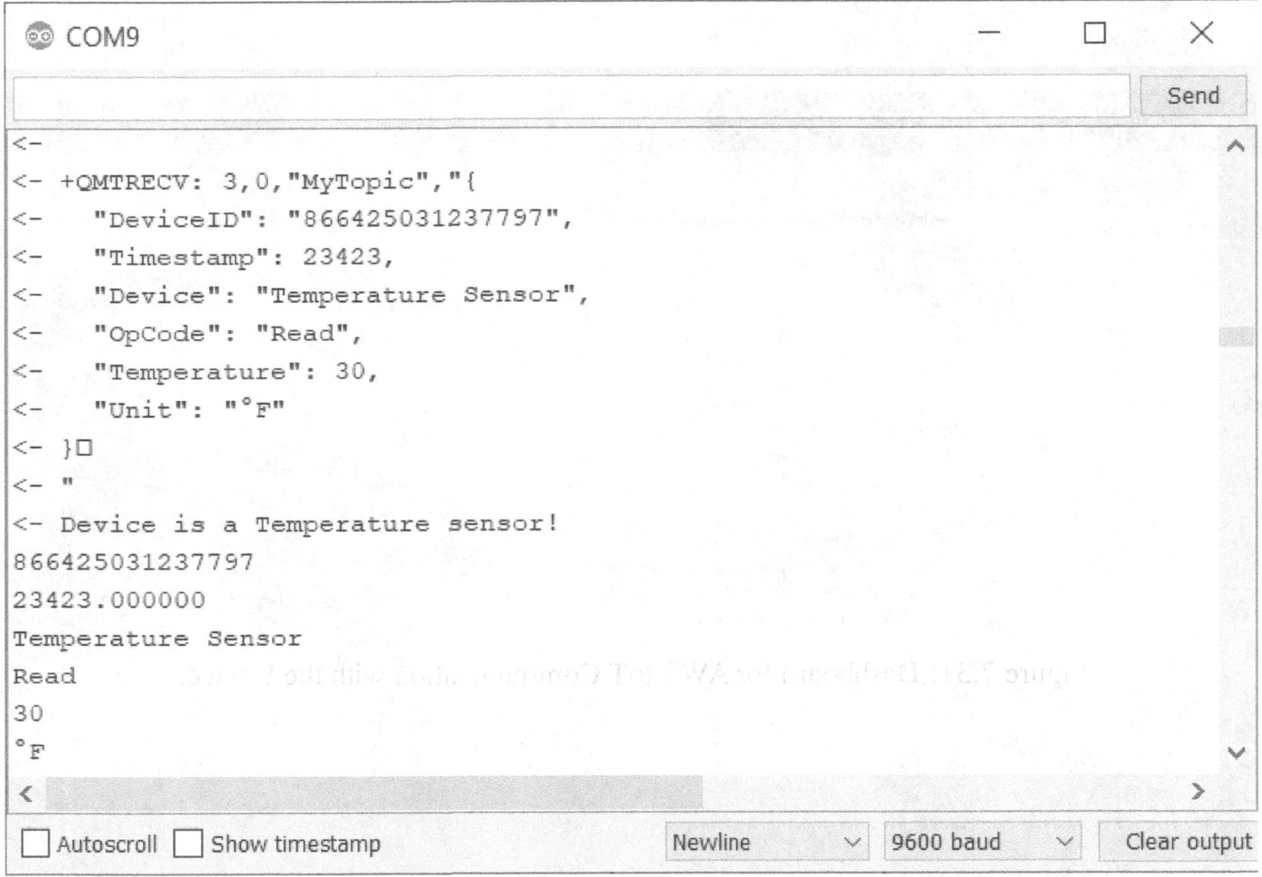

Figure 7.30: Serial Monitor Output when JSON Data is Received on the Device.

7.8 AWS IoT Device Communication and Testing

In the previous section you have added a new NB-IoT device (thing) into AWS IoT and configured it. By now, you have made the NB-IoT device connect, transmit, and receive messages with the cloud. In the menu bar on the AWS IoT dashboard in Figure 7.3, click **Test**. This brings the MQTT dashboard, shown in Figure 7.31, where you can specify a topic to Publish/Subscribe and see all messages received from the device or you can transmit a message to the device.

Under the **Subscription topic**, enter **MyTopic**. Remember that **MyTopic** was added to the policy document which states that any device can publish, subscribe, and receive on this topic. After entering the topic name to the box, click **Subscribe to topic**.

The topic name, **MyTopic**, is now shown on the sidebar, as in Figure 7.32, and any message transmitted from the device will show up here. You can send a message to the device by clicking **Publish to a topic** and enter the message to be transmitted to the device. You can also receive a message from the device by clicking **subscribe to MyTopic**.

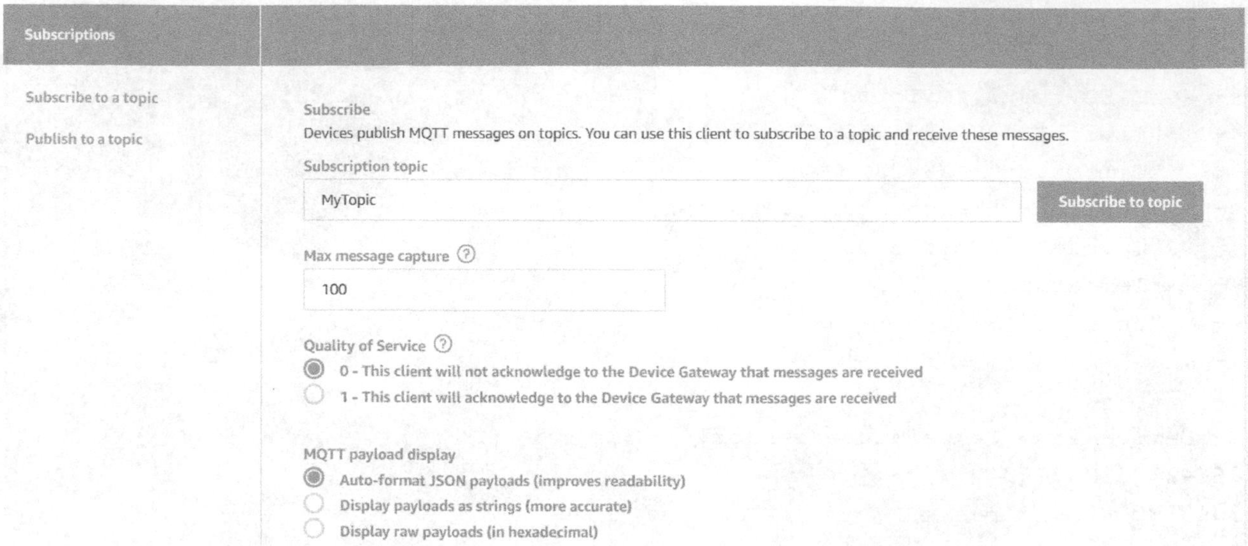

Subscriptions

Subscribe to a topic

Publish to a topic

Subscribe

Devices publish MQTT messages on topics. You can use this client to subscribe to a topic and receive these messages.

Subscription topic

MyTopic

Subscribe to topic

Max message capture

100

Quality of Service

0 - This client will not acknowledge to the Device Gateway that messages are received

1 - This client will acknowledge to the Device Gateway that messages are received

MQTT payload display

Auto-format JSON payloads (improves readability)

Display payloads as strings (more accurate)

Display raw payloads (in hexadecimal)

Figure 7.31: Dashboard for AWS IoT Communication with the Device.

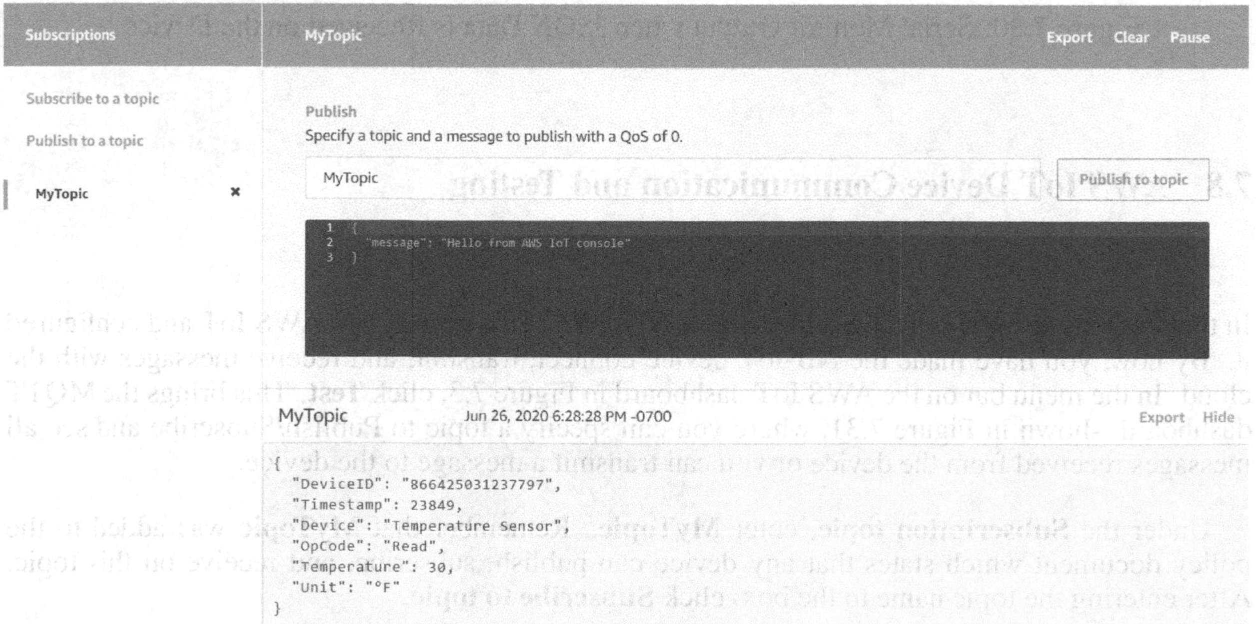

Figure 7.32: Dashboard for AWS IoT When the Device Publishes a JSON Data.

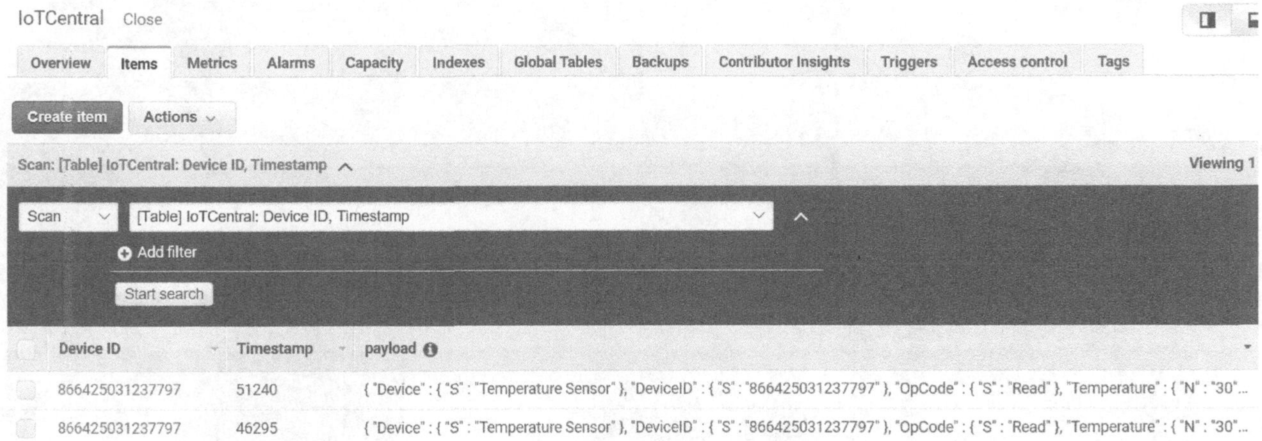

Figure 7.33: Data Stored in the Dynamo Database.

When you connect an NB-IoT device to the AWS IoT and if the device transmits the JSON message shown in Listing 7.4, the message is received and shows up on AWS IoT as in Figure 7.32.

```
{
    "DeviceID": "866425031237797",
    "Timestamp": 36918,
    "Device":
    "Temperature Sensor",
    "OpCode": "Read",
    "Temperature": 30,
    "Unit": "°F"
}
```

Listing 7.4: JSON Data Published by the Device.

Go to the DynamoDB table and refresh the table and you can see all messages received from the NB-IoT devices are stored in the DynamoDB.

As the data is stored in the DynamoDB, you can build your own web application that can read this data, analyze it, or visualize it in a different way. Chapter 8 explains data visualization and how to read records stored in DynamoDB and visualize data in a web application.

Chapter 8

Data Visualization

Data visualization is the graphical representation of information and data. With visual elements like maps and charts, data visualization provides an accessible way to see and understand trends, outliers, and patterns in data. In the world of big data, data visualization tools are essential to analyze massive amounts of information coming from the NB-IoT devices and make data-driven decisions. In this chapter, you will learn how to use Google map to visualize the GPS location of the NB-IoT device. You will also learn how to use the Chart.js, one of the top JavaScript libraries for charts, to visualize sensor data such as temperature readings. Google map and charts can be used to create attractive and data-rich dashboard for your NB-IoT devices.

8.1 Accessing AWS DynamoDB Data

As explained Chapter 7, the DynamoDB has now been created and holds different items (or records) from the NB-IoT device. You can access these records one by one or all of them so that you can parse the data, visualize them, or have many statistics or insight about the data. In this chaper, you will use Node.js and JavaScript programming language to access DynamoDB records. JavaScript can be easily used in web pages and script to display the information in a web browser. Let us go step by step on how to access the records in the DynamoDB.

8.2 Setting AWS Credentials and Region

To connect to DynamoDB and access it uses Java programming language, AWS SDK for Java needs to be installed. You must provide AWS credentials. The credentials consist of the following:

ACCESS_KEY: It is an access key for using DynamoDB. You can generate this key, using AWS management console.

SECRET_KEY: It is a secret key of above-mentioned access key.

The AWS SDK looks for AWS credentials in several different places, including local AWS configuration file stored on the Windows computer. You can set AWS credentials in the AWS credentials profile file on your Windows computer located at:

```
C:\Users\USERNAME\.aws\credentials
```

This file contains the following lines:

```
[default]
aws_access_key_id = AKIAINI2AIGLQ6TGM
aws_secret_access_key = f5skN9dDRvpGcE1oAPLxHbVdrHPax86
```

Listing 8.1: AWS credentials File.

In addition, you need to set up a default AWS region that is used for accessing the DynamoDB with AWS SDK for Java. You can set the AWS region in the AWS config file on a file stored on your Windows computer. Set the AWS region in the AWS config file on your local system, located at:

```
C:\Users\USERNAME\.aws\config
```

This file contains lines in the following format which specify the "us-west-2" region as the region where the DynamoDB is hosted.

```
[default]
region=us-west-2
```

Listing 8.2: AWS config File.

By setting up the AWS credentials and region file, you are now ready to start accessing DynamoDB records.

8.3 Using Node.js and JavaScript APIs for AWS SDK

JavaScript is a scripting and browser dynamic programming language used with HTML to control how web pages interact with users. JavaScript is used extensively for displaying and rendering web elements such as charts, maps, or any other visualization on web pages and providing the ability for users to interact with these web elements such as displaying statistics.

JavaScript has a wide variety of constructs, applications, and practices that takes considerable time to master at a professional level. However, there are some fundamental elements that can be learned quickly, and by the conclusion of the following code exercises, you shall be able to copy, understand, and customize simple scripts. If JavaScript is entirely new to you, and/or you find this tutorial challenging, you may wish to work through some of tutorials available on the Internet such as the W3 Schools JavaScript tutorial [28] to give you a firmer foundation on the basics of JavaScript.

Node.js is an open-source, cross-platform, asynchronous, event-driven JavaScript runtime environment that executes JavaScript code outside a web browser. Node.js lets a developer use JavaScript to write command line tools and for server-side scripting. Developer can run scripts on server-side to produce dynamic web page content before the page is sent to the user web browser. Node.js is a unifying web-application development around a single programming language, rather than different languages for server- and client-side scripts. Node.js is designed to build scalable network applications. In the following Sections, you will use Node.js and JavaScript to visualize the data stored in the DynamoDB by the NB-IoT devices.

8.4 Read Single Records in DynamoDB

To read an item in DynamoDB, it requires using **getItem(.)** API, and specifying the table name and item primary key. The table name in the previous DynamoDB is "IoTCentral" and its primary key is composed of two attributes which is "Device ID" and "Timestamp". Chapter 7 explained how to build the DynamoDB and store records in it.

When you perform a read operation, the complete primary key composing of the two attributes, must be included in the parameters of the **getItem(.)** API. Be sure to include the complete primary key rather than omitting a portion.

The **getItem(.)** operation returns the "payload" attribute for the item with the given primary key. If there is no matching item, **getItem (.)** does not return any data and there will be no item element in the response.

When the **getItem(.)** is called, it makes a request through the AWS SDK which is asynchronous and use a callback interface. **getItem(.)** kicks off a request and returns an **AWS.Request** object that you can use to register callbacks.

The parameter params in the **getItem(.)** API, provides parameters such as table name and primary key. The callback parameter is called when a response from the service is returned.

```
getItem(params = {}, callback)⇒ AWS.Request
```

Listing 8.3: **getItem(.)** API.

8.5 JavaScript for Reading the DynamoDB

The following JavasScript code is an example of how to read a single item from the DynamoDB. This example can be run using Node.js in Visual Studio Code (VSC). Launch Visual Studio Code

(VSC) and run this code to read a single item from the DynamoDB. The steps to use the AWS SDK to read a single item from the DynamoDB are as follows:

- Instantiate a DynamoDB object, this object is used to call the **getItem(.)** API.
- For the **getItem(.)** API parameters, set the name of the table. In this case, it is "IoTCentral".
- For the **getItem(.)** API parameters, set the primary key value to be retrieved. In this case, it is "Device ID" and "Timestamp" and their value are set.
- Invoke the **getItem(.)** API on **ddb** object and passing parameters and callback to be called when the API response returns.

The JavaScript file, **DynamoDBRead.js**, as in Listing 8.4, shows how to use the **getItem(.)** API.

```
// Load the AWS SDK for Node.js
var AWS = require('aws-sdk');

// Create the DynamoDB service object
var ddb = new AWS.DynamoDB();

var params = {
  TableName: "IoTCentral",
  Key: {
    'Device ID': {S: '866425031237797'},
    'Timestamp': {S: '84810'}
  }
};

// Call DynamoDB to read the item from the table
ddb.getItem(params, function(err, data) {
    data = JSON.stringify(data.Item);
    dataParse= JSON.parse(data)
    IMEI = dataParse["Device ID"];
    Timestamp = dataParse["Timestamp"];
    dataPayloadParse = dataParse["payload"].M
    console.log("DeviceID: ",IMEI.S);
    console.log("Timestamp: ",Timestamp.S);
    console.log("payload: ",dataPayloadParse);
});
```

Listing 8.4: DynamoDBRead.js with **getItem(.)** API.

Run the JavaScript program in Visual Studio Code. You can open the terminal window from the menu **View->Terminal** and type **node** `.\DynamoDBRead.js` which produces the output as in Figure 8.1.

8.6 Read All Records in DynamoDB

You can read all records in the DynamoDB and not only a single item. The **getItem(.)** API reads only a single record.

```
PROBLEMS   OUTPUT   TERMINAL   DEBUG CONSOLE                1: powershell
PS C:\AWS> node .\DynamoDBRead.js
DeviceID:  866425031237797
Timestamp:  84810
payload:  {
  Temperature: { S: '50' },
  Unit: { S: '°F' },
  Device: { S: 'Temperature Sensor' },
  OpCode: { S: 'Read' }
}
PS C:\AWS>
```

Figure 8.1: Output of DynamoDBRead.js.

DynamoDB offers scan functionality through **scan(.)** API. Scan fetches all the items in the DynamoDB table. Therefore, scan does not require to provide primary key values. Instead, scan only require the table name to be provided along with the callback function.

The JavaScript code below shows how to use **scan(.)** API to read all records in the DynamoDB. Inside the **scan(.)** callback function, there is for-loop that iterates over all items read and display them.

```
// Load the AWS SDK for Node.js
var AWS = require('aws-sdk');

// Create the DynamoDB service object
var ddb = new AWS.DynamoDB();

var params = {
  TableName: "IoTCentral"
};

// Call DynamoDB to read the item from the table
var count = 0;
ddb.scan(params, function(err, data) {
      data.Items.forEach(function(itemdata)
      {
          console.log("Record :", ++count);
          data = JSON.stringify(itemdata);
          dataParse = JSON.parse(data)
          IMEI = dataParse["Device ID"];
          Timestamp = dataParse["Timestamp"];
          dataPayloadParse = dataParse["payload"].M
          console.log("IMEI: ",IMEI.S);
          console.log("Timestamp: ",Timestamp.S);
          console.log("payload: ",dataPayloadParse);
      });
});
```

Listing 8.5: DynamoDBScan.js with **scan(.)** API.

The DynamoDB table has only two items as in Figure 8.2

Run the JavaScript program in Visual Studio Code. You can open the terminal window from the menu **View->Terminal** and type **node .\DynamoDBScan.js**. You will see the two items now displayed as in Figure 8.3.

The **scan(.)** API is run asynchronously. This means that when the **scan(.)** API is called, it does not wait until the response come back from the AWS server. Instead the next line of code

Device ID	Timestamp	payload
866425031237797	84810	{ "Device" : { "S" : "Temperature Sensor" }, "OpCode" : { "S" : "Read" }, "Temperature" : { "S" : "50" }, "...
866425031237797	84820	{ "Device" : { "S" : "Temperature Sensor" }, "OpCode" : { "S" : "Read" }, "Temperature" : { "S" : "42" }, "...

Figure 8.2: DynamoDB with Only two Items.

after **scan(.)** API can start executing while the response has not been received yet from the AWS server. In order to make the **scan(.)** API runs synchronously which means that it has to wait until the response is fully received before the next line of code is executed, you can use the Promise in JavaScript. Promise means that the **scan(.)** API has to be fully completed and finished before starting to execute the next line of code. This acts as if **scan(.)** API is run synchronously. The following line of code can be used to call **scan(.)** API synchronously.

```
// Call DynamoDB to read the item from the table
var result = await ddb.scan(params).promise();

var count = 0;
result.Items.forEach(function(itemdata)
    {
      console.log("Record :", ++count);
      data = JSON.stringify(itemdata);
      dataParse = JSON.parse(data)
      IMEI = dataParse["Device ID"];
      Timestamp = dataParse["Timestamp"];
      dataPayloadParse = dataParse["payload"].M
      console.log("IMEI: ",IMEI.S);
      console.log("Timestamp: ",Timestamp.S);
      console.log("payload: ",dataPayloadParse)
    });
```

Listing 8.6: DynamoDBScan.js with **scan(.)** API.

```
Record : 1
IMEI:  866425031237797
Timestamp:  84810
payload:  {
  Temperature: { S: '50' },
  Unit: { S: '°F' },
  Device: { S: 'Temperature Sensor' },
  OpCode: { S: 'Read' }
}
Record : 2
IMEI:  866425031237797
Timestamp:  84820
payload:  {
  Temperature: { S: '42' },
  Unit: { S: '°F' },
  Device: { S: 'Temperature Sensor' },
  OpCode: { S: 'Read' }
}
PS C:\AWS>
```

Figure 8.3: Output of DynamoDBScan.js.

8.7 Visualizing GPS Geo-Location Using Google Maps

Google provides APIs that be called from JavaScript to display and plot geo-locations on a geographical map. Google has JavaScript APIs to control and interact with the map. These APIs let you customize the map with your own content and imagery for display on web pages and mobile devices. The JavaScript APIs feature four basic map types (roadmap, satellite, hybrid, and terrain) which you can modify using layers and styles, controls and events, and various services and libraries.

One of the important application of NB-IoT device is to use it as a GPS tracker to track objects such as moving vehicles, human, or even a child or a pet. Thus, using NB-IoT devices to collect and emits GPS locations and display these locations on Google map is one important application that can be used by NB-IoT devices.

In this section, you will learn, step by step, how to make the NB-IoT device emits GPS location and importantly how to use Google map APIs to plot and display them on a map in a web browser. The Google map project in this section, involves two sides. The NB-IoT device side which emits the GPS location and the server side which reads the data emitted by the NB-IoT device and display them on the Google map.

For the NB-IoT device side, run the Arduino sketch in Chapter 13 on the NB-IoT device so that the device can emit the GPS location. The NB-IoT device can be stationary device or attached to any moving object such as vehicle, human, pet, or a child to track their geo-locations and visually plot their locations.

On your computer you can display a web page with Google map inside it as illustrated in Listing 8.11. It is an HTML page, **GoogleMap.html**, that contains JavaScript code and HTML elements to display Google map and NB-IoT device GPS geo-location on the map. In the next section, it will be explained step by step.

8.7.1 Get the Google Maps API

To use the Google map JavaScript APIs, you must have an API key. The API key is a unique identifier that is used to authenticate requests associated with your project for usage and billing purposes. To get the Google map API key:

- Go to the Google cloud platform console [29].
- Click the project drop-down and select or create the project for which you want to add an API key.
- Click the menu button and select **APIs & Services->Credentials**.
- On the **Credentials page**, click Create **credentials->API key**. The API key created dialog displays your newly created API key.
- Click **Close**. The new API key is listed on the **Credentials** page under **API keys**.

Insert the API key as a query string on the end of the script URL as in Listing 8.7.

```
<script src="https://maps.googleapis.com/maps/api/js?key=YOUR_API_KEY"></script>
```

Listing 8.7: Google Map API Key.

8.7.2 Initializing Google Maps Using JavaScript API

The first step to display Google map, is to initialize it. The Google map JavaScript API is loaded using a script tag, which can be added inline in your HTML file as in Listing 8.8.

```
<script async defer src="https://maps.googleapis.com/maps/api/js?key=YOUR_API_KEY&callback=
    initMap">
</script>
```

Listing 8.8: Google Map Initialization.

Notice in this example listing above that several attributes are set on the "script" HTML tag, which are:

- **src**: The URL where the maps JavaScript API is loaded from, including all of the symbols and definitions you need for using the maps JavaScript API. The URL has two parameters: key, where you provide your API key and **initMap(.)** which is a callback API representing the name of a global function to be called once the maps JavaScript API loads completely.
- **async**: Asks the browser to render the rest of your website while the maps JavaScript API loads. When the API is ready, it will call the function specified using the **initMap(.)** parameter.
- **defer**: Asks the browser to parse the HTML document first before loading the script.

The callback API is **initMap(.)** and it initializes the Google map which is displayed in the web browser. In the following code, it has the class called **google.maps.Map**. The JavaScript class that represents a map is the **Map** class. Objects of this class define a single map on a web page. You create a new instance of this class using the JavaScript new operator.

```
map = new google.maps.Map(document.getElementById("googleMap"),{...});
```

Listing 8.9: Google Map Object.

When you create a new map instance, you specify a <div> HTML element in the page as a container for the map. HTML nodes are children of the JavaScript document object, and you obtain a reference to this element via the **document.getElementById()** method.

```
<div id="googleMap"></div>
```

Listing 8.10: Google Map div.

The code in Listing 8.11 defines a variable named **map** and assigns it a new object of type **Map**. The function **Map(.)** is known as a constructor which accepts parameters as the <DIV> id and map option. The map option has two parameters, the GPS location defined as latitude and longitude and zoom. The map options have the following two options:

- Center: lat: -25.344, lng: 131.036
- Zoom level which is an integer number from 1 to 20 determining the zoom level on the map

Google map defines what is called a marker. A marker identifies a location on a map. By default, a marker uses a standard image set by Google map.

The **google.maps.Marker** is the JavaScript class. When you instantiate an object of this class, the constructor takes a single **Marker options** object literal, specifying the initial properties of the marker. The following fields are particularly important and commonly set when constructing a marker:

- **position**: specifies a latitude and longitude identifying the initial location of the marker.
- **map**: specifies the map on which to place the marker.

The complete code for initializing the Google map using **initMap(.)** is shown in Listing 8.11 which displays the Google map using a GPS location near Australia (lat: -25.344, lng: 131.036).

8.7.3 Retrieving the GPS location from the DynamoDB

When you run the Arduino sketch in Chapter 13, the NB-IoT device emits its GPS location and these locations for all NB-IoT devices are stored in DynamoDB. The DynamoDB is as shown in Figure 8.4 which contains records for GPS locations emitted by an NB-IoT device. The payload is a JSON-formatted string and has a position key and its value contains the detailed GPS location according to Table 13.1.

Similar to the JavaScript in Listing 8.4, you can implement a JavaScript code that reads the DynamoDB records and parses the payload field to extract the latitude and longitude and display them on the Google map. The **ReadDB(.)** API code is shown is Listing 8.11. This API is implemented as a JavaScript inside an HTML page so that it can be displayed in a web browser. The **ReadDB(.)** API does the following:

Scan: [Table] IoTCentral: Device ID, Timestamp

Device ID	Timestamp	payload
866425031237797	84810	{ "Device" : { "S" : "GPS" }, "OpCode" : { "S" : "Read" }, "Position" : { "S" : "063729.0,47.82670,-122.20605,1.1,14.0,2,0.00,0.0,0...
866425031237797	84880	{ "Device" : { "S" : "GPS" }, "OpCode" : { "S" : "Read" }, "Position" : { "S" : "063729.0,47.82670,-122.20605,1.1,14.0,2,0.00,0.0,0...

Figure 8.4: DynamoDB snapshot with NB-IoT Device GPS Geo-Location.

- Initialize the AWS region, access keys required to use the AWS SDK to read the item from the DynamoDB.
- Specify the parameters needed to call **getItem(.)** API includes the primary key values which consists of the "Device ID" and "Timestamp".
- Once the item is retrieved from the DynamoDB in a JSON format, it is converted into a string and the payload field is parsed to extract the latitude and longitude. Notice that the value of the position key inside the **payload** field follows the format in Table 13.1.
- Once the latitude and longitude are extracted, the marker object **setPoistion(.)** API is used to set the GPS location on the map. Next, the marker object API, **panTo(.)**, is used which changes the center of the Google map to the new latitude and longitude.

```
<h3>NB-IoT Device using Google map</h3>
<script src="https://sdk.amazonaws.com/js/aws-sdk2.7.16.min.js"></script>
<div id="googleMap" style="width:100%;height:400px;"></div>
<div style="width:100%;height:50;text-align:center"></div>
<div style="width:100%;height:200;text-align:center">
    <button type="button" onclick="readDB()">Read GPS Position!</button>
</div>

<script async defer
src="https://maps.googleapis.com/maps/api/js?key=YOUR_KEY&callback=initMap">
</script>

<script>
    var map, marker;

    function initMap()
    {
        var uluru = {lat: -25.344, lng: 131.036};
        map = new google.maps.Map(document.getElementById("googleMap"), {zoom: 6, center: uluru})
    ;
        marker = new google.maps.Marker({position: uluru, draggable: true, map: map});
    }
    AWS.config.update({
    region: "us-west-2",
    accessKeyId:"AKIAINI2AIGLQ6TGM",
    secretAccessKey: "f5skN9dDRvpGcE1oAPLxHbVdrHPax86"
    });

    function readDB()
    {
      var ddb = new AWS.DynamoDB();

      var params = {
        TableName: "IoTCentral",
        Key: {
          'Device ID': {S: '866425031237797'},
          'Timestamp': {S: '84810'}
        }
      };

      ddb.getItem(params, function(err, data) {
         data = JSON.stringify(data.Item);
         dataParse = JSON.parse(data)
         IMEI = dataParse["Device ID"];
         Timestamp = dataParse["Timestamp"];
         dataPayloadParse = dataParse["payload"].M
```

```
          Device = dataPayloadParse["Device"];
          OpCode = dataPayloadParse["OpCode"];
          Position = dataPayloadParse["Position"];
          dataGNSS = Position.S.split(',');
          marker.setPosition(dataGNSS[1], dataGNSS[2]);
         map.panTo( new google.maps.LatLng(dataGNSS[1], dataGNSS[2]));
      });
    }
</script>
```

Listing 8.11: An HTML page GoogleMap.html to Display Google Map.

8.7.4 Displaying the GPS Geo-Location in a Web Browser

The final step is to run the HTML page in Listing 8.11 inside a browser to display the Google map and see how reading the GPS location from the DynamoDB is displayed and visualized in the web browser.

With Node.js, you can write a simple web server that can run as a web server on your local computer that loads the HTML page in Listing 8.11. The web server code is few lines of codes as in Listing 8.12. It creates a web server that listens on port 8000. To access the web page from any web browser on your Windows computer, launch the browser and put the URL: `http://localhost:8000/`.

```
let http = require('http');
let fs = require('fs');

let handleRequest = (request, response) => {
    response.writeHead(200, {
        'Content-Type': 'text/html'
    });
    fs.readFile('GoogleMap.html', null, function (error, data) {
            response.write(data);
        response.end();
    });
};
http.createServer(handleRequest).listen(8000);
```

Listing 8.12: JavaScript to Create a Web Server for Data Visualization.

Inside Visual Studio Code, run the web server code in Listing 8.12. Then, launch a web browser (such as Microsoft Edge), and type the URL: `http://localhost:8000/`. The web page in Listing 8.11 is displayed in the browser as in the screen shot in Figure 8.5. As the **initMap(.)** API initializes the map with a location near Australia, that location is displayed on Google map.

There is a button on the web page. When this button is pressed, the item in the DynamoDB for the NB-IoT device is retrieved and read as in **readDB(.)** API in Listing 8.11. The GPS location retrieved from the DynamoDB is latitude: 47.82670 and longitude: -122.20605. This GPS location is displayed on the Google map as in Figure 8.6 which is location near Seattle area, Washington, USA.

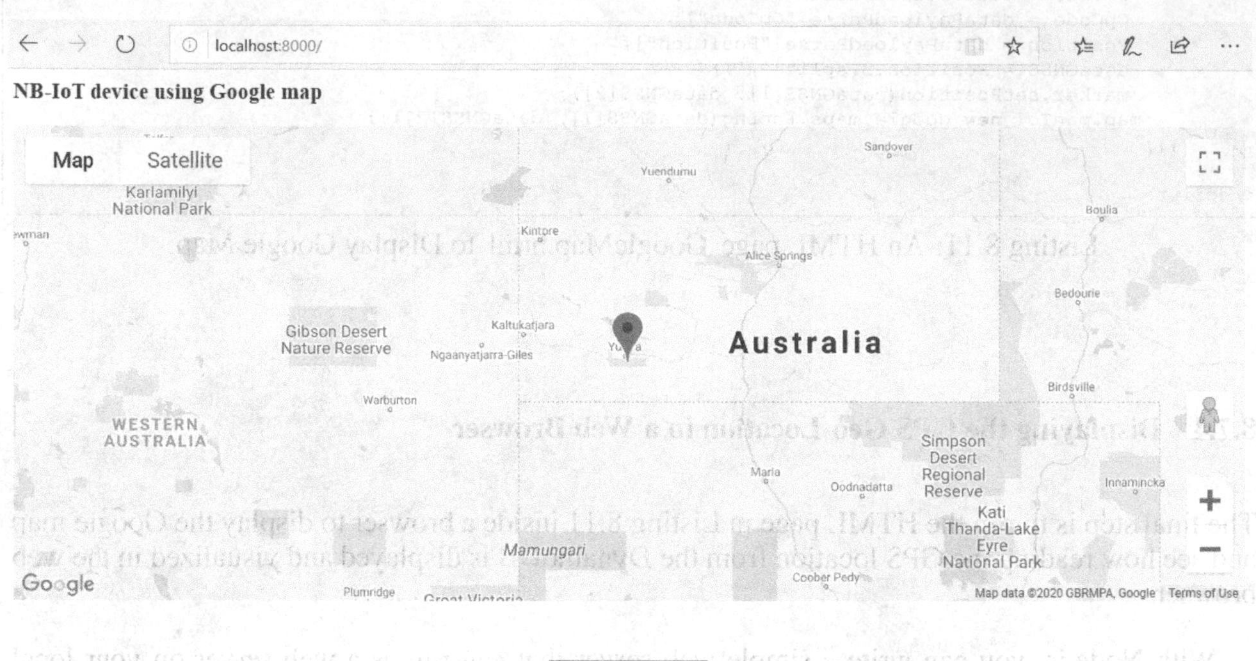

Figure 8.5: Google Map after Calling **initMap(.)** API.

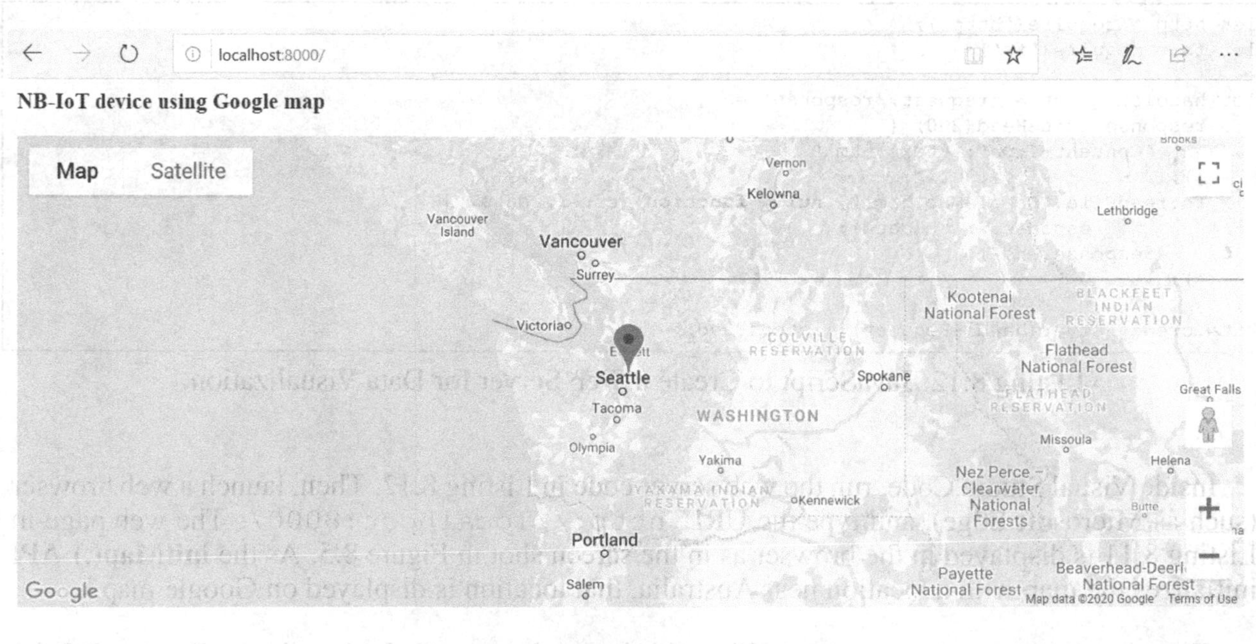

Figure 8.6: Google Map after Reading an Item from the DynamoDB.

By this step you are now able to make the device emits its GPS location to the DynamoDB as in Chapter 13, store the GPS location in DynamoDB, and uses Google map API, JavaScript, and HTML web page to visualize the device GPS geo-location.

If you have multiple NB-IoT devices emitting their GPS locations to the DynamoDB and you want display all of their GPS locations on the Google map, then you can use the DynamoDB **scan(.)** API to read all items in the DynamoDB, and plot each GPS location on the map using similar JavaScript code as in Listing 8.5 and Listing 8.11.

8.8 Data Visualization Using Charts

It is attractive to use charts to visualize your data. Charts can have different shapes and colors such as pie, bar, line, doughnut, or other shapes and with full range of colors that make it attractive and useful to visualize your NB-IoT device data such as temperature readings or other sensor and measurements readings.

Chart.js [30] is a popular open source library that can be used to visualize NB-IoT data in web applications. It is highly customizable and configurable. Chart.js allows you to draw different types of charts by using the HTML5 canvas element.

A good feature of Chart.js is that the charts are responsive, so they adapt based on the space available. Importantly Chart.js provides extensive library and different chart shapes and colors, they are very easy to use for web or data visualization applications, and you get beautiful and attractive charts.

8.8.1 Installing Chart.js Library

Chart.js can be downloaded and installed from a Content Delivery Network (CDN) which is a repository for storing JavaScipt libraries.

The first step is to add the Chart.js to a web page so that you can use the library. At the time of writing this book, the latest version of the Chart.js library is 2.9.3. Include the following line in a web page to add Chart.js

```
<script src="https://cdnjs.cloudflare.com/ajax/libs/Chart.js/2.9.3/Chart.min.js"></script>
```

Listing 8.13: Adding JavaScript Chart.js.

8.8.2 Prepare an Area in Web Page to Render Chart

The next step before you visualize your data is to define an area in the HTML page where you want to draw the chart. For Chart.js, you do this by adding a canvas tag element, and setting width and height to define the proportions of your graph. This is shown below.

Scan: [Table] IoTCentral: Device ID, Timestamp

Device ID	Timestamp	payload
866425031237797	84810	{ "Device" : { "S" : "Temperature Sensor" }, "OpCode" : { "S" : "Read" }, "Temperature" : { "S" : "50" }, "...
866425031237797	84820	{ "Device" : { "S" : "Temperature Sensor" }, "OpCode" : { "S" : "Read" }, "Temperature" : { "S" : "42" }, "...
866425031237797	84830	{ "Device" : { "S" : "Temperature Sensor" }, "OpCode" : { "S" : "Read" }, "Temperature" : { "S" : "46" }, "...
866425031237797	84840	{ "Device" : { "S" : "Temperature Sensor" }, "OpCode" : { "S" : "Read" }, "Temperature" : { "S" : "44" }, "...
866425031237797	84850	{ "Device" : { "S" : "Temperature Sensor" }, "OpCode" : { "S" : "Read" }, "Temperature" : { "S" : "34" }, "...
866425031237797	84860	{ "Device" : { "S" : "Temperature Sensor" }, "OpCode" : { "S" : "Read" }, "Temperature" : { "S" : "33" }, "...
866425031237797	84870	{ "Device" : { "S" : "Temperature Sensor" }, "OpCode" : { "S" : "Read" }, "Temperature" : { "S" : "36" }, "...
866425031237797	84880	{ "Device" : { "S" : "Temperature Sensor" }, "OpCode" : { "S" : "Read" }, "Temperature" : { "S" : "35" }, "...
866425031237797	84890	{ "Device" : { "S" : "Temperature Sensor" }, "OpCode" : { "S" : "Read" }, "Temperature" : { "S" : "44" }, "...
866425031237797	84900	{ "Device" : { "S" : "Temperature Sensor" }, "OpCode" : { "S" : "Read" }, "Temperature" : { "S" : "45" }, "...

Figure 8.7: DynamoDB Records for Temperature Sensor.

Notice that there is an id (myChart) added to the canvas element that you can later use to reference your designated graph element in JavaScript. What this ID is set to has no significance for Chart.js; you can name it whatever you want. What matters is that you use the exact same ID when you reference it in JavaScript. If you are adding several graphs to a page, just make sure that every ID is unique (you could for example give your graphs more specific names, like TemperatureChart or HumidityChart).

```
<canvas id="myChart" width="1600" height="900"></canvas>
```

Listing 8.14: Canvas for Chart.js.

8.8.3 Reading and Preparing the Data from DynamoDB

The NB-IoT devices are emitting their data to AWS IoT and the data is stored in the DynamoDB. Now, you can access and read this data from the DynamoDB and visualize it on a chart. You are going to use the records stored in the DynamoDB for temperature sensor. The DynamoDB has ten records stored from a single NB-IoT device acting as a temperature sensor. The temperature sensor is explained in Chapter 30 Temperature and Humidity Sensor.

To visualize these temperature sensor data, you can use Charts.js. To draw bar chart and add labels along the x-axis and y-axis, Chart.js expects the data to be passed in the form of a set of arrays like [50, 30, 36]. You are going to use two arrays. One array is used on the x-axis and represents the timestamp attribute of the record in the DynamoDB. Second array represents the temperature readings parsed from the payload attribute. All you need to do is read or use

DynamoDB **scan(.)** API to read all records and then parse each record and store the timestamp attribute and the temperature value into the two arrays.

8.8.4 Draw the Bar Chart

The next step is to draw your chart. You will draw a bar chart. For displaying temperature dataset, you can choose charts from line, bar, or other type of chart as you like. Let us use the bar chart and visualize all temperature dataset read from the DynamoDB.

For drawing the chart, all you need to do is define what chart you want to draw, and pass in the data that you want to visualize. To draw the chart, you need to call the following Chart.js API. This JavaScript code first locates canvas element that reserve space for the chart. Then the chart itself is created by calling the **Chart(.)** API and passing all configuration and datasets to be displayed on the chart.

```
<script>
var ctx = document.getElementById("myChart");
var myChart = new Chart(ctx, {...});
</script>
```

Listing 8.15: Creating Chart.js Object.

8.8.5 Create Complete Web Page

Now, you can create your web page or HTML page that contains all the JavaScript programming to fully visualize the DynamoDB temperature records and visualize it on the bar chart. The complete web page is shown in Listing 8.16. To explain this web page, it contains the following:

- It includes the JavaScript libraries used which are the AWS SDK and Charts API.
- It defines canvas element which is used to draw graphics on a web page.
- It configures AWS SDK by specifying the region, access key, and secret access key.
- It calls the **Chart(.)** API to draw the chart.
- It implements two APIs:

  - **readDB(.)** which reads all records in the DynamoDB.

  - **replaceData(.)** which is used to set the dataset on the x-axis, y-axis, and legend of the chart and render the chart.

Let us now explain in more details what **Chart(.)** API does. This API is called to configure and render the chart, the following parameters are passed to this API to display and render the chart on the web page:

- **ctx:** this contains the canvas area on the web page to draw this chart.
- **type**: this defines the chart type which is set to be bar chart.
- **data**: the data to be displayed on x-axis and y-axis. This represents plotting timestamp attribute on x-axis and temperature reading on y-axis. It also include the legend of the chart. This parameter contains the following parameters:

  - **labels**: this is the dataset for the x-axis which represents the timestamp attribute in the DynamoDB records.

  - **legendText**: this is the chart legend which is set to the IMEI attribute in the DynamoDB.

  - **datasets**: this is the y-axis dataset which represents the temperature value in the payload attribute in the DynamoDB. You can define the color of each bar.
- **options**: this represents additional options which includes:

  - **title**: the title to be displayed on the top of the chart along with its font color and size.

  - **legend**: represent the location where the chart legend is to be displayed and its font color.

  - **scales**: this define the string labels to be displayed on the x-axis or y-axis and their font colors. For the y-axis, it also defines the minimum and maximum value to be displayed which is set to be between 20 and 100.

Notice that the web page defines **onload** which calls the **readDB(.)** API once the web page is loaded or re-loaded.

```
<!DOCTYPE html>
<html>
    <body onload="readDB()">
    <head>
        <title>Temperature Sensor</title>
<script src="https://sdk.amazonaws.com/js/aws-sdk2.7.16.min.js"></script>
<script src="https://cdnjs.cloudflare.com/ajax/libs/Chart.js/2.9.3/Chart.js">
</script>
        <style type="text/css">
            .wrapper { max-width: 800px; margin: 50px auto; }
        </style>
    </head>

    <div class="wrapper">
        <canvas id="myChart" width="1600" height="900"></canvas>
    </div>

    <script>
        AWS.config.update({
        region: "us-west-2",
        accessKeyId: "AKIAINI2AIGLQ6TGM",
        secretAccessKey: "f5skN9dDRvpGcE1oAPLxHbVdrHPax86"
        });

        var ctx = document.getElementById("myChart");
        var myChart = new Chart(ctx, {
        type: 'bar',
        data: {
            labels: timeStampArray,
```

```
        legendText: 'IMEI',
        datasets: [
            {
                label: 'Timestamp',
                data: tempArray,
                backgroundColor:
                [
         "#566573", "#99a3a4", "#dc7633", "#f5b041", "#f7dc6f",
         "#82e0aa", "#73c6b6", "#5dade2", "#a569bd", "#ec7063"
                ],
            }
         ]
        },
        options:
        {
            title:
            {
                display: true,
                text: "Temperature readings from NB-IoT device",
                fontColor: "green",
                fontSize: "20"
            },
            legend:
            {
                display: true,
                position: "bottom",
                labels:
                {
                    fontColor: 'rgb(255, 0, 0)'
                }
            },
            scales:
            {
                xAxes:
                [
                    {
                        scaleLabel:
                        {
                            display: true,
                            labelString: "Timestamp (ms)",
                            fontColor: "red"
                        }
                    }
                ],
                yAxes:
                [
                    {
                        scaleLabel:
                        {
                            display: true,
                            labelString: "Temperature (F)",
                            fontColor: "blue"
                        },
                        ticks:
                        {
                            suggestedMin: 20,
                            suggestedMax: 100
                        }
                    }
                ]
            }
        }
        });
```

```
        async function readDB()
        {
            var ddb = new AWS.DynamoDB();

            var params = {
                TableName: "IoTCentral"
            };

            var result = await ddb.scan(params).promise();

            var count = 0;
            result.Items.forEach(function(itemdata)
                    {
                        data = JSON.stringify(itemdata);
                        dataParse = JSON.parse(data)
                        IMEI = dataParse["Device ID"].S;
                        Timestamp = dataParse["Timestamp"].S;
                        dataPayloadParse = dataParse["payload"].M
                        Temperature = dataPayloadParse["Temperature"].S;

                        timeStampArray[count] = Timestamp;
                        tempArray[count] = Temperature;

                        count++;
                    });

            replaceData(myChart, timeStampArray, tempArray, IMEI) ;
        }

        function replaceData(chart, label, data, legend)
        {
            chart.data.labels= label;
            chart.data.datasets[0].data = data;
            chart.data.datasets[0].label = legend;
            chart.update();
        }

    </script>
    </body>
</html>
```

Listing 8.16: An HTML page Temperature.html to Visualize Temperature Readings.

8.8.6 Rendering the Chart

The last step is to load the above the web page with the chart displayed on it. Run the JavaScript in Listing 8.12 to create the web server and replace the HTML page name to be **Temperature.html**. Run it and you will be able to load the chart at the URL `http://localhost:8000/` as shown below.

You can change the chart type from bar to line and then display it again, it will show up the following chart:

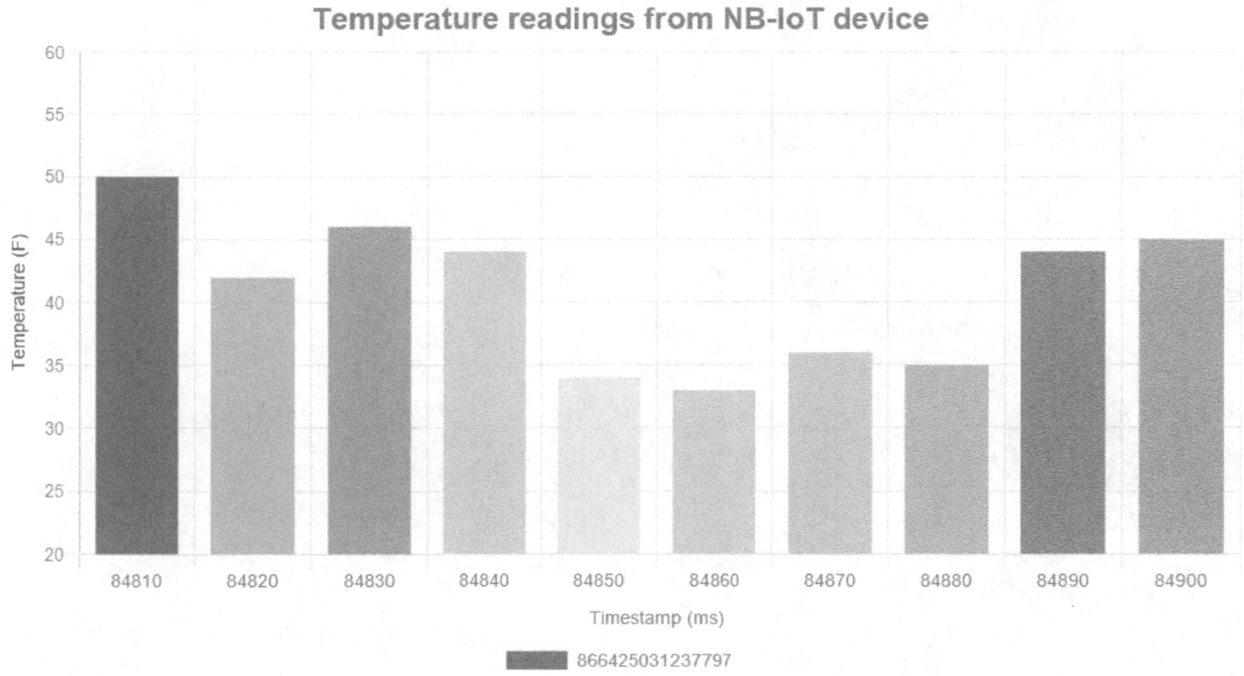

Figure 8.8: Bar Chart for the Temperature Sensor.

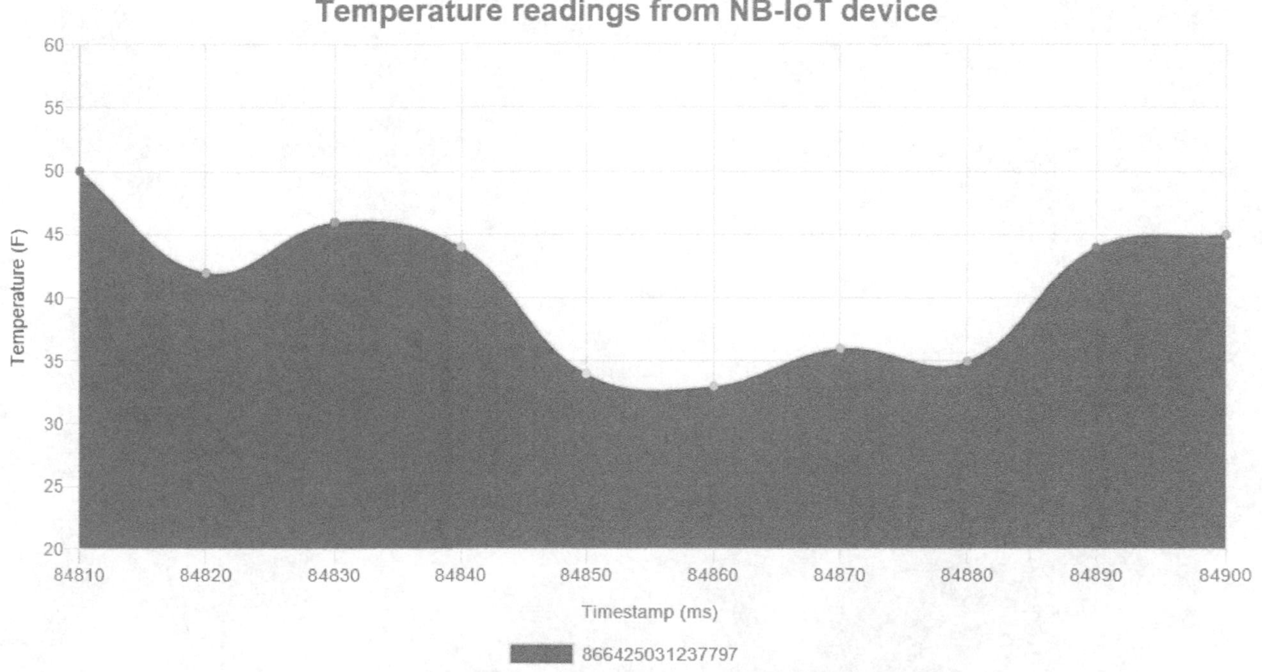

Figure 8.9: Line Chart for the Temperature Sensor.

Part I

Networking

Chapter 9

Turning on the Modem

In this chapter, you will learn how to write an Arduino sketch that turns on the modem, connects it to the mobile operator network, and communicates to the Internet from your computer.

9.1 Hardware and Software Component Required

- 1 x NB-IoT hardware board
- 2 x Micro USB cable
- 1 x LTE & GNSS Antenna
- Install Quectel BG96 Driver for Windows

9.2 Setup Steps and Diagram

The first step is to turn on the NB board and make the modem registers with the mobile operator and connects to an APN and to the Internet.

1. Insert a USIM into the USIM card slot on the NB board.
2. Connect the LTE/GPS antenna to the MAIN and GNSS antenna ports respectively on the NB board.
3. Connect the USB cable between the MCU port and the computer to power on the board and use Arduino IDE.
4. Connect the second USB cable between the modem port and the computer to detect the modem on the Windows computer.

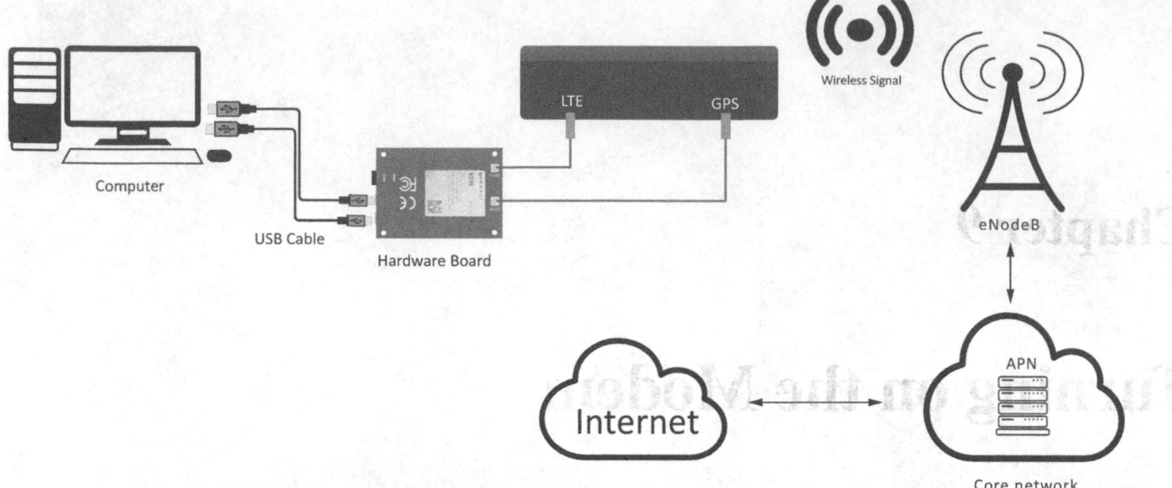

Figure 9.1: NB-IoT Hardware Board Connected to the Internet.

Figure 9.1 shows the setup of the board when connected to the computer and to the antenna.

> **NOTE:**
> Connecting the second USB between the computer and the modem USB port is optional.

9.3 Arduino Sketch

The following is the Arduino sketch that shows how the MCU is turning on the modem. When the sketch is uploaded to the board and starts running on the MCU, the MCU initializes two serial interfaces; one UART that connects the MCU to the modem and second USB interface which connects the board to the computer. The sketch programs LED1 and LED2 as output and initializes the modem by turning the modem power on and set the APN name to that of the AT&T mobile operator network. The loop is simply toggling the two LEDs on and off while the modem is turned on.

```
#include <board.h>

#define DSerial SerialUSB
#define ATSerial Serial1

char APN[] = "m2mNB16.com.attz";
unsigned int comm_pdp_index = 1;  // The range is 1 ~ 16

_5G_NB_IoT_TCPIP _5GNBIoT(ATSerial, DSerial);

void setup()
{
    DSerial.begin(115200);
```

```
    while (DSerial.read() >= 0);
    DSerial.println("This is the _5GNBIoT Debug Serial!");

    ATSerial.begin(115200);
    while (ATSerial.read() >= 0);
    delay(1000);

    pinMode(LED1, OUTPUT);
    pinMode(LED2, OUTPUT);

    _5GNBIoT.InitModule();
    DSerial.println("\r\n_5GNBIoT.InitModule() OK!");

    char apn_error[64];
    _5GNBIoT.InitAPN(comm_pdp_index, APN, "", "", apn_error);
}

void loop()
{
    digitalWrite(LED1, LOW);
    digitalWrite(LED2, HIGH);
    delay(500); // wait for a 0.5 second
    digitalWrite(LED1, HIGH);
    digitalWrite(LED2, LOW);
    delay(500); // wait for a 0.5 second
}
```

Listing 9.1: Turning on the Modem Arduino Sketch.

The **InitModule(.)** API is a simple API that turns on the modem as in Listing 9.2. The MCU powers on the modem through a modem power pin connected from the MCU to the modem. To turn on the modem, it has to follow the signaling and timing as in Figure 9.2 where a pulse of LOW duration of 500 ms or more is to be applied to turn on the modem.

```
bool _5G_NB_IoT_Common::InitModule()
{
  pinMode(POWKEY_PIN, OUTPUT);
  digitalWrite(POWKEY_PIN, HIGH);
  delay(600);
  digitalWrite(POWKEY_PIN, LOW);
  delay(600);
  digitalWrite(POWKEY_PIN, HIGH);
  return true;
}
```

Listing 9.2: Arduino Sketch for Turning on the Modem.

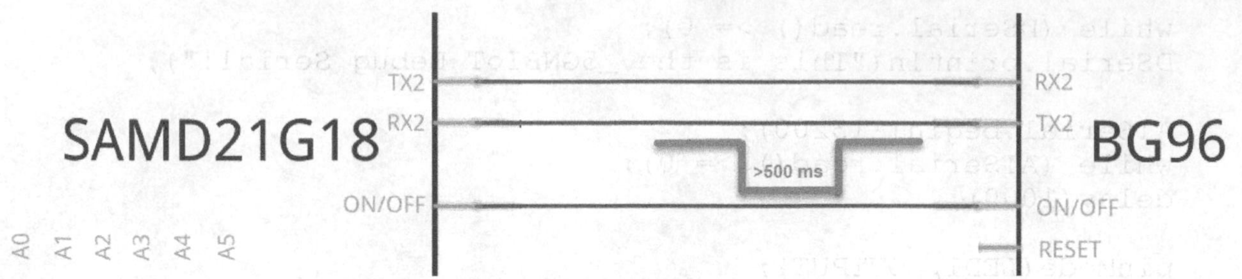

Figure 9.2: Powering on the Modem from the MCU.

After uploading this sketch to the NB board, you will see the AT commands on the Serial Monitor indicating that the device is registered on AT&T network (+CEREG: 1,1), connected to the APN name (m2mNB16.com.attz), and assigned an IP address (10.64.157.122).

After powering on the modem, the **InitAPN(.)** API is called which set the APN name to that of the AT&T network. Before you upload the Arduino sketch, install the BG96 driver for windows and connect the second USB cable to the modem USB port. After uploading the Arduino sketch, open the Windows device manager and verify that the modem is listed under **Modems** and **Ports** as in the Figure below.

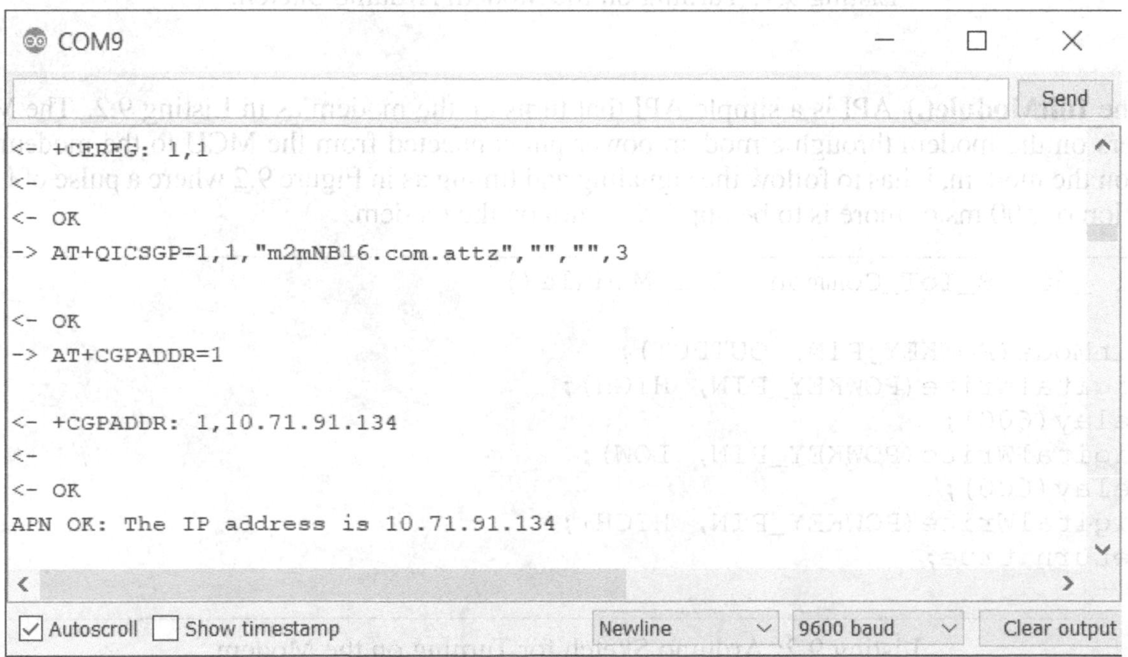

Figure 9.3: AT Commands when turning on the Modem.

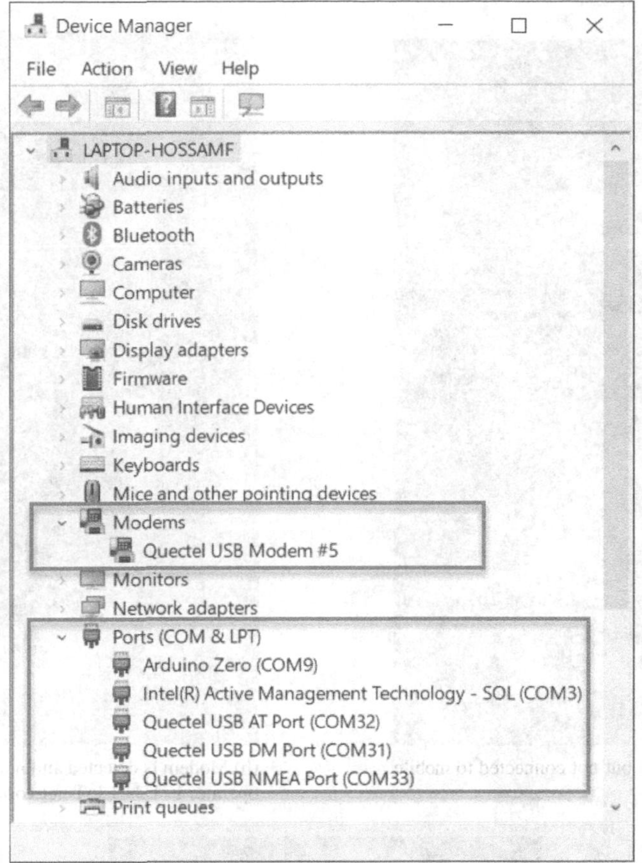

Figure 9.4: Windows Device Manager.

On the Windows computer connected to the board, click the WiFi or cellular icon at the task bar. This pops up a Window that shows that the computer detects an AT&T cellular LTE network, but the modem is not connected yet to the mobile operator network. This is shown in Figure 9.5. Click **Connect** and the modem open a connection to the mobile operator network and got assigned an IP address. Once the modem is connected, you can use the computer to access the Internet as if you are using WiFi or Ethernet networks. To verify the modem is connected to the mobile operator network, open a command Windows on the computer and runs the **ipconfig** command, which displays the cellular modem interface as one of the networks available on the computer as shown in Figure 9.6. You can also run **ping** command to ping any website and this shows that the modem is communicating and connected to the Internet over AT&T network of LTE NB-IoT.

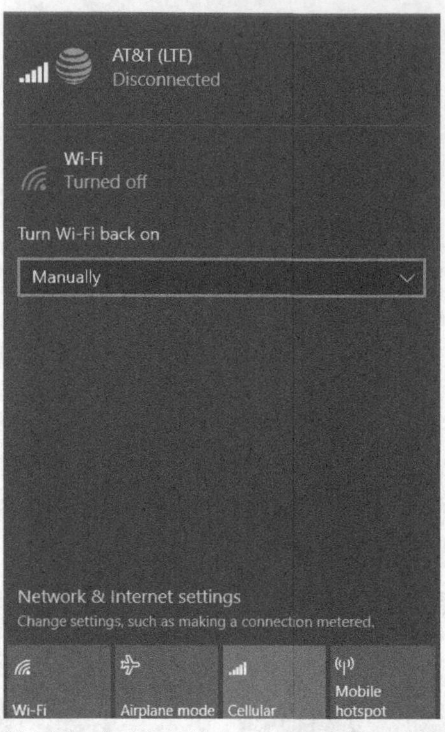

(a) Modem is detected but not connected to mobile operator network.

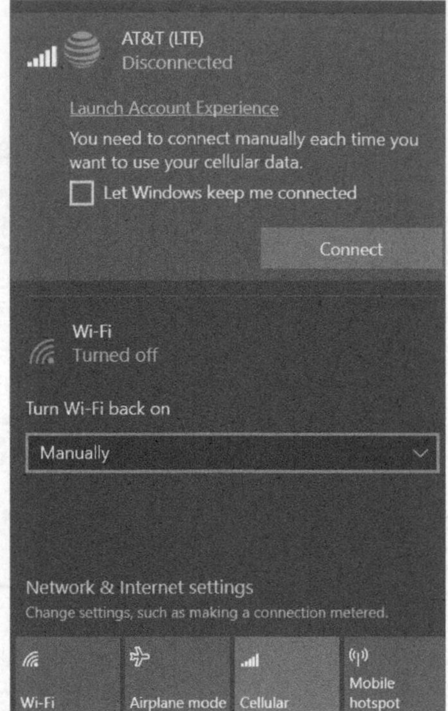

(b) Modem is detected and not connected to mobile operator LTE NB-IoT network.

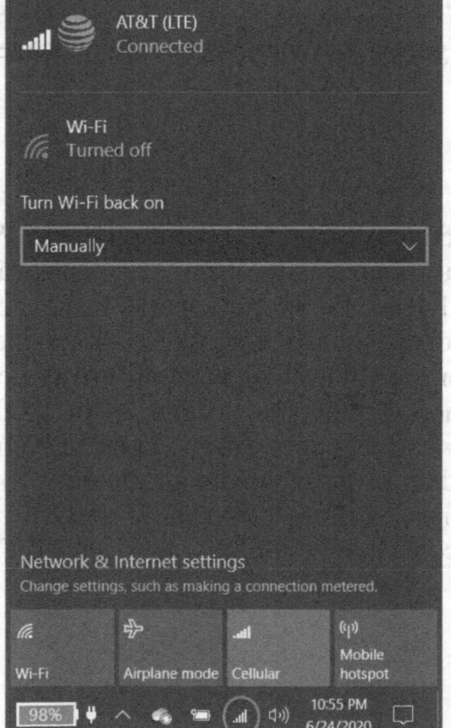

(c) Modem is connected. Cellular bars icon indicating signal strength is displayed on the task bar.

Figure 9.5: Windows Network & Internet Settings.

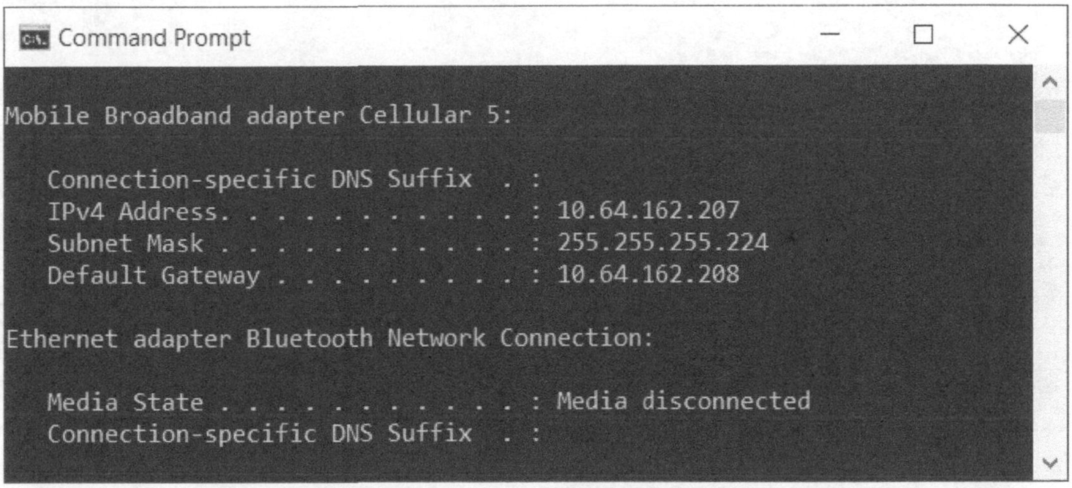

Command Prompt

```
Mobile Broadband adapter Cellular 5:

   Connection-specific DNS Suffix  . :
   IPv4 Address. . . . . . . . . . . : 10.64.162.207
   Subnet Mask . . . . . . . . . . . : 255.255.255.224
   Default Gateway . . . . . . . . . : 10.64.162.208

Ethernet adapter Bluetooth Network Connection:

   Media State . . . . . . . . . . . : Media disconnected
   Connection-specific DNS Suffix  . :
```

(a) Run ipconfig command and it shows the LTE cellular network.

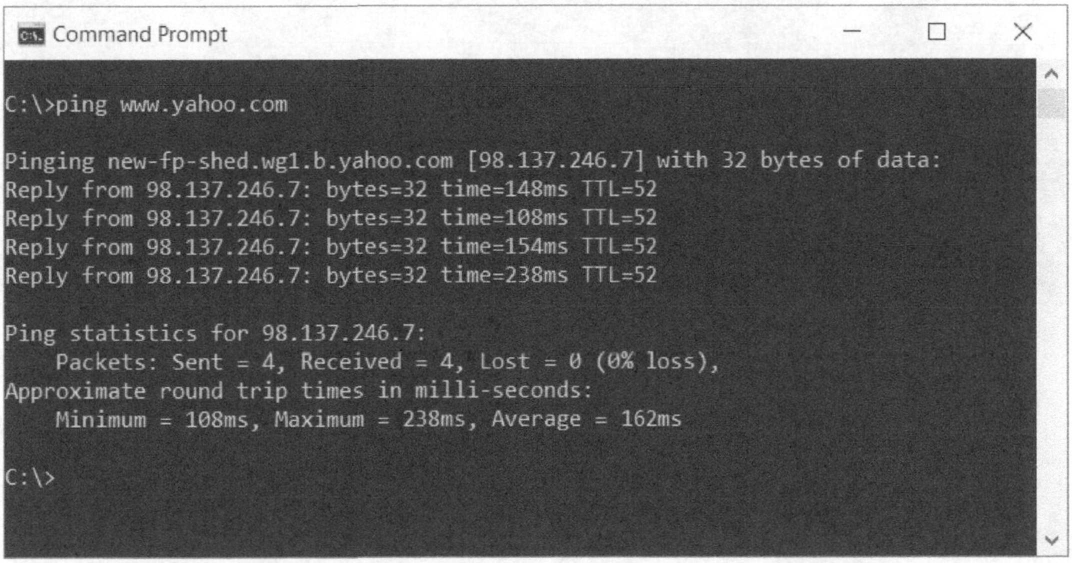

Command Prompt

```
C:\>ping www.yahoo.com

Pinging new-fp-shed.wg1.b.yahoo.com [98.137.246.7] with 32 bytes of data:
Reply from 98.137.246.7: bytes=32 time=148ms TTL=52
Reply from 98.137.246.7: bytes=32 time=108ms TTL=52
Reply from 98.137.246.7: bytes=32 time=154ms TTL=52
Reply from 98.137.246.7: bytes=32 time=238ms TTL=52

Ping statistics for 98.137.246.7:
    Packets: Sent = 4, Received = 4, Lost = 0 (0% loss),
Approximate round trip times in milli-seconds:
    Minimum = 108ms, Maximum = 238ms, Average = 162ms

C:\>
```

(b) Run ping command to yahoo to verify the modem is connected to the Internet over LTE NB-IoT network.

Figure 9.6: Windows Networks & Ping.

Chapter 10

Transmission Control Protocol (TCP)

In this chapter, you will use socket and AT commands to configure TCP/IP socket on the modem and send and receive TCP data. TCP is a connection-oriented protocol, which means a connection is established and maintained between a client and a server. TCP determines how to send application data as packets that traverse the network to the receiver. TCP sends packets to and accepts packets from the network layer, manages flow control, and handles retransmission of dropped or corrupted packets as well as acknowledgement of all packets that arrive. In the Open Systems Interconnection (OSI) communication model, TCP is a protocol of layer 4, the Transport layer.

10.1 Hardware Setup, Steps, and Diagram

Follow the same steps and diagram as in Chapter 9 and Figure 9.1.

10.2 Arduino Sketch

The following is the Arduino sketch that configures the TCP socket and sends some data. In the sketch and in the setup() API, it configures two serial interfaces, initialize the modem , sets the APN name, opens a TCP socket to an IP address **mbed.org** and port number **80**, and sends data over this socket.

In the loop() API, it waits for an TCP event such as closing socket, or receiving data from the remote server, or deactivation of the PDP context.

```
#include <board.h>

#define DSerial SerialUSB
#define ATSerial Serial1

char APN[] = "m2mNB16.com.attz";
char LOGIN[] = "";
char PASSWORD[] = "";

char tcp_ip[] = "mbed.org";
int tcp_port = 80;
char send_data[] = "GET /media/uploads/mbed_official/hello.txt
   HTTP/1.0\r\n\r\n";
unsigned int comm_pdp_index = 1;  // The range is 1 ~ 16
unsigned int comm_socket_index = 1;  // The range is 0 ~ 11
Socket_Type_t socket = TCP_CLIENT;

_5G_NB_IoT_TCPIP _5GNBIoT(ATSerial, DSerial);

void setup()
{
  DSerial.begin(115200);
  while (DSerial.read() >= 0);
  DSerial.println("This is the _5GNBIoT Debug Serial!");

  ATSerial.begin(115200);
  while (ATSerial.read() >= 0);
  delay(1000);

  _5GNBIoT.InitModule();
  DSerial.println("\r\n_5GNBIoT.InitModule() OK!");

  _5GNBIoT.SetDevCommandEcho(false);

  char inf[64];
  if (_5GNBIoT.GetDevInformation(inf))
  {
    DSerial.println(inf);
  }

  char apn_error[64];
  _5GNBIoT.InitAPN(comm_pdp_index, APN, LOGIN, PASSWORD,
   apn_error);

  _5GNBIoT.OpenSocketService(comm_pdp_index, comm_socket_index,
  Socket, tcp_ip, tcp_port, 0, BUFFER_MODE);
  DSerial.println("\r\nOpen Socket Service Success!");
```

```
  if (_5GNBIoT.SocketSendData(comm_socket_index, socket,
   send_data,
  "", tcp_port))
  {
    DSerial.println("\r\nSocket Send Data Success!");
  }
}

void loop()
{
  char m_event[16];
  unsigned int index;
  char recv_data[128];
  Socket_Event_t ret = _5GNBIoT.WaitCheckSocketEvent(m_event, 2);
  switch (ret)
  {
    case SOCKET_CLOSE_EVENT:
    index = atoi(m_event);
    if (_5GNBIoT.CloseSocketService(index))
    {
      DSerial.println("\r\nClose Socket Success!");
    }
    break;
    case SOCKET_RECV_DATA_EVENT:
    index = atoi(m_event);
    if (_5GNBIoT.SocketRecvData(index, 128, socket, recv_data))
    {
      DSerial.println("\r\nSocket Recv Data Success!");
      DSerial.println("");
      DSerial.println(recv_data);
      DSerial.println("");
    }
    break;
    case SOCKET_PDP_DEACTIVATION_EVENT:
    index = atoi(m_event);
    if (_5GNBIoT.DeactivateDevAPN(index))
    {
      DSerial.println("\r\nPlease reconfigure APN!");
    }
    break;
    default:
    break;
  }
}
```

Listing 10.1: TCP Arduino Sketch.

The following is the AT commands output of the previous Arduino sketch. After the modem completes registration successfully with the mobile operator LTE network (+CEREG: 1,1) it configures the TCP/IP context AT+QICSGP, and the modem is assigned an IP address from the network (10.69.112.187). The modem opens a TCP socket AT+QIOPEN to server mbed.org on port 80 (HTTP port) and transmits a message that gets a text file stored on the server. When the modem receives an event for closing the socket, it closes the socket using AT+QICLOSE.

```
_5GNBIoT.InitModule() OK!

-> ATE0
ATE0

<- OK
-> ATI

<- Quectel
<- BG96
<- Revision: BG96MAR02A07M1G
<-
<- OK
Quectel
BG96
Revision: BG96MAR02A07M1G

-> AT+CPIN?

<- +CPIN: READY
-> AT+CEREG?

<- +CEREG: 1,1
<-
<- OK
-> AT+QICSGP=1,1,"m2mNB16.com.attz","","",3

<- OK
-> AT+CGPADDR=1

<- +CGPADDR: 1,10.69.112.187
<-
<- OK
APN OK: The IP address is 10.69.112.187

-> AT+QIOPEN=1,1,"TCP","mbed.org",80,0,0

<- OK
<-
<- +QIOPEN: 1,0
<-
```

```
Open Socket Service Success!

-> AT+QISEND=1,55

<- >
GET /media/uploads/mbed_official/hello.txt HTTP/1.0

Send Data len :55

<- SEND OK
Socket Send Data Success!

<-
<- +QIURC: "closed",1
<-
-> AT+QICLOSE

<- OK
Close Socket Success!
```

Listing 10.2: AT Commands Output for TCP.

Chapter 11

Secure Socket Layer (SSL) Connection

In this chapter, you will use secure socket layer (SSL) and AT commands to establish a secure connection to a server. The communication between the server and the modem is encrypted so that it prevents eavesdropping, tampering, or forging during exchanging data and information.

Secure Sockets Layer (SSL) is widely deployed cryptographic protocol to provide security when communicating over the internet. SSL provides a secure channel between two devices or between a client and a server operating over the internet or an internal network. One common example is when SSL is used to secure communication between an NB-IoT device and a server.

11.1 Hardware Setup, Steps, and Diagram

Follow the same steps and diagram as in Chapter 9 and Figure 9.1.

11.2 Arduino Sketch

The following is the Arduino sketch that configures a secure socket and sends some data. The board opens a secure socket with AWS IoT server. Communication between the board and AWS IoT is protected using security certificates. There are two certificates and one key; root certificate, the client certificate, and the private key.

The sketch starts by configuring two serial interfaces, turn on the modem, and then do the following steps:

Step 1: Configure the SSL version, cipher suite, store certificates and key on modem storage, and set the security level for the specified SSL context by AT+QSSLCFG.

Step 2: Configure the APN name and other parameters of a PDP context by issuing AT+QICSGP.

Step 3: Activate the PDP context by AT+QIACT. The modem is assigned an IP address.

Step 4: Open SSL client connection by AT+QSSLOPEN.

Step 5: After the SSL connection has been established, data is sent or received via the SSL connection.

```
#include <board.h>

#define DSerial SerialUSB
#define ATSerial Serial1

char pem_CA[] = "
-----BEGIN CERTIFICATE-----\n\
MIIEDzCCAvegAwIBAgIBADANB\n\
-----END CERTIFICATE-----\n";

// "The certificate for this thing"
char pem_cert[] = "
-----BEGIN CERTIFICATE-----\n\
MIIDWTCCAkGgAwIBAgIUWermTFtq\n\
-----END CERTIFICATE-----\n";

// "The private key of the thing". The public key is not needed
    here.
char pem_pkey[] = "
-----BEGIN RSA PRIVATE KEY-----\n\
MIIEowIBAAKCAQEAtqUK+kXqFRyk\n\
-----END RSA PRIVATE KEY-----\n";

char APN[] = "m2mNB16.com.attz";
char LOGIN[] = "";
char PASSWORD[] = "";

char ssl_ip[] = "a3kjt69iibf2h0-ats.iot.us-west-2.amazonaws.com";
char ssl_cmd[] = "GET / HTTP/1.1\r\n\r\n";
int ssl_port = 8883;
unsigned int comm_pdp_index = 1;  // The range is 1 ~ 16
unsigned int comm_socket_index = 1;  // The range is 0 ~ 11
unsigned int comm_ssl_index = 1;  // The range if 0 ~ 5

_5G_NB_IoT_SSL _5GNBIoT(ATSerial, DSerial);

void setup()
{
    DSerial.begin(115200);
    while (DSerial.read() >= 0);
```

```
    DSerial.println("This is the _5GNBIoT Debug Serial!");

    ATSerial.begin(115200);
    while (ATSerial.read() >= 0);
    delay(1000);

    _5GNBIoT.InitModule();
    DSerial.println("\r\n_5GNBIoT.InitModule() OK!");

    _5GNBIoT.SetDevCommandEcho(false);

    char inf[64];
    if (_5GNBIoT.GetDevInformation(inf))
    {
        DSerial.println(inf);
    }

    _5GNBIoT.DeleteFiles("*");

    char ssl_error[128];
    _5GNBIoT.InitSSL(comm_ssl_index, pem_CA, pem_cert, pem_pkey,
    ssl_error);

    char apn_error[64];
    _5GNBIoT.InitAPN(comm_pdp_index, APN, "", "", apn_error);

    _5GNBIoT.OpenSSLSocket(comm_pdp_index, comm_ssl_index,
    comm_socket_index, ssl_ip, ssl_port, BUFFER_MODE);
    DSerial.println("\r\nConnect the SSL Sever Success!");

    if (_5GNBIoT.SSLSocketSendData(comm_socket_index, ssl_cmd))
    {
        DSerial.println("\r\nSSL Socket Send Data Success!");
    }
}

void loop()
{
    char ssl_event[16];
    unsigned int index;
    char recv_data[128];
    SSL_Socket_Event_t ret = _5GNBIoT.WaitCheckSSLSocketEvent(
   ssl_event,2);
    switch (ret)
    {
        case SSL_SOCKET_CLOSE_EVENT:
        index = atoi(ssl_event);
        if (_5GNBIoT.CloseSSLSocket(index))
```

```
        {
            DSerial.println("\r\nClose SSL Socket Success!");
        }
    break;
    case SSL_SOCKET_RECV_EVENT:
    index = atoi(ssl_event);
    if (_5GNBIoT.SSLSocketRecvData(index, 128, recv_data))
    {
        DSerial.println("\r\nSSL Socket Recv Data Success!");
        DSerial.println("");
        DSerial.println(recv_data);
        DSerial.println("");
    }
    break;
    default:
    break;
    }
}
```

Listing 11.1: SSL Socket Arduino Sketch.

The following is the AT commands output of the SSL socket sketch. After initializing the SSL socket and opens a socket connection successfully, the board sends data to the AWS IoT.

```
_5GNBIoT.InitModule() OK!

-> ATE0
ATE0

<- OK
-> ATI

<- Quectel
<- BG96
<- Revision: BG96MAR02A07M1G
<-
<- OK
Quectel
BG96
Revision: BG96MAR02A07M1G

-> AT+QFDEL="*"

<- OK
-> AT+QSSLCFG="sslversion",1,3

<- OK
-> AT+QSSLCFG="ciphersuite",1,0X0035
```

```
<- OK
-> AT+QSSLCFG="negotiatetime",1,300

<- OK
-> AT+QFUPL="ca_cert.pem",1457

<- CONNECT
-----BEGIN CERTIFICATE-----
MIIEDzCCAvegAwIBAgIBADANB
-----END CERTIFICATE-----

Send Data len :1457
+QFUPL: 1457,6b3e
<-
<- OK
-> AT+QFUPL="client_cert.pem",1211

<- CONNECT
-----BEGIN CERTIFICATE-----
MIIDWTCCAkGgAwIBAgIUWermTFtq
-----END CERTIFICATE-----

Send Data len :1211
+QFUPL: 1211,3f06
<-
<- OK
-> AT+QFUPL="client_key.pem",1662
<- CONNECT
-----BEGIN RSA PRIVATE KEY-----
MIIEowIBAAKCAQEAtqUK+kXqFRyk
-----END RSA PRIVATE KEY-----

Send Data len :1662
+QFUPL: 1662,380f
<-
<- OK
-> AT+QSSLCFG="seclevel",1,2

<- OK
-> AT+QSSLCFG="cacert",1,"ca_cert.pem"

<- OK
-> AT+QSSLCFG="clientcert",1,"client_cert.pem"

<- OK
-> AT+QSSLCFG="clientkey",1,"client_key.pem"
```

```
<- OK
-> AT+QSSLCFG="ignorelocaltime",1

<- +QSSLCFG: "ignorelocaltime",1,1
<-
<- OK
SSL OK: The ssl were successfully initialized.


-> AT+CPIN?

<- +CPIN: READY
-> AT+CEREG?

<- +CEREG: 1,1
<-
<- OK
-> AT+QICSGP=1,1,"m2mNB16.com.attz","","",3

<- OK
-> AT+CGPADDR=1

<- +CGPADDR: 1,10.70.109.229
<-
<- OK
APN OK: The IP address is 10.70.109.229

-> AT+QSSLOPEN=1,1,1,"a3kjt69iibf2h0-ats.iot.us-west-2.amazonaws.
   com",8883,0

<- OK
<-
<- +QSSLOPEN: 1,0
<-
Connect the SSL Sever Success!

-> AT+QSSLSEND=1,18

<- >
GET / HTTP/1.1

Send Data len :18

<- SEND OK
SSL Socket Send Data Success!
```

Listing 11.2: AT Commands Output for SSL.

Chapter 12

Message Queue Telemetry Transport (MQTT)

MQTT is the common protocol used for NB-IoT devices and other IoT clients. It is a lightweight protocol with a small footprint that makes it popular to be used with IoT device. In this chapter, you will learn how to use MQTT with the AWS IoT cloud.

12.1 Hardware Setup, Steps, and Diagram

Follow the same steps and diagram as in Chapter 9 and Figure 9.1.

12.2 Arduino Sketch

The Arduino sketch used to communicates with AWS IoT cloud is explained in Listing 7.1 and Listing 7.2. After uploading this sketch to the NB board, the following output shows AT commands and data transmission that occurred by the modem. In the AT commands output, the following configuration and events occurred:

1. The modem is tuned on and queried for its product information and IMEI using ATI and AT+CGSN.

2. The modem is initialized and the APN name of the mobile operator is set to m2mNB16.com.attz. Modem starts to search for a mobile operator network. When the modem registers successfully to the network, the TCP/IP context is configured.

3. The secure socket layer is configured through a series of AT+QSSLCFG commands.

4. The root certificate, client certificate, and client keys are uploaded to the modem file storage and is stored so that it can be used during MQTT connection establishment between the modem and the AWS IoT.
5. The MQTT configuration is done through a series of AT+MQTCFG commands.
6. MQTT AT commands are used to open an MQTT connection to AWS IoT, subscribe to the topic, **MyTopic**, and starts publishing message to the same topic.
7. The NB board publishes its temperature sensor data which is the temperature in Fahrenheit.

```
InitModule() OK!

-> ATE0
ATE0

<- OK
-> ATI

<- Quectel
<- BG96
<- Revision: BG96MAR02A07M1G
<-
<- OK
Quectel
BG96
Revision: BG96MAR02A07M1G

-> AT+CGSN

<- 866425031237797
<-
<- OK866425031237797

-> AT+QFDEL="*"

<- OK
-> AT+CPIN?

<- +CPIN: READY
-> AT+CEREG?

<- +CEREG: 1,1
<-
<- OK
-> AT+QICSGP=1,1,"m2mNB16.com.attz","","",3

<- OK
-> AT+CGPADDR=1
```

```
<- +CGPADDR: 1,10.64.31.150
<-
<- OK
APN OK: The IP address is 10.64.31.150


-> AT+QSSLCFG="sslversion",2,3

<- OK
-> AT+QSSLCFG="ciphersuite",2,0X0035

<- OK
-> AT+QSSLCFG="negotiatetime",2,300

<- OK
-> AT+QFUPL="ca_cert.pem",1457

<- CONNECT
-----BEGIN CERTIFICATE-----
MIIEDzCCAvegAwIBAgIBADANB
-----END CERTIFICATE-----

Send Data len :1457
+QFUPL: 1457,6b3e
<-
<- OK
-> AT+QFUPL="client_cert.pem",1211

<- CONNECT
-----BEGIN CERTIFICATE-----
MIIDWTCCAkGgAwIBAgIUWermTFtq
-----END CERTIFICATE-----

Send Data len :1211
+QFUPL: 1211,3f06
<-
<- OK
-> AT+QFUPL="client_key.pem",1662

<- CONNECT
-----BEGIN RSA PRIVATE KEY-----
MIIEowIBAAKCAQEAtqUK+kXqFRyk
-----END RSA PRIVATE KEY-----

Send Data len :1662
+QFUPL: 1662,380f
<-
```

```
<- OK
-> AT+QSSLCFG="seclevel",2,2

<- OK
-> AT+QSSLCFG="cacert",2,"ca_cert.pem"

<- OK
-> AT+QSSLCFG="clientcert",2,"client_cert.pem"

<- OK
-> AT+QSSLCFG="clientkey",2,"client_key.pem"

<- OK
-> AT+QSSLCFG="ignorelocaltime",1

<- +QSSLCFG: "ignorelocaltime",1,1
<-
<- OK
SSL OK: The ssl were successfully initialized.


Start Config the MQTT Parameter!

-> AT+QMTCFG="version",3,3

<- OK
-> AT+QMTCFG="pdpcid",3,1

<- OK
-> AT+QMTCFG="keepalive",3,150

<- OK
-> AT+QMTCFG="session",3,0

<- OK
Config the MQTT Parameter Success!

-> AT+QMTCFG="ssl",3,1,2

<- OK
SetMQTTEnableSSL the MQTT Parameter Success!

-> AT+QMTOPEN=3,"a3kjt69iibf2h0-ats.iot.us-west-2.amazonaws.com"
   ,8883

<- OK
<-
<- +QMTOPEN: 3,0
```

```
<-
Set the MQTT Service Address Success!

-> AT+QMTCFG="timeout",3,10,5,1

<- OK
Start Create a MQTT Client!

-> AT+QMTCONN=3,"basicPubSub"

<- OK
<-
<- +QMTCONN: 3,0,0
<-
Create a MQTT Client Success!

Start MQTT Subscribe Topic!

-> AT+QMTSUB=3,1,"MyTopic",0

<- OK
<-
<- +QMTSUB: 3,1,0,0
<-
MQTT Subscribe Topic Success!

-> AT+QMTPUB=3,1,1,0,"MyTopic"

<- >
{
  "DeviceID": "866425031237797",
  "Timestamp": 22933,
  "Device": "Temperature Sensor",
  "OpCode": "Read",
  "Temperature": 30,
  "Unit": "°F"
}
Send Data len :157

<- OK
<-
<-
<- +QMTRECV: 3,0,"MyTopic","{
  <-    "DeviceID": "866425031237797",
  <-    "Timestamp": 22933,
  <-    "Device": "Temperature Sensor",
  <-    "OpCode": "Read",
  <-    "Temperature": 30,
```

```
  <-   "Unit": "°F"
  <- }"
<-
<- +QMTPUB: 3,1,0
<- Publish Succeded!
```

Listing 12.1: AT Commands Output of the MQTT Described in Listing 7.2.

This MQTT Arduino sketch is the backbone for communication between the NB-IoT device and the cloud. Using this sketch, the NB-IoT device can emit JSON-formatted messages containing sensor and measurement readings and information.

Chapter 13

Location and GPS Tracking

In this chapter, you will learn how to use GNSS and GPS system. GNSS is a satellite navigation system of satellites that provides geo-spatial positioning with global coverage and allow NB-IoT devices to determine location (longitude, latitude, and altitude/elevation) using time signals transmitted along a line of sight by radio from satellites.

13.1 Hardware Setup, Steps, and Diagram

Follow the same steps and diagram as in Chapter 9 and Figure 9.1.

13.2 Arduino Sketch

Global Navigation Satellite System (GNSS) is a system that includes all global satellite positioning systems. This includes several satellites orbiting over the earth's surface and continuously transmitting signals that enable NB-IoT devices to determine their position.

The Global Positioning System (GPS) is one component of GNSS developed by USA. Besides GPS, the GNSS also includes the Russian GLONASS, European Galileo, and China Beidou. The modem on the NB board supports all these GNSS systems. Example of GNSS applications are tracking devices, location-based advertising, geo-fencing, sea vessels, air navigation, asset tracking, and automobiles. You can visualize GPS location of the device on Google maps using the Arduino sketch in this chapter and follow the steps described before in Chapter 8.

For accurate position information, the GNSS receiver needs to receive good unobstructed signals from the satellite constellation. GNSS receiver receives data from satellites moving at relativistic orbital speeds, over 10,000 miles away, and so they need somewhat of a clear view of the sky. GPS sensitivity and accuracy are dependent on environmental conditions. Not only does this include physical objects, like trees, earth, and structures, but also includes atmospheric effects, space weather, the overall health of the GPS constellation, and multipath interactions, all of which contribute to constant variability in receiving the GPS signal.

13.3 Arduino Sketch

The following Arduino sketch shows how to use the GNSS capability of the modem. After turning on the modem, the following steps are done to read the positioning information,

Step 1: Configure GNSS parameters via AT+QGPSCFG. The second UART on the BG96 is used to output NMEA sentences. NMEA (National Marine Electronics Association) sentence, is a defined format of the positing and GPS information that can be used interchangeably between different hardware and devices.

Step 2: Turn on GNSS via AT+QGPS.

Step 3: After GNSS is turned on and position is fixed successfully, the positioning information can be obtained by issuing AT+QGPSLOC which is used to obtain positioning information directly, such as latitude, longitude, height, GNSS positioning mode, time, number of satellites, and more information.

```
#include "5G-NB-IoT_GNSS.h"

#define DSerial SerialUSB
#define ATSerial Serial1
#define UART_DEBUG

GNSS_Work_Mode_t mode = STAND_ALONE;

_5G_NB_IoT_GNSS _5GNBIoT(ATSerial, DSerial);

void setup()
{
  DSerial.begin(115200);
  while (DSerial.read() >= 0);
  DSerial.println("This is the _5GNBIoT Debug Serial!");

  ATSerial.begin(115200);
  while (ATSerial.read() >= 0);
  delay(1000);

  _5GNBIoT.InitModule();
```

```
  DSerial.println("\r\n_5GNBIoT.InitModule() OK!");

  _5GNBIoT.SetGNSSOutputPort(UARTNMEA);

  _5GNBIoT.SetDevCommandEcho(false);
  delay(100);

  char inf[64];
  if (_5GNBIoT.GetDevInformation(inf))
  {
    DSerial.println(inf);
  }

  _5GNBIoT.TurnOnGNSS(mode, WRITE_MODE);
  DSerial.println("\r\nOpen the GNSS Function Success!");
}

void loop()
{
  char gnss_posi[128];
  _5GNBIoT.GetGNSSPositionInformation(gnss_posi);
  DSerial.println("\r\nGet the GNSS Position Success!");
  DSerial.println(gnss_posi);
}
```

Listing 13.1: GPS Arduino Sketch.

The following shows the AT commands output of the Arduino sketch.

```
_5GNBIoT.InitModule() OK!

-> AT+QGPSCFG="outport","uartnmea"
<- OK

-> ATE0
<- OK
-> ATI

<- Quectel
<- BG96
<- Revision: BG96MAR02A07M1G
<-
<- OK
Quectel
BG96
Revision: BG96MAR02A07M1G
```

```
-> AT+QGPS=1

<- OK
Open the GNSS Function Success!

-> AT+QGPSLOC=2

<- +QGPSLOC: 063729.0,47.82670,-122.20605,1.1,14.0,
             2,0.00,0.0,0.0,161119,06
<-
<- OK
Get the GNSS Position Success!
063729.0,47.82670,-122.20605,1.1,14.0,
2,0.00,0.0,0.0,161119,06

-> AT+QGPSLOC=2

<- +QGPSLOC: 063729.0,47.82670,-122.20605,1.1,14.0,
             2,0.00,0.0,0.0,161119,06
<-
<- OK
Get the GNSS Position Success!
063729.0,47.82670,-122.20605,1.1,14.0,
2,0.00,0.0,0.0,161119,06
```

Listing 13.2: AT Commands Output of the GPS.

In the above output, the position information returned from the GNSS is:

+QGPSLOC: 063729.0,47.82670,-122.20605,1.1,14.0,2,0.00,0.0,0.0,161119,06

According to the AT commands for GNSS, this maps to the following information: <UTC>, <latitude>,<longitude>,<hdop>,<altitude>,<fix>,<cog>,<spkm>, <spkn>,<date>,<nsat>

Which translates to the following information in Table 13.1:

You can use the latitude and longitude to get the location. For example, open a browser and go to Google map and type the two numbers from the latitude and longitude and you will get this location displayed on Google map as in this screen shoot in Figure 13.1.

Table 13.1: Interpretation of the GPS Information.

UTC	063729.0 (time is 6 AM, 37 minutes, 29 seconds)
latitude	47.82670
longitude	-122.20605
hdop	1.1
altitude	14
fix	2 (2 means 2D positioning)
cog	0.00 (Course Over Ground based on true north)
spkm	0.0 (Speed over ground in Km/hr. The NB-IoT device is stationary and not moving)
spkn	0.0 (Speed over ground in Knots. The NB-IoT device is stationary and not moving)
date	161119 (Date is November 16th, 2019)
nsat	06 (Number of satellites is 6)

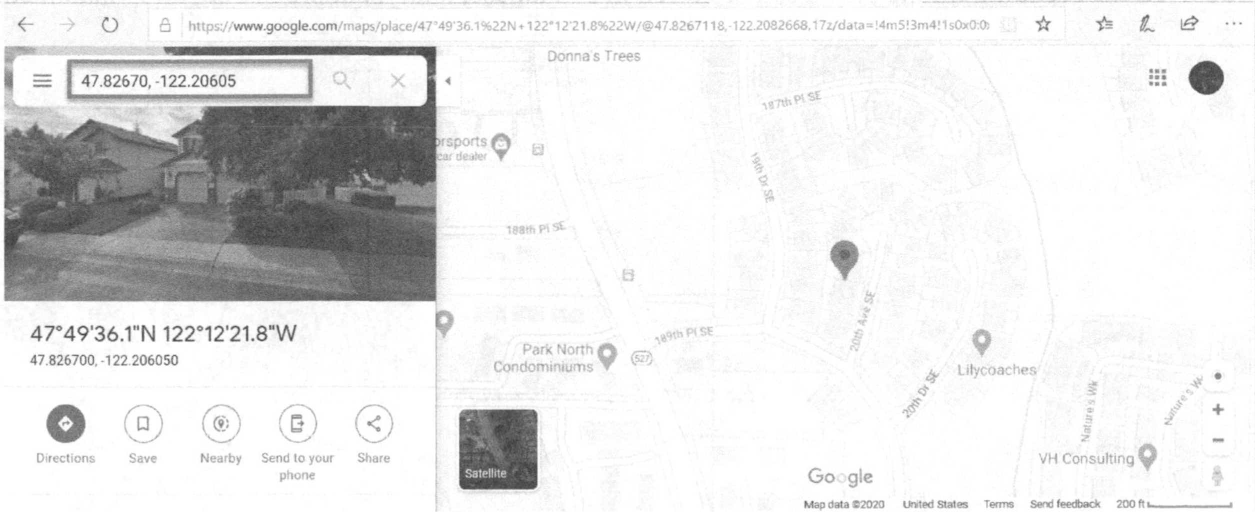

Figure 13.1: Latitude and Longitude on Google Maps.

13.4 Interface with the Cloud

The GPS information, especially latitude, longitude, and altitude, can be uploaded to the cloud and stored. GPS data on the cloud can be used for smart applications such as vehicle tracking, fleet management, child tracking, or even to track prisoners and law-enforcements purposes. Chapter 8 explains how to visualize GPS location on Google map.

To make the Arduino sketch upload the GPS position information to the AWS cloud, add the following Arduino lines of codes in Listing 13.3 to the above sketch and use the MQTT codes as explained in Listing 7.1 and Listing 7.2. Use the following JSON format to upload the GPS location readings to the cloud.

```
// ...... Previous code lines go here

docInput["DeviceID"] = IMEI;
docInput["Timestamp"] = millis();
docInput["Device"] = "GPS";
docInput["OpCode"] = "Read";
docInput["Position"] = gnss_posi;
serializeJsonPretty(docInput, payload);

// ..... Next code lines go here
```

Listing 13.3: JSON Document for GPS Position.

Upload the final sketch to the NB board and notice the output on the Serial Monitor as shown below. The GPS position is uploaded to the cloud and can be interpreted as in Table 13.1. Go to the AWS IoT, and the JSON data received by the cloud is displayed on AWS dashboard. The received data reading on the cloud can be stored in a database, analyzed, processed, and visualized.

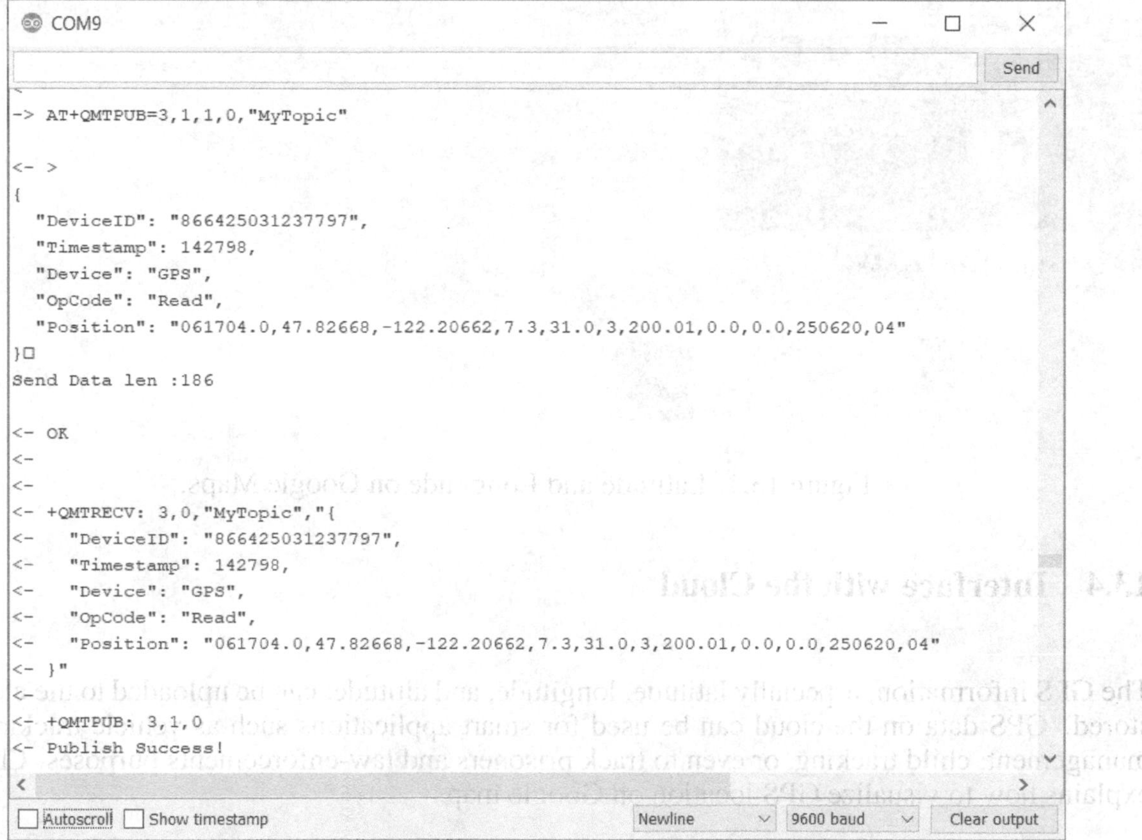

Figure 13.2: Serial Monitor Output for GPS Position.

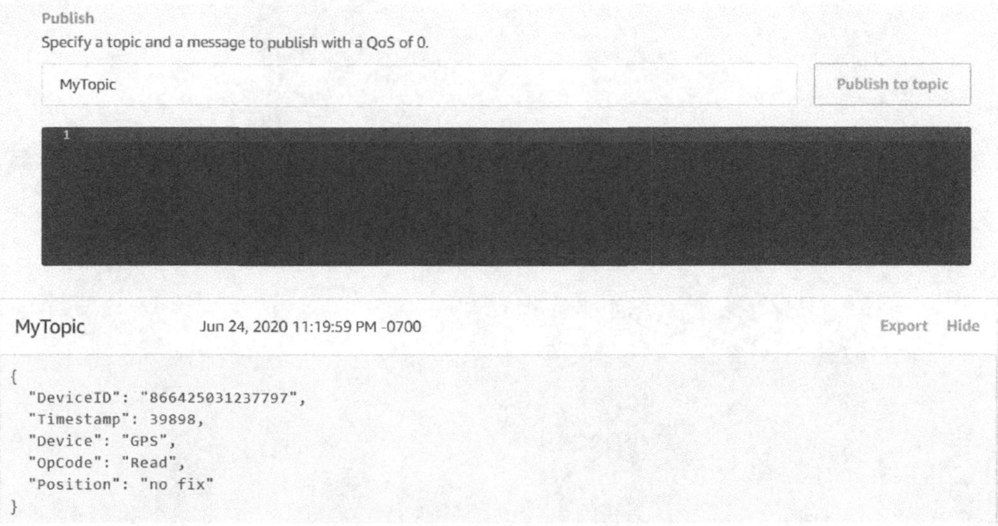
Publish
Specify a topic and a message to publish with a QoS of 0.
MyTopic
Publish to topic
MyTopic
Jun 24, 2020 11:19:59 PM -0700
Export
Hide
{
"DeviceID": "866425031237797",
"Timestamp": 39898,
"Device": "GPS",
"OpCode": "Read",
"Position": "no fix"
}

Figure 13.3: GPS JSON Data on AWS IoT.

Chapter 14

Hypertext Transfer Protocol (HTTP)

Hyper Text Transfer Protocol (HTTP) is a protocol for World Wide Web (WWW) communication between web clients and servers. Communication between client computers and web servers is done by sending HTTP requests and receiving HTTP responses. Clients are often browsers (Chrome, Edge, Safari), but they can be any type of program or device. Servers can be in the cloud. HTTPS is the secure version of HTTP. HTTPS is encrypted in order to increase security of data transfer. Every time you visit a website starting with HTTPS, a public/private key encryption is being used. It is the basis of SSL and TLS encryption, which is employed for HTTPS communications. In this chapter, you will learn how to use HTTP and HTTPS using the NB board.

14.1 Hardware Setup, Steps, and Diagram

Follow the same steps and diagram as in Chapter 9 and Figure 9.1.

14.2 Arduino Sketch

The Arduino sketch for running HTTP is shown the Listing 14.1. The sketch configures the HTTP, transmit HTTP GET request to the web site, `http://httpbin.org/ip` and then read the response from the server. The sketch does the following steps:

Step 1: Configure the APN name and other parameters of PDP context by AT+QICSGP. When the PDP context is activated, the modem is assigned an IP address which can be queried by AT+QIACT?.

Step 2: Configure HTTP by setting the PDP context ID, request header, and content type, through AT+QHTTPCFG command.

Step 3: If HTTPS is to be used, then SSL context parameters is configured by AT+QSSLCFG command.

Step 4: Set HTTP URL by AT+QHTTPURL command.

Step 5: Send HTTP request. AT+QHTTPGET command can be used for sending HTTP GET request.

Step 6: Read HTTP(S) response information by AT+QHTTPREAD command.

```
#include <board.h>

#define DSerial SerialUSB
#define ATSerial Serial1

char APN[] = "m2mNB16.com.attz";
char LOGIN[] = "";
char PASSWORD[] = "";

char http_url[] = "http://httpbin.org/ip";
unsigned int comm_pdp_index = 1;
HTTP_Body_Data_Type_t  http_type =
  APPLICATION_X_WWW_FORM_URLENCODED;

_5G_NB_IoT_HTTP _5GNBIoT(ATSerial, DSerial);
void setup()
{
  DSerial.begin(115200);
  while (DSerial.read() >= 0);
  DSerial.println("This is the _5GNBIoT Debug Serial!");

  ATSerial.begin(115200);
  while (ATSerial.read() >= 0);
  delay(1000);

  _5GNBIoT.InitModule();
  DSerial.println("\r\n_5GNBIoT.InitModule() OK!");

  _5GNBIoT.SetDevCommandEcho(false);

  char inf[64];
  if (_5GNBIoT.GetDevInformation(inf))
  {
    DSerial.println(inf);
  }

  char apn_error[64];
  _5GNBIoT.InitAPN(comm_pdp_index, APN, LOGIN, PASSWORD,
   apn_error);
```

```
  _5GNBIoT.SetHTTPConfigParameters(comm_pdp_index, false, false,
  http_type);
  DSerial.println("\r\nConfig the HTTP Parameter Success!");

  _5GNBIoT.HTTPURL(http_url, WRITE_MODE);
  DSerial.println("\r\Set the HTTP URL Success!");
}

void loop()
{
  char recv_data[128];
  !_5GNBIoT.HTTPGET(80);
  DSerial.println("\r\nHTTP GET Success!");

  if (_5GNBIoT.HTTPRead(recv_data, 80))
  {
    DSerial.println("\r\nHTTP Read Success!");
    DSerial.println("");
    DSerial.println(recv_data);
    DSerial.println("");
  }
  while (1);
}
```

Listing 14.1: HTTP Arduino Sketch.

The following are the AT commands output after running the sketch. The modem connects to the website, `http://httpbin.org/ip`, using HTTP protocol. The modem then posts a GET message on port 80. Once the response is received, it is read and displayed.

```
_5GNBIoT.InitModule() OK!
-> ATE0
ATE0

<- OK
-> ATI

<- Quectel
<- BG96
<- Revision: BG96MAR02A07M1G
<-
<- OK
Quectel
BG96
Revision: BG96MAR02A07M1G

-> AT+CPIN?
```

```
<- +CPIN: READY
-> AT+CEREG?

<- +CEREG: 1,1
<-
<- OK
-> AT+QICSGP=1,1,"m2mNB16.com.attz","","",3

<- OK
-> AT+CGPADDR=1

<- +CGPADDR: 1,10.64.102.200
<-
<- OK
APN OK: The IP address is 10.64.102.200

-> AT+QHTTPCFG="contextid",1

<- OK
-> AT+QHTTPCFG="requestheader",0

<- OK
-> AT+QHTTPCFG="responseheader",0

<- OK
-> AT+QHTTPCFG="contenttype",0

<- OK
Config the HTTP Parameter Success!

-> AT+QHTTPURL=21

<- CONNECT
http://httpbin.org/ip
Send Data len :21

<- OK
Set the HTTP URL Success!

-> AT+QHTTPGET=80

<- OK
<-
<- +QHTTPGET: 0,200,49
<-
HTTP GET Success!

-> AT+QHTTPREAD=80
```

```
<- CONNECT
<- {
  <-    "origin": "12.153.230.187, 12.153.230.187"
  <- }
<-
<- OK
<-
<- +QHTTPREAD: 0
<-
HTTP Read Success!

{
  "origin": "12.153.230.187, 12.153.230.187"
}
```

Listing 14.2: AT Commands Output of HTTP.

Chapter 15

NB-IoT Modem Firmware Update

NB-IoT modem requires occasional Over-The-AIR (OTA) firmware update. This update is needed to address many issues such as bug fixes for the firmware, adding new features, or updating the software logic of the GPS and sensors. In addition, this firmware update process needs to be suitable for constrained modem and for the limited bandwidth available on the wireless channel. In this chapter, you learn how to do OTA firmware update for the NB-IoT modem.

15.1 Hardware Setup, Steps, and Diagram

Follow the same steps and diagram as in Chapter 9 and Figure 9.1.

15.2 Arduino Sketch

Firmware update to the NB-IoT modem is expected to occur occasionally. This includes software reconfiguration of NB-IoT modem or application upgrade such as updating the GPS or sensor software. Payload of such upgrades is expected to be small file sizes or delta firmware and not the full firmware. This is because the upgrade happens over the air and only a small footprint of the firmware to be communicated to the NB-IoT modem to update its firmware.

Firmware update can be conveyed to the NB-IoT modem through different means such as USB or UART. Delta Firmware Over-the-air (DFOTA) upgrade is another way to upgrade the NB-IoT modem firmware over the air. Using DFOTA, it can either upgrade the firmware to a new version or revert to the old version. DFOTA uses a delta firmware which contains only the difference between the existing firmware and new firmware. This reduces the amount of data transmitted and accelerates the speed of firmware upgrade.

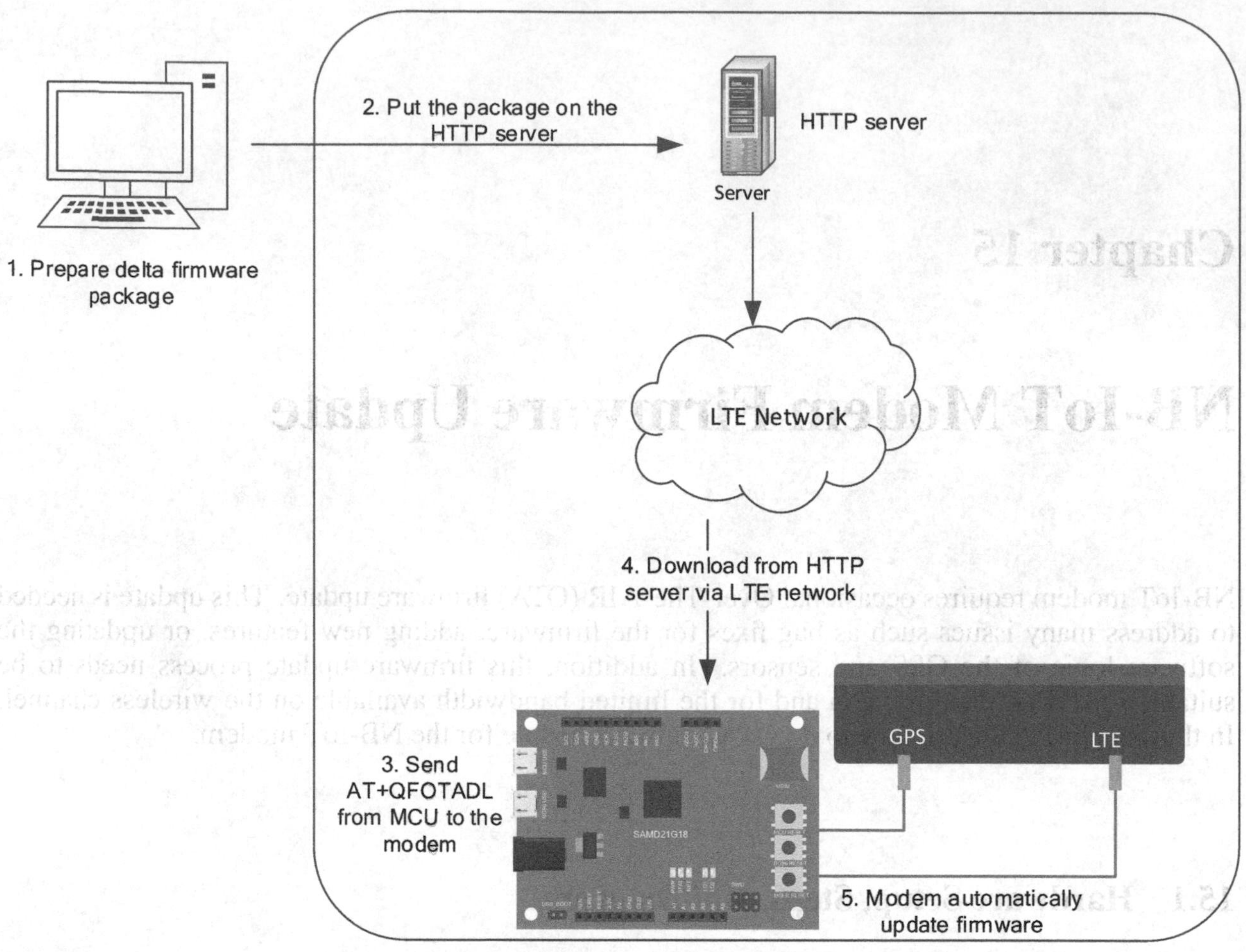

Figure 15.1: Firmware Upgrade Using DFOTA.

Figure 15.1 shows the steps needed to upgrade the firmware when the firmware package is stored on HTTP(S) server:

Step 1: Prepare the delta firmware package. Typically, this package is prepared or provided by the modem manufacturer.

Step 2: Put the delta firmware on HTTP(S) server.

Step 3: Execute **AT+QFOTADL** command. Then the modem downloads the package from HTTP(S) server via the LTE network (**Step 4**) and automatically upgrade its firmware (**Step 5**).

The Arduino sketch for running HTTP is shown the Listing 15.1. The sketch does the following:

Step 1: Configure the APN name and make the modem registers to mobile operator network. The modem is assigned an IP address.

Step 3: Configure DFOTA by specifying the HTTP URL to download the delta firmware from.

Step 4: The modem starts downloading and finish downloading.

Step 5: The modem automatically starts updating its firmware and finish.

```
#include <board.h>

#define DSerial SerialUSB
#define ATSerial Serial1

char APN[] = "m2mNB16.com.attz";
char LOGIN[] = "";
char PASSWORD[] = "";

const char DFOTA[] = "+QFOTADL";
const char http_url[] =
"http://95.171.16.128/DeltaFW.zip";
const char FOTA_HTTPSTART[] =
"+QIND: \"FOTA\",\"HTTPSTART\"";
const char FOTA_HTTPEND[] =
"+QIND: \"FOTA\",\"HTTPEND\",0";
const char FOTA_START[] =
"+QIND: \"FOTA\",\"START\"";
const char FOTA_UPDATING[] =
"+QIND: \"FOTA\",\"UPDATING\"";
const char FOTA_RESTORE[] =
"+QIND: \"FOTA\",\"RESTORE\"";
const char FOTA_END[] =
"+QIND: \"FOTA\",\"END\",0";
unsigned int comm_pdp_index = 1;
unsigned int comm_socket_index = 1;

_5G_NB_IoT_TCPIP _5GNBIoT(ATSerial, DSerial);

bool dfota()
{
  char cmd[16];
  int timeout = 200;

  strcpy(cmd, DFOTA);
  strcat(cmd, "=\"");
  strcat(cmd, http_url);
  strcat(cmd, "\"");
  _5GNBIoT.sendAndSearch(cmd, RESPONSE_OK, 2);

  //+QIND: "FOTA","HTTPSTART"
  _5GNBIoT.readResponseAndSearch(FOTA_HTTPSTART, timeout);
  DSerial.println("\r\HTTPSTART OK!");

  //+QIND: "FOTA","HTTPEND",0
```

```
  _5GNBIoT.readResponseAndSearch(FOTA_HTTPEND, timeout);
  DSerial.println("\r\HTTPEND OK!");

  //+QIND: "FOTA","START"
  _5GNBIoT.readResponseAndSearch(FOTA_START, timeout);
  DSerial.println("\r\FOTA_START OK!");

  //+QIND: "FOTA","UPDATING", 1%
  do
  {
    ret = _5GNBIoT.readResponseAndSearch(FOTA_UPDATING, timeout);
    DSerial.println("\r\FOTA_UPDATING OK!");
  } while (ret == SUCCESS_RESPONSE);

  //+QIND: "FOTA","RESTORE", 1%
  do
  {
    ret = _5GNBIoT.readResponseAndSearch(FOTA_RESTORE, timeout);
  } while (ret == SUCCESS_RESPONSE);

  //+QIND: "FOTA","END",0
  ret = _5GNBIoT.readResponseAndSearch(FOTA_END, timeout);
  DSerial.println("\r\FOTA_END OK!");
}

void setup()
{
  DSerial.begin(115200);
  while (DSerial.read() >= 0);

  ATSerial.begin(115200);
  while (ATSerial.read() >= 0);
  delay(1000);

  _5GNBIoT.InitModule();
  DSerial.println("\r\n_5GNBIoT.InitModule() OK!");

  char apn_error[64];
  _5GNBIoT.InitAPN(comm_pdp_index, APN, LOGIN, PASSWORD,
   apn_error);
  DSerial.println(apn_error);

  if (dfota())
  DSerial.println("\nDFOTA successful!");
  else
  DSerial.println("\nDFOTA fail!");
}
```

```
void loop()
{
}
```

Listing 15.1: DFOTA Arduino Sketch.

The following are the AT commands output after running the sketch. The modem downloads the delta firmware and updates its firmware automatically and then finish updating.

```
<- +CEREG: 1,1
<-
<- OK
-> AT+QICSGP=1,1,"m2mNB16.com.attz","","",3

<- OK
-> AT+CGPADDR=1

<- +CGPADDR: 1, 10.64.102.200
<-
<- OK
APN OK: The IP address is 10.64.102.200

-> AT+QFOTADL="http://95.171.16.128/DeltaFW.zip"

<- OK
<-
<- +QIND: "FOTA","HTTPSTART"
<- +QIND: "FOTA","HTTPEND",0
<- +QIND: "FOTA","START"
<- +QIND: "FOTA","UPDATING", 1%
<- +QIND: "FOTA","UPDATING", 2%
...
<- +QIND: "FOTA","UPDATING", 100%
<- +QIND: "FOTA","RESTORE", 1%
<- +QIND: "FOTA","RESTORE", 2%
...
<- +QIND: "FOTA","RESTORE", 100%
<- +QIND: "FOTA","END",0
<-
DFOTA successful!
```

Listing 15.2: AT Commands Output of DFOTA.

Part II

Microcontroller

Chapter 16

RGB LED

RGB LED is a Light Emitting Diode that emits light using three colors; red, green and blue. It is the simplest and fundamental project in any hardware electronic project to get familiar with the software and hardware board. An RGB LED is equivalent to three regular LEDs in one LED. An RGB LED operates the same way as a single LED.

The RGB LED used in this chapter is a common cathode(GND or negative) which uses a common GND on a common pin. A resistor is connected to each other pin of the RGB LED to limit the current flowing in this PIN and not to damage the LED.

In this project, the RGB LED is put in the red-color state, then it fades to green, then fades to blue and finally back to the red color. By doing this, the RGB LED is cycling through the colors that can be illuminated.

16.1 Hardware Component Required

- 1 x NB-IoT hardware board
- 1 x Micro USB cable
- 1 x F-M wires
- 1 x RGB LED
- 3 x 220 Ω resistors

16.2 Circuit Operation

An RGB LED and a regular LED are alike. Inside the RGB LED, there are three LEDs, one red, one green and one blue. By controlling the brightness of each of the individual LEDs you can mix

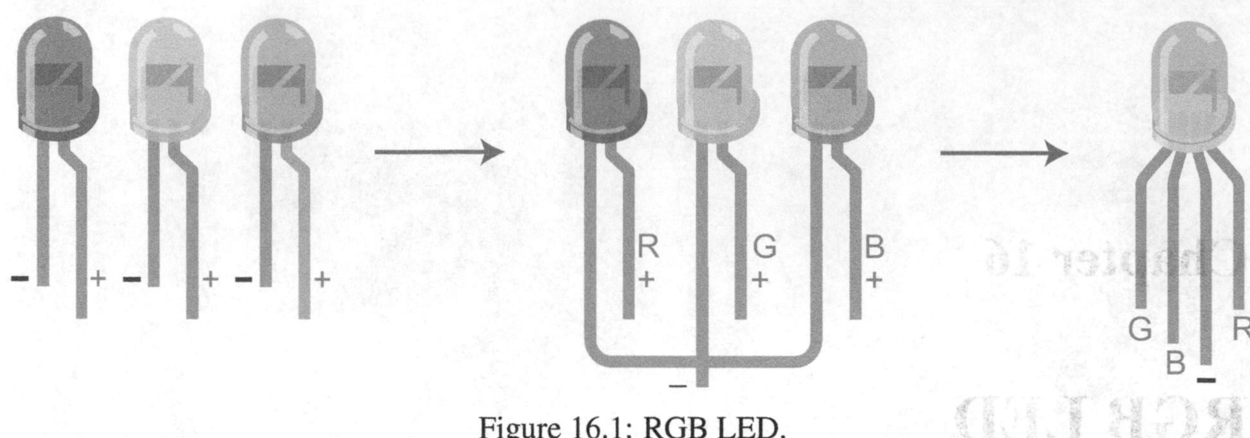

Figure 16.1: RGB LED.

pretty much any color you want. Colors are mixed the same way a paint is mixed on a palette; by adjusting the brightness of each of the three LEDs. The hardware board supports an analogWrite() function that writes an analog value (PWM) to a PIN.

The RGB LED has four pins. There is one pin going to the positive connection of each of the single LED within the RGB LED and a single pin that is connected to all three negative sides of the three LEDs.

In Figure 16.1, you can see four electrodes. A separate pin for red or green or blue color is called Anode. The anode (+) is always connected to the red, green, or blue pin while the cathode

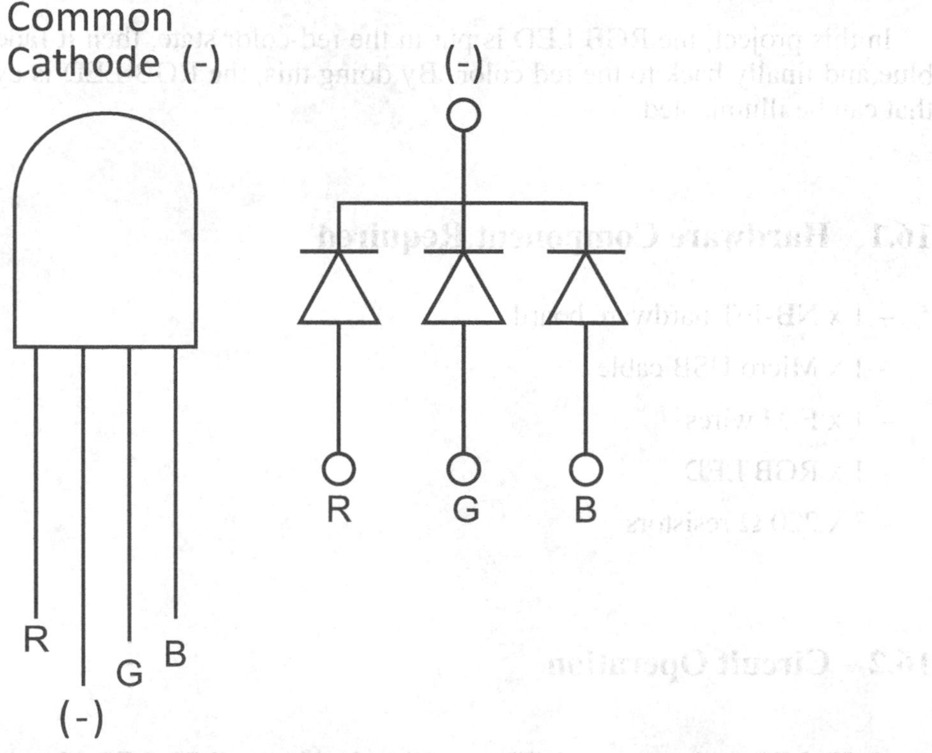

Figure 16.2: RGB LED Structure.

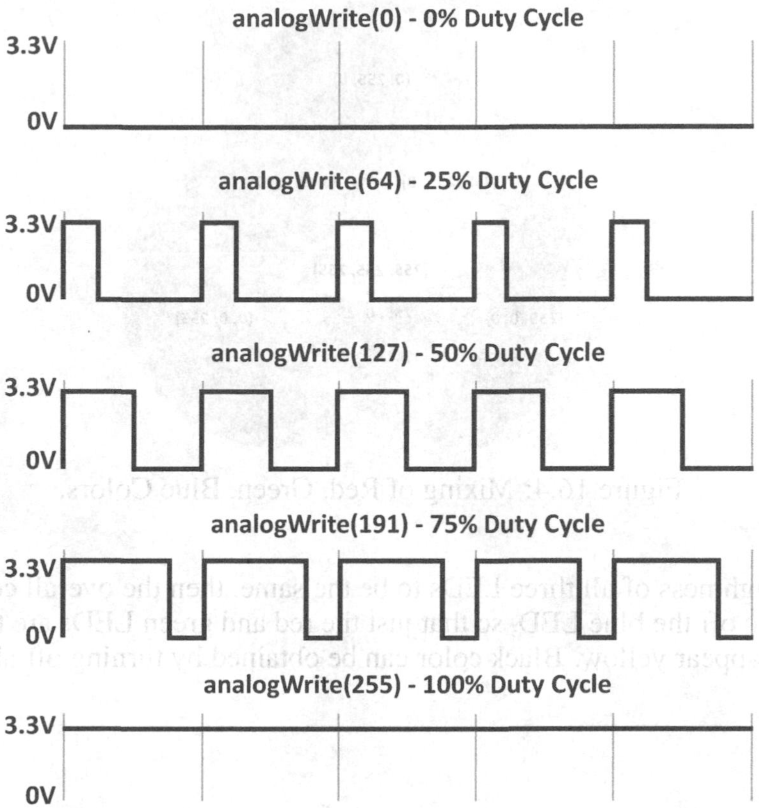

Figure 16.3: Pulse Width Modulation (PWM).

goes to ground (-). The common negative pin of the RGB LED is the longest of the four pins and is connected to the ground. Each LED inside the RGB LED is connected to its own 220Ω resistor to prevent too much current flowing through it. The three positive pins of the RGB LED are connected to pins on the NB board using three resistors.

The RGB LED is controlled using Pulse Width Modulation (PWM) which converts a digital value to an analog output. The analog output is a square wave signal that varies in the duration of its peak (on period) and its low (off period). This on-off pattern simulates analog voltages between a value of 3.3V and a value of 0V by changing the duration of the time the signal stays on versus the time that the signal stays off. The duration of "on" time is called the duty cycle. To get varying analog values the duty cycle is changed. In Figure 16.3, the blue lines represent the PWM frequency which is at 732Hz or 1/732 = 1.4 ms. A call to the analogWrite(), with a value in the range of 0 âĂŞ 255, generates a PWM with duty cycle in the range of 0 to 100%. In other words, a value of 255 generates a 100% duty cycle (always on) while a value of zero generates 0% duty cycle (always off).

Figure 16.4 shows the different colors that can be generated from the RGB LED using PWM with different values as arguments for the analogWrite(). The brightness of each of the red, green and blue parts of the RGB LED can then be controlled separately by passing different digital value, making it possible to mix large number of colors.

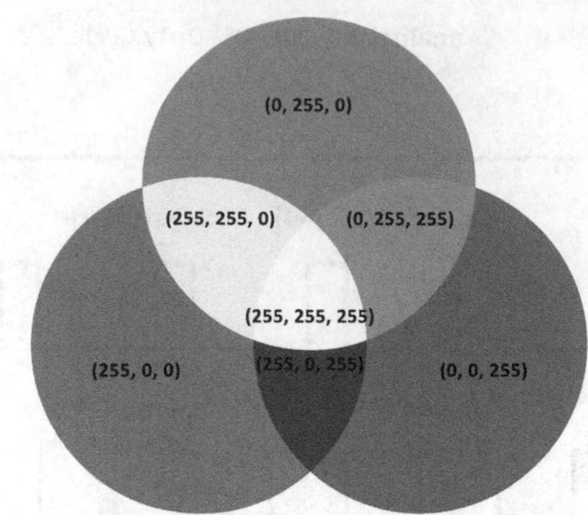

Figure 16.4: Mixing of Red, Green, Blue Colors.

If we set the brightness of all three LEDs to be the same, then the overall color of the light will be white. If we turn off the blue LED, so that just the red and green LEDs are the same brightness, then the light will appear yellow. Black color can be obtained by turning off all three colors of the RGB LED.

16.3 Schematic Diagram

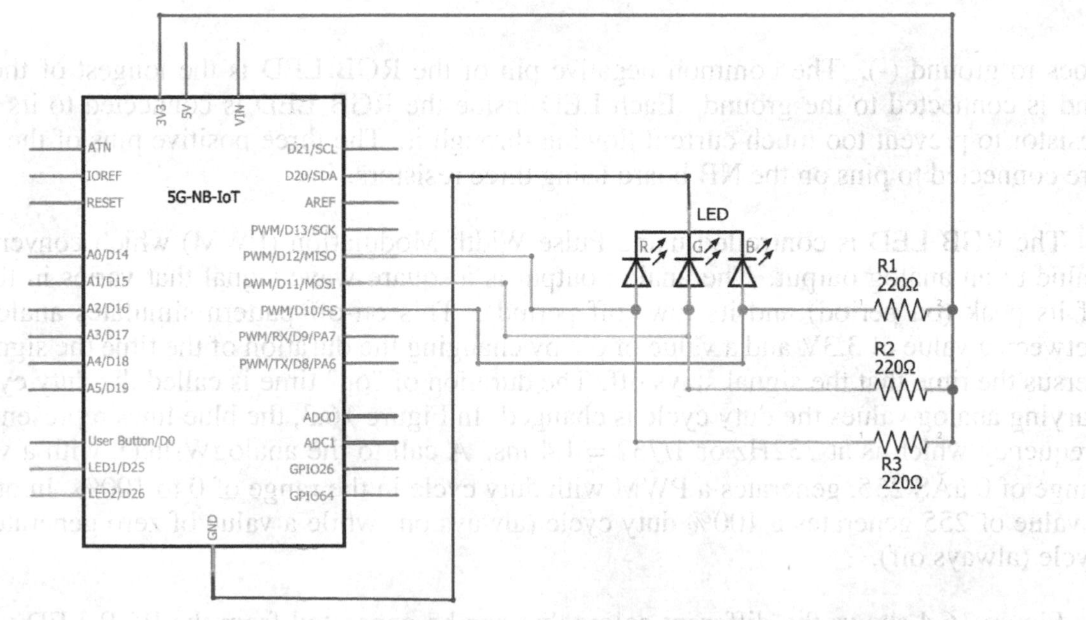

Figure 16.5: Schematic Diagram for the RGB LED Circuit.

16.4 Breadboard Diagram

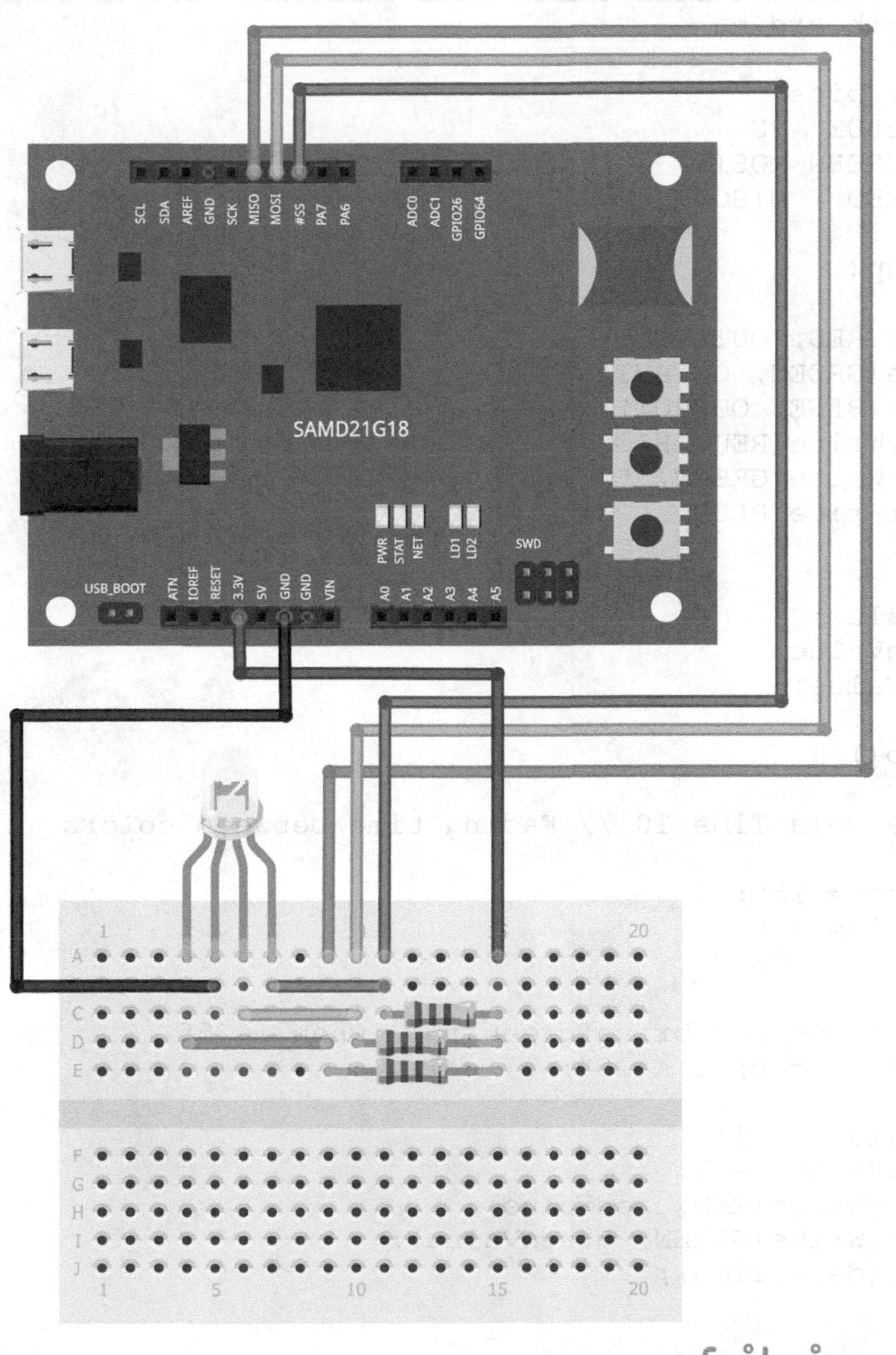

Figure 16.6: Breadboard Diagram for the RGB LED Circuit.

16.5 Arduino Sketch

The following Arduino Sketch starts by turning on the red LED. Then, it fades the red LED while starting to bring the green LED to full on. Then, it fades out green LED and brings blue LED to full on. Finally, it fades out the blue LED and bring the red LED to full on.

```
#include <board.h>

// Define pins
#define BLUE  SS
#define GREEN MOSI
#define RED   MISO

void setup()
{
  pinMode(RED, OUTPUT);
  pinMode(GREEN, OUTPUT);
  pinMode(BLUE, OUTPUT);
  digitalWrite(RED, HIGH);
  digitalWrite(GREEN, LOW);
  digitalWrite(BLUE, LOW);
}

int redValue;
int greenValue;
int blueValue;

void loop()
{
  #define delayTime 10 // Fading time between colors

  redValue = 255;
  greenValue = 0;
  blueValue = 0;

  // Fades out red bring green full when i=255
  for (int i = 0; i < 255; i += 1)
  {
    redValue -= 1;
    greenValue += 1;
    analogWrite(RED, redValue);
    analogWrite(GREEN, greenValue);
    delay(delayTime);
  }

  redValue = 0;
  greenValue = 255;
  blueValue = 0;
```

```
  // Fades out green bring blue full when i=255
  for (int i = 0; i < 255; i += 1)
  {
    greenValue -= 1;
    blueValue += 1;
    analogWrite(GREEN, greenValue);
    analogWrite(BLUE, blueValue);
    delay(delayTime);
  }

  redValue = 0;
  greenValue = 0;
  blueValue = 255;

  // Fades out blue bring red full when i=255
  for (int i = 0; i < 255; i += 1)
  {
    blueValue -= 1;
    redValue += 1;
    analogWrite(BLUE, blueValue);
    analogWrite(RED, redValue);
    delay(delayTime);
  }
}
```

Listing 16.1: RGB LED Arduino Sketch.

Chapter 17

Making Sound Using Active Buzzer

In this chapter, you will learn how to generate a sound with an active buzzer. Electronic buzzers are DC-powered integrated circuit. They are used in computers, printers, photocopiers, alarms, electronic toys, automotive electronic devices, telephones, timers and other electronic products for voice devices. Buzzers can be categorized as active and passive ones.

17.1 Hardware Component Required

- 1 x NB-IoT hardware board
- 1 x Micro USB cable
- 1 x KY-012 Active buzzer
- 1 x F-M wires

17.2 Circuit Operation

Active buzzer has a built-in oscillating source, so it generates a sound when electrified. A passive buzzer does not have such a source, so it does not tweet if DC signals are used; instead, you need to use square waves whose frequency is between 2KHz and 5KHz to drive it. The active buzzer is often more expensive than the passive one because of multiple built-in oscillating circuits.

The KY-012 active buzzer module consists of an active piezoelectric buzzer. It generates a sound of approximately 2.5kHz when signal is high.

Figure 17.1: Active Buzzer.

17.3 Schematic Diagram

Connect signal (S) to pin PA6 and ground (-) to GND on the NB board. The active buzzer is now ready to generate sounds.

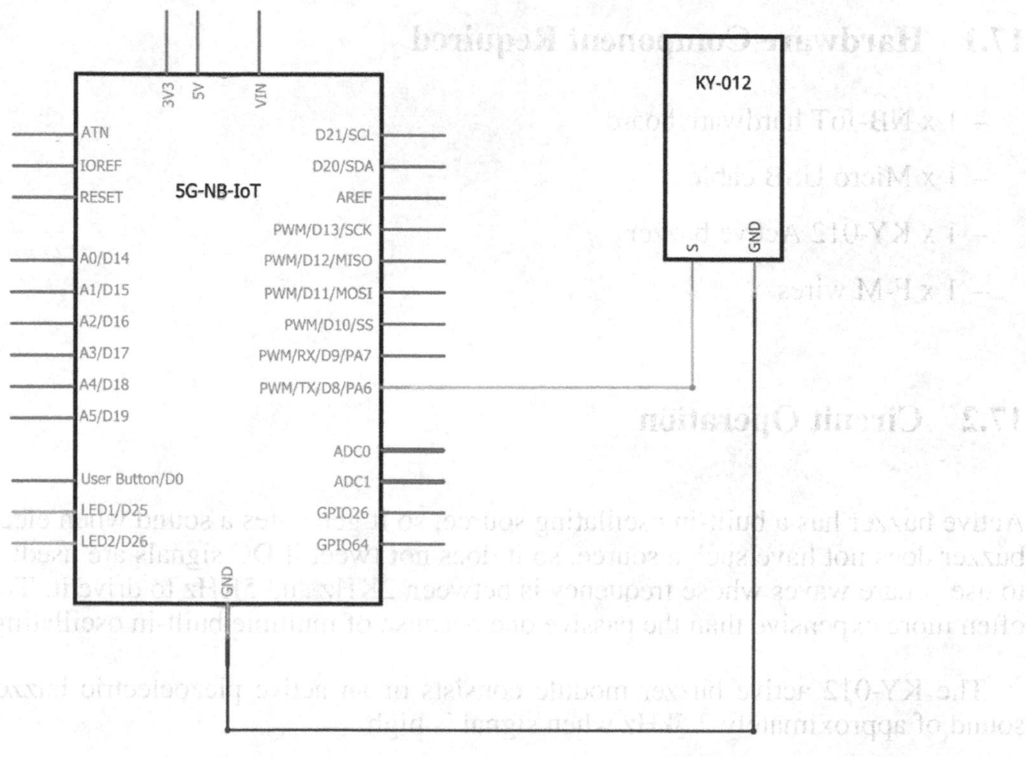

Figure 17.2: Schematic Diagram for the Active Buzzer.

17.4 Breadboard Diagram

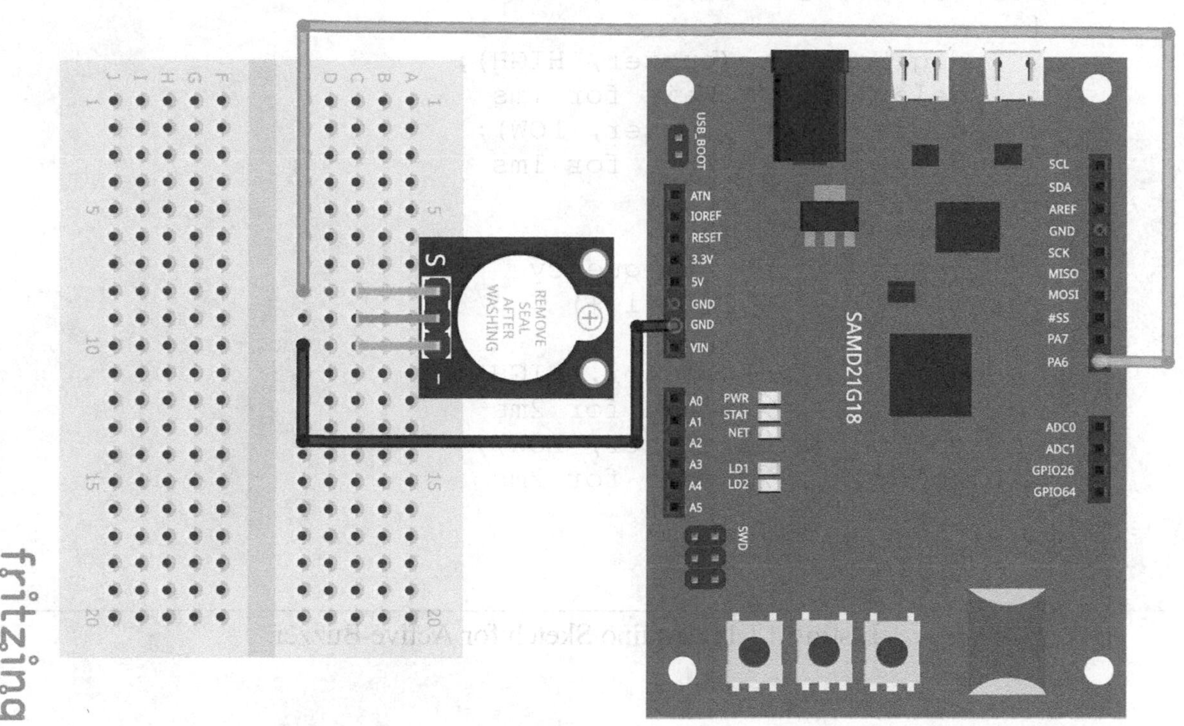

Figure 17.3: Breadboard Diagram for the Active Buzzer.

17.5 Arduino Sketch

The following Arduino sketch continually turns the buzzer on and off with delay in-between thus generating a series of short high-pitched beeps.

```
#include <board.h>

// Pin of the active buzzer
int buzzer = PA6;

void setup()
{
    pinMode(buzzer, OUTPUT); // Initialize the buzzer pin as an
   output
}

void loop()
{
    unsigned char i;
    while (1)
```

```
    {
        // Output an frequency
        for (i = 0; i < 80; i++)
        {
            digitalWrite(buzzer, HIGH);
            delay(1); // Wait for 1ms
            digitalWrite(buzzer, LOW);
            delay(1); // Wait for 1ms
        }

        // Output another frequency
        for (i = 0; i < 100; i++)
        {
            digitalWrite(buzzer, HIGH);
            delay(2); // Wait for 2ms
            digitalWrite(buzzer, LOW);
            delay(2); // Wait for 2ms
        }
    }
}
```

Listing 17.1: Arduino Sketch for Active Buzzer.

Chapter 18

Making Sound Using Passive Buzzer

In this chapter, you will learn how to use a passive buzzer. Using the passive buzzer, you can generate eight different sounds, each sound lasting 0.5 second: from Alto Do (523Hz), Re (587Hz), Mi (659Hz), Fa (698Hz), So (784Hz), La (880Hz), Si (988Hz) to Treble Do (1047Hz).

18.1 Hardware Component Required

- 1 x NB-IoT hardware board
- 1 x Micro USB cable
- 1 x Passive buzzer
- 1 x F-M wires

18.2 Circuit Operation

Passive buzzer is using Pulse Width Modulation (PWM) and generates audio to make the air vibrates. When the vibration frequency changes, it can generate different sounds. For example, sending a pulse of 523Hz, it can generate Alto Do, a pulse of 587Hz, it can generate midrange Re, and a pulse of 659Hz, it can produce midrange Mi. Using the passive buzzer, you can play a song.

Figure 18.1: Passive Buzzer.

18.3 Schematic Diagram

The passive buzzer is connected to the NB board, the positive pin is connected to pin PA6 and the black wire (negative) to the GND.

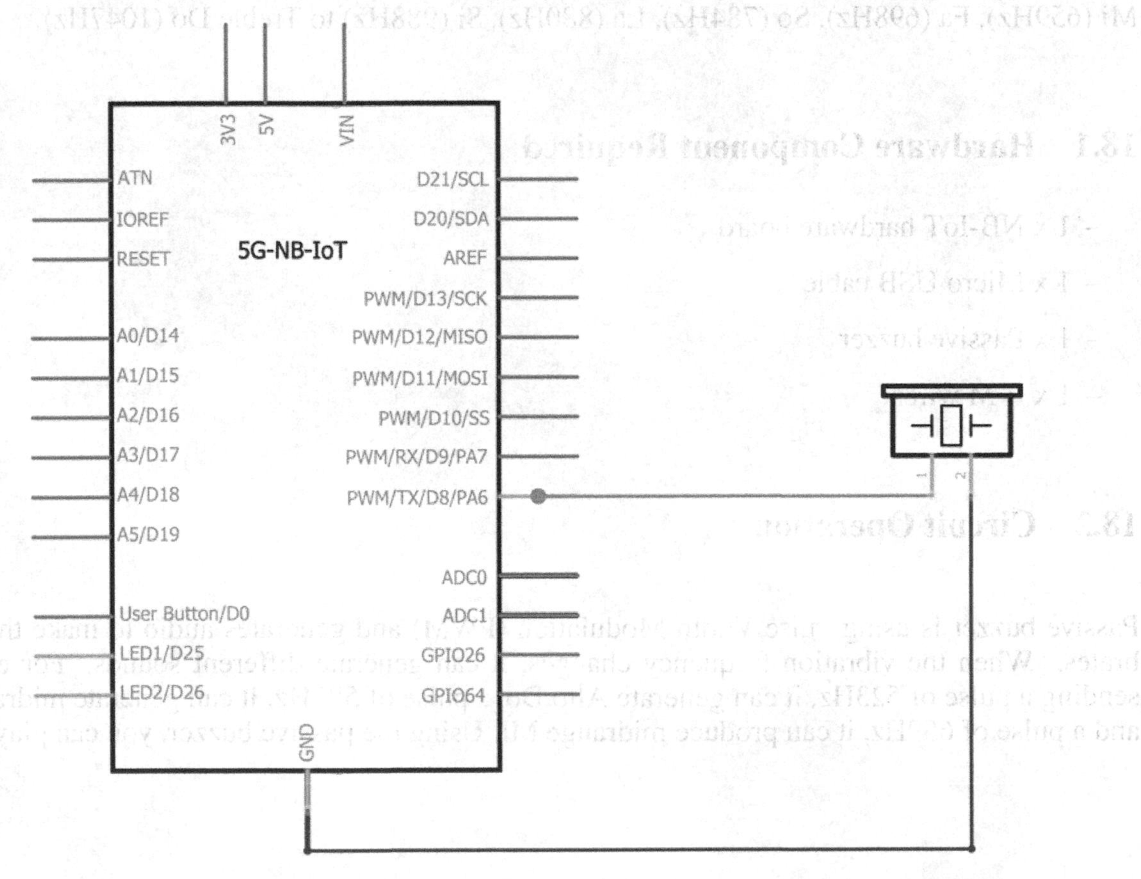

Figure 18.2: Schematic Diagram for the Passive Buzzer.

18.4 Breadboard Diagram

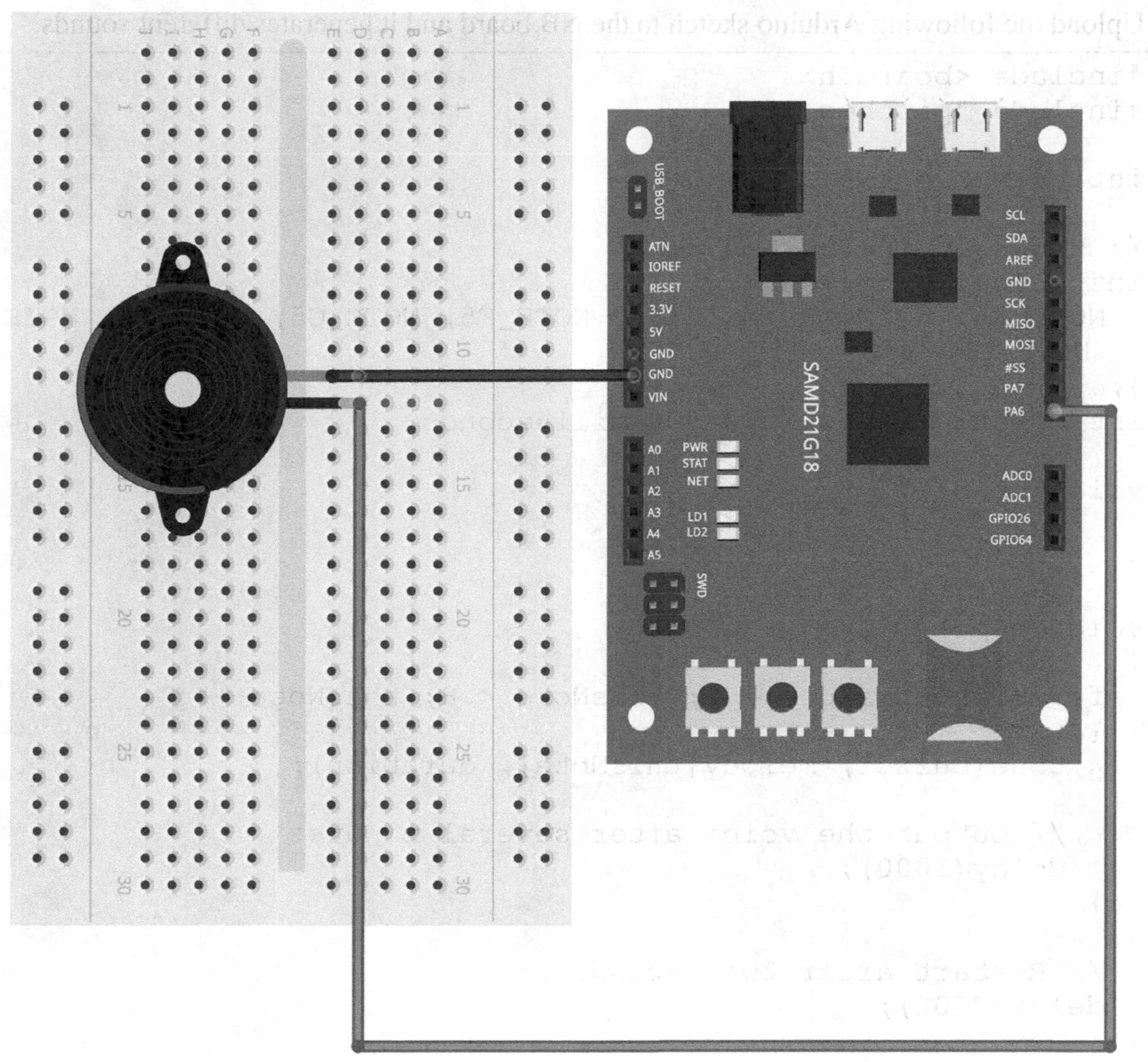

Figure 18.3: Breadboard Diagram for the Passive Buzzer.

18.5 Arduino Sketch

Upload the following Arduino sketch to the NB board and it generates different sounds.

```
#include <board.h>
#include "pitches.h"

int buzzer = PA6;

// Notes in the melody:
int melody[] = {
  NOTE_C5, NOTE_D5, NOTE_E5, NOTE_F5, NOTE_G5, NOTE_A5, NOTE_B5,
   NOTE_C6
};
int duration = 500; // 500 miliseconds

void setup()
{
}

void loop()
{
  for (int thisNote = 0; thisNote < 8; thisNote++)
  {
    tone(buzzer, melody[thisNote], duration);

    // Output the voice after several minutes
    delay(1000);
  }

  // Restart after two seconds
  delay(2000);
}
```

Listing 18.1: Arduino Sketch for Passive Buzzer.

Chapter 19

Keypad Switch

In this chapter, you will learn how to integrate a keyboard with the NB board so that the board can read the keys being pressed by a user. Keypads are used in all types of devices such as cell phones, fax machines, microwaves, ovens, door locks. Keypad is also called membrane switch.

19.1 Hardware Component Required

- 1 x NB-IoT hardware board
- 1 x Micro USB cable
- 1 x Membrane switch module
- 1 x F-M wires

19.2 Circuit Operation

A matrix keypad is used. This is a keypad that follows an encoding scheme that allows it to have much less output pins than its keys. For example, the matrix keypad we are using has 16 keys (0-9, A-D,$*$, #), with only 8 output pins. With a linear keypad, there would have to be 17 output pins (one for each key and a ground pin) in order to work.

The buttons on a keypad are arranged in rows and columns. A 4x4 keypad has 4 rows and 4 columns. Pressing a button closes the switch between a column and a row trace, allowing current to flow between a column pin and a row pin. The schematic for a 4x4 keypad shows how the rows and columns are connected.

The hardware board detects which button is pressed by detecting the row and column pin that is connected to the button. This happens as follows:

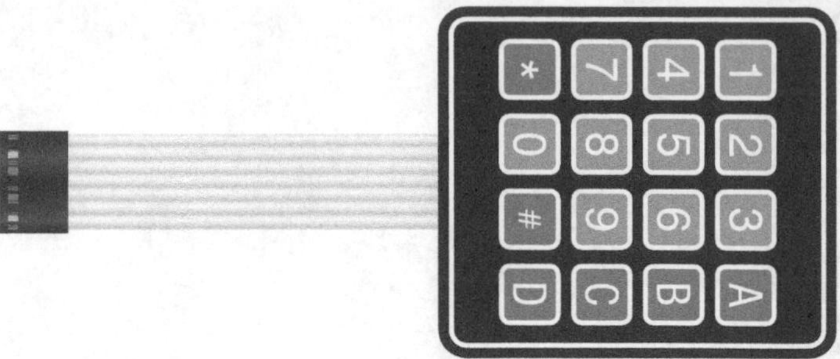

Figure 19.1: 4x4 Keyboard.

1. When no buttons are pressed, all the column pins are held HIGH, and all the row pins are held LOW.

2. When a button is pressed, the column pin is pulled LOW since the current from the HIGH column flows to the LOW row pin.

3. The hardware pin now knows which column the button is in; it just needs to find the row the button is in. It does this by switching each one of the row pins HIGH, and at the same time reading all the column pins to detect which column pin returns to HIGH.

4. When the column pin goes HIGH again, the board has found the row pin that is connected to the button.

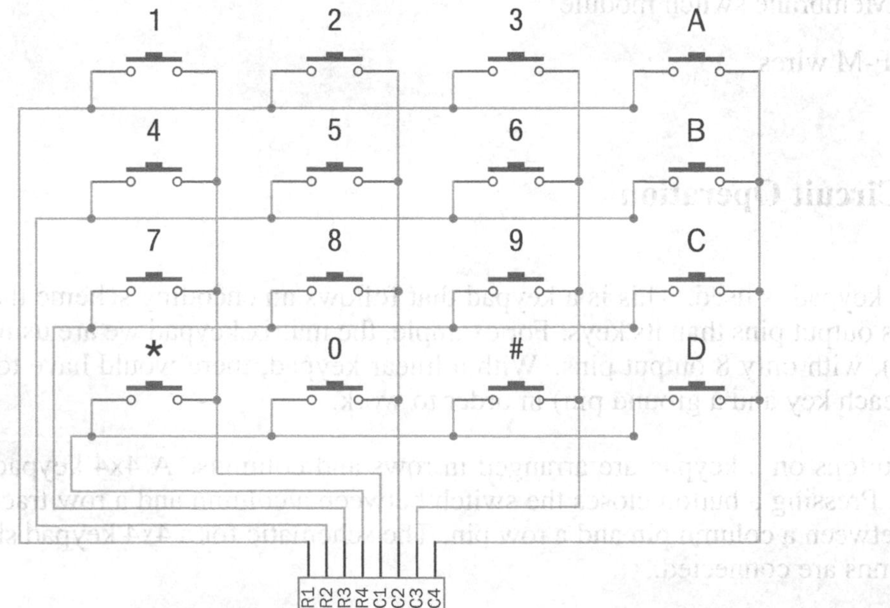

Figure 19.2: Keyboard Circuit Schematic.

19.3 Schematic Diagram

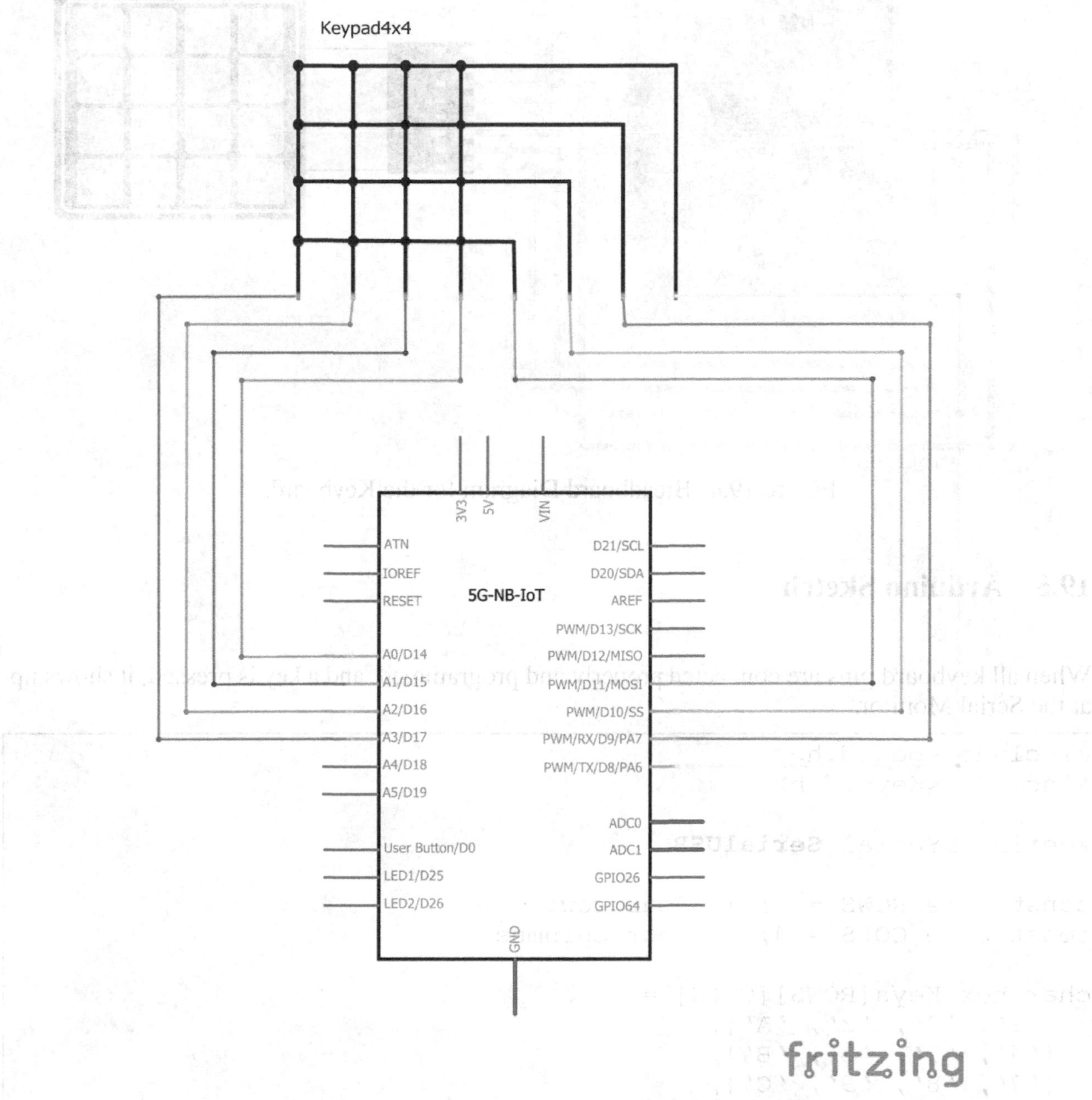

Figure 19.3: Schematic Diagram of the Keyboard.

19.4 Breadboard Diagram

When connecting the pins to the NB board, the row pins are connected to the digital output pins, D8-D11, and columns pins to digital output pins, D14-D17.

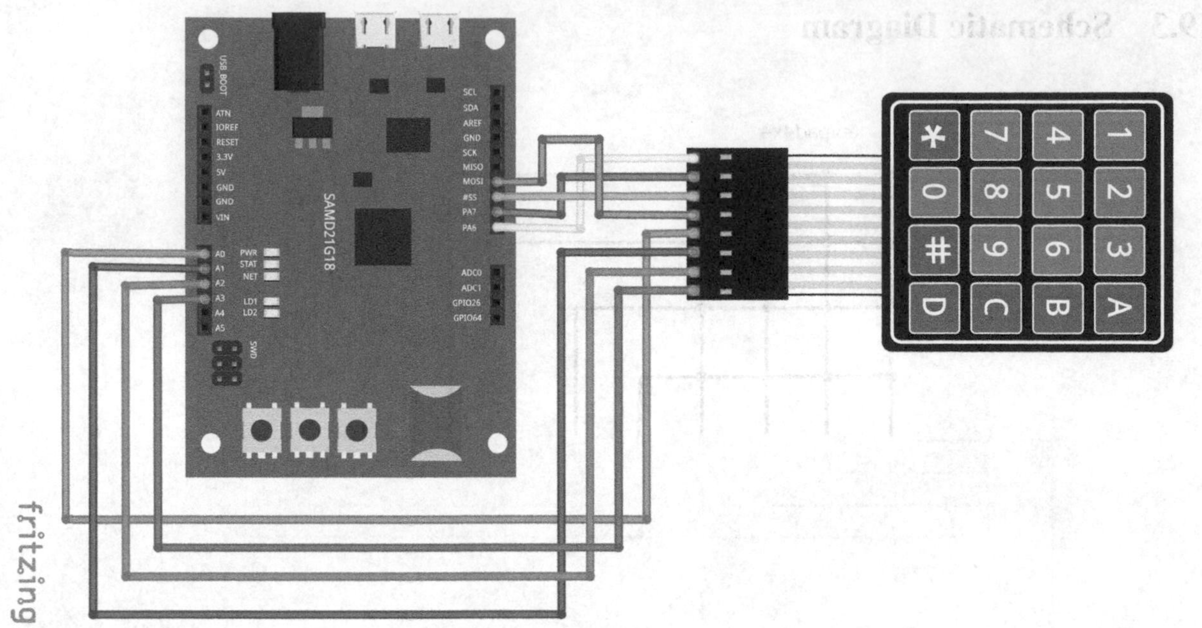

Figure 19.4: Breadboard Diagram for the Keyboard.

19.5 Arduino Sketch

When all keyboard pins are connected properly and programmed, and a key is pressed, it shows up at the Serial Monitor.

```
#include <board.h>
#include <Keypad.h>

#define DSerial SerialUSB

const byte ROWS = 4; // Four rows
const byte COLS = 4; // Four columns

char hexaKeys[ROWS][COLS] = {
  {'1', '2', '3', 'A'},
  {'4', '5', '6', 'B'},
  {'7', '8', '9', 'C'},
  {'*', '0', '#', 'D'}
};

// Connect to the row pinouts of the keypad
byte rowPins[ROWS] = {MOSI, SS, PA7, PA6};
// Connect to the column pinouts of the keypad
byte colPins[COLS] = {A0, A1, A2, A3};

// Initialize an instance of class Keypad
```

```
Keypad customKeypad = Keypad( makeKeymap(hexaKeys), rowPins,
   colPins, ROWS, COLS);

void setup()
{
  DSerial.begin(9600);
}

void loop()
{
  char customKey = customKeypad.getKey();

  if (customKey)
  {
    DSerial.println(customKey);
  }
}
```

Listing 19.1: Arduino Sketch for Membrane Switch.

With this code, once we press a key on the keypad, it shows up on the Serial Monitor output as shown.

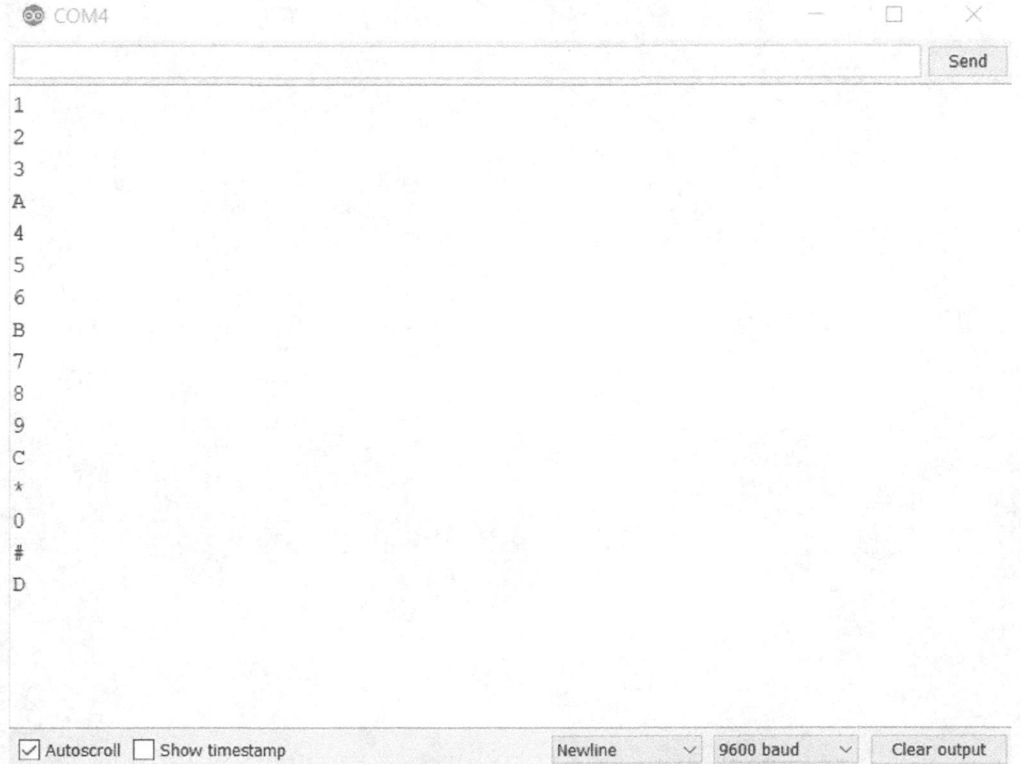

Figure 19.5: Serial Monitor Output for Keyboard.

Chapter 20

Push Button

In this chapter, you will learn how to use push buttons to control an LED by turning it on and off. Pressing the first push button will turn the LED on and pressing the second button will turn the LED off.

20.1 Hardware Component Required

- 1 x NB-IoT hardware board
- 1 x Micro USB cable
- 1 x Red LED
- 1 x 220Ω resistor
- 2 x Push button
- 1 x F-M wires

20.2 Circuit Operation

Buttons are simple components. When you press a button, it connects two contacts together so that electricity can flow through them. The little tactile button that is used in this chapter has four connections.

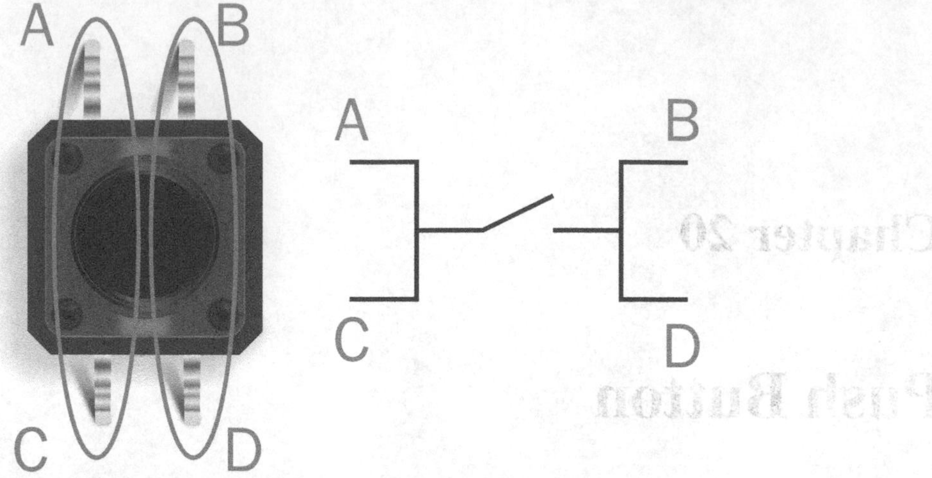

Figure 20.1: Push Button Diagram and Circuit.

In a tactical button, there are only two electrical connections. Inside the switch package, pins A and C are connected, and pins B and D are connected.

When you press the button, all four connections are connected and act as a single point. If the button is released, the connections are disconnected from each other

Figure 20.2: Push Button When Pressed and When Released.

Figure 20.3 and Figure 20.4 show the circuit used. It has two push buttons and one LED. Pressing the left button will turn the LED on while pressing the right button will turn it off.

The pin mode used on the NB board is INPUT_PULLUP which means that the pin is pulled up to a HIGH value. In other words, the default value for the input is HIGH, unless it is pulled LOW by the action of pressing the button.

Each push button is connected to GND. When a button is pressed, it connects the input pin to GND and it is no longer HIGH. In the Arduino sketch the input pin level (HIGH or LOW) is detected and the LED is either controlled to be on or off.

20.3 Schematic Diagram

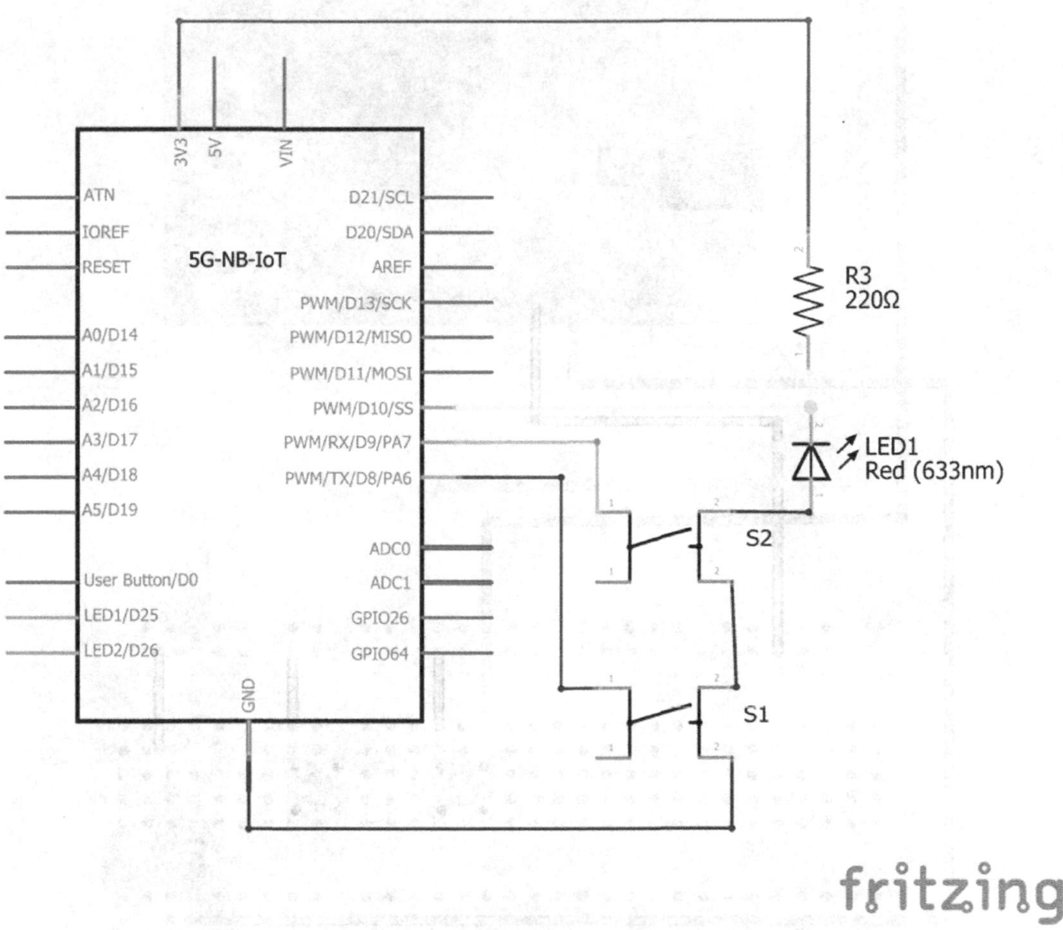

Figure 20.3: Schematic Diagram for Push Button and LED.

20.4 Breadboard Diagram

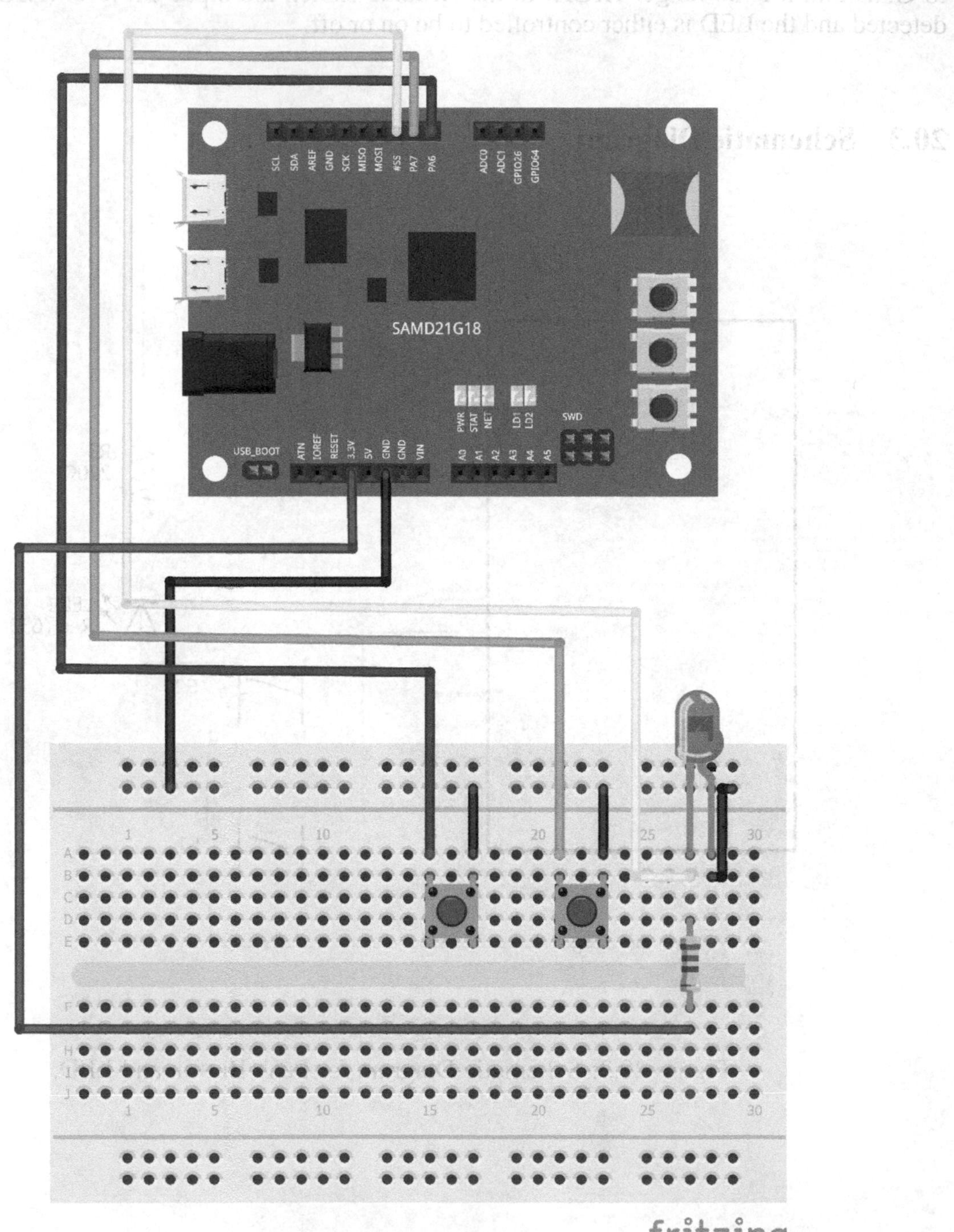

Figure 20.4: Breadboard Diagram for Push Button and LED.

20.5 Arduino Sketch

The Arduino code is shown in Listing 20.1. The first part of the sketch defines three variables for the three pins that are being used. The **ledPin** is the output pin and **buttonApin** refers to the switch on the right side of the breadboard and **buttonBpin** to the other switch. The setup() function defines the **ledPin** as being an OUTPUT as normal, but now there are two input pins to deal with. In this case, pinMode() is used to set the input pins to be INPUT_PULLUP.

In the loop() function, there are two if-statements. One for each button. If the button is pressed, the corresponding input will be LOW, if button A is low, then a digitalWrite() on the **ledPin** turns it on. Similarly, if button B is pressed, a LOW is written to the **ledPin**.

```
#include <board.h>

int ledPin = SS;
int buttonApin = PA7;
int buttonBpin = PA6;

byte leds = 0;

void setup()
{
  pinMode(ledPin, OUTPUT);
  pinMode(buttonApin, INPUT_PULLUP);
  pinMode(buttonBpin, INPUT_PULLUP);
}

void loop()
{
  if (digitalRead(buttonApin) == LOW)
  {
    digitalWrite(ledPin, HIGH);
  }
  if (digitalRead(buttonBpin) == LOW)
  {
    digitalWrite(ledPin, LOW);
  }
}
```

Listing 20.1: Arduino Sketch for Push Buttons.

Chapter 21

Analog Joystick

Analog joysticks are a great way to add some control in your projects. In this chapter, you we will learn how to use the analog joystick module.

21.1 Hardware Component Required

– 1 x NB-IoT hardware board

– 1 x Micro USB cable

– 1 x Joystick module

– 1 x F-M wires

21.2 Circuit Operation

The basic idea of a joystick is to translate the stick position on **two axes**; the **X-axis** (left and right) and the **Y-axis** (up and down) into electronic information which the NB board can process. The design of the joystick consists of two potentiometers that interprets the position of the X and Y position of the joystick as an analog reading. if you push the stick all the way forward, it turns the potentiometer contact arm to one end of the track, and if you pull it back toward you, it turns the contact arm the other way. Additionally, the Joystick can be pressed down to activate a "press to select" push button.

To read the joystick physical position, the change in resistance of the potentiometer is measured. This change can be read by the ADC analog pin on the NB board.

The joystick module has 5 pins: VCC, GND, X, Y, push-button key. As the board has an ADC resolution of 10 bits, the values on each analog channel (axis) can vary from 0 to 1023. So, if the

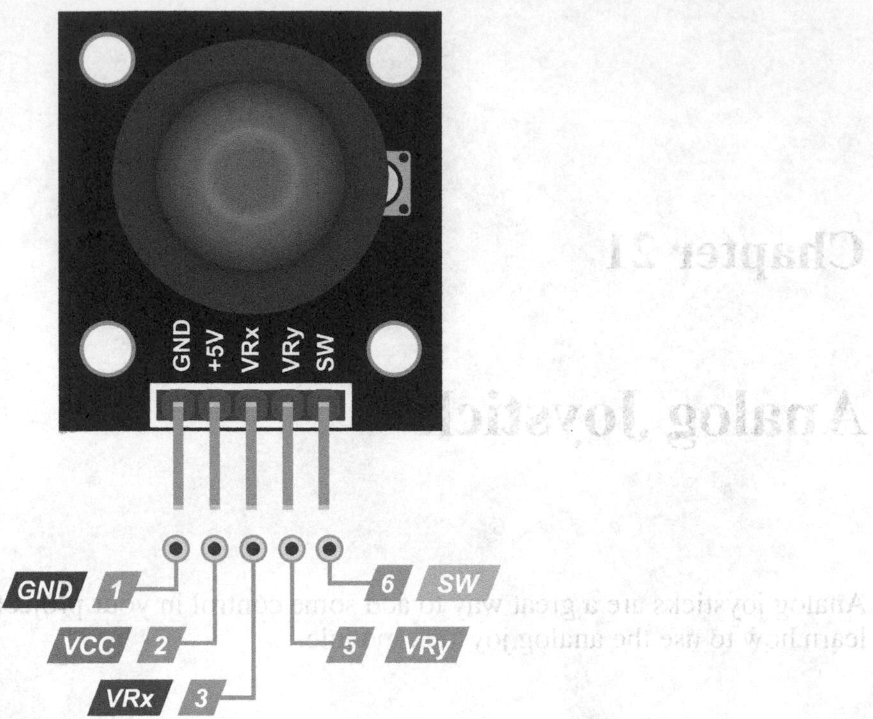

Figure 21.1: Joystick Module.

stick is moved on X axis from one end to the other, the X values will change from 0 to 1023 and similar thing happens when moved along the Y axis. When the joystick stays in its center position the value is around 512.

We use analog pins to read the data from the X/Y pins, and a digital pin to read the button. The push-button key pin is connected to ground when the joystick is pressed down and is floating

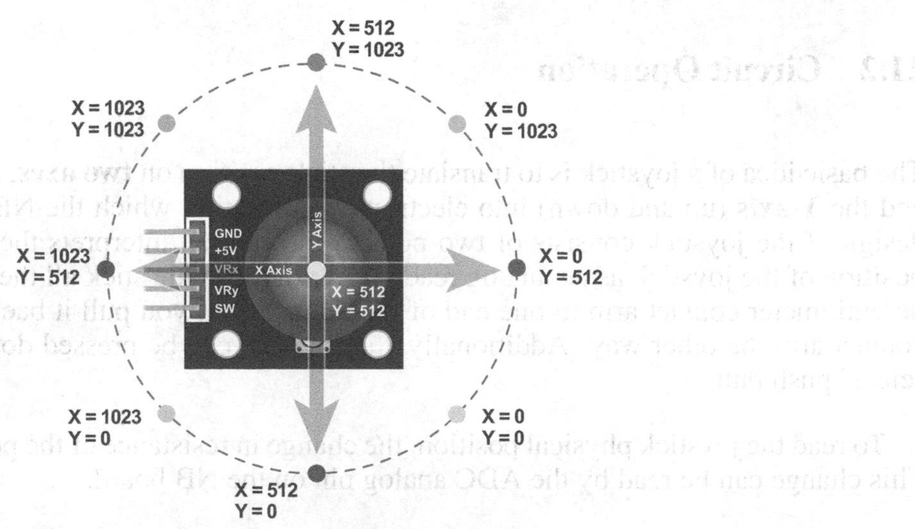

Figure 21.2: Joystick Analog X/Y Positions.

otherwise. To get stable readings from the key pin, it needs to be connected to VCC via a pull-up resistor. The built-in resistors on the NB board digital pins can be used.

21.3 Schematic Diagram

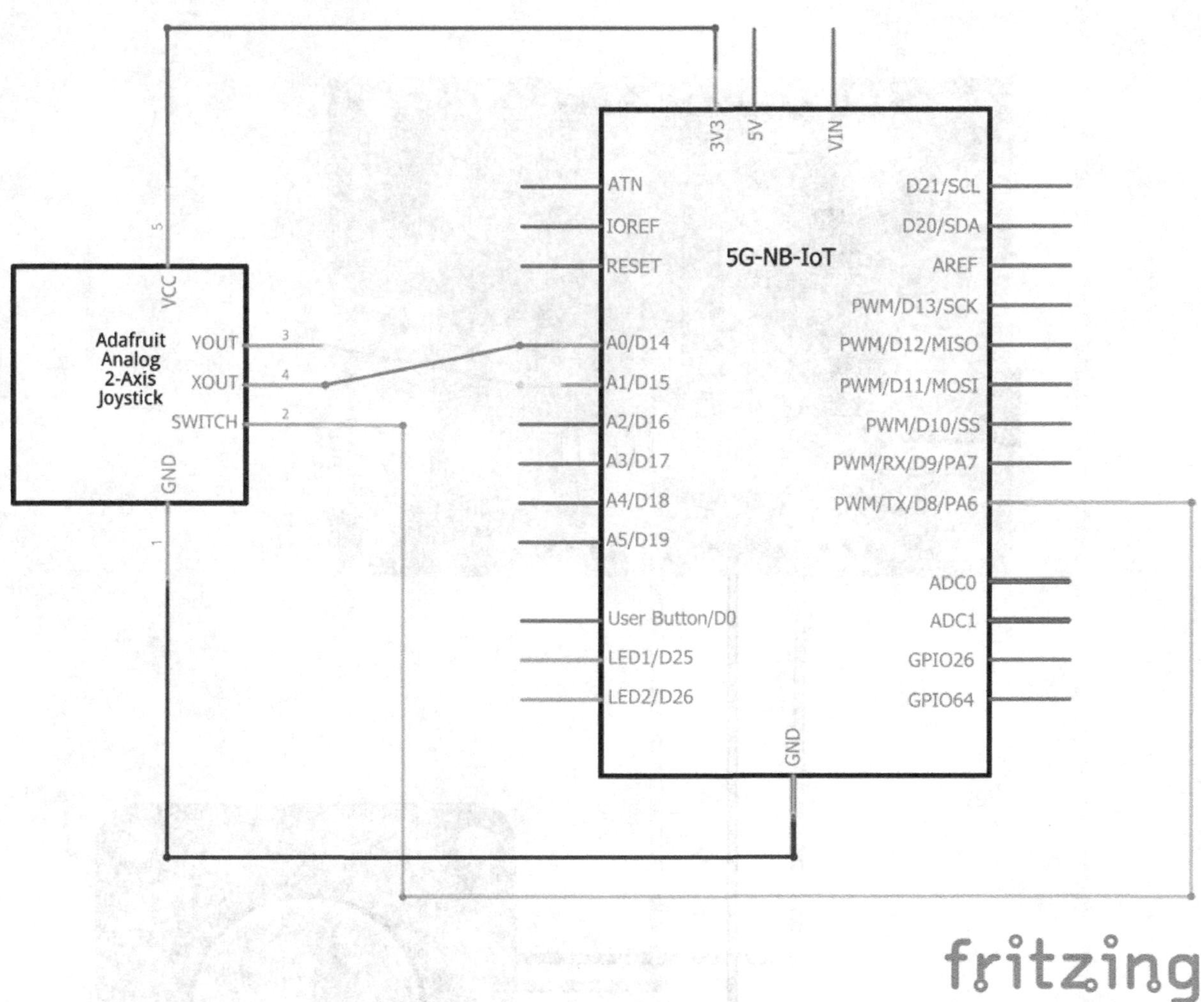

Figure 21.3: Schematic Diagram for the Analog Joystick.

21.4 Breadboard Diagram

Five connections to the joystick are needed. The connections are: Key, Y, X, VCC and GND. Y and X are analog, and key is digital. If the switch is not needed, then only 4 pins can be used.

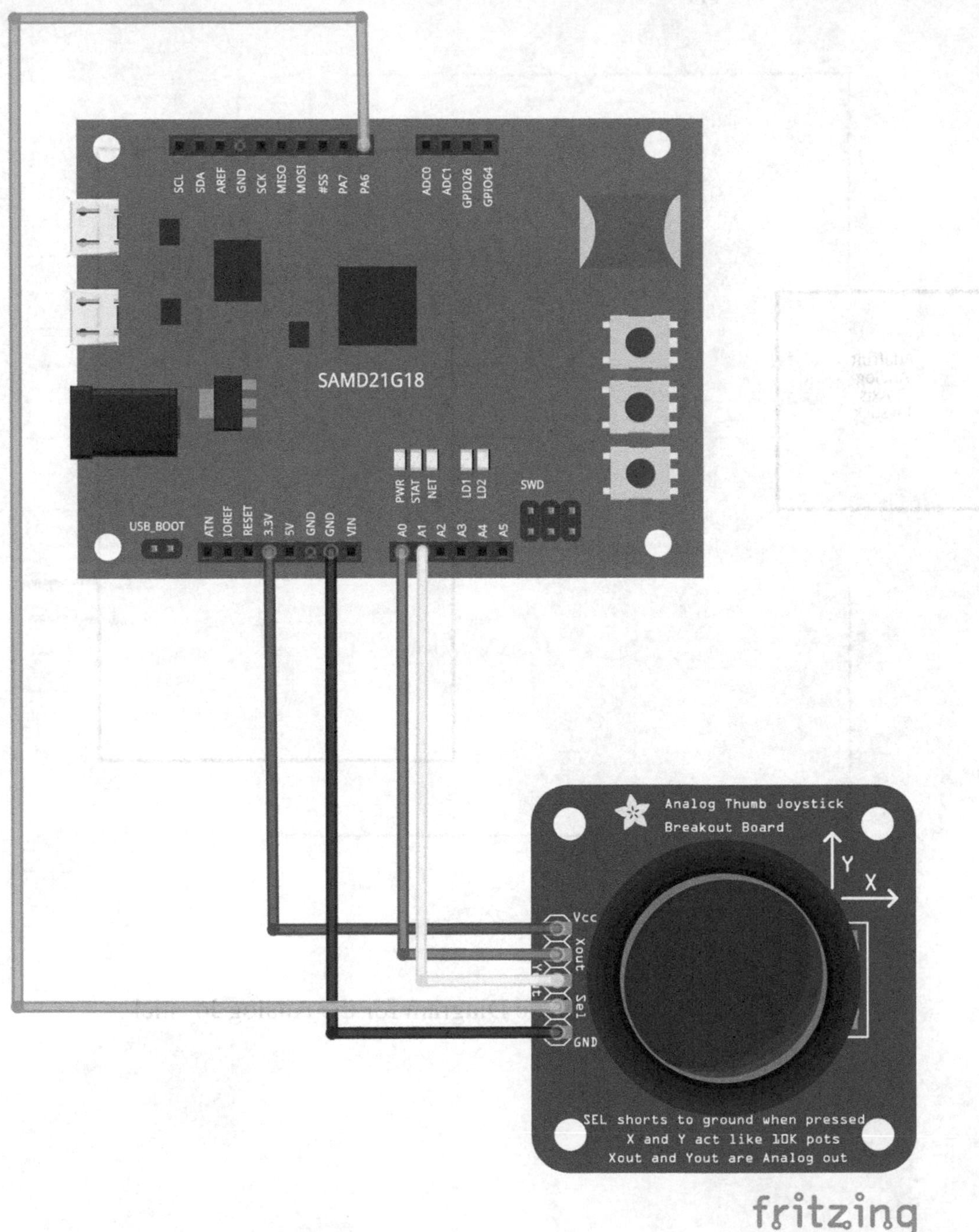

Figure 21.4: Breadboard Diagram for the Analog Joystick.

21.5 Arduino Sketch

Arduino sketch to read the analog joystick X/Y position and key pin is shown below.

```
#include <board.h>
#define DSerial SerialUSB

// Arduino pin numbers
const int SW_pin = PA6;
const int X_pin = A0;
const int Y_pin = A1;

void setup()
{
  DSerial.begin(9600);
  while (!DSerial);
  delay(1000);

  pinMode(SW_pin, INPUT);
  digitalWrite(SW_pin, HIGH);
}

void loop()
{
  DSerial.print("Switch:  ");
  DSerial.print(digitalRead(SW_pin));
  DSerial.print("\n");
  DSerial.print("X-axis: ");
  DSerial.print(analogRead(X_pin));
  DSerial.print("\n");
  DSerial.print("Y-axis: ");
  DSerial.println(analogRead(Y_pin));
  DSerial.print("\n\n");
  delay(500);
}
```

Listing 21.1: Arduino Sketch for Analog Joystick.

After uploading the Arduino sketch to the NB board and starting to move the analog joystick, the output is shown on the Serial Monitor as below.

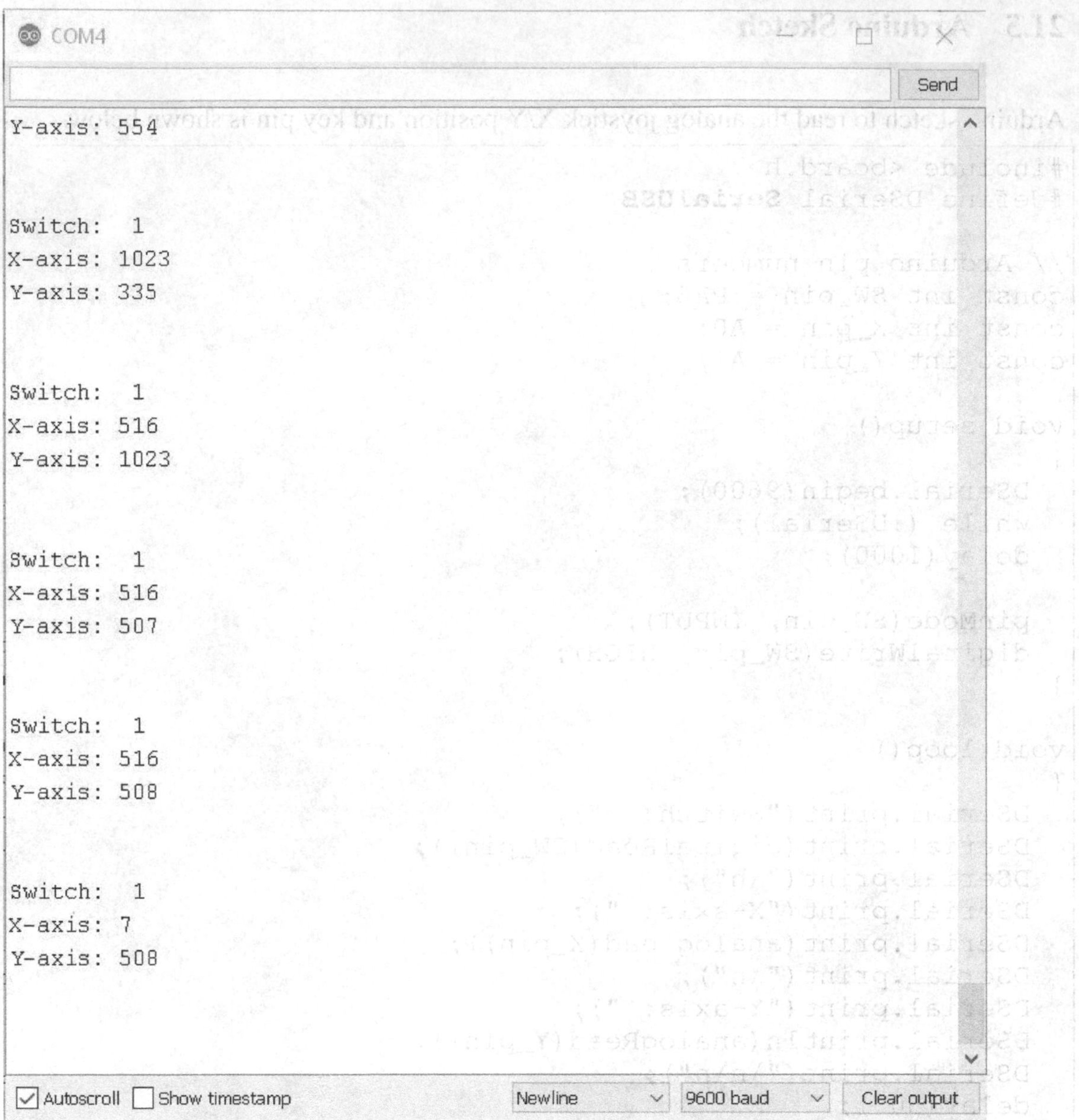

Figure 21.5: Serial Monitor Output for the Joystick.

Chapter 22

Infra-Red (IR) Receiver

In this chapter, you will learn how to use IR sensor and IR remote to control remote object. IR remote generate hexadecimal codes and can be detected by the IR detector when received on the NB board.

22.1 Hardware Component Required

- 1 x NB-IoT hardware board
- 1 x Micro USB cable
- 1 x AX-1838HS IR receiver module
- 1 x IR remote
- 1 x F-M wires

22.2 Circuit Operation

An IR sensor is an electronic instrument that scans IR signals in specific frequency ranges defined by standards and converts them to electric signals on its output pin (typically called signal pin). The IR signals are typically transmitted by IR remote over the air on short distances (typically few meters) like those used by TV remote controls or other similar electronic device. Inside the remote control is a matching IR LED, which emits IR pulses to tell the TV to turn on, off or change channels. IR light is not visible to the human eye, which means it takes a little more work to test a setup.

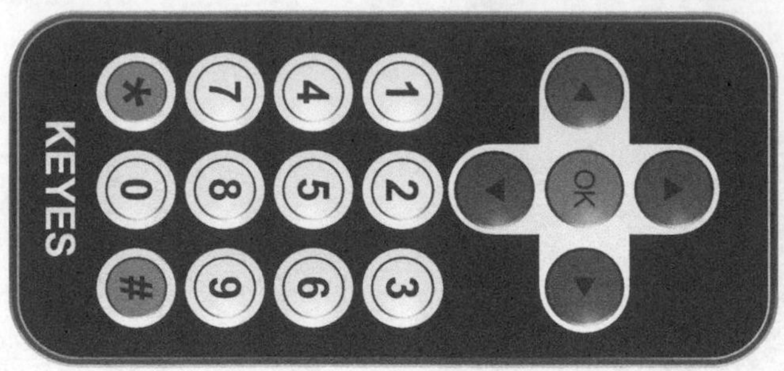

Figure 22.1: IR Remote.

Each signal represents a specific code. Electric signals can be converted back to the actual data/code that IR remote has sent. When you press a button on the IR remote control, it generates a signal corresponding to the button code (e.g. On/Off, Volume Up, etc.) and sends it to the IR sensor. Both IR remote and sensor agree on a set of codes so that the sensor knows what to do based on each code. The way a code should be modulated (modeled) as a signal is defined in different standard and each sensor manufacturer normally tries to produce a product compatible with them so that it could be used in different devices.

IR detectors are digital out. That is, they either detect 38KHz IR signal and output low (0V) or they do not detect any and output high (5V).

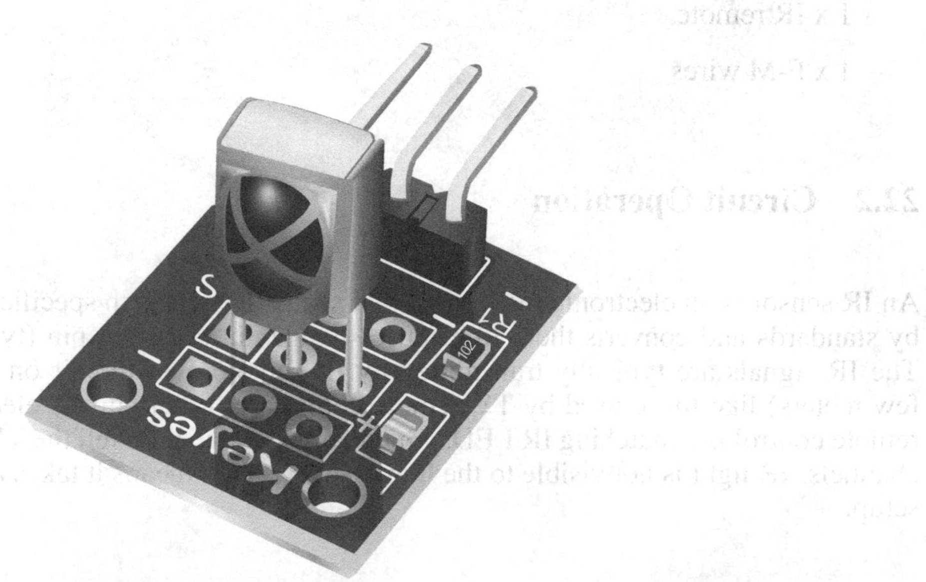

Figure 22.2: IR Sensor (Detector).

22.3 Schematic Diagram

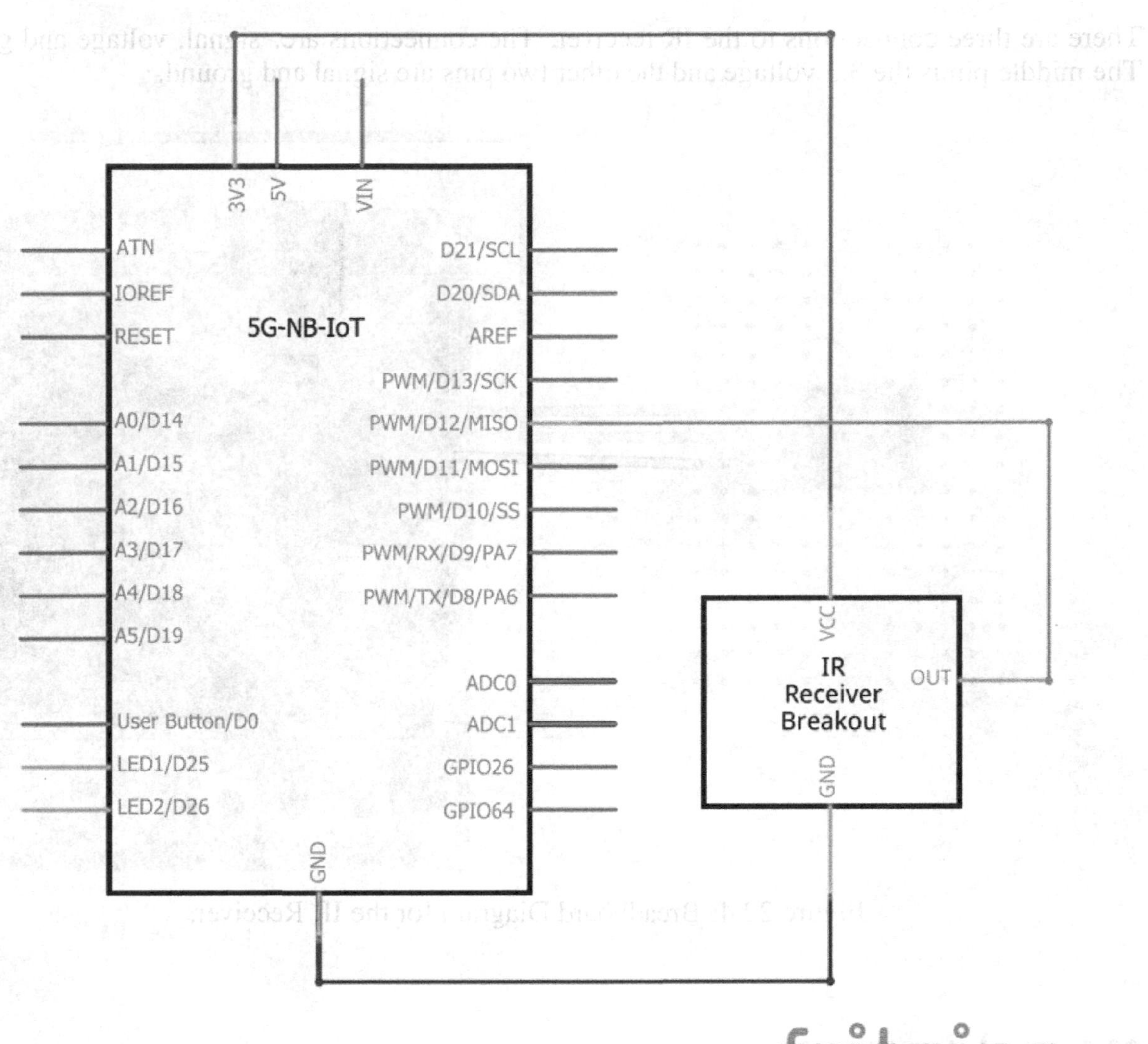

Figure 22.3: Schematic Diagram for the IR Receiver.

22.4 Breadboard Diagram

There are three connections to the IR receiver. The connections are: signal, voltage and ground. The middle pin is the 3.3 voltage and the other two pins are signal and ground.

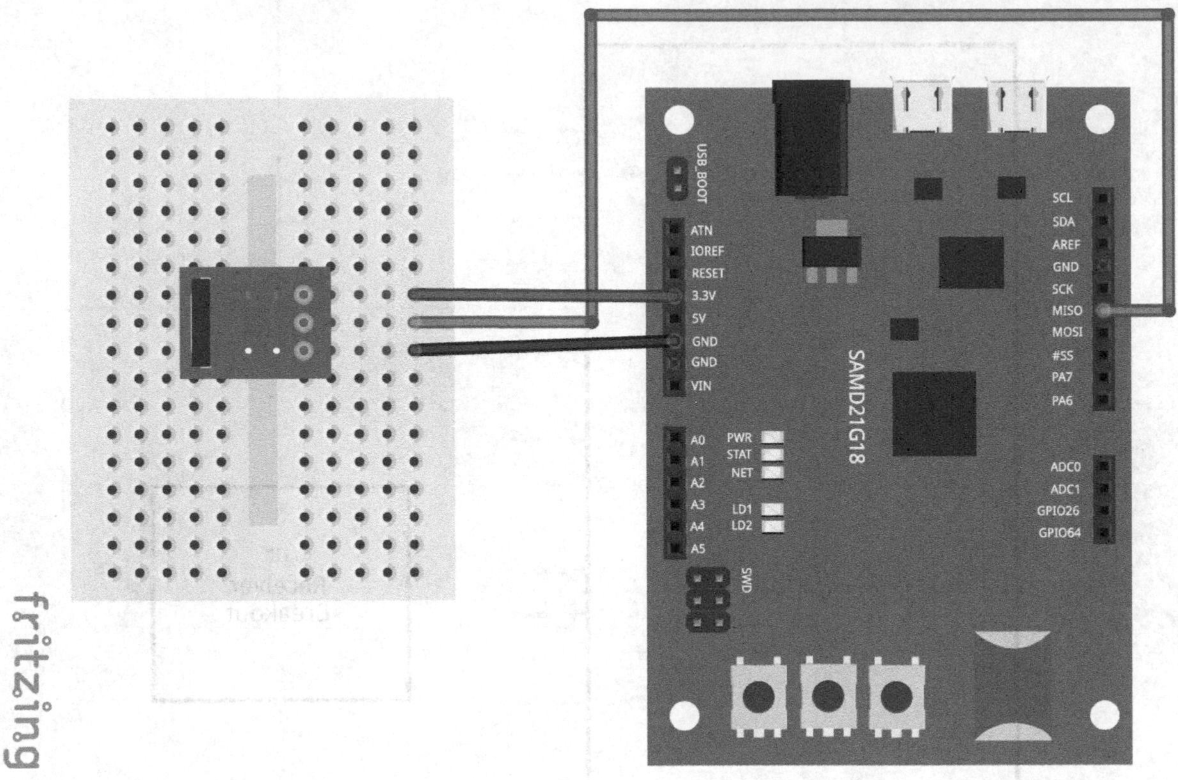

Figure 22.4: Breadboard Diagram for the IR Receiver.

22.5 Arduino Sketch

When you press a key on the IR remote, there is a hexadecimal code for that key. The sketch below reads the received hexadecimal code and prints the corresponding key pressed. Upon detecting a key press, you can control other objects such as turning volume up/down, turning led on/off, move a motor clockwise/anti-clockwise.

```
#include <board.h>
#include <IRLibAll.h>

IRrecv myReceiver(MISO);
IRdecode myDecoder;

#define DSerial SerialUSB

```

```
void setup()
{
    // Initialize serial communications with the PC
  DSerial.begin(9600);
    // Do nothing if no serial port is opened
    while (!DSerial);
  delay(1000);
  DSerial.println("IR Receiver Button Decode");
  myReceiver.enableIRIn(); // Start the receiver
}

void loop()
{
  if (myReceiver.getResults()) {
    myDecoder.decode();
    if (myDecoder.protocolNum == NEC) {
      switch (myDecoder.value) {
        case 0xFFA25D: DSerial.println("POWER");        break;
        case 0xFFE21D: DSerial.println("FUNC/STOP");    break;
        case 0xFF629D: DSerial.println("VOL+");         break;
        case 0xFF22DD: DSerial.println("FAST BACK");    break;
        case 0xFF02FD: DSerial.println("PAUSE");        break;
        case 0xFFC23D: DSerial.println("FAST FORWARD"); break;
        case 0xFFE01F: DSerial.println("DOWN");         break;
        case 0xFFA857: DSerial.println("VOL-");         break;
        case 0xFF906F: DSerial.println("UP");           break;
        case 0xFF9867: DSerial.println("EQ");           break;
        case 0xFFB04F: DSerial.println("ST/REPT");      break;
        case 0xFF6897: DSerial.println("0");            break;
        case 0xFF30CF: DSerial.println("1");            break;
        case 0xFF18E7: DSerial.println("2");            break;
        case 0xFF7A85: DSerial.println("3");            break;
        case 0xFF10EF: DSerial.println("4");            break;
        case 0xFF38C7: DSerial.println("5");            break;
        case 0xFF5AA5: DSerial.println("6");            break;
        case 0xFF42BD: DSerial.println("7");            break;
        case 0xFF4AB5: DSerial.println("8");            break;
        case 0xFF52AD: DSerial.println("9");            break;
        case 0xFFFFFFFF: DSerial.println(" REPEAT");    break;

        default:
        DSerial.println(" other button   ");
      }

      delay(500); // Do not get immediate repeat

      myReceiver.enableIRIn(); //Restart the receiver
    }
```

```
  }
}
```

Listing 22.1: Arduino Sketch for IR Receiver Module.

The output can be seen on the Serial Monitor as shown below.

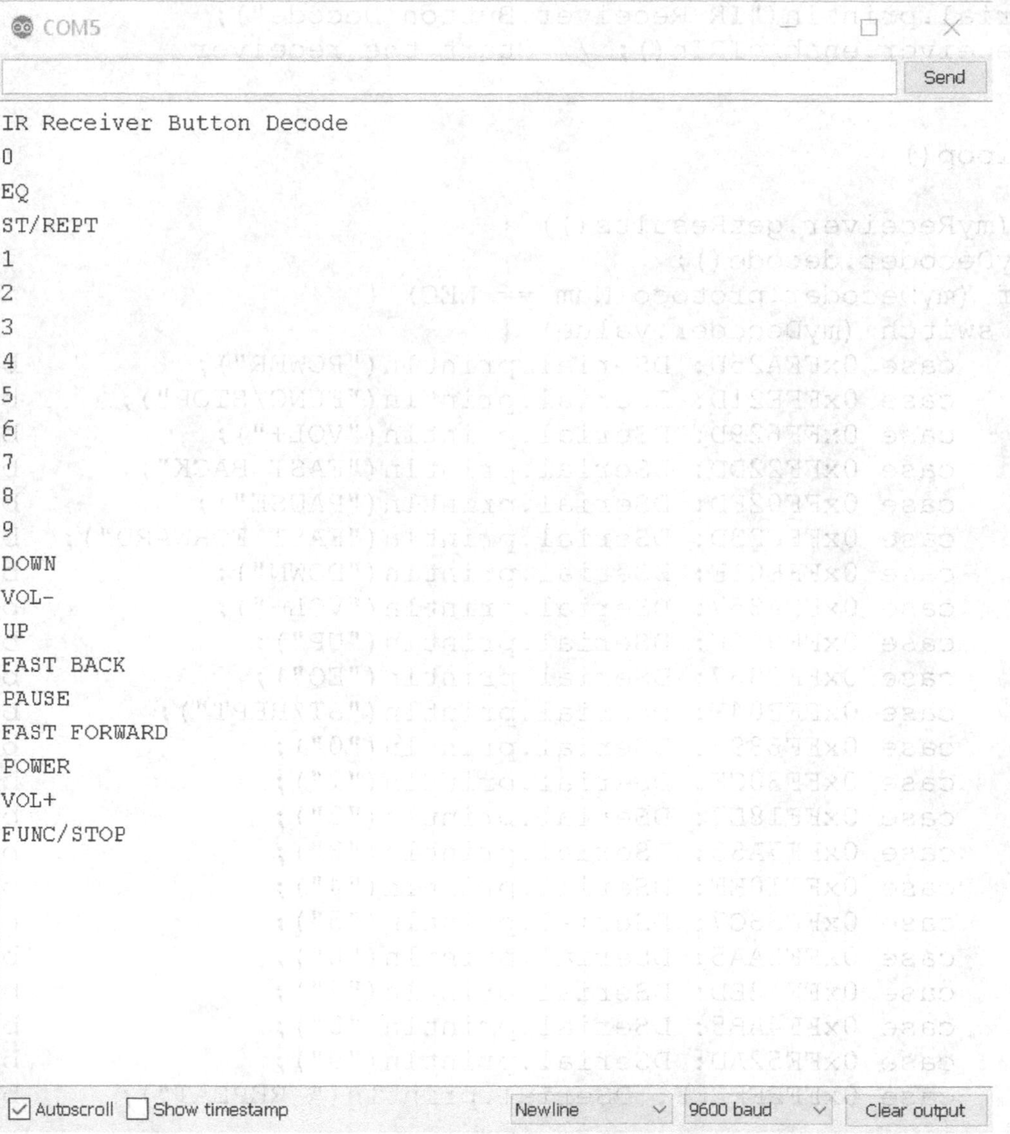

Figure 22.5: Serial Monitor Output for the IR Receiver.

Chapter 23

Radio Frequency Identification

In this chapter you will learn how to use RFID for tracking and identification. RFID stands for **Radio Frequency IDentification** and it is a short-distance RF technology that is used for many applications such as personnel tracking, security access control, supply chain management, asset tracking and management, gate and door systems.

You will use the RC522 RFID reader module with the NB board. This module uses the Serial Peripheral Interface (SPI) bus to communicate with hardware boards such as Raspberry Pi boards.

23.1 Hardware Component Required

- 1 x NB-IoT hardware board
- 1 x Micro USB cable
- 1 x MFRC522 RFID module
- 1 x F-M wires

23.2 Circuit Operation

The RFID system consists of two components, a transponder or a tag which is located on the object that is to be identified such as door or a book, and a transceiver or a reader. The **reader** sends a signal to the tag and reads its response back.

Figure 23.1: Different RFID Tags.

The RFID reader consists of a radio frequency module, a control unit, and an antenna coil which generates a high frequency electromagnetic field. On the other hand, the tag is usually a passive component, which consists of just an antenna and an electronic microchip, so when it gets near the electromagnetic field of the transceiver, due to induction, a voltage is generated in its antenna coil and this voltage serves as a power for the microchip.

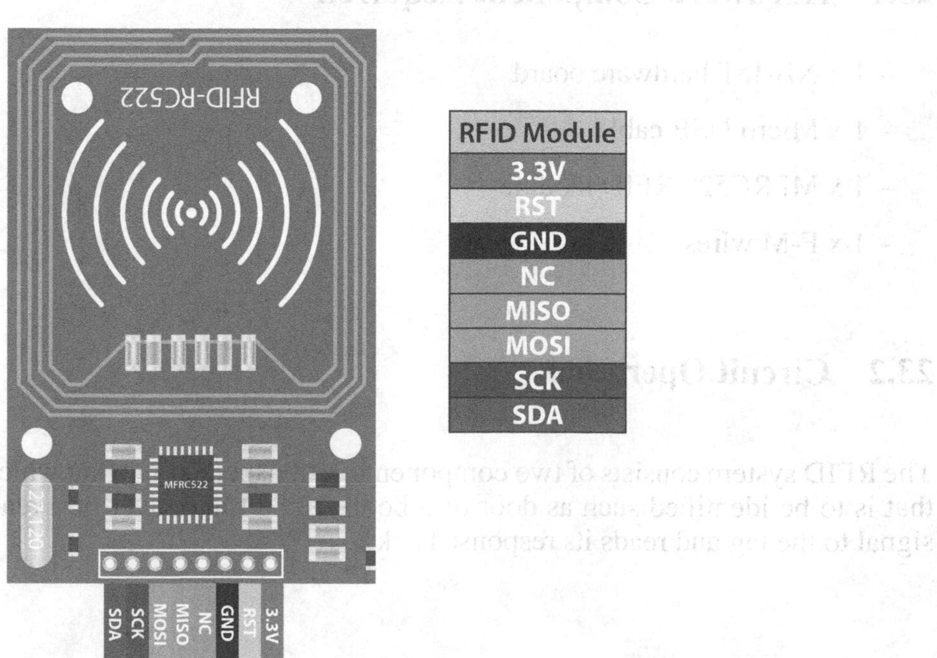

Figure 23.2: RFID Reader/Writer.

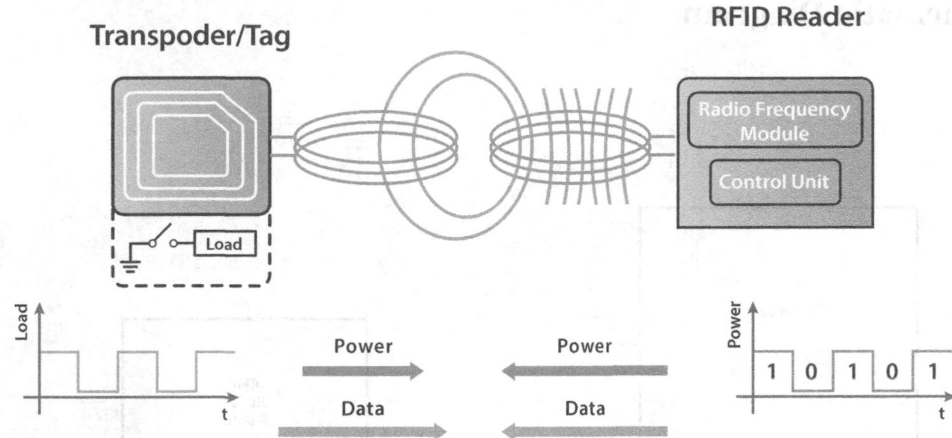

Figure 23.3: RFID Communication between the Tag and Reader.

When the tag is powered, it can extract the transmitted message coming from the reader, and for sending message back to the reader, it uses a technique called load manipulation. Switching on and off a load at the antenna of the tag affects the power consumption of the reader antenna which can be measured as voltage drop. The changes in the voltage are captured as ones and zeros and that is how the data is transferred from the tag to the reader.

The MFRC522 is an RFID highly integrated reader and writer for RF communication at 13.56 MHz at range of 10 cm (4 inches). The MFRC522 reader supports MIFARE® protocol. The MFRC522 internal transmitter drives a reader/writer antenna designed to communicate with an MIFARE® capable cards and tags without additional active circuitry. The receiver part provides a robust and efficient implementation of a demodulation and decoding circuitry for signals from MIFARE® compatible cards. The digital part handles the complete framing and error detection (Parity & CRC). The MFRC522 supports contactless communication using MIFARE higher transfer speeds up to 848 Kbps in both directions.

The RFID module uses SPI interface to communicate with the NB board. The figure below shows how the RFID system is communicating with a tag or a card.

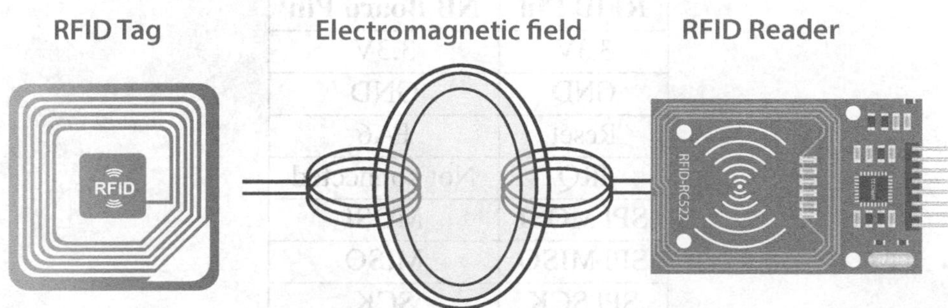

Figure 23.4: Communication between the Tag and Reader.

23.3 Schematic Diagram

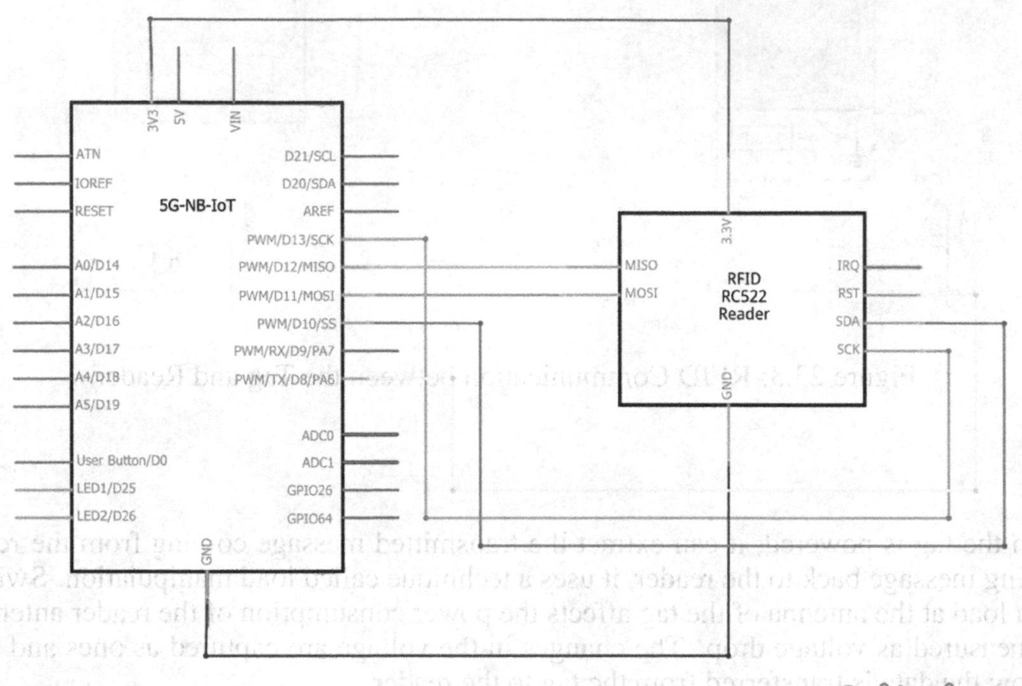

Figure 23.5: Schematic Diagram for the RFID.

23.4 Breadboard Diagram

The RFID uses SPI to communicate with the NB board. The following table shows how the RFID pins are connected to the pins on the NB board.

Table 23.1: RFID Pins Mapping.

RFID Pin	NB Board Pin
3.3V	3.3V
GND	GND
Reset	PA6
IRQ	Not connected
SPI MOSI	MOSI
SPI MISO	MISO
SPI SCK	SCK
SDA	SS

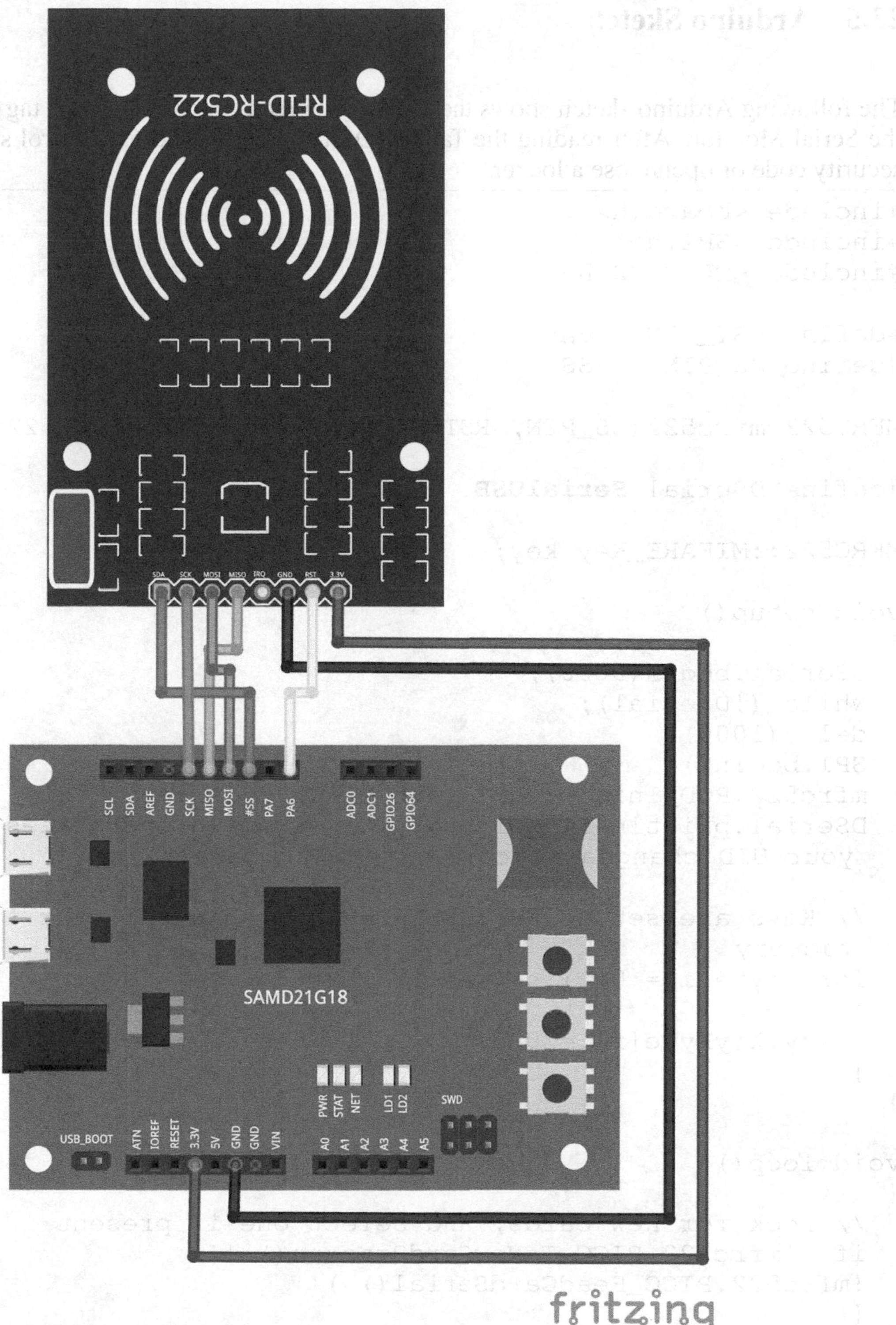

Figure 23.6: Breadboard Diagram for the RFID.

23.5 Arduino Sketch

The following Arduino sketch shows the code which reads the RFID on the tag and displays it on the Serial Monitor. After reading the Tag RFID, it can control access control such as open/close security code or open/close a locker.

```
#include <board.h>
#include <SPI.h>
#include <MFRC522.h>

#define RST_PIN   PA6
#define SS_PIN    SS

MFRC522 mfrc522(SS_PIN, RST_PIN);   // Create MFRC522 instance

#define DSerial SerialUSB

MFRC522::MIFARE_Key key;

void setup()
{
  DSerial.begin(9600);
  while (!DSerial);
  delay(1000);
  SPI.begin();          // Init SPI bus
  mfrc522.PCD_Init();   // Init MFRC522 card
  DSerial.println(F("Warning: this example overwrites the UID of
   your UID changeable card, use with care!"));

  // Keys are set to FFFFFFFFFFFFh at chip delivery from the
   factory
  for (byte i = 0; i < 6; i++)
  {
    key.keyByte[i] = 0xFF;
  }
}

void loop()
{
  // Look for new cards, and select one if present
  if (!mfrc522.PICC_IsNewCardPresent() ||
  !mfrc522.PICC_ReadCardSerial() )
  {
    delay(50);
    return;
  }

  // Dump UID
```

```
  DSerial.print(F("Card UID:"));
  for (byte i = 0; i < mfrc522.uid.size; i++)
  {
    DSerial.print(mfrc522.uid.uidByte[i] < 0x10 ? " 0" : " ");
    DSerial.print(mfrc522.uid.uidByte[i], HEX);
  }
  DSerial.println();

  // Dump PICC type
  MFRC522::PICC_Type piccType = mfrc522.PICC_GetType(mfrc522.uid.
   sak);
  DSerial.print(F("PICC type: "));
  DSerial.print(mfrc522.PICC_GetTypeName(piccType));
  DSerial.print(F(" (SAK "));
  DSerial.print(mfrc522.uid.sak);
  DSerial.print(")\r\n");
  DSerial.println();

  while (true) {}
}
```

Listing 23.1: Arduino Sketch for RFID Module.

The output from the Serial Monitor is shown below and displays the card identification (UID).

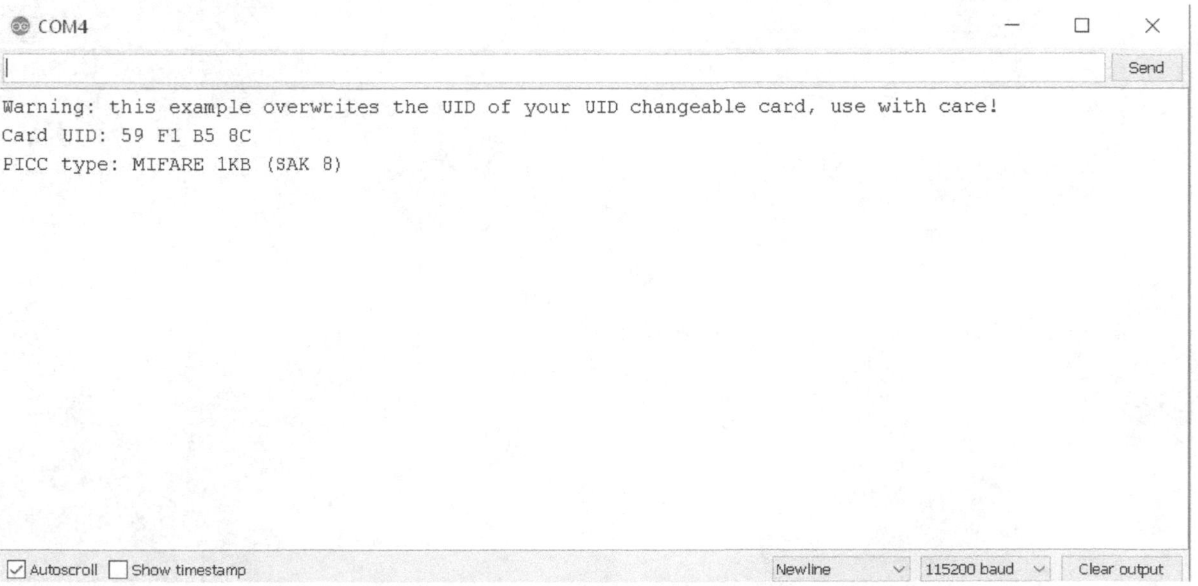

Figure 23.7: Serial Monitor Output for the RFID.

Chapter 24

Eight LED and Shift Register

In this chapter, you will control eight LEDs without the need of eight pins to use on the NB board. If each of the eight LEDs is to be connected to a separate pin, it needs eight separate pins which is inefficient use of the hardware resources. The chipset, 74HC595, which is a serial to parallel converter can be used. Using this chip, the eight LEDs can be controlled using three pins on the NB board.

24.1 Hardware Component Required

- 1 x NB-IoT hardware board
- 1 x Micro USB cable
- 8 x LEDs
- 8 x 220Ω resistors
- 1 x 74HC595 IC
- 1 x F-M wires
- 1 x M-M wires

24.2 Circuit Operation

The chip, 74HC595, is a shift register. This chip has eight outputs and three inputs that are used to feed data into it one bit at a time. This chip makes it a little slower to drive the LEDs since bits inputs to the chip need to be serialized (i.e., fed one bit by one bit). However, it is still fast and fast enough for many applications.

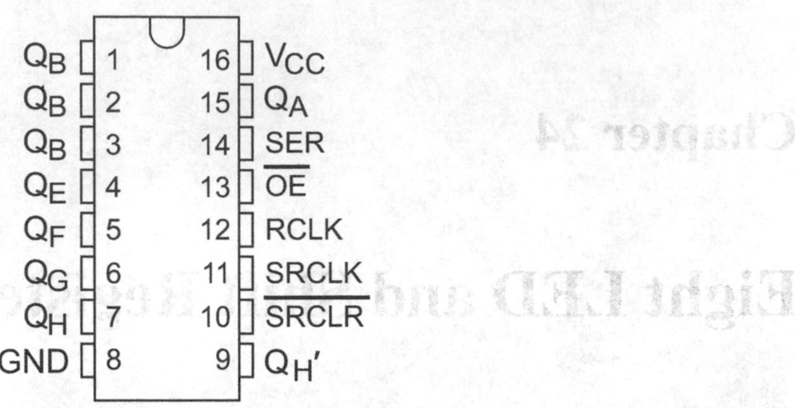

Figure 24.1: 74HC595 Chip.

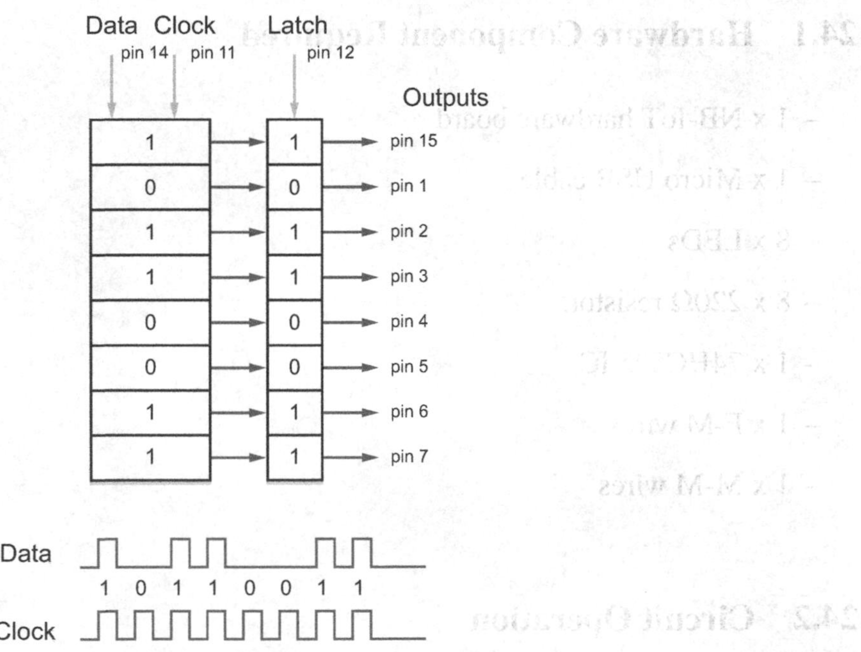

Figure 24.2: Block Diagrams of the Shift Register.

A shift register is a type of hardware logic that stores the bit value (either binary 1 or 0), shift it to the next register and store it. To store a binary 1 or 0 into each register, data is fed into the 74HC595 using the (Data) and (Clock) pins of the chip.

The clock pin needs to receive eight clocks (or pulses). At each clock, if the data pin is high, then a binary 1 gets pushed into the shift register; otherwise, a binary 0 is pushed. When all eight pulses have been received, enabling the (Latch) pin (also called storage pin) copies those eight values to the latch register. This is necessary as the values in the latch register are to stay permanently thus controlling the LEDs.

The chip also has an output enable (OE) pin, which is used to enable or disable the outputs all at once. This pin is active low, so we connect it to GND.

24.3 Schematic Diagram

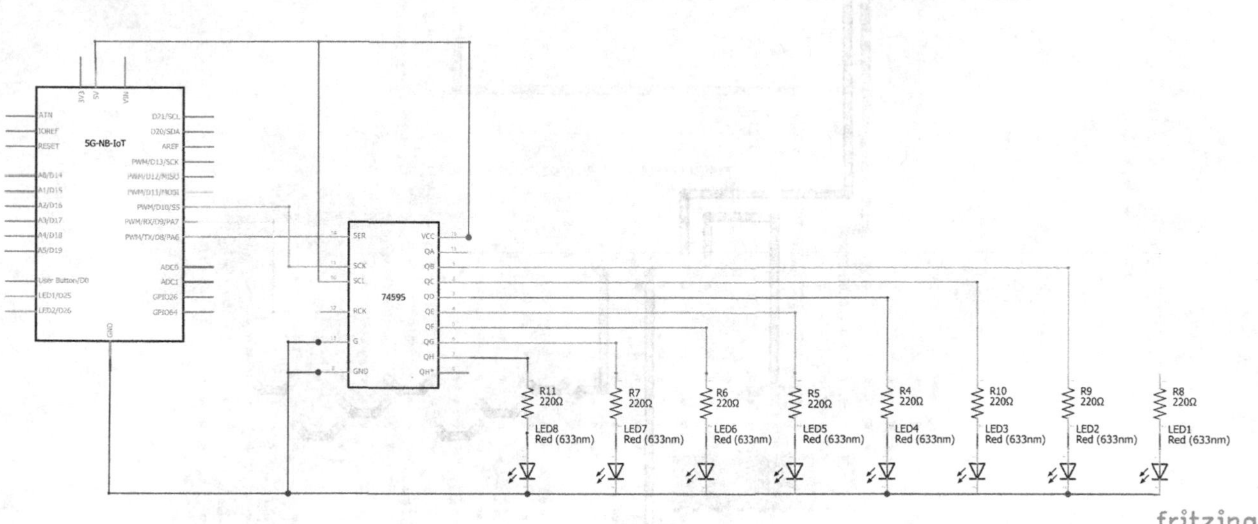

Figure 24.3: Schematic Diagram of the LEDs and Shift Register.

24.4 Breadboard Diagram

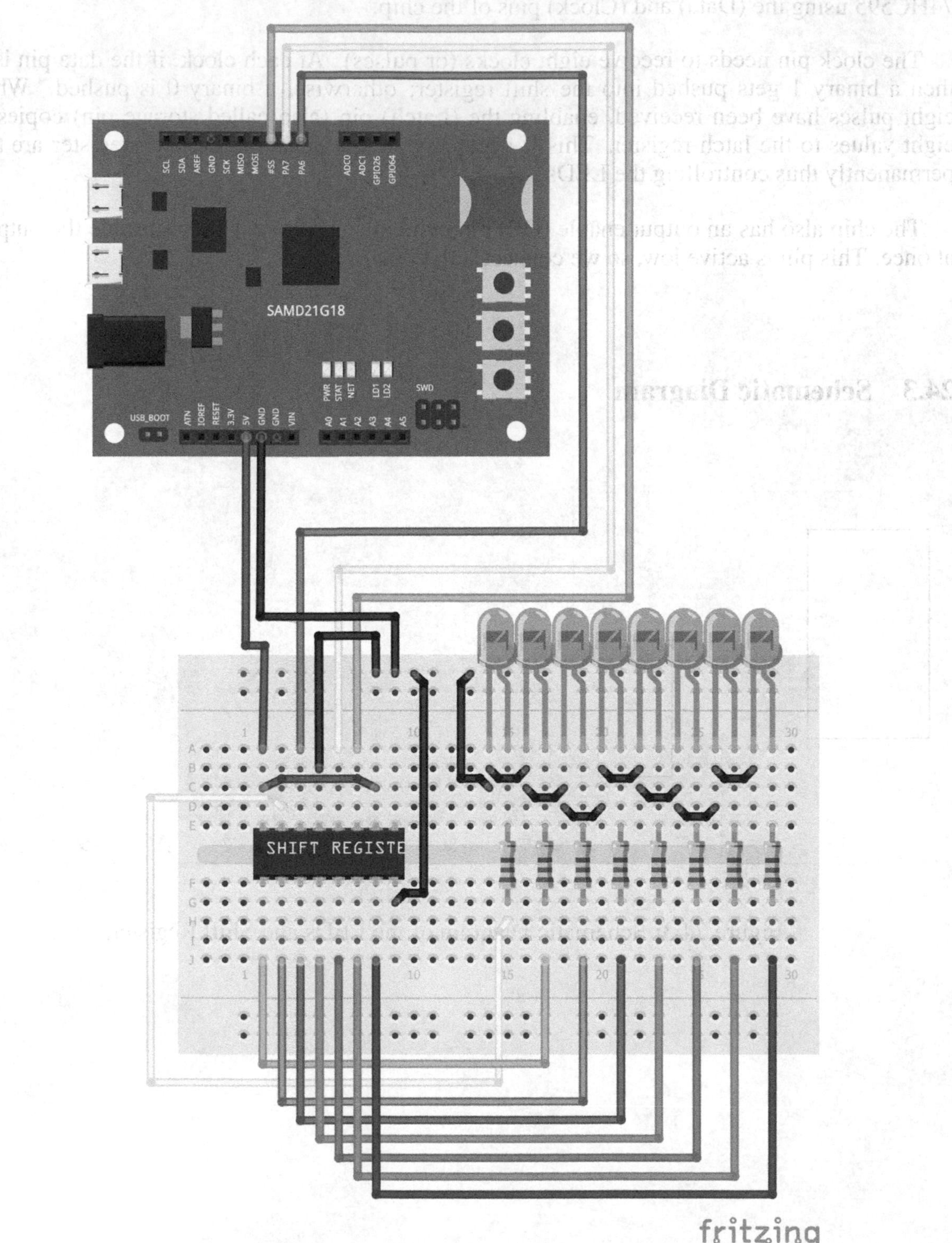

Figure 24.4: Breadboard Diagram of the LEDs and Shift Register.

As there are eight LEDs and eight resistors to connect. You can start by putting the 74HC595 chip in first and then connect LEDs and resistors to it.

Next, place the LEDs on the breadboard. Attach the jumper leads as shown above. Pin 8 of the IC is connected to the GND column of the breadboard.

24.5 Arduino Sketch

Load up the sketch into the NB board. Each LED lights in turn until all the LEDs are on, and then they all go off and this cycle keep repeating.

In the Arduino sketch, the three pins that are going to be used are defined The pins on the NB board, PA7, PA6, and SS are connected to the latch, data, and clock pins on the 74HC595chip respectively.

A variable called **leds** is defined. This is used to hold the pattern of which LEDs are currently turned on or off. A byte is a type of data which represents a number using eight bits. Each bit can be either on or off, so this is perfect for keeping track of which of the eight LEDs are on or off.

The setup() function sets the three pins used to be digital outputs. In the loop() function, it initially turns all the LEDs off, by giving the variable **leds** the value 0. It then calls **updateShiftRegister()** that sends the **leds** pattern to the shift register so that all the LEDs are turned off. The loop() function pauses for 100 ms and then begins to count from 0 to 7. Each time, it uses the Arduino function bitSet() to set the bit that controls that LED in the variable **leds**. It then also calls **updateShiftRegister()** so that the LEDs are updated to reflect what is in the variable **leds**. There is 100 ms delay until the next LED is turned on.

The function **updateShiftRegister()** sets the **latchPin** to low, then calls the shiftOut() before putting the **latchPin** high again. This takes four parameters, the first two are the pins to use for (Data) and (Clock) respectively.

The third parameter specifies which end of the data you want to start at. You are going to start with the right most bit, which is referred to as the Least Significant Bit (LSB). The last parameter is the actual data to be shifted into the shift register, which in this case is **leds**.

If any of the LED is to be turned off rather than on, the Arduino function bitClear() can be used with the **leds** variable. This sets that bit of **leds** to be 0 and then follow it with a call to **updateShiftRegister()** to update the actual LEDs.

```
#include <board.h>

int tDelay = 100;
int latchPin = PA7;
int clockPin = SS;
int dataPin = PA6;

byte leds = 0;

void updateShiftRegister()
{
  digitalWrite(latchPin, LOW);
  shiftOut(dataPin, clockPin, LSBFIRST, leds);
  digitalWrite(latchPin, HIGH);
}

void setup()
{
  pinMode(latchPin, OUTPUT);
  pinMode(dataPin, OUTPUT);
  pinMode(clockPin, OUTPUT);
}

void loop()
{
  leds = 0;
  updateShiftRegister();
  delay(tDelay);
  for (int i = 0; i < 8; i++)
  {
    bitSet(leds, i);
    updateShiftRegister();
    delay(tDelay);
  }
}
```

Listing 24.1: Arduino Sketch for LEDs and Shift Register.

24.6 Arduino Sketch Using the Serial Monitor

You can also modify the Arduino sketch to control eight LEDs from your computer using the Arduino IDE Serial Monitor. The Serial Monitor is the tether between the computer and the NB board. Serial monitor lets you send and receive text messages, handy for debugging and controlling the hardware board from the keyboard. You can send commands from your computer to turn on LEDs.

In the loop() function, it reads user input from the Serial Monitor and turns on the corresponding LED accordingly. If the user enters **x** in the Serial Monitor, then all LEDs are cleared. Load up the sketch below. Based on the LED number provided in the Serial Monitor, it turns on that LED. If you enter **x**, it turns off all LEDs

```
#include <board.h>

#define DSerial SerialUSB

int latchPin = PA7;
int clockPin = SS;
int dataPin = PA6;

byte leds = 0;
void updateShiftRegister()
{
  digitalWrite(latchPin, LOW);
  shiftOut(dataPin, clockPin, LSBFIRST, leds);
  digitalWrite(latchPin, HIGH);
}
void setup()
{
  pinMode(latchPin, OUTPUT);
  pinMode(dataPin, OUTPUT);
  pinMode(clockPin, OUTPUT);
  updateShiftRegister();

  DSerial.begin(115200);
  while (DSerial.read() >= 0);
  DSerial.println("Enter LED Number 0 to 7 or 'x' to clear");
}

void loop()
{
  if (DSerial.available())
  {
    char ch = DSerial.read();
    if (ch >= '0' && ch <= '7')
    {
      int led = ch - '0';
      bitSet(leds, led);
      updateShiftRegister();
      DSerial.print("Turned on LED ");
      DSerial.println(led);
    }
    if (ch == 'x')
```

```
    {
      leds = 0;
      updateShiftRegister();
      DSerial.println("Cleared");
    }
  }
}
```

Listing 24.2: Arduino Sketch for the LEDs and Shift Register.

After this sketch is uploaded to the NB board, launch the Serial Monitor.

The message "Enter LED Number 0 to 7 or 'x' to clear" has been sent by the hardware board. It is telling what command you can send to the NB board: either send the **x** (to turn all the LEDs off) or the number of the LED you want to turn on (where 0 is the bottom LED, 1 is the next one up, all the way to 7 for the top LED). Try typing any number from 0 to 7 or **x** into the top area of the Serial Monitor and click the **Send** button, and you will get the following Window.

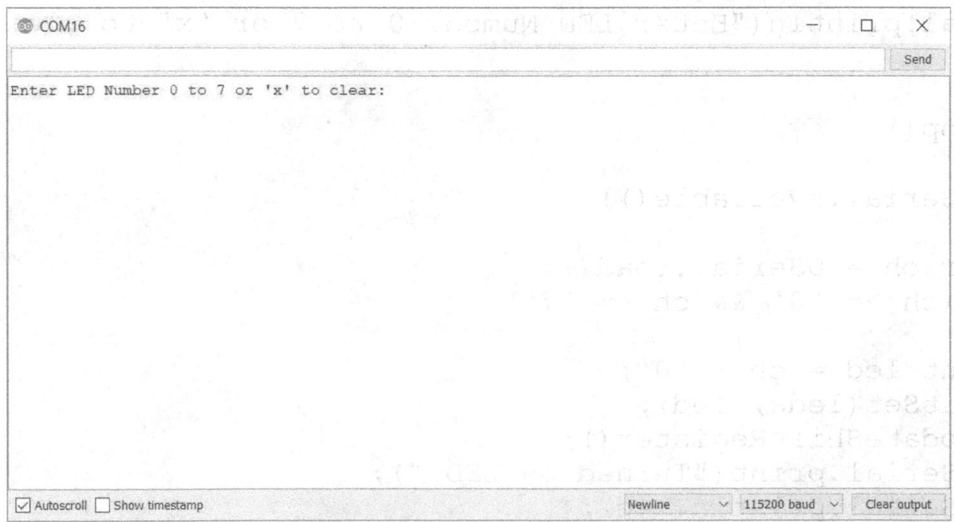

Figure 24.5: Serial Monitor Output for Controlling LEDs and Shift Register.

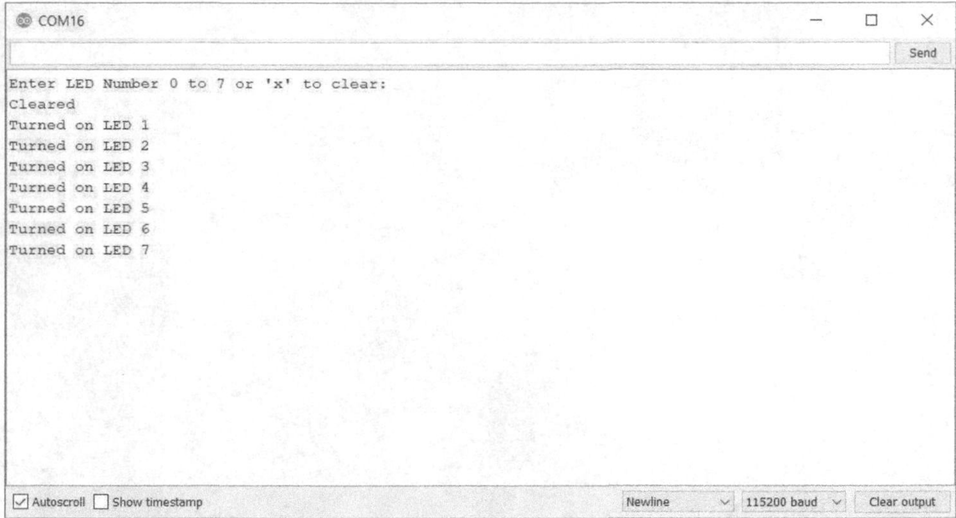

Figure 24.6: Serial Monitor Output When Clearing and Turning on LEDs.

Chapter 25

Seven-Segment Display

In this chapter, you will use a seven-segment (7-segment) display. The seven-segment display is a small display that can display one digit or one character.

25.1 Hardware Component Required

- 1 x NB-IoT hardware board
- 1 x Micro USB cable
- 1 x 74HC595 IC
- 1 x 1 Digit 7-segment display
- 8 x 220Ω resistors
- 1 x F-M wires
- 1 x M-M wires

25.2 Circuit Operation

Below is the seven-segment pin diagram. It consists of 7-segments and one Decimal Point (DP). They are all LEDs which when they are illuminated in certain pattern, it displays a numeric digit or a single character

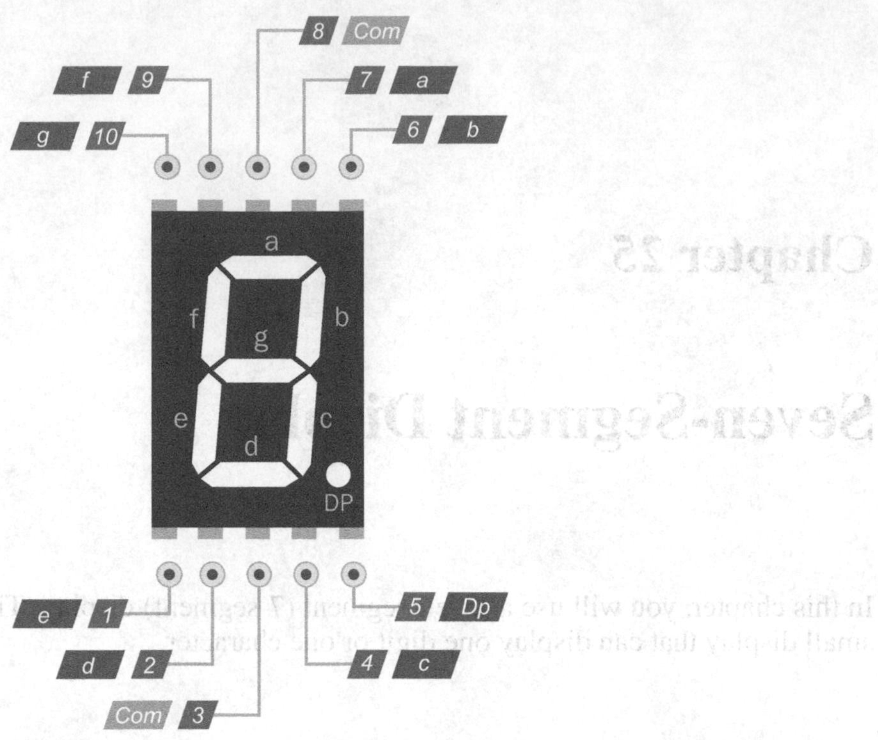

Figure 25.1: 7-Segement Display.

The following table shows the binary values that needs to apply to each pin to display a numeric digit. For example, to display digit zero, binary one is to be applied to all pins except pin g. The pin Dp can be used if a decimal point needs to be displayed.

Table 25.1: Digit representation on a 7-Segement.

Displayed Digit	Dp	a	b	c	d	E	f	g
0	0	1	1	1	1	1	1	0
1	0	0	1	1	0	0	0	0
2	0	1	1	0	1	1	0	1
3	0	1	1	1	1	0	0	1
4	0	0	1	1	0	0	1	1
5	0	1	0	1	1	0	1	1
6	0	1	0	1	1	1	1	1
7	0	1	1	1	0	0	0	0
8	0	1	1	1	1	1	1	1
9	0	1	1	1	1	0	1	1

25.3 Schematic Diagram

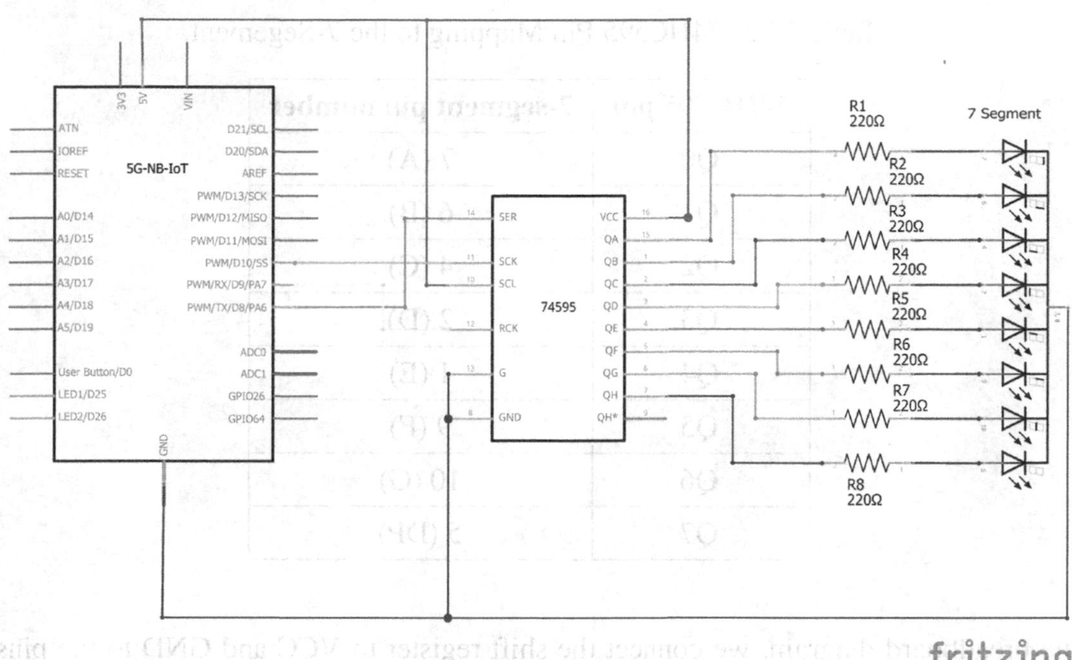

Figure 25.2: Schematic Diagram for 7-Segment.

25.4 Breadboard Diagram

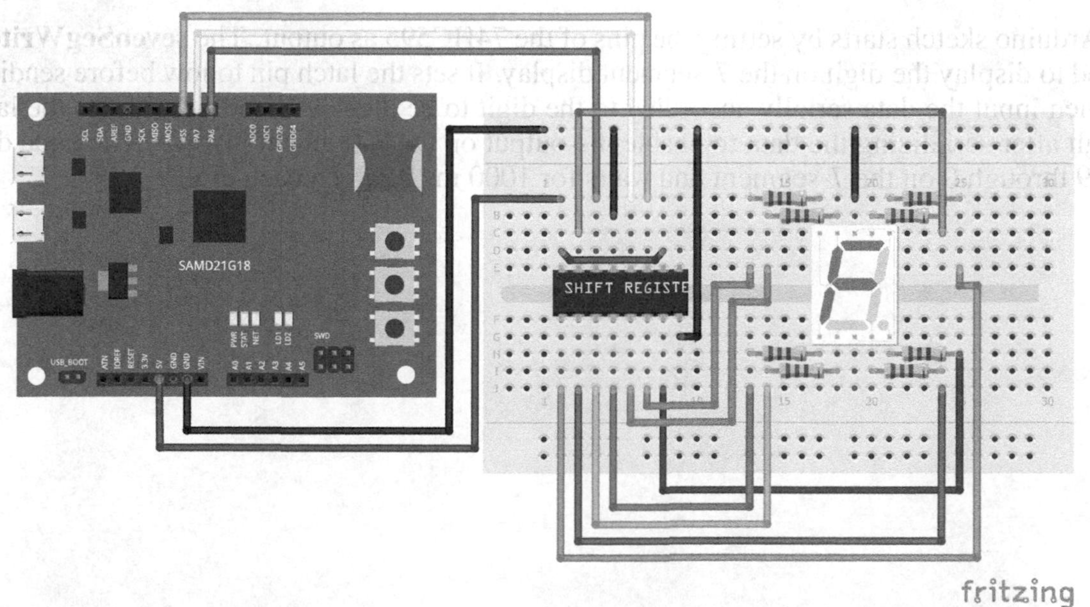

Figure 25.3: Breadboard Diagram for 7-Segment.

The shift register, 74HC595, is going to be used to control the pins of the 7-segment. The following table shows the 74HC595 pin number connected to the corresponding pin of the 7-segment.

Table 25.2: 74HC595 Pin Mapping to the 7-Segement.

74HC595 pin	7-segment pin number
Q0	7 (A)
Q1	6 (B)
Q2	4 (C)
Q3	2 (D)
Q4	1 (E)
Q5	9 (F)
Q6	10 (G)
Q7	5 (DP)

In the breadboard diagram, we connect the shift register to VCC and GND to the pins on the NB board. We use pins PA7, PA6, and SS on the hardware to connect to latch, data, and clock pins of the 74HC595.

25.5 Arduino Sketch

The Arduino sketch starts by setting the pins of the 74HC595 as output. The **sevenSegWrite()** API is used to display the digit on the 7-segment display. It sets the latch pin to low before sending data and then input the data serially according to the digit to be displayed and finally sets the latch pin to high after serializing the data to enable the output on the 7-segment display. The code displays digit 9 through 0 on the 7-segment and waits for 1000 ms between each digit.

```
#include <board.h>

byte seven_seg_digits[10] =
{
    B11111100,  // = 0
    B01100000,  // = 1
    B11011010,  // = 2
    B11110010,  // = 3
    B01100110,  // = 4
    B10110110,  // = 5
    B10111110,  // = 6
    B11100000,  // = 7
    B11111110,  // = 8
    B11100110   // = 9
};

int latchPin = PA7;
int clockPin = SS;
int dataPin = PA6;

void setup()
{
  // Set latchPin, clockPin, dataPin as output
  pinMode(latchPin, OUTPUT);
  pinMode(clockPin, OUTPUT);
  pinMode(dataPin, OUTPUT);
}

void sevenSegWrite(byte digit)
{
  digitalWrite(latchPin, LOW);
  shiftOut(dataPin, clockPin, LSBFIRST, seven_seg_digits[digit]);
  digitalWrite(latchPin, HIGH);
}

void loop()
{
  // Count from 9 to 0
  for (byte digit = 10; digit > 0; --digit)
  {
    delay(1000);
    sevenSegWrite(digit - 1);
  }
  delay(3000);
}
```

Listing 25.1: Arduino Sketch for 7-Segment Display.

Chapter 26

Real-Time Clock

In this chapter, you will learn how to use Real-Time Clock (RTC) module. It is a low-power chip. Address and data are transferred serially through an I^2C. DS1307 provides seconds, minutes, hours, day, date, month, and year information. Timekeeping operation continues while the part operates from the backup supply.

26.1 Hardware Component Required

- 1 x NB-IoT hardware board
- 1 x Micro USB cable
- 1 x DS1307 RTC (PCF8523 module)
- 1 x F-M wires

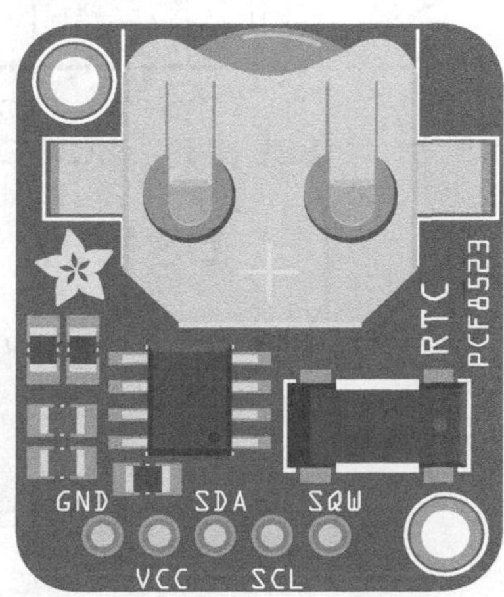

Figure 26.1: DS1307-based (PCF8523) Real-Time Clock.

26.2 Circuit Operation

DS1307 is a low cost, easy to handle, real-time clock chip works on a very small coin cell and lasts for years. DS1307 has a built-in power-sense circuit that detects power failures and automatically switches to the backup supply. Timekeeping operation continues while the part operates from the backup supply. You must have the 3V coin cell (lithium battery) installed for the RTC to work. In case of no coin cell, the battery pin (VBAT) should be pulled to low.

The DS1307 serial real-time clock is a low power, full Binary Coded Decimal (BCD) clock-/calendar plus 56 bytes of NV SRAM. Address and data are transferred serially through an I^2C, bidirectional bus. The 24-hour/12-hour format clock/calendar provides seconds, minutes, hours, day, date, month, and year information, including corrections for leap year. The clock operates in either the 24-hour or 12-hour format with AM/PM indicator.

The DS1307 has SCL (Serial Clock) and SDA (Serial Data) which is used to communicate to the NB board, both these pins have to be pulled high using a resistor. The I^2C can be powered by providing 3.3V on the VCC pin, when the power fails it will automatically switch to battery operated mode in which it will obtain power with lithium cell connected to pin VBAT and GND. The pins X1 and X2 are used to connect the crystal oscillator. Typically, a 32.7KHz Quartz crystal is used.

The SQuare Wave/Output Driver (SQW/OUT) pin outputs one of four square-wave frequencies (1Hz, 4kHz, 8kHz, 32kHz). The SQW/OUT pin is open drain and requires an external pullup resistor. SQW/OUT operates with either VCC or VBAT applied. The pullup voltage can be up to 5.5V regardless of the voltage on VCC. If not used, this pin can be left floating.

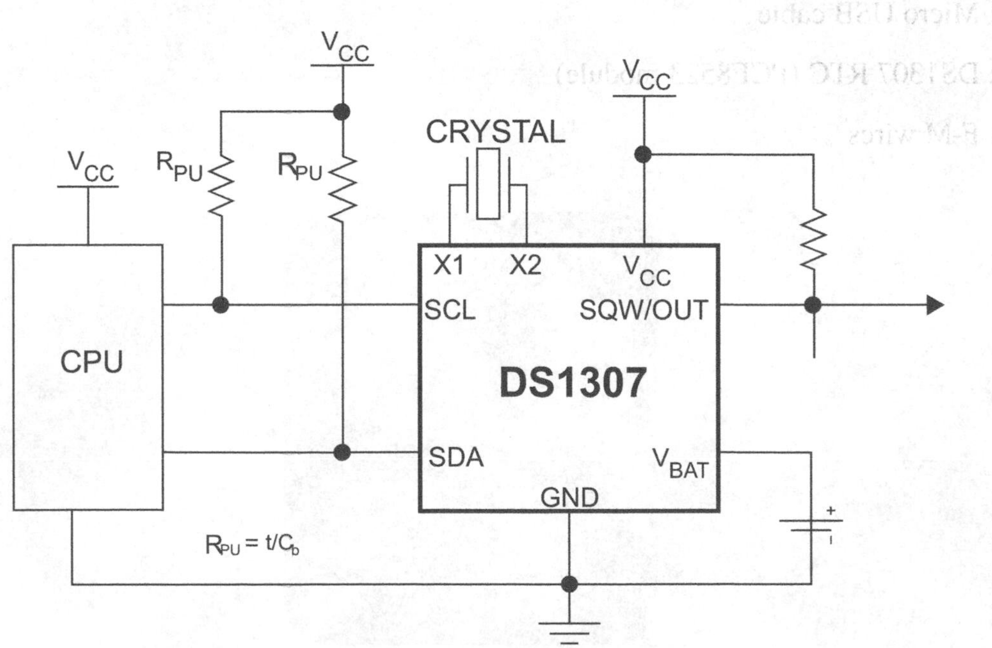

Figure 26.2: DS1307 Circuit Diagram.

26.3 Schematic Diagram

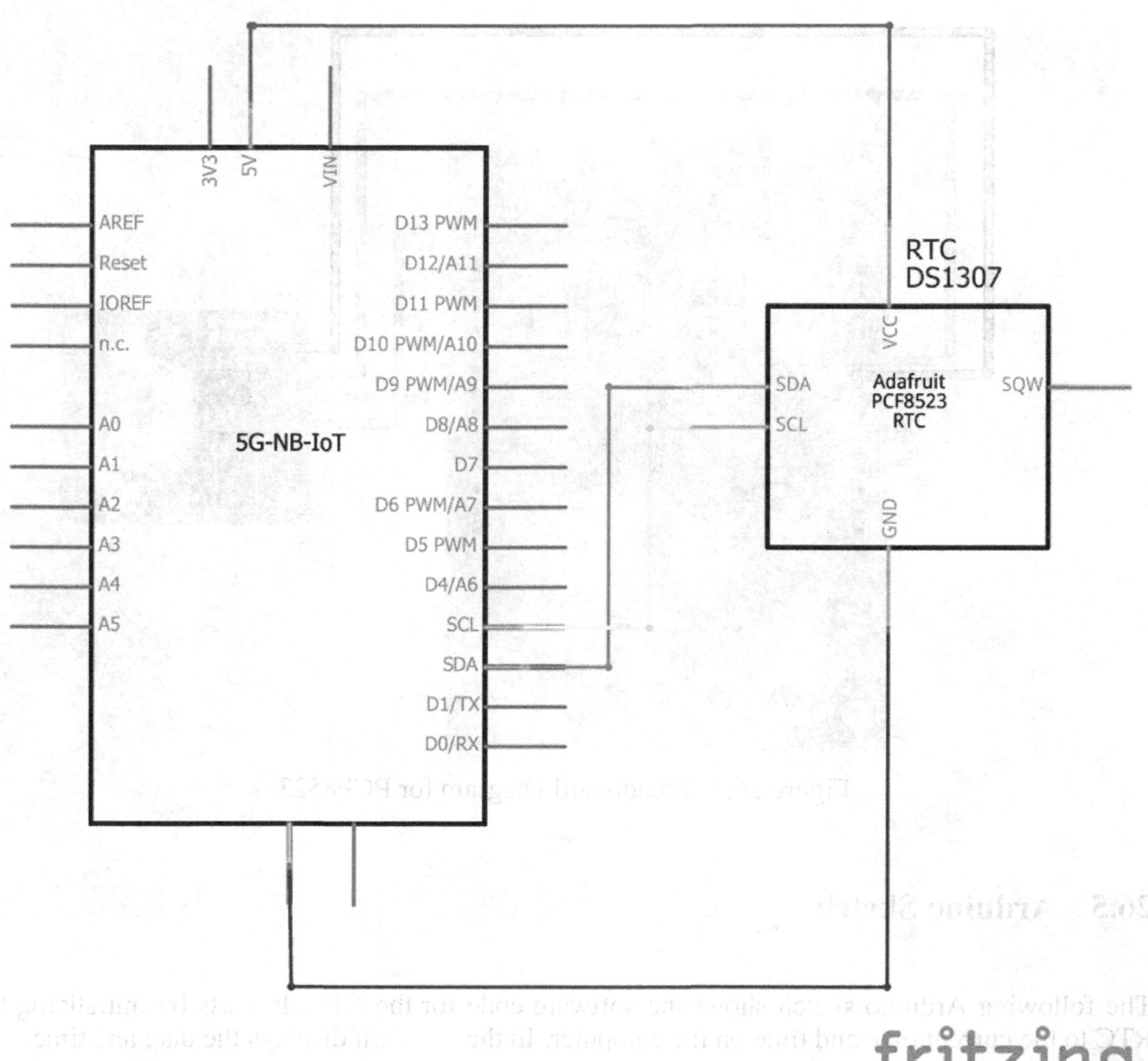

Figure 26.3: Schematic Diagram for PCF8523.

26.4 Breadboard Diagram

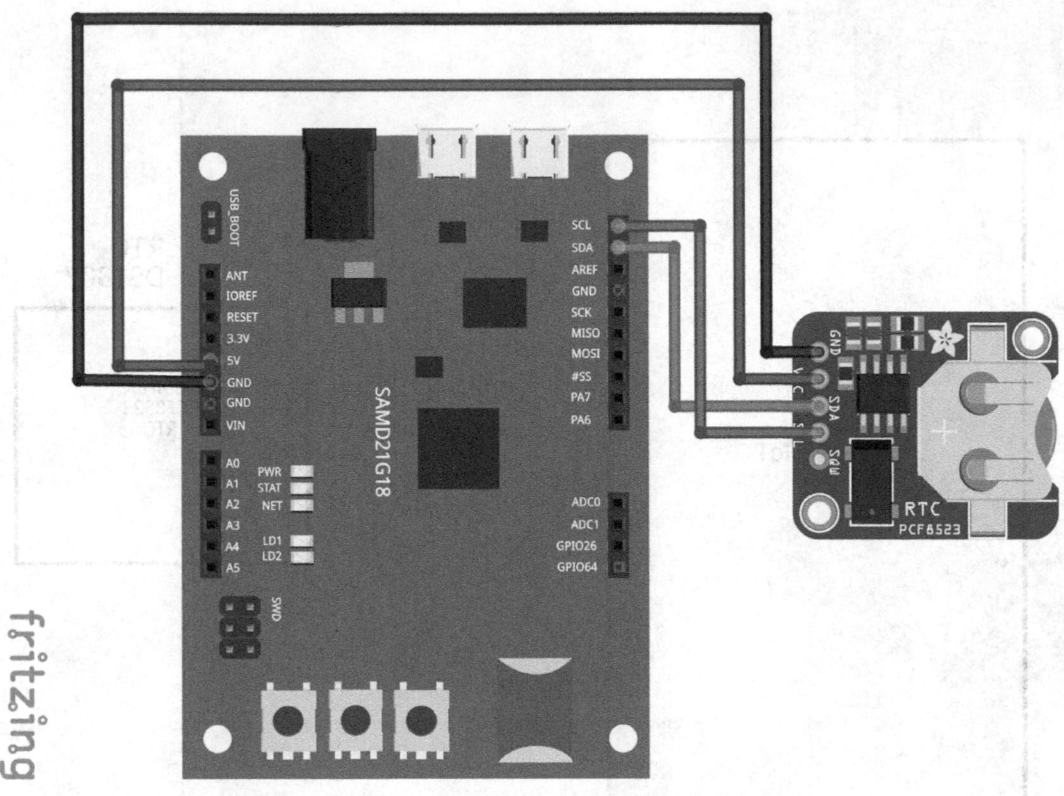

Figure 26.4: Breadboard Diagram for PCF8523.

26.5 Arduino Sketch

The following Arduino sketch shows the software code for the RTC. It starts by initializing the RTC to the current date and time on the computer. In the loop(), it displays the date and time.

```
#include <board.h>
#include <Wire.h>
#include <RtcDS1307.h>

#define DSerial SerialUSB

RtcDS1307<TwoWire> rtc(Wire);

void setup()
{
  DSerial.begin(9600);

  DSerial.println("Initialize RTC module");
```

```
  // Initialize RTC
  rtc.Begin();

  RtcDateTime compiled = RtcDateTime(__DATE__, __TIME__);
  printDateTime(compiled);
  DSerial.println();

  if (!rtc.IsDateTimeValid())
  {

    DSerial.println("RTC lost confidence in the DateTime!");
    rtc.SetDateTime(compiled);
  }
}
void loop()
{
  RtcDateTime now = rtc.GetDateTime();

  printDateTime(now);
  DSerial.println();

  if (!now.IsValid())
  {
    DSerial.println("RTC lost confidence in the DateTime!");
  }

  delay(1000); // One seconds
}

#define countof(a) (sizeof(a) / sizeof(a[0]))
void printDateTime(const RtcDateTime& dt)
{
  char datestring[20];

  snprintf_P(datestring,
  countof(datestring),
  PSTR("%02u/%02u/%04u %02u:%02u:%02u"),
  dt.Month(),
  dt.Day(),
  dt.Year(),
  dt.Hour(),
  dt.Minute(),
  dt.Second() );
  DSerial.print(datestring);
}
```

Listing 26.1: Arduino Sketch for Real-Time Clock.

On the Serial Monitor, it shows up the data and time stored in the RTC.

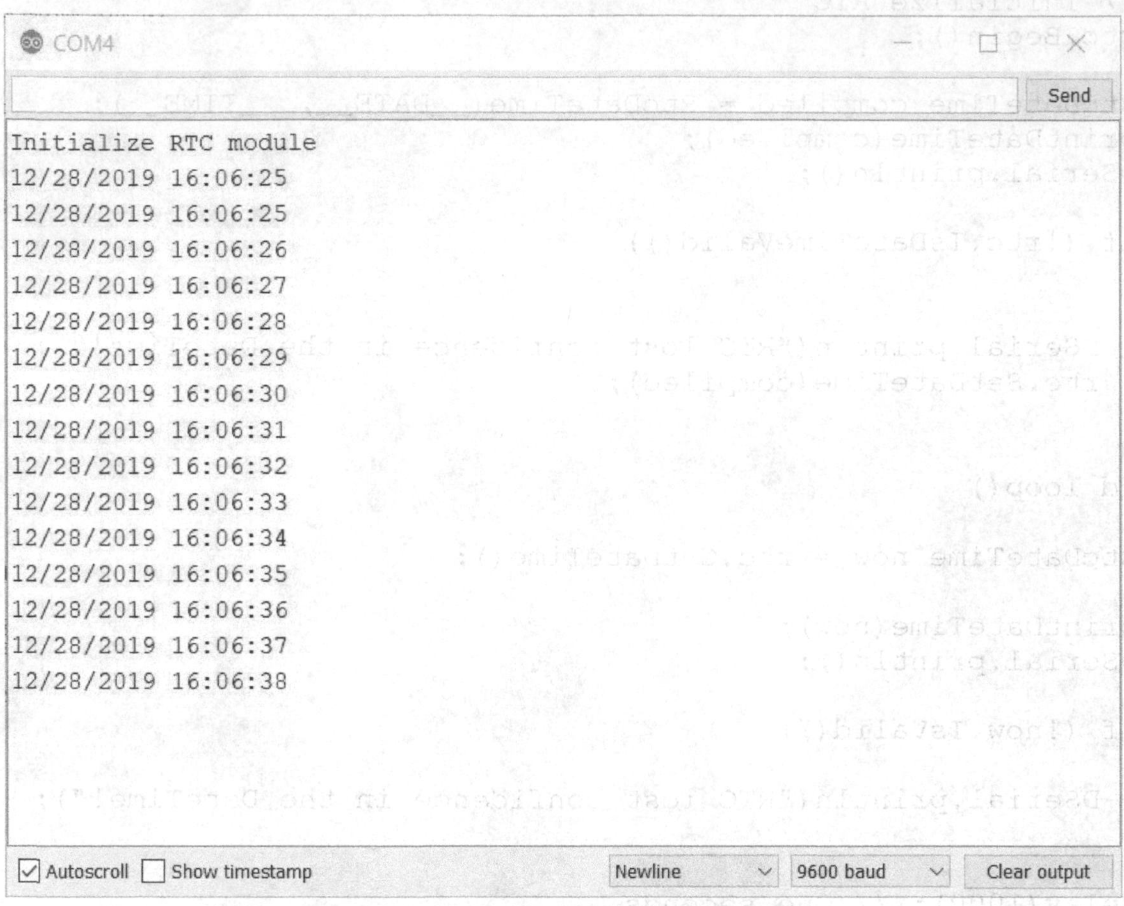

Figure 26.5: Serial Monitor Output for the Clock.

Part III

Sensors

Chapter 27

Tilt Sensor Switch

In this chapter, you will learn how to use a tilt sensor switch which is used to detect small angle of inclination.

27.1 Hardware Component Required

– 1 x NB-IoT hardware board

– 1 x Micro USB cable

– 1 x Tilt ball switch

– 1 x F-M wires

27.2 Circuit Operation

Tilt sensors (tilt ball switch) allow to detect orientation or inclination. They are small, inexpensive, low-power and easy-to-use. Their simplicity makes them popular for toys, gadgets and appliances. Sometimes, they are referred to as "mercury switches", "tilt switches" or "rolling ball sensors".

They are usually made up of cylindrical cavity with a conductive free conductive rolling ball inside. One end of the cavity has two conductive poles. When the sensor is oriented so that end is downwards, the mass rolls onto the poles and shorts them thus allowing current to flow. When the sensor is tilted, the ball does not touch the poles, the poles are open, and current does not flow.

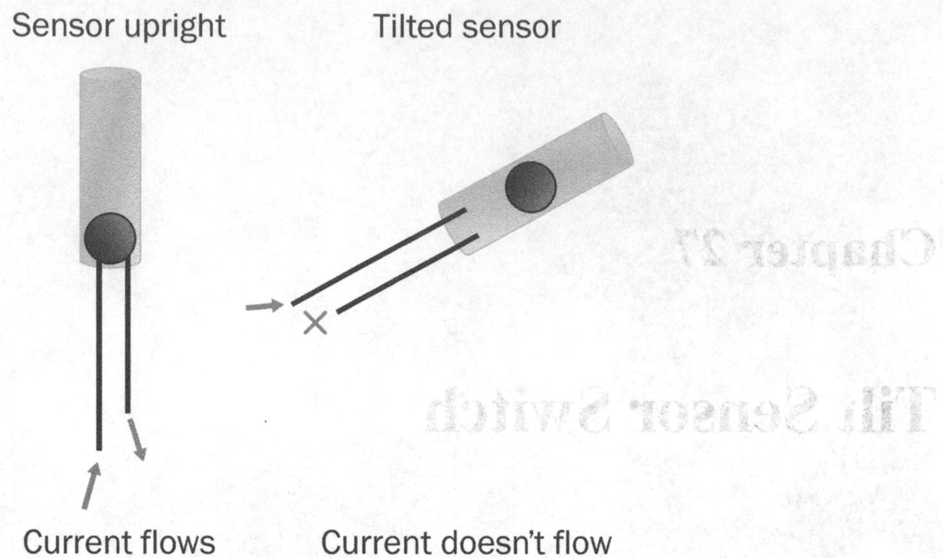

Figure 27.1: Tilt Sensor in Upright and Tilted Position.

27.3 Schematic Diagram

To use the tilt sensor, connect one pin to a digital pin (D8) on the NB board and ground to GND. You will also need to activate the NB board internal pull-up resistor for the digital pin to which the sensor is connected to. Otherwise, you should use a 10KΩ pull up resistor in the circuit.

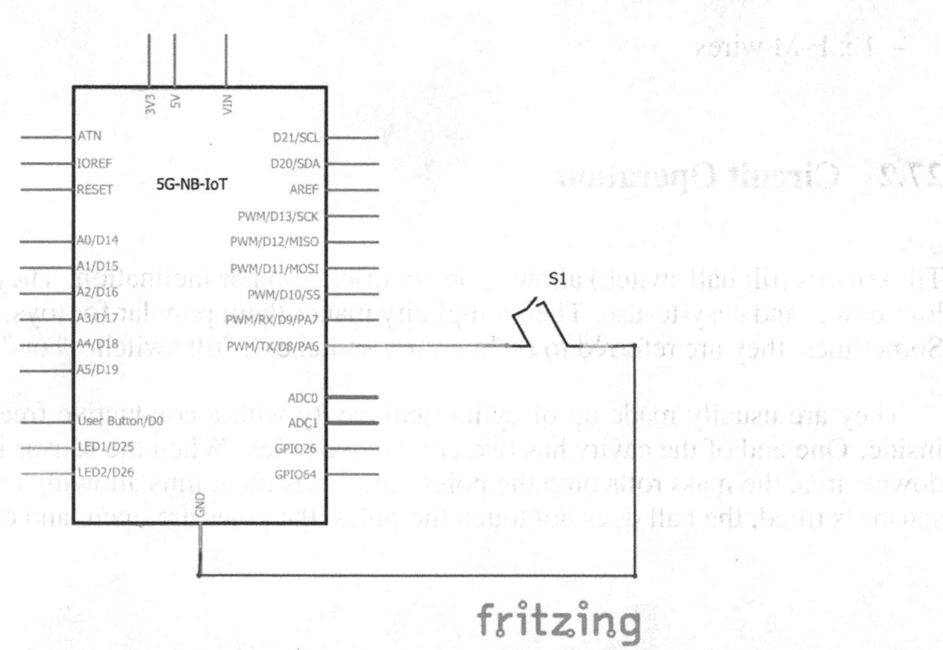

Figure 27.2: Schematic Diagram for Tilt Sensor.

27.4 Breadboard Diagram

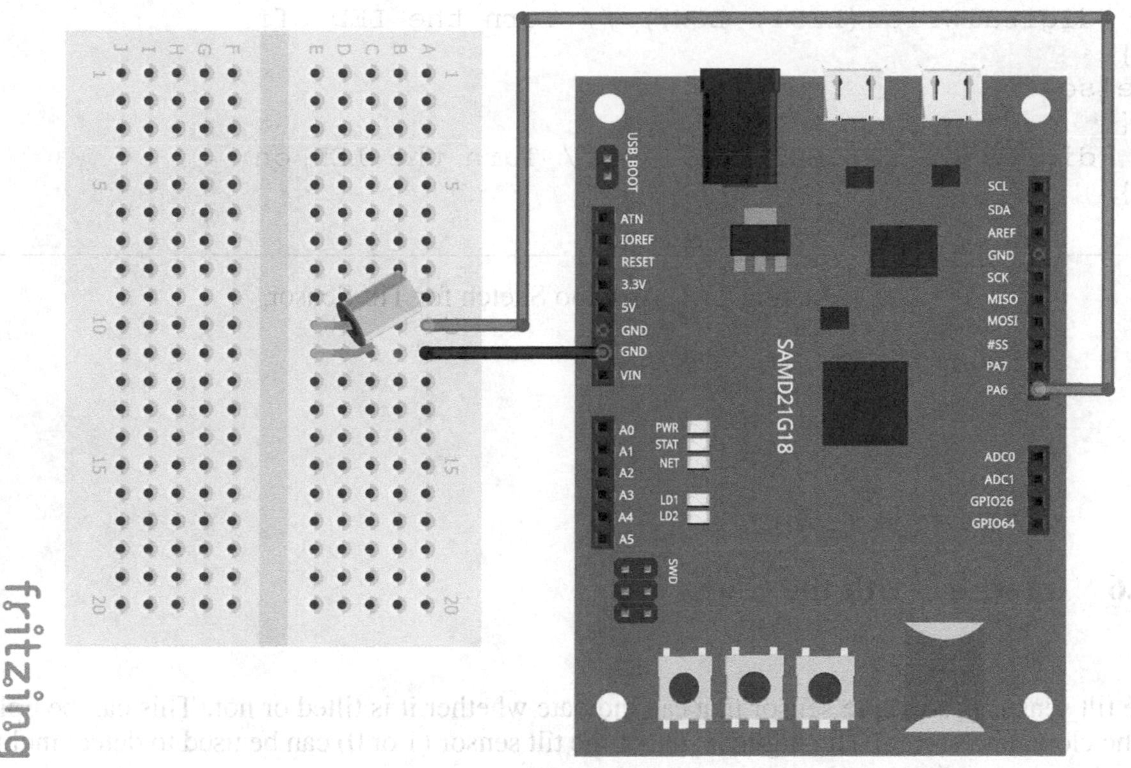

Figure 27.3: Breadboard Diagram for Tilt Sensor.

27.5 Arduino Sketch

In the Arduino sketch, an LED will be turned off if the sensor is upright and will be turned on if the sensor is tilted.

```
#include <board.h>

void setup()
{
  pinMode(LED1, OUTPUT); // Initialize LED1 as an output
  pinMode(PA6, INPUT);
  digitalWrite(PA6, HIGH);
}

void loop()
{
```

```
  int digitalVal = digitalRead(PA6);
  if (HIGH == digitalVal)
  {
    digitalWrite(LED1, LOW); // Turn the LED off
  }
  else
  {
    digitalWrite(LED1, HIGH); // Turn the LED on
  }
}
```

Listing 27.1: Arduino Sketch for Tilt Sensor.

27.6 Interface with the Cloud

The tilt sensor is a simple sensor that can indicate whether it is tilted or not. This can be uploaded to the cloud and stored. The digital value of the tilt sensor (1 or 0) can be used to detect inclination in gadgets or appliances.

To make the Arduino sketch uploads the readings to the AWS cloud, add the following Arduino lines of codes to the above sketch and use the MQTT codes as explained in Listing 7.1 and Listing 7.2. Use the following JSON format to upload the tilt sensor readings to the cloud.

```
// ...... Previous code lines go here

docInput["DeviceID"] = IMEI;
docInput["Timestamp"] = millis();
docInput["Device"] = "Tilt Sensor";
docInput["OpCode"] = "Read";
docInput["Value"] = digitalVal;
serializeJsonPretty(docInput, payload);

// ..... Next code lines go here
```

Listing 27.2: JSON document for Tilt Sensor.

Upload the final sketch to the NB board and notice the output on the Serial Monitor as shown below.

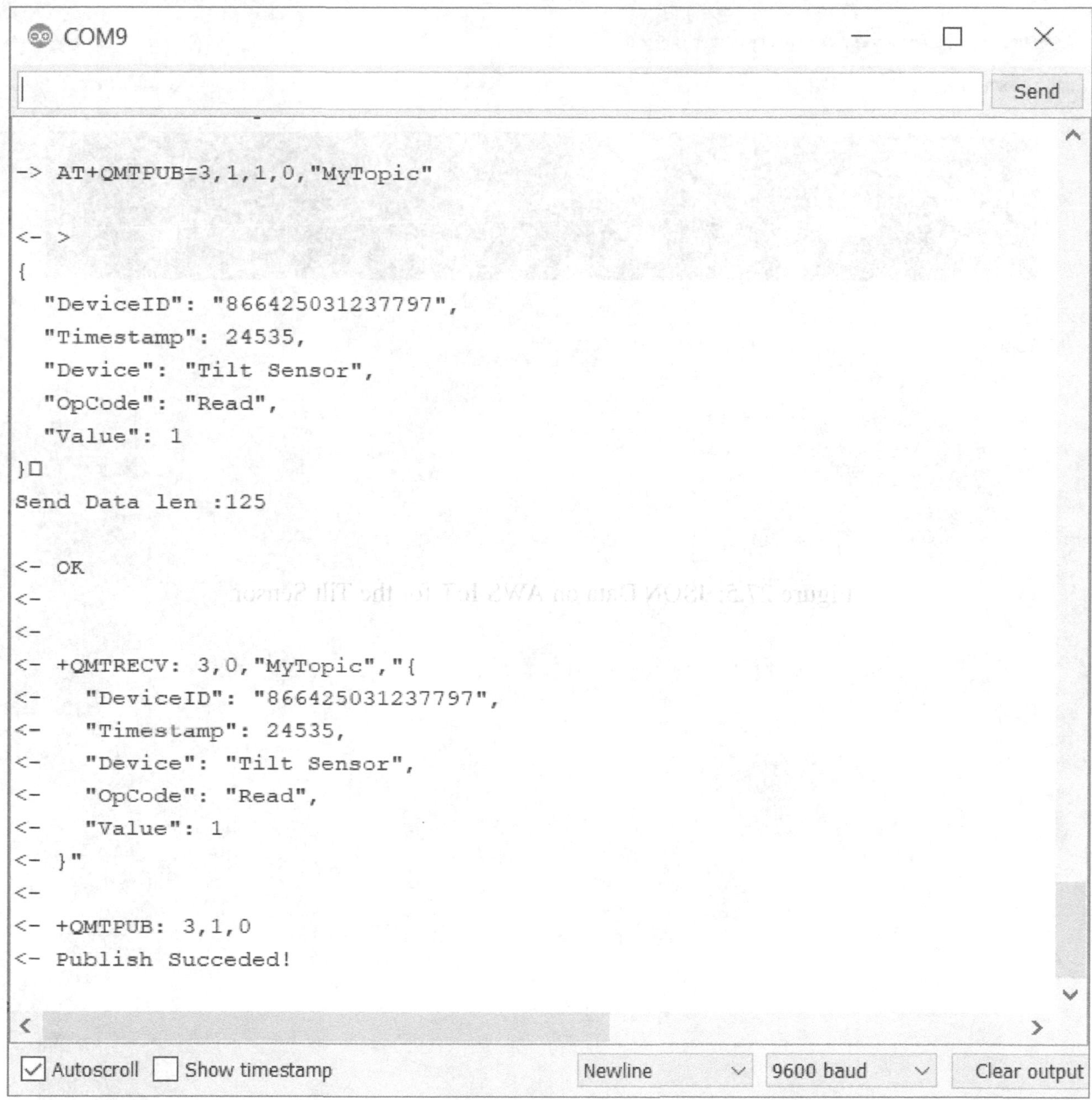

Figure 27.4: Serial Monitor Output for JSON Data Published by the Tilt Sensor.

Go to the AWS IoT, and the JSON data received at the cloud is displayed on AWS dashboard. The received data on the cloud can be stored in a database, analyzed, visualized, and used to control appliances.

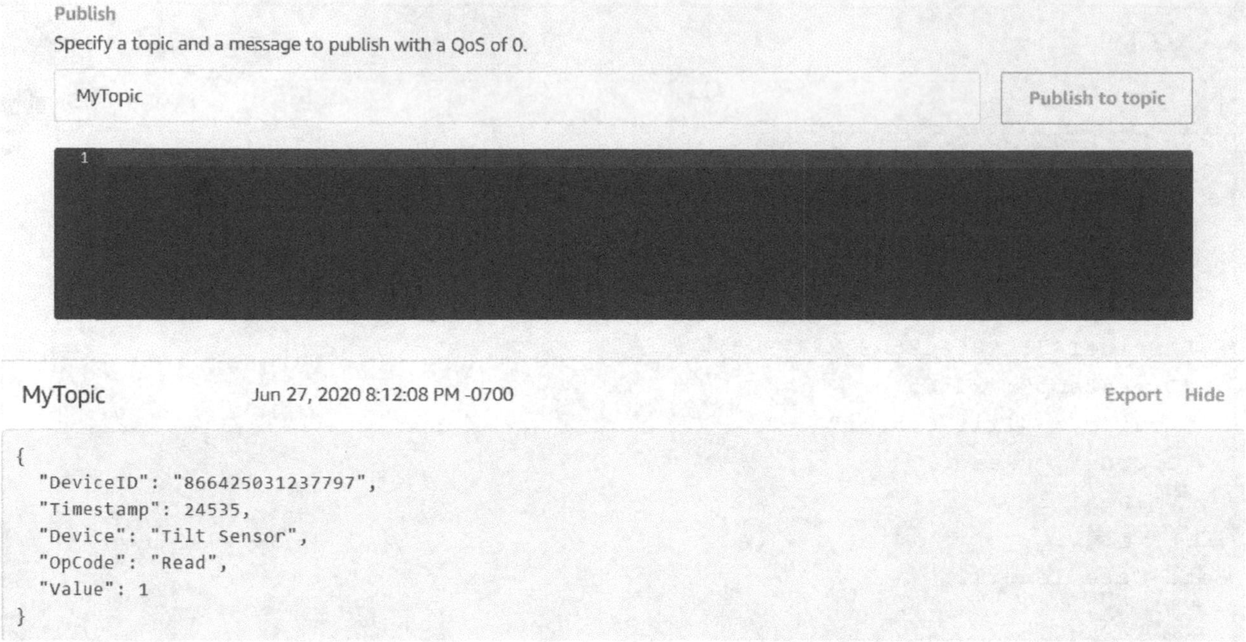

```
{
  "DeviceID": "866425031237797",
  "Timestamp": 24535,
  "Device": "Tilt Sensor",
  "OpCode": "Read",
  "Value": 1
}
```


Figure 27.5: JSON Data on AWS IoT for the Tilt Sensor.

Chapter 28

Photocell

In this chapter, you will learn how to measure light intensity using an analog Input. You will also use the level of light to control the number of LEDs to be lit.

28.1 Hardware Component Required

- 1 x NB-IoT hardware board
- 1 x Micro USB cable
- 8 x LEDs
- 8 x 220Ω resistors
- 1 x 1KΩ resistor
- 1 x 74HC595 IC
- 1 x Photoresistor (Photocell)
- 1 x F-M wires

28.2 Circuit Operation

The photocell used is of a type called a Light Dependent Resistor (LDR). Photocell acts as a variable resistor where the resistance changes in response to how much light is falling on them. The photocell used in this chapter has a resistance of about 50KΩ in near darkness and 500Ω in bright light. To convert this variable resistance into something we can measure on the analog input of the NB board, it needs to be converted into a voltage. The simplest way to do this is to combine it with a fixed resistor.

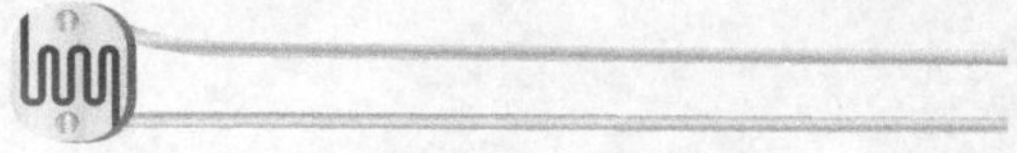

Figure 28.1: Photocell.

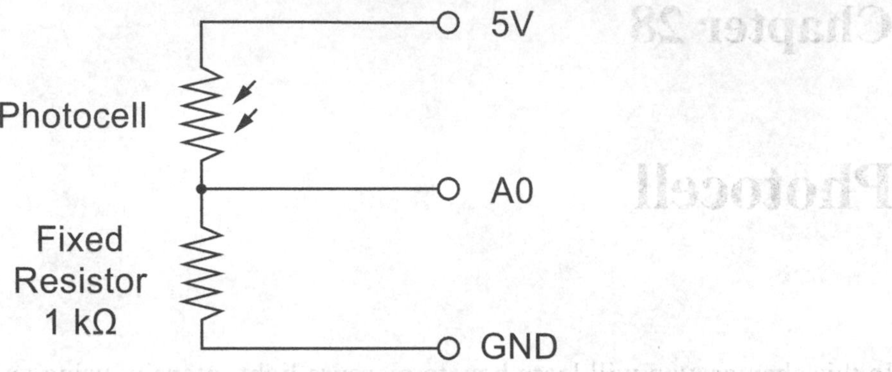

Figure 28.2: Photocell in a Voltage Divider.

The resistor and photocell together behave like a voltage divider or a knob. When the light is very bright, then the resistance of the photocell is very low compared with the fixed value resistor, and so it is as if the knob were turned to maximum. When the photocell is in dark, the resistance becomes greater than the fixed 1KΩ resistor and it is as if the knob were being turned towards GND. Upload the sketch given in the next section and cover the photocell with your hand, and then holding it near a light source to see how the photocell detects lights.

28.3 Schematic Diagram

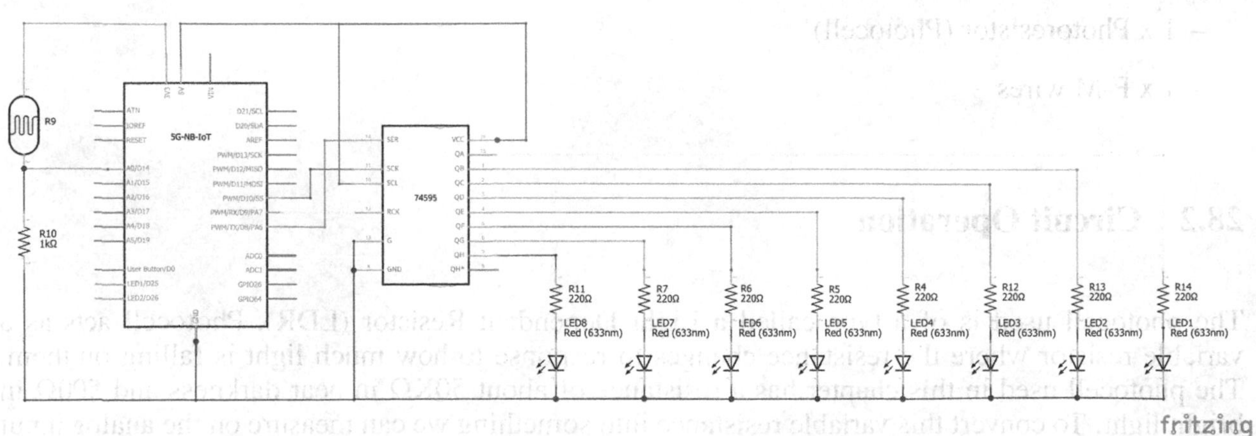

Figure 28.3: Schematic Diagram for the Photocell.

28.4 Breadboard Diagram

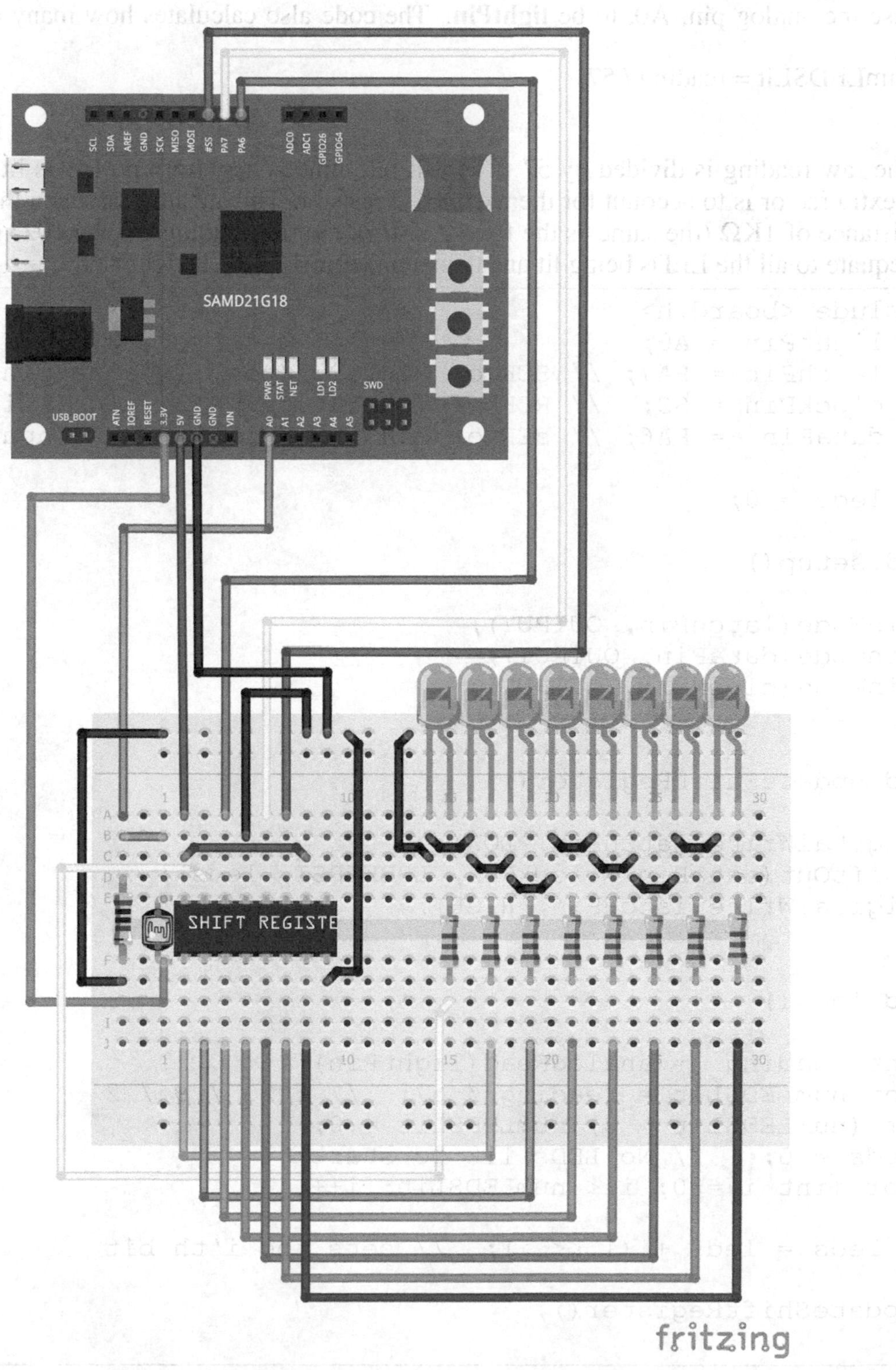

Figure 28.4: Breadboard Diagram for the Photocell.

28.5 Arduino Sketch

We use the analog pin, A0, to be **lightPin**. The code also calculates how many of the LEDs to light:
int numLEDSLit = reading / 57;

The raw reading is divided by 57 to split it into nine zones, from no LEDs lit to all eight lit. This extra factor is to account for the fixed 1KΩ resistor. This means that when the photocell has a resistance of 1KΩ (the same as the fixed resistor), the raw reading will be 1023 / 2 = 511. This will equate to all the LEDs being lit and then a bit (**numLEDSLit**) will be 8.

```
#include <board.h>
int lightPin = A0;
int latchPin = PA7; // SCK of 74HC595 (pin 11,latch pin)
int clockPin = SS;  // RCK of 74HC595 (pin 12, clock pin)
int dataPin  = PA6; // sER of 74HC595 (pin 14, SER Input)

int leds = 0;

void setup()
{
  pinMode(latchPin, OUTPUT);
  pinMode(dataPin, OUTPUT);
  pinMode(clockPin, OUTPUT);
}

void updateShiftRegister()
{
  digitalWrite(latchPin, LOW);
  shiftOut(dataPin, clockPin, LSBFIRST, leds);
  digitalWrite(latchPin, HIGH);
}

void loop()
{
  int reading  = analogRead(lightPin);
  int numLEDSLit = reading / 57;  // 1023 / 9 / 2
  if (numLEDSLit > 8) numLEDSLit = 8;
  leds = 0;   // No LEDs lit to start
  for (int i = 0; i < numLEDSLit; i++)
  {
    leds = leds + (1 << i);  // sets the i'th bit
  }
  updateShiftRegister();
}
```

Listing 28.1: Arduino Sketch for Photocell.

28.6 Interface with the cloud

The photocell sensor can upload its readings to the cloud and store it there. The analog readings can be used for smart applications such as smart building to turn on/off building lights based on sun light.

To make the Arduino sketch uploads the readings to the AWS cloud, add the following Arduino lines of codes to the above sketch and use the MQTT codes as explained in Listing 7.1 and Listing 7.2. Use the following JSON format to upload the photocell sensor readings to the cloud.

```
// ..... Previous code lines go here

docInput["DeviceID"] = IMEI;
docInput["Timestamp"] = millis();
docInput["Device"] = "Photocell Sensor";
docInput["OpCode"] = "Read";
docInput["Analog"] = reading;
docInput["Unit"] = "V";
serializeJsonPretty(docInput, payload);

// ..... Next code lines go here
```

Listing 28.2: JSON Document for Photocell.

Upload the final sketch to the board and notice the output on the Serial Monitor as shown below.

Figure 28.5: Serial Monitor Output for JSON Data Published by the Photocell.

Go to the AWS IoT, and the JSON data received at the cloud are displayed on AWS dashboard. The received data on the cloud can be stored in a database, analyzed, visualized, and used to control other appliances.

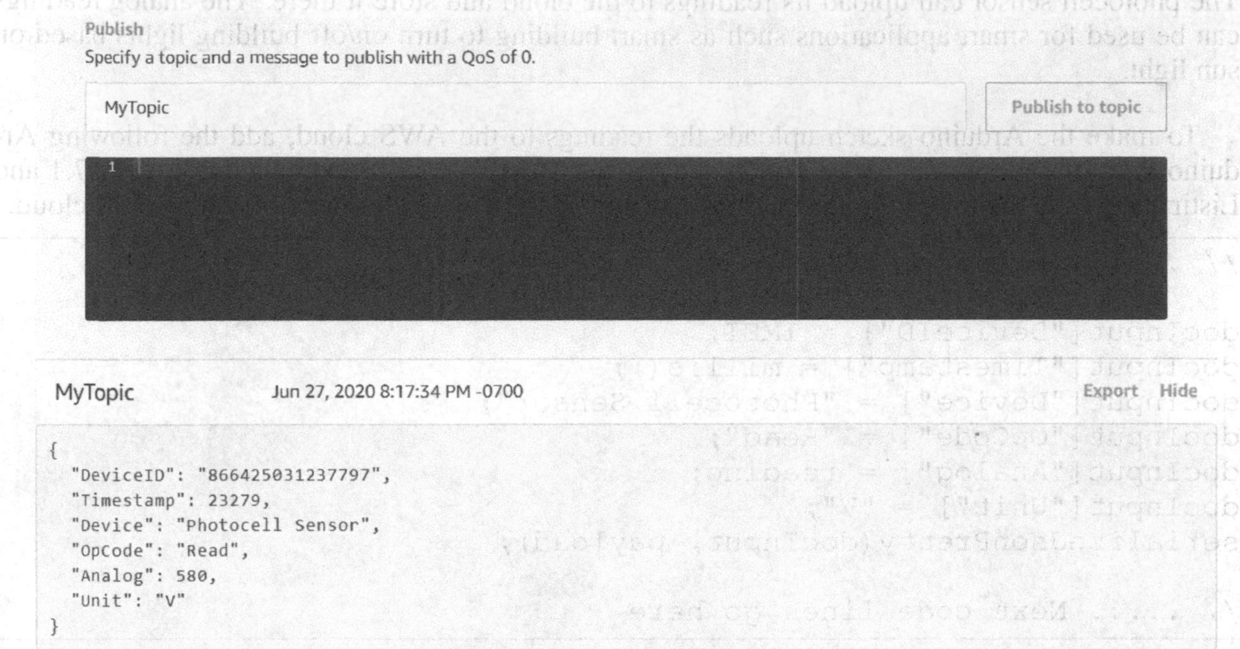
Publish
Specify a topic and a message to publish with a QoS of 0.
MyTopic
Publish to topic
1
MyTopic
Jun 27, 2020 8:17:34 PM -0700
Export
Hide
{
"DeviceID": "866425031237797",
"Timestamp": 23279,
"Device": "Photocell Sensor",
"OpCode": "Read",
"Analog": 580,
"Unit": "V"
}

Figure 28.6: JSON Data on AWS IoT for the Photocell.

Chapter 29

Ultrasonic Sensor

The ultrasonic sensor is used for measuring distances and proximity to detect objects and obstacles. It can be used for smart parking, smart city, or as a traffic sensor. It emits an ultrasound at 40 KHz which travels through the air and if there is an object or obstacle in its path, it bounces back to the sensor. Considering the travel time and the speed of the sound you can calculate the distance. Ultrasonic sensors can be used for smart parking applications.

29.1 Hardware Component Required

- 1 x NB-IoT hardware board
- 1 x Micro USB cable
- 1 x Ultrasonic sensor
- 1 x F-M wires

29.2 Circuit Operation

The Ultrasonic sensor, HC-SR04, has 4 pins; VCC, GND, Trig and Echo. The GND and the VCC pins of the sensor are connected to the ground and the 5V pins on the NB board respectively and the Trig and Echo pins are connected to any Digital I/O pin on the board.

Ultrasonic sensor HC-SR04 detects a range from 2 cm to 400 cm. The ranging accuracy can reach to 3 mm. The sensor includes ultrasonic transmitter, receiver and control circuit. Ultrasonic sensors work by emitting sound waves with a frequency that is too high for a human to hear. These sound waves travel through the air at the speed of sound, roughly 343 m/s. If there is an object in front of the sensor, the sound waves are reflected back, and the receiver of the ultrasonic sensor

Figure 29.1: Ultrasonic sensor.

detects them. By measuring how much time passed between sending and receiving the sound waves, the distance between the sensor and the object can be calculated.

At 20°C the speed of sound is roughly 343 m/s or 0.034 cm/μs. Assuming a time between sending and receiving the sound waves of 2000 microseconds. Multiplying the speed of sound by the time the sound waves traveled, the distance that the sound waves traveled can be calculated from the following equation:

$$\textbf{Distance = Speed} \times \textbf{Time}$$

However, the distance between the sensor and the object is half this distance calculated because the sound waves traveled from the sensor to the object and back from the object to the sensor. As a result, the calculated distance needs to be divided by two as in the following equation:

$$\textbf{Distance (cm) = Speed of sound (cm/}\mu\textbf{s)} \times \textbf{Time (}\mu\textbf{s) / 2}$$

Calculating this for this example, it becomes:

$$\textbf{Distance (cm) = 0.0343 (cm/}\mu\textbf{s)} \times \textbf{2000 (}\mu\textbf{s) / 2 = 34.3 cm}$$

At the front of the ultrasonic sensor, there are two silver cylinders (ultrasonic transducers), one is the transmitter of the sound waves and the other is the receiver. The sensor generates a sonic

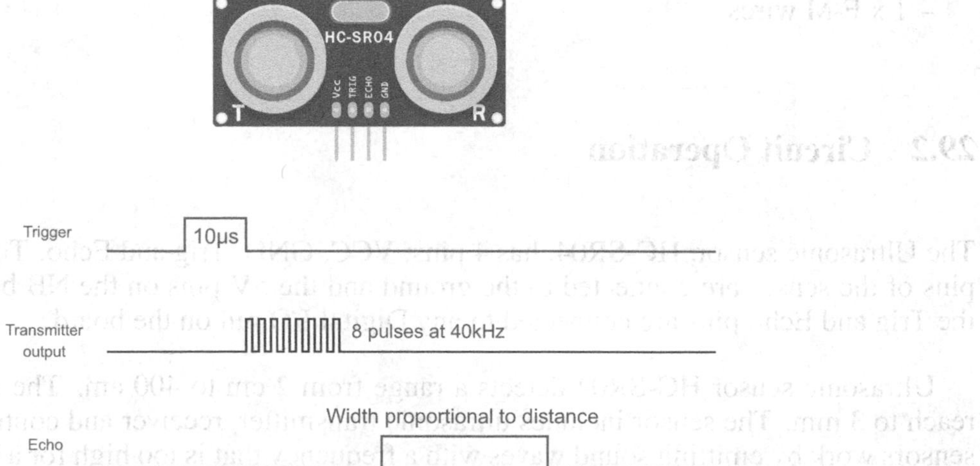

Figure 29.2: Sonic waves of the Ultrasonic sensor.

burst by setting the Trig pin high for at least 10 μs. The sensor then creates 8 cycles burst of ultrasound at 40 KHz.

The sonic burst travels at the speed of sound, bounces back and gets received by the receiver of the sensor. The Echo pin then outputs the time that the sound waves traveled in microseconds.

As an example, if there is an object at 100 cm away from the sensor, and the speed of the sound is 340 m/s, the sound wave needs to travel about 2.94 ms. The ultrasonic Echo pin will produce double of that number (2.94 x 2 = 5.88 ms) because the sound wave needs to travel round trip distance (a distance from the sensor to the object and then back to the sensor again). To calculate the distance based on the output from the Echo pin, multiply the received travel time value from the echo pin by 0.034 and divide it by 2.

29.3 Schematic Diagram

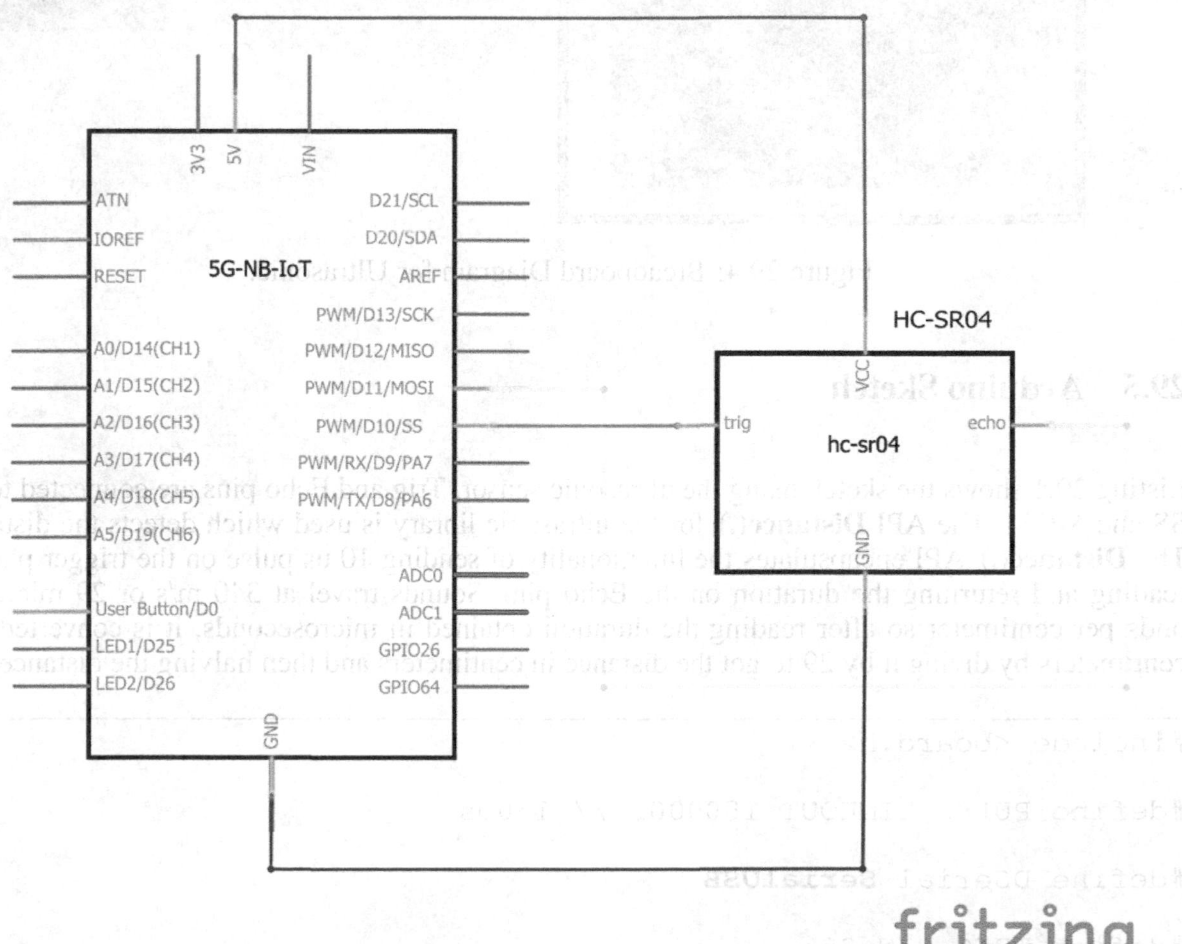

Figure 29.3: Schematic Diagram for Ultrasonic.

29.4 Breadboard Diagram

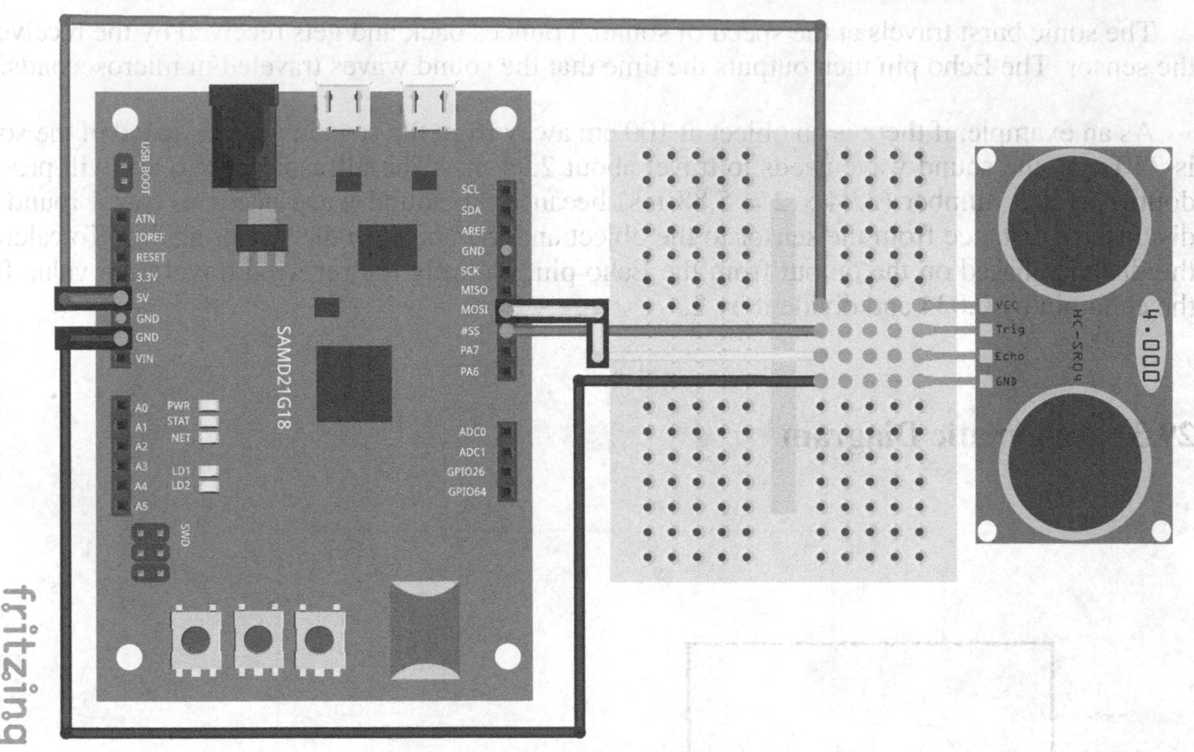

Figure 29.4: Breadboard Diagram for Ultrasonic.

29.5 Arduino Sketch

Listing 29.1 shows the sketch using the ultrasonic sensor. Trig and Echo pins are connected to pin SS and MOSI. The API **Distance(.)** for the ultrasonic library is used which detects the distance. The **Distance(.)** API encapsulates the functionality of sending 10 us pulse on the trigger pin and reading and returning the duration on the Echo pin. Sounds travel at 340 m/s or 29 microseconds per centimeter so after reading the duration obtained in microseconds, it is converted into centimeters by diving it by 29 to get the distance in centimeters and then halving the distance.

```
#include <board.h>

#define PULSE_TIMEOUT 150000L // 150ms

#define DSerial SerialUSB

#define TRIG_PIN SS
#define ECHO_PIN MOSI

long a;
```

```
void setup()
{
  DSerial.begin(9600);
  delay(1000);

  pinMode(ECHO_PIN, INPUT);
  pinMode(TRIG_PIN, OUTPUT);
}

void loop()
{
  a = Distance();
  DSerial.print(a);
  DSerial.println("cm");
  delay(1000);
}

long Distance()
{
  long d = 0;
  long _duration = 0;
  digitalWrite(TRIG_PIN, LOW);
  delayMicroseconds(2);
  digitalWrite(TRIG_PIN, HIGH);
  delayMicroseconds(10);
  digitalWrite(TRIG_PIN, LOW);
  delayMicroseconds(2);
  _duration = pulseIn(ECHO_PIN, HIGH, PULSE_TIMEOUT);
  d = microsecondsToCentimeters(_duration);
  delay(25);
  return d;
}
long microsecondsToCentimeters(long microseconds)
{
  return microseconds / 29 / 2;
}
```

Listing 29.1: Arduino Sketch for Ultrasonic Sensor.

The following output on Serial Monitor is shown when you upload and run the Arduino sketch and it displays the distance at which an object is detected.

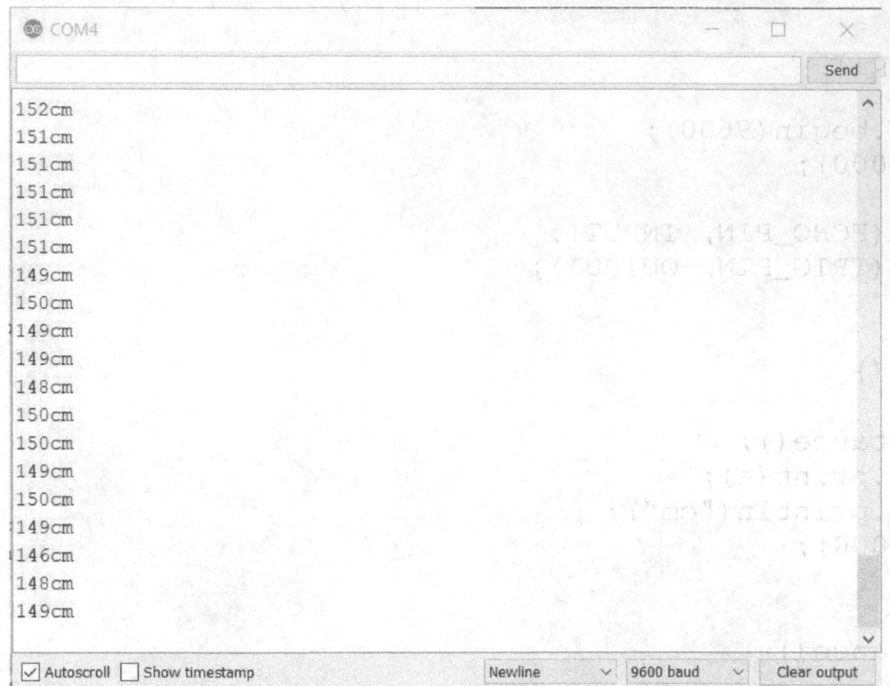

Figure 29.5: Serial Monitor Output for Ultrasonic.

29.6 Interface with the Cloud

The ultrasonic sensor can upload the distance readings to the cloud and store it there. These distances can be used for smart applications such as smart parking where the ultrasonic sensor can be used to determine whether a parking space is occupied or empty. This decision can be done based on the distance detected of a parking vehicle.

To make the Arduino sketch uploads the readings to the AWS cloud, add the following Arduino lines of codes to the above sketch and use the MQTT codes as explained in Listing 7.1 and Listing 7.2. Use the following JSON format to upload the ultrasonic readings to the cloud.

```
// ...... Previous code lines go here

docInput["DeviceID"] = IMEI;
docInput["Timestamp"] = millis();
docInput["Device"] = "UltraSonic Sensor";
docInput["OpCode"] = "Read";
docInput["Distance"] = a;
docInput["Unit"] = "cm";
serializeJsonPretty(docInput, payload);

// ..... Next code lines go here
```

Listing 29.2: JSON Document for Ultrasonic Sensor.

Upload the final sketch to the board and notice the output on the Serial Monitor as shown below.

```
COM9
Send
-> AT+QMTPUB=3,1,1,0,"MyTopic"

<- >
{
  "DeviceID": "866425031237797",
  "Timestamp": 23379,
  "Device": "UltraSonic Sensor",
  "OpCode": "Read",
  "Distance": 58,
  "Unit": "cm"
}□
Send Data len :152

<- OK
<-
<-
<- +QMTRECV: 3,0,"MyTopic","{
<-    "DeviceID": "866425031237797",
<-    "Timestamp": 23379,
<-    "Device": "UltraSonic Sensor",
<-    "OpCode": "Read",
<-    "Distance": 58,
<-    "Unit": "cm"
<- }"
<-
<- +QMTPUB: 3,1,0
<- Publish Succeded!
Autoscroll  Show timestamp    Newline   9600 baud   Clear output
```

Figure 29.6: Serial Monitor Output for JSON Data Published by the Ultrasonic.

Go to the AWS IoT, and the JSON data received at the cloud are displayed on AWS dashboard. The received data readings on the cloud can be stored in a database, analyzed, processed, and visualized.

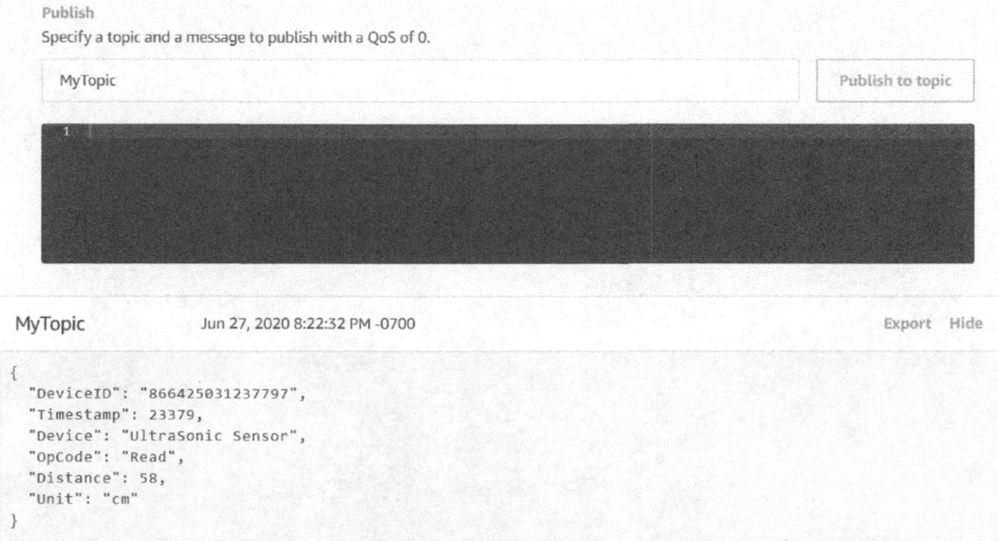
Publish
Specify a topic and a message to publish with a QoS of 0.
MyTopic
Publish to topic
MyTopic
Jun 27, 2020 8:22:32 PM -0700
Export
Hide
{
"DeviceID": "866425031237797",
"Timestamp": 23379,
"Device": "UltraSonic Sensor",
"OpCode": "Read",
"Distance": 58,
"Unit": "cm"
}

Figure 29.7: JSON Data on AWS IoT for the Ultrasonic.

Chapter 30

Temperature and Humidity Sensor

In this chapter, you will learn how to use a temperature and humidity sensor. It can keep track for climate and atmosphere changes, humidity and temperature readings. The sensor can be used in applications such as smart home environmental control, and farm or garden monitoring systems, HVAC, dehumidifier, testing and inspection equipment, consumer goods, automotive, automatic control, data loggers, weather stations, humidity regulator, medical and other humidity measurement and control.

30.1 Hardware Component Required

– 1 x NB-IoT hardware board

– 1 x Micro USB cable

– 1 x DHT11 Temperature and humidity sensor

– 1 x F-M wires

30.2 Circuit Operation

DHT11 digital temperature and humidity sensor is a composite sensor which contains a calibrated digital signal output for the temperature and humidity. The dedicated digital module collection technology and the temperature and humidity sensing technology are applied to ensure that the product has high reliability and excellent long-term stability. The sensor includes a resistive sense of wet components and a Negative Temperature Coefficient (NTC) temperature measurement device that is connected with a high-performance 8-bit microcontroller. NTC thermistors are resistors with a negative temperature coefficient which means that the resistance decreases with increasing temperature.

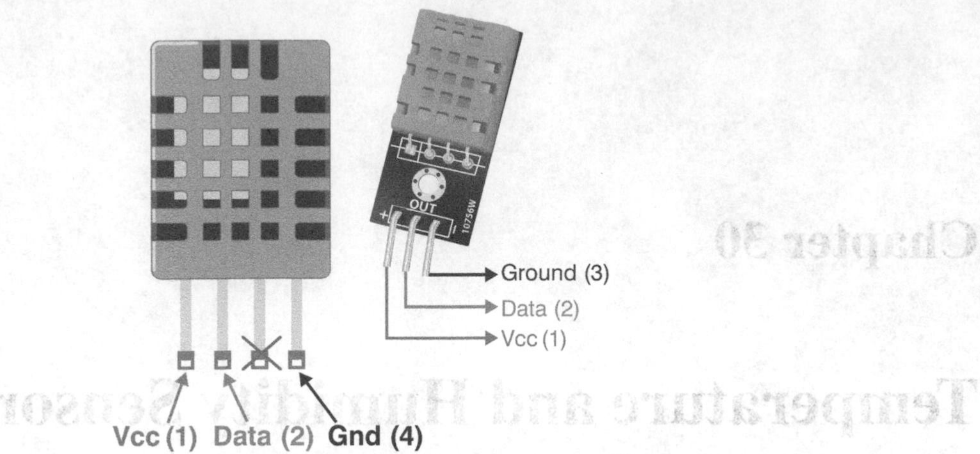

Figure 30.1: Temperature and Humidity Sensor.

30.3 Schematic Diagram

Figure 30.2 shows how to connect the sensor. Three connections are only needed to the sensor, since one of the pins is not used. The connections are: VCC, GND, and signal which can be connected to any pin on the NB board.

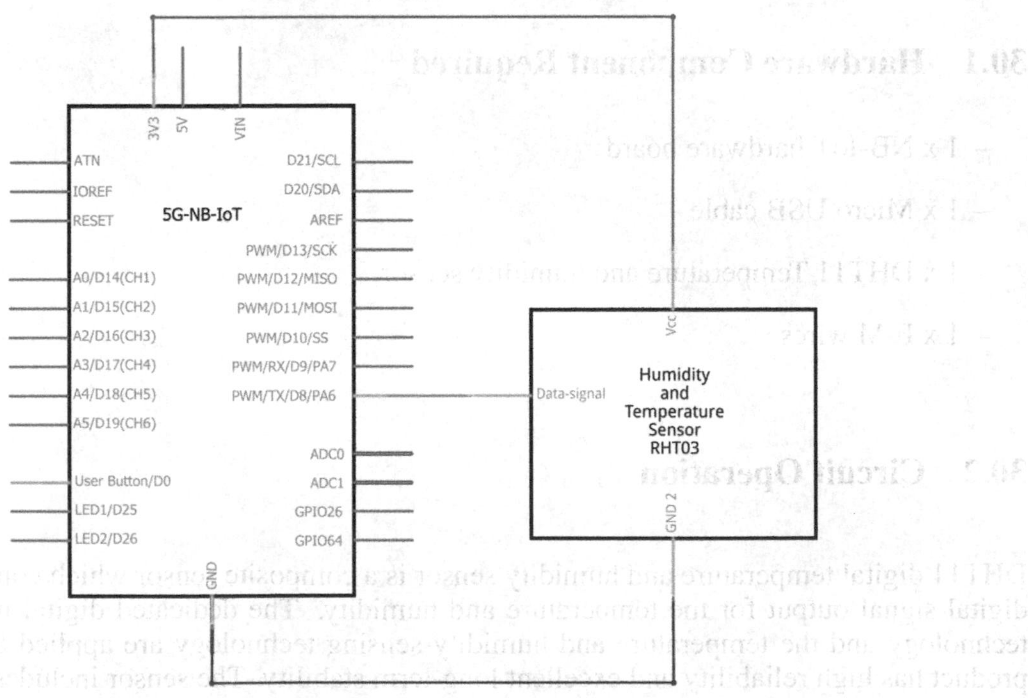

Figure 30.2: Sensor Schematic Diagram for Temperature and Humidity.

30.4 Breadboard Diagram

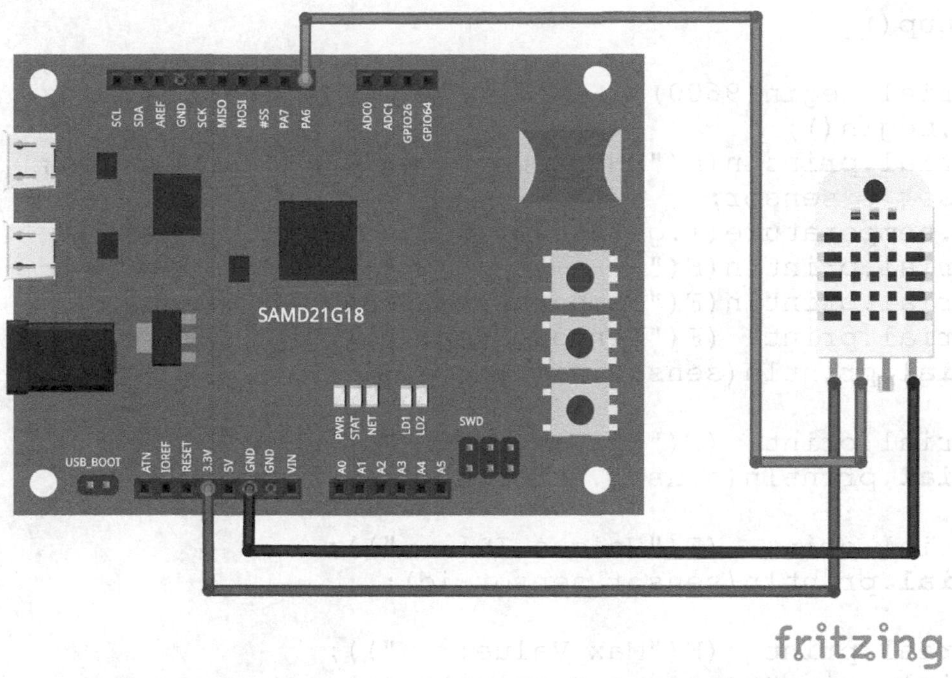

Figure 30.3: Breadboard Diagram for Temperature and Humidity Sensor.

30.5 Arduino Sketch

Listing 30.1 shows the sketch using the temperature and humidity sensor where its signal pin is connected to pin PA6 on the hardware kit. The sensor is initialized, and its specification is displayed and then readings of temperature and humidity are displayed.

```
#include <board.h>
#include <Adafruit_Sensor.h>
#include <DHT.h>
#include <DHT_U.h>

#define DSerial SerialUSB

#define DHTPIN PA6

#define DHTTYPE    DHT11

DHT_Unified dht(DHTPIN, DHTTYPE);
```

```
uint32_t delayMS;

void setup()
{
    DSerial.begin(9600);
    dht.begin();
    DSerial.println(F("DHTxx Unified Sensor Example"));
    sensor_t sensor;
    dht.temperature().getSensor(&sensor);
    DSerial.println(F("------------------------------------"));
    DSerial.println(F("Temperature Sensor"));
    DSerial.print  (F("Sensor Type: "));
    Serial.println(sensor.name);

    DSerial.print  (F("Driver Ver:  "));
    Serial.println(sensor.version);

    DSerial.print  (F("Unique ID:   "));
    Serial.println(sensor.sensor_id);

    DSerial.print  (F("Max Value:   "));
    Serial.print(sensor.max_value);
    Serial.println(F("°C"));

    DSerial.print  (F("Min Value:   "));
    Serial.print(sensor.min_value);
    Serial.println(F("°C"));

    DSerial.print  (F("Resolution:  "));
    Serial.print(sensor.resolution);
    Serial.println(F("°C"));
    DSerial.println(F("------------------------------------"));
    // Print humidity sensor details.
    dht.humidity().getSensor(&sensor);
    DSerial.println(F("Humidity Sensor"));
    DSerial.print  (F("Sensor Type: "));
    Serial.println(sensor.name);

    DSerial.print  (F("Driver Ver:  "));
    Serial.println(sensor.version);

    DSerial.print  (F("Unique ID:   "));
    Serial.println(sensor.sensor_id);

    DSerial.print  (F("Max Value:   "));
    Serial.print(sensor.max_value);
```

```
    Serial.println(F("%"));

    DSerial.print  (F("Min Value:   "));
    Serial.print(sensor.min_value);
    Serial.println(F("%"));

    DSerial.print  (F("Resolution:  "));
    Serial.print(sensor.resolution);
    Serial.println(F("%"));
    DSerial.println(F("------------------------------------"));
    // Set delay between sensor readings based on sensor details.
    delayMS = sensor.min_delay / 1000;
}

void loop()
{
    delay(delayMS); // Delay between measurements.
    // Get temperature event and print its value.
    sensors_event_t event;
    dht.temperature().getEvent(&event);
    DSerial.print(F("Temperature: "));
    DSerial.print(event.temperature);
    DSerial.println(F("°C"));

    // Get humidity event and print its value.
    dht.humidity().getEvent(&event);
    DSerial.print(F("Humidity: "));
    DSerial.print(event.relative_humidity);
    DSerial.println(F("%"));
}
```

Listing 30.1: Arduino Sketch for Temperature and Humidity Sensor.

The Serial Monitor displays the following output which shows the sensor specifications and then it displays the temperature and humidity readings.

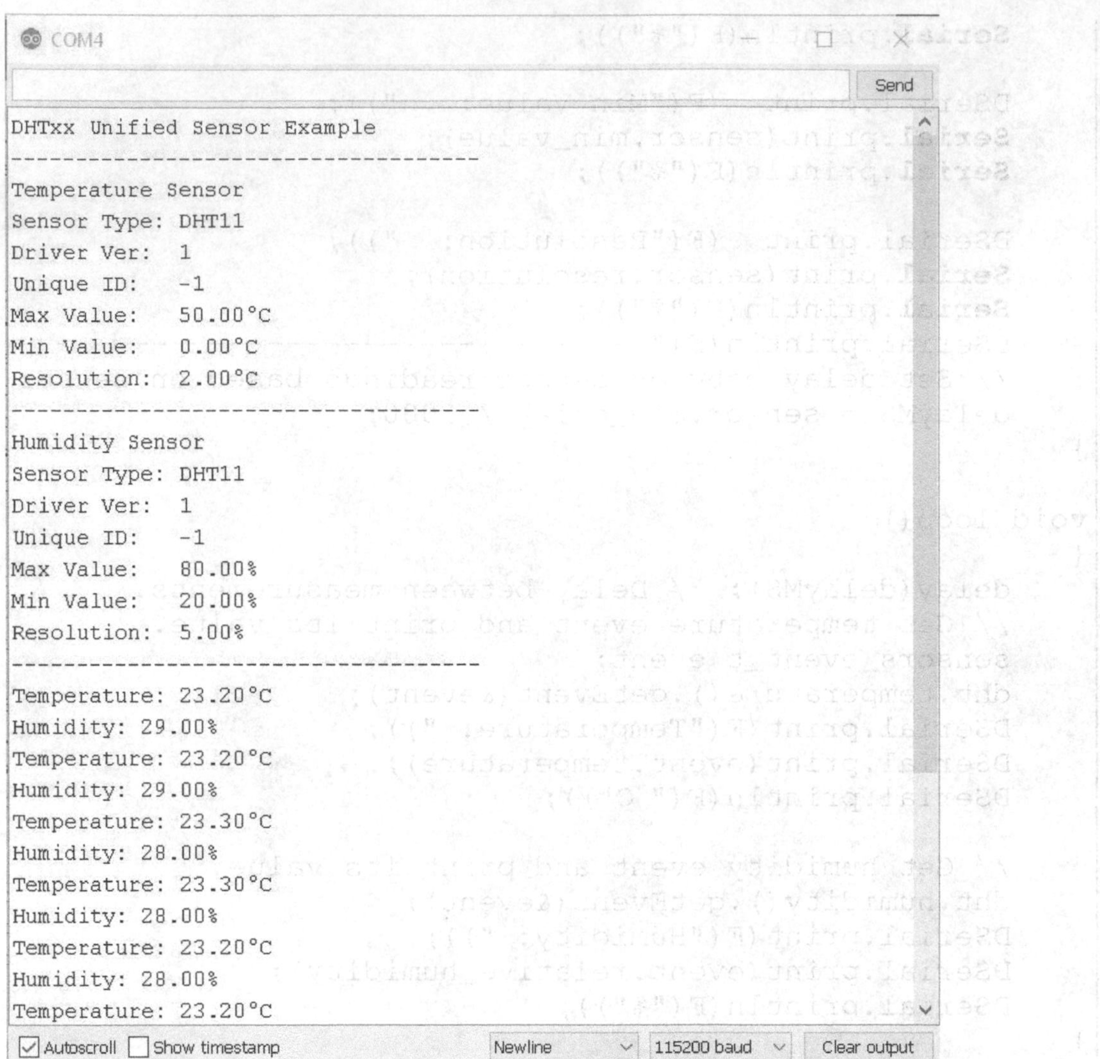

Figure 30.4: Serial Monitor Output for the Temperature and Humidity Sensor.

30.6 Interface with the Cloud

The temperature and humidity sensor can upload its weather readings to the cloud and store it there. These weather reading can be used for smart buildings or home to detect weather conditions, turn on/off heaters and air conditions, or adjust climate control appliances.

To make the Arduino sketch uploads the readings to the AWS cloud, add the following Arduino lines of codes to the above sketch and use the MQTT codes as explained in Listing 7.1 and Listing 7.2. Use the following JSON format to upload the water sensor readings to the cloud.

```
// ...... Previous code lines go here

docInput["DeviceID"] = IMEI;
```

```
docInput["Timestamp"] = millis();
docInput["Device"] = "Temperature and Humidity Sensor";
docInput["OpCode"] = "Read";
docInput["Temperature"] = event.temperature;
docInput["Unit"] = "°C";
docInput["Humidity"] = event.relative_humidity;
serializeJsonPretty(docInput, payload);

// ..... Next code lines go here
```

Listing 30.2: JSON Document for Temperature and Humidity Sensor.

Upload the final sketch to the board and notice the output on the Serial Monitor as shown below.

Figure 30.5: Serial Monitor Output for JSON Data Published by the Temperature and Humidity Sensor.

Go to the AWS IoT, and the JSON data received at the cloud are displayed on AWS dashboard. The received data readings on the cloud can be stored in a database and analyzed.

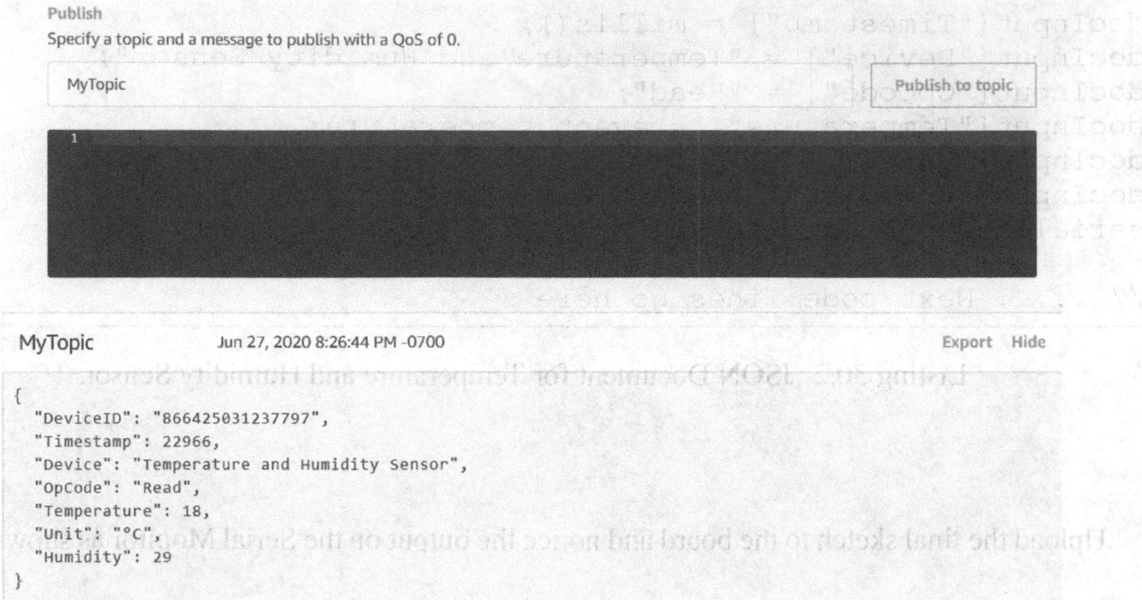

Figure 30.6: JSON Data on AWS IoT for the Temperature and Humidity Sensor.

Chapter 31

Water Level Detection Sensor

In this chapter, you will learn how to use a water level detection sensor. This sensor can perceive the depth of water and the core component is an amplifying circuit which is made up of a transistor and several pectinate PCB routings. When the sensor is put into the water, these routings will present a resistor that can change along with the change of water level. Then, the signal of water depth is converted into the electrical signal, and you can know the change of water depth through the ADC function of hardware kit.

31.1 Hardware Component Required

- 1 x NB-IoT hardware board
- 1 x Micro USB cable
- 1 x Water lever detection sensor
- 1 x F-M wires

31.2 Circuit Operation

A water sensor is designed for water level detection, which can be widely used in sensing the rainfall, water level, and even the water leakage. The sensor is composed of three parts: an electronic brick connector, a 1 MΩ resistor, and several lines of bare conducting wires.

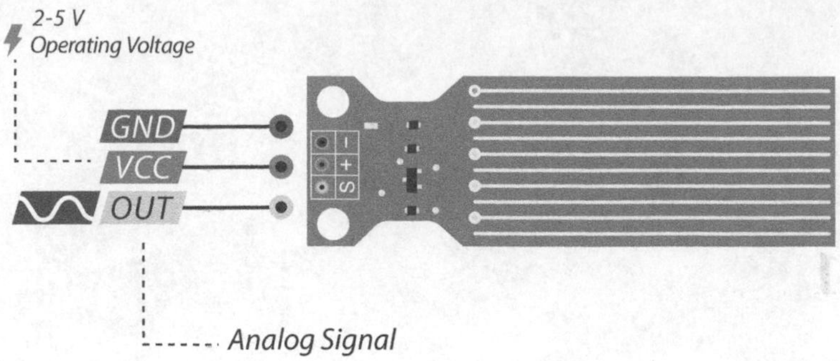

Figure 31.1: Water Level Sensor.

This sensor works by having a series of five exposed traces connected to ground. Interlaced between each two ground traces are a sense trace. The sensor traces have a weak pull-up resistor of 1 MΩ. The resistor will pull the sensor trace value high until a drop of water shorts the sensor trace to the ground trace. This detects the level of water. The sensor outputs an analog signal that is proportional to the resistance between the sense traces.

31.3 Schematic Diagram

The schematic diagram is shown. The power supply (+) is connected to 3.3V of the NB board, ground electrode (-) is connected to GND. Signal output (S) is connected to the A0 pin which have the function of receiving analog signal on the NB board.

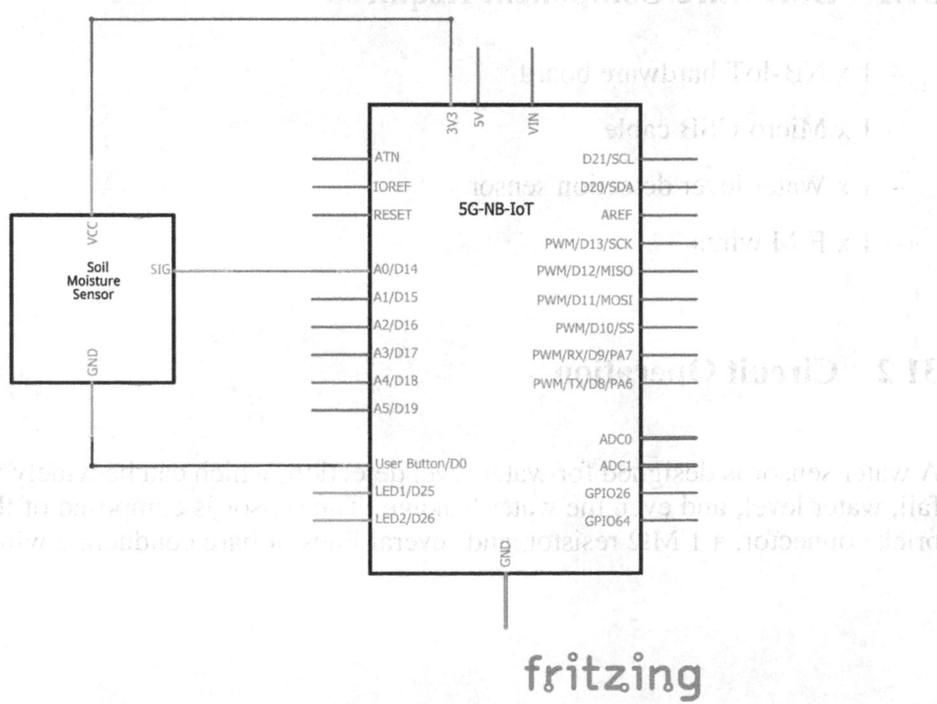

Figure 31.2: Schematic Diagram for Water Level Sensor.

31.4 Breadboard Diagram

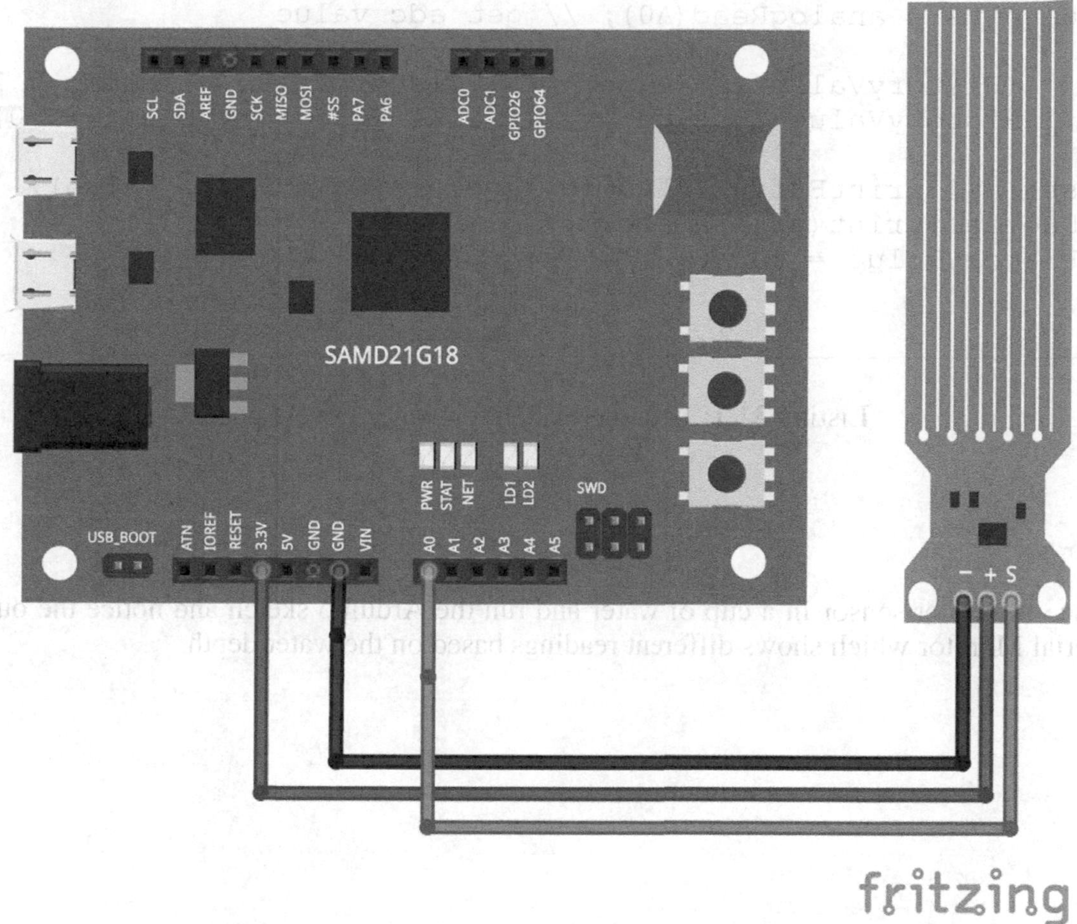

Figure 31.3: Breadboard Diagram for Water Level Sensor.

31.5 Arduino Sketch

The analog output from the sensor produces an analog value that increases depending on the sensor surface is covered with water. This is because the water acts as a conductor.

```
#define DSerial SerialUSB

int HistoryValue = 0;
char printBuffer[128];

void setup()
{
  DSerial.begin(9600);
}
```

```
void loop()
{
  int value = analogRead(A0); // get adc value

  if (((HistoryValue >= value) && ((HistoryValue - value) > 10))
  || ((HistoryValue < value) && ((value - HistoryValue) > 10)))
  {
    sprintf(printBuffer, "ADC%d level is %d\n", A0, value);
    DSerial.print(printBuffer);
    HistoryValue = value;
  }
}
```

Listing 31.1: Arduino Sketch for Water Level Sensor.

Place the water sensor in a cup of water and run the Arduino sketch and notice the output on the Serial Monitor which shows different readings based on the water depth.

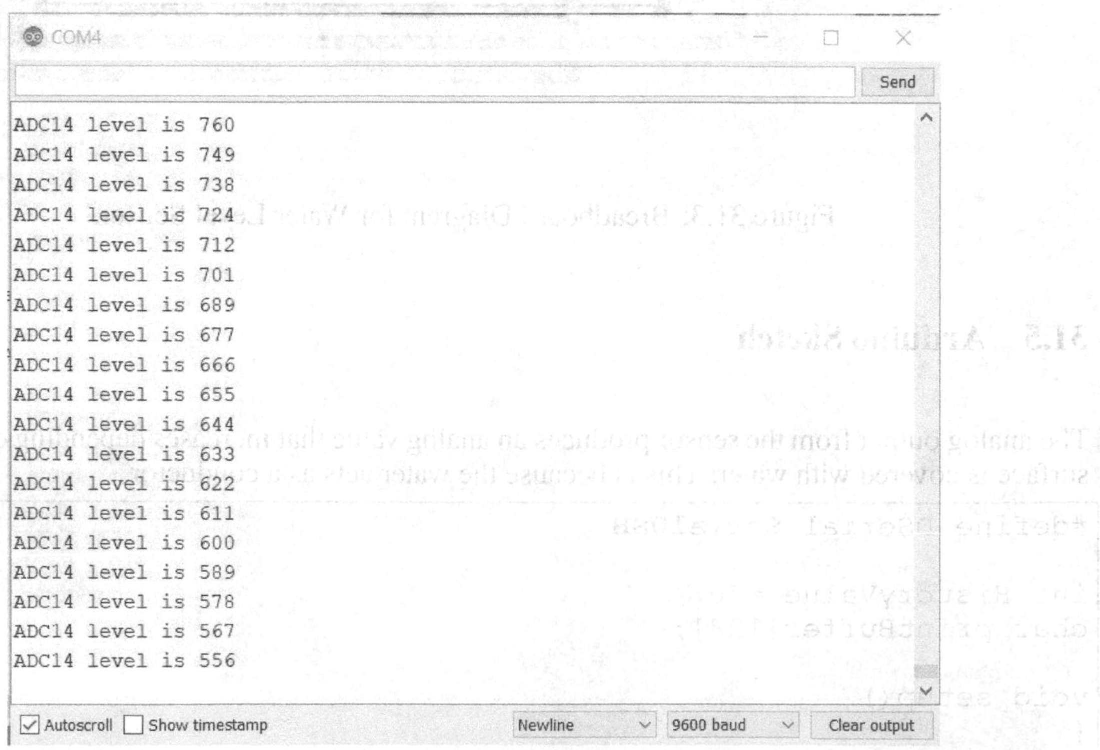

Figure 31.4: Serial Monitor Output for the Water Level Sensor.

31.6 Interface with the Cloud

The water level sensor can upload the water level readings to the cloud and store it there. The water level readings on the cloud can be analyzed, processed, and provides insights for central operator or a function.

To make the Arduino sketch upload the readings to the AWS cloud, add the following Arduino lines of codes to the above sketch and use the MQTT codes as explained in Listing 7.1 and Listing 7.2. Use the following JSON format to upload the water sensor readings to the cloud.

```
// ...... Previous code lines go here

docInput["DeviceID"] = IMEI;
docInput["Timestamp"] = millis();
docInput["Device"] = "Water Level Sensor";
docInput["OpCode"] = "Read";
docInput["WaterLevel"] = value;
docInput["Unit"] = "Analog";
serializeJsonPretty(docInput, payload);

// ..... Next code lines go here
```

Listing 31.2: JSON Document for Water Level Sensor.

Upload the final sketch to the board and notice the output on the Serial Monitor as shown below.

```
COM9
Send
-> AT+QMTPUB=3,1,1,0,"MyTopic"

<- >
{
  "DeviceID": "866425031237797",
  "Timestamp": 25303,
  "Device": "Water Level Sensor",
  "OpCode": "Read",
  "WaterLevel": 160,
  "Unit": "Analog"
}
Send Data len :160

<- OK
<-
<-
<- +QMTRECV: 3,0,"MyTopic","{
<-    "DeviceID": "866425031237797",
<-    "Timestamp": 25303,
<-    "Device": "Water Level Sensor",
<-    "OpCode": "Read",
<-    "WaterLevel": 160,
<-    "Unit": "Analog"
<- }"
<-
<- +QMTPUB: 3,1,0
<- Publish Succeded!
Autoscroll  Show timestamp    Newline    9600 baud    Clear output
```

Figure 31.5: Serial Monitor Output for JSON Data Published by the Water Level Sensor.

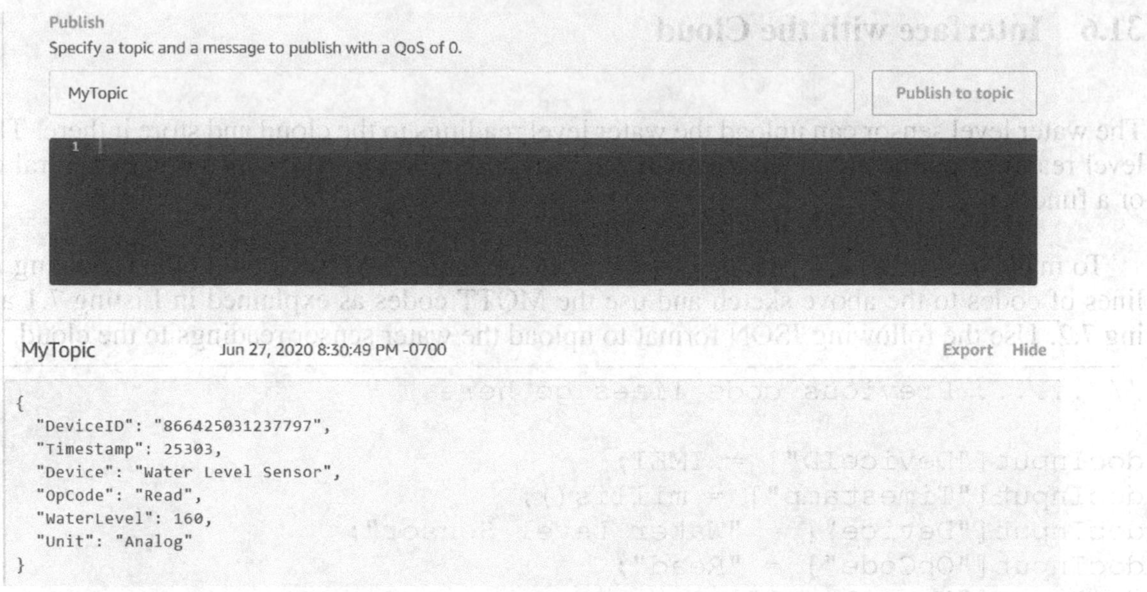
Publish
Specify a topic and a message to publish with a QoS of 0.
MyTopic
Publish to topic
MyTopic
Jun 27, 2020 8:30:49 PM -0700
Export
Hide
{
"DeviceID": "866425031237797",
"Timestamp": 25303,
"Device": "Water Level Sensor",
"OpCode": "Read",
"WaterLevel": 160,
"Unit": "Analog"
}

Figure 31.6: JSON Data on AWS IoT for the Water Level Sensor.

Go to the AWS IoT, and the JSON data received at the cloud are displayed on AWS dashboard. The received data readings on the cloud can be stored in a database, analyzed, processed, and visualized.

Chapter 32

Microphone Sound Sensor

Sound sensor detects voice with different intensity. The sensor detects sound when the sound exceeds a selected set point. Sound is detected via a microphone and fed into an op-amp. The sound level set point is adjusted via an on-board potentiometer. When the sound level exceeds the set point, an LED on the module is turned on and the output is sent low.

To make sure the microphone can detect voice, the sensitivity of the sensor can be adjusted by turning the blue precise potentiometer on the module.

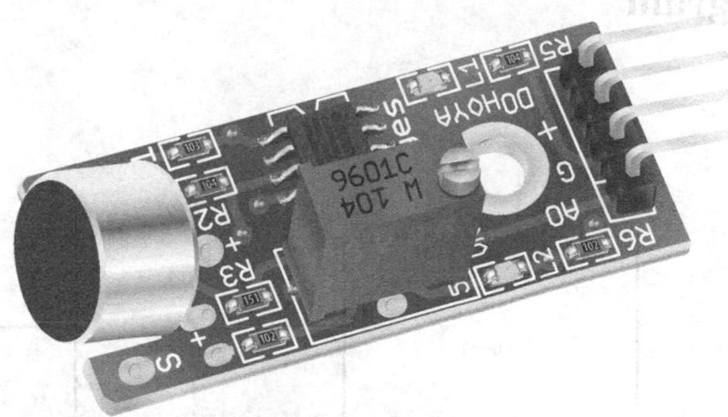

Figure 32.1: Microphone Sound Sensor.

- AO (Analog Output): real-time output voltage signal of microphone
- DO (Digital Output): when the intensity of the sound reaches a certain level, the output is a high- or low-level signal. The threshold sensitivity can be achieved by adjusting the potentiometer.

32.1 Hardware Component Required

– 1 x NB-IoT hardware board

- 1 x Micro USB cable
- 1 x Sound sensor
- 1 x F-M wires

32.2 Circuit Operation

The sound sensor provides an easy way to detect sound and is generally used for detecting sound intensity. The sensor can be used for security and sound monitoring applications. Its accuracy can be easily adjusted for the convenience of usage. It uses a microphone which supplies the input to an amplifier, peak detector and buffer. When the sensor detects a sound, it processes an output signal voltage which is sent to a microcontroller which performs necessary processing.

This microphone can be used to detect sound or air vibration which in turn are converted to electrical signals for further use. The microphone has a solid conducting metal body which encapsulates the various parts of the microphone. The top face is covered with a porous material. It acts as a filter for the dust particles. The sound signals and air vibrations pass through the porous material and falls on the diaphragm through the hole shown in the image above.

32.3 Schematic Diagram

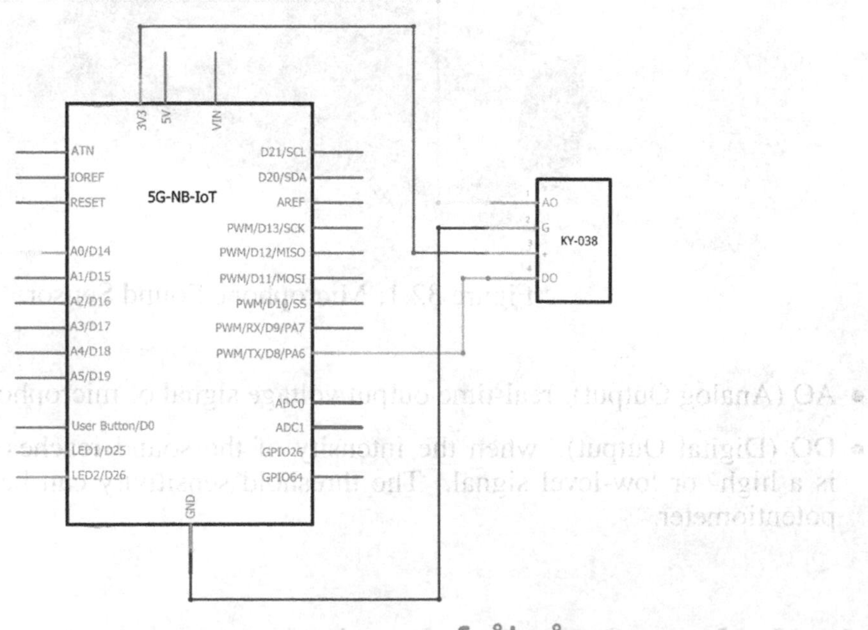

Figure 32.2: Schematic Diagram for Microphone Sound Sensor.

32.4 Breadboard Diagram

The analog output, AO, is connected to A0 on the NB board while the digital output, DO, is connected to PA6.

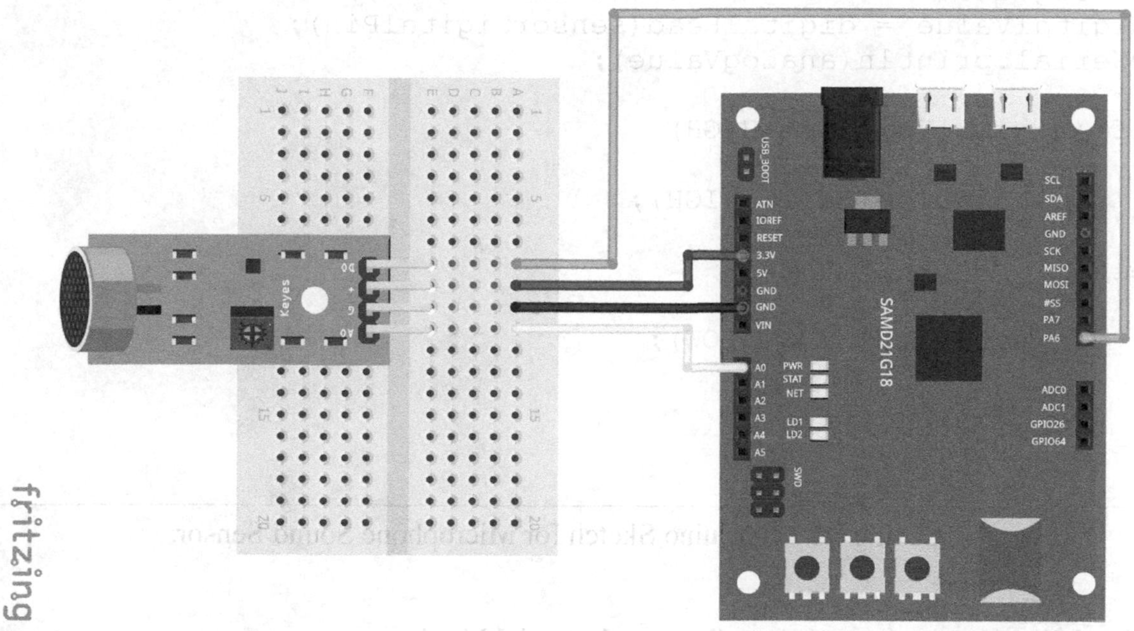

Figure 32.3: Breadboard Diagram for Microphone Sound Sensor.

32.5 Arduino Sketch

The following Arduino sketch reads the sound from the analog input. It displays the analog sound readings on Serial Monitor. It uses LED1 as output and turns it on when the sound threshold is reached.

```
#include <board.h>

#define DSerial SerialUSB

int  sensorAnalogPin = A0;
int  sensorDigitalPin = PA6;
int  analogValue = 0;
int  digitalValue;

void setup()
{
  DSerial.begin(9600);
  pinMode(sensorDigitalPin, INPUT);
```

```
  pinMode(LED1, OUTPUT);
}

void loop()
{
  analogValue = analogRead(sensorAnalogPin);
  digitalValue = digitalRead(sensorDigitalPin);
  DSerial.println(analogValue);

  if (digitalValue == HIGH)
  {
    digitalWrite(LED1, HIGH);
  }
  else
  {
    digitalWrite(LED1, LOW);
  }

  delay(50);
}
```

Listing 32.1: Arduino Sketch for Microphone Sound Sensor.

The following are the sound readings on the Serial Monitor.

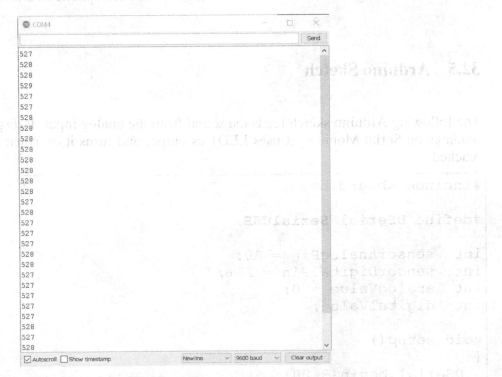

Figure 32.4: Serial Monitor Output for the Microphone Sensor.

In the Arduino IDE, select **Tools->Serial Plotter**. When you speak into the microphone or inflate, you can observe the waveform changes in correlation with the input sound. This is displayed as a waveform as shown in the following:

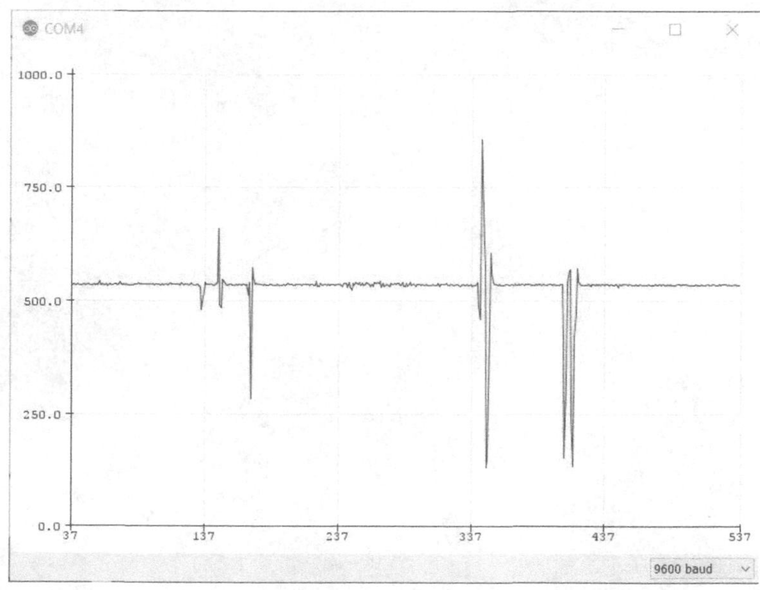

Figure 32.5: Serial Plotter Output for the Microphone Sensor.

32.6 Interface with the Cloud

The sound level sensor can upload the sound analog readings to the cloud and store it there. The analog sound level on the cloud can be analyzed, processed, and sound can be detected to develop voice assistant or speech recognition application.

To make the Arduino sketch uploads the readings to the AWS cloud, add the following Arduino lines of codes to the above sketch and use the MQTT codes as explained in Listing 7.1 and Listing 7.2. Use the following JSON format to upload the water sensor readings to the cloud.

```
// ...... Previous code lines go here

docInput["DeviceID"] = IMEI;
docInput["Timestamp"] = millis();
docInput["Device"] = "Sound Sensor";
docInput["OpCode"] = "Read";
docInput["Analog"] = analogValue;
docInput["Unit"] = "V";
serializeJsonPretty(docInput, payload);

// ..... Next code lines go here
```

Listing 32.2: JSON Document for Microphone Sound Sensor.

Upload the final sketch to the board and notice the output on the Serial Monitor as shown below.

Figure 32.6: Serial Monitor Output for JSON Data Published by the Microphone Sensor.

Go to the AWS IoT, and the JSON data received at the cloud are displayed on AWS dashboard. The received data on the cloud can be stored in a database and analyzed.

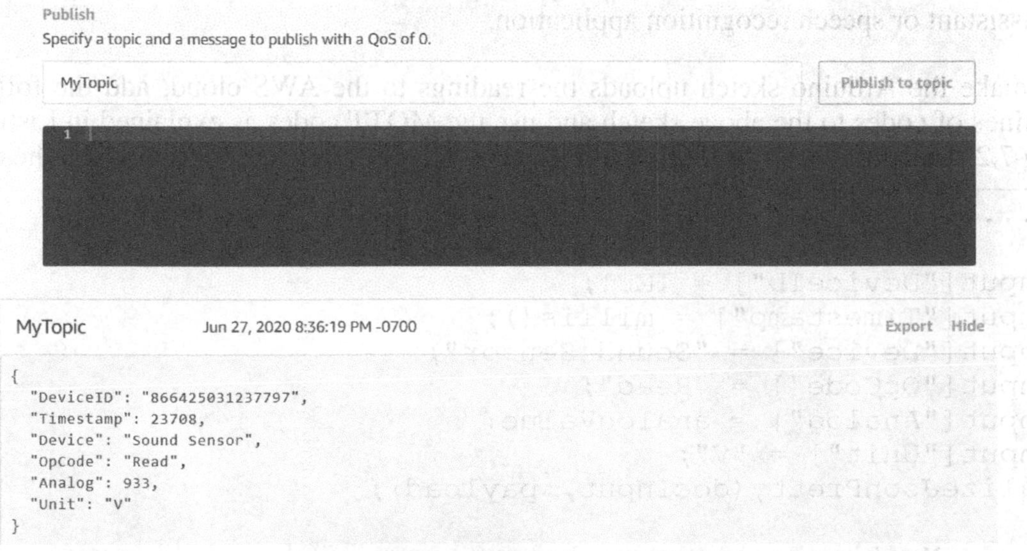

Figure 32.7: JSON Data on AWS IoT for the Microphone Sensor.

Chapter 33

Thermometer

In this chapter, a thermometer is used to measure the temperature and display it on an LCD. Thermometer is used in many appliances, medical devices, and for industrial control applications to measure climate temperatures.

33.1 Hardware Component Required

- 1 x NB-IoT hardware board
- 1 x Micro USB cable
- 1 x LCD1602 Module
- 1 x 10 KΩ resistor
- 1 x 10 KΩ Thermistor
- 1 x Potentiometer
- 1 x F-M wires
- 1 x M-M wires

33.2 Circuit Operation

A thermistor is a thermal resistor. It is a resistor that changes its resistance with temperature. In fact, all resistors are thermistors (their resistance changes slightly with temperaturc) but the change is usually very small and difficult to measure. Thermistors are made so that the resistance changes drastically with temperature so that it can be 100 Ω of resistance or more of change per degree.

There are two kinds of thermistors, NTC (negative temperature coefficient) and PTC (positive temperature coefficient) . In NTC sensor, the resistance decreases with increasing temperature. PTC sensors are often used as resettable fuses. In PTC sensors, when there is an increase in temperature, it increases the resistance which means that less current is flowing in the resistor. As a result, as the resistor heats up, it limits the current flow and hence as a protecting circuit and fuse.

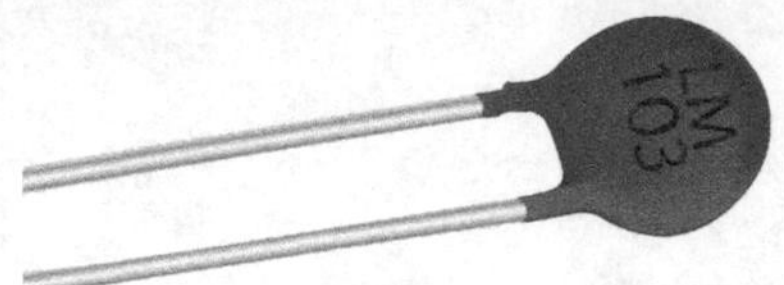

Figure 33.1: 10 KΩ Thermistor.

To convert resistance to temperature, it has been determined that **Steinhart and Hart Equation** is the empirical expression that is the best mathematical expression for resistance temperature relationship of NTC thermistor. Steinhart-Hart equation expresses the temperature in unit of degree Kelvin as follows:

Steinhart-Hart Equation	$T = \dfrac{1}{A + B\ln(R) + C(\ln(R))^3}$

Where

$$A = 0.001125308852122$$
$$B = 0.000234711863267$$
$$C = 0.000000085663516.$$

The circuit diagram for using the thermistor is shown in Figure 33.2. The voltage is measured at a point between the thermistor and a known resistor. This is known as a voltage divider. The equation for a voltage divider of $R2$ and $R3$ can be calculated at the analog input, $A0$, as:

$$V(A0) = R2 * 3.3V/(R2 + 10000)$$

But since A0 is an analogue input to the 10-bit ADC (10 bits divides the 3.3V into 1024 levels) thus yielding the following:

$$V(A0) = R2 * 3.3V * 1023/V(AREF)/(R2 + 10000)$$

As V(AREF) is the analog reference voltage which is the same value at 3.3V, this equation yields:

$$V(A0) = R2 * 1023/(R2 + 10000)$$

And re-arranging for $R2$, yields the thermistor resistance $R2$ can be expressed as:

$$R2 = 10000 * (1023/V(A0) - 1)$$

To convert temperature in degree Kelvin to Celsius, subtract 273.15.

33.3 Schematic Diagram

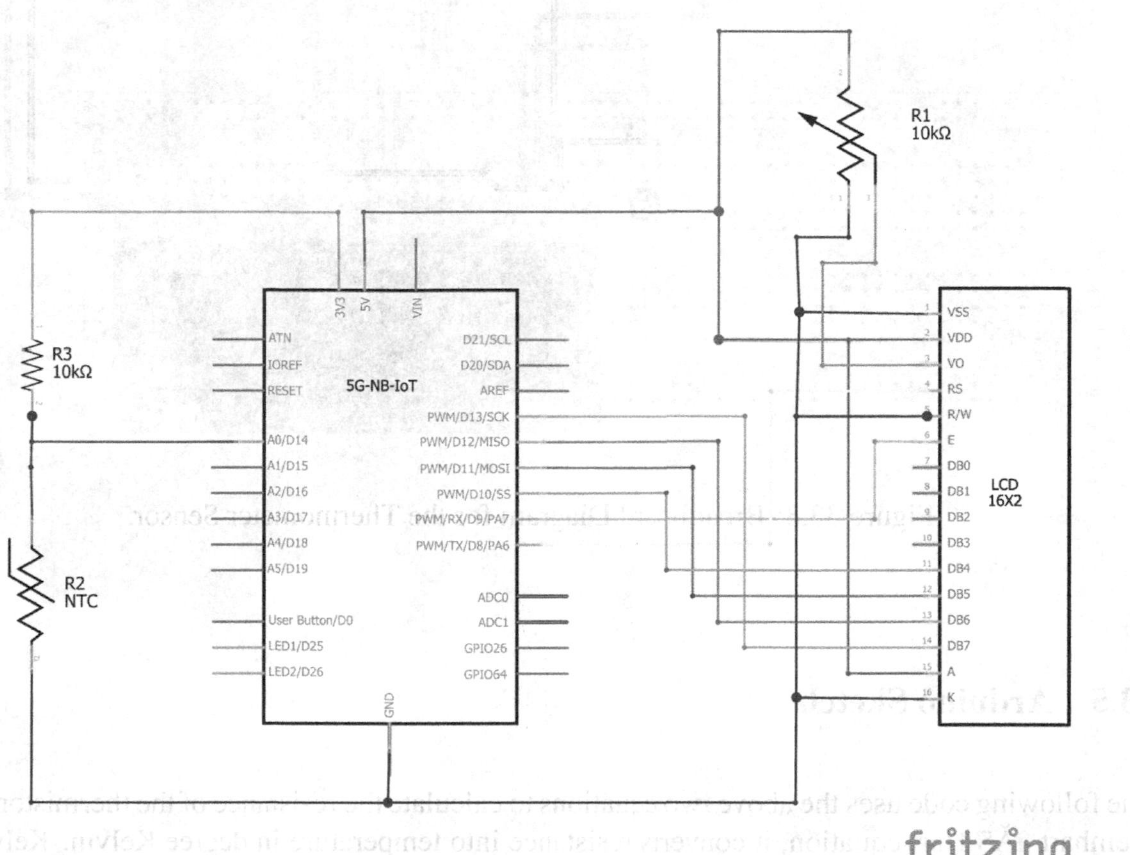

Figure 33.2: Schematic Diagram for the Thermometer Sensor.

33.4 Breadboard Diagram

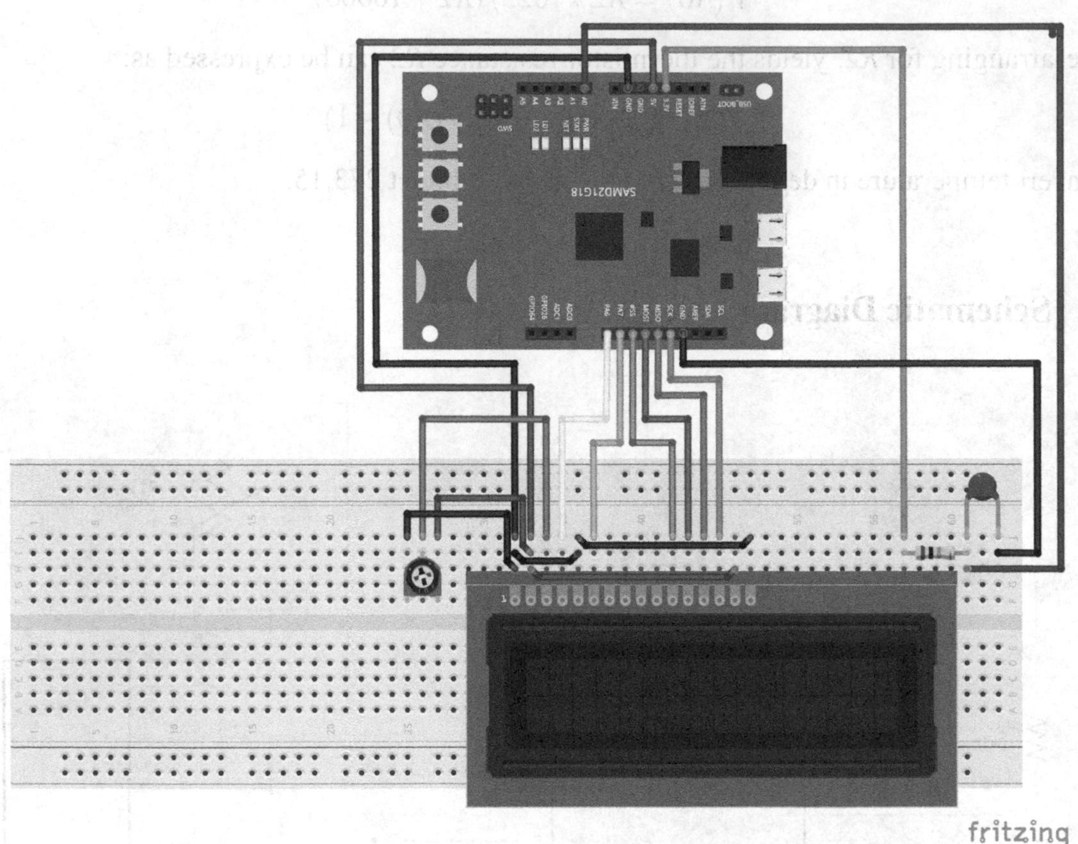

Figure 33.3: Breadboard Diagram for the Thermometer Sensor.

33.5 Arduino Sketch

The following code uses the above two equations to calculate the resistance of the thermistor. Using Steinhart âĂŞ Hart equation, it converts resistance into temperature in degree Kelvin. Kelvin unit is converted to Celsius and Fahrenheit. After the temperature is obtained, it can be displayed on LCD display.

```
#include <board.h>
#include <LiquidCrystal.h>

int tempPin = A0;
LiquidCrystal lcd(PA6, PA7 SS, MOSI, MISO, SCK);

```

```
void setup()
{
  lcd.begin(16, 2);
}

void loop()
{
  int Vout = analogRead(tempPin);
  double logR = log(10000.0 * ((1023.0 / Vout - 1)));
  tempK = 1 / (0.001129148 + (0.000234125 + (0.0000000876741 *
   logR * logR)) * logR);

    // Convert Kelvin to Celcius
    float tempC = tempK - 273.15;

    // Convert Celcius to Fahrenheit
  float tempF = (tempC * 9.0) / 5.0 + 32.0;

  // Display Temperature in C
  lcd.setCursor(0, 0);
  lcd.print("Temp         C  ");

  // Display Temperature in F
  lcd.setCursor(6, 0);

  // Display Temperature in F
  lcd.print(tempF);

  delay(500);
}
```

Listing 33.1: Arduino Sketch for Thermometer.

33.6 Interface with the Cloud

The thermistor readings can be uploaded to the cloud and stored there. The thermistor readings can be analyzed on the cloud and used to triggers different applications such as smart home where the air condition or heater temperature in the home can be adjusted accordingly.

To make the Arduino sketch upload the readings to the AWS cloud, add the following Arduino lines of codes to the above sketch and use the MQTT codes as explained in Listing 7.1 and Listing 7.2. Use the following JSON format to upload the water sensor readings to the cloud.

```
// ...... Previous code lines go here

docInput["DeviceID"] = IMEI;
docInput["Timestamp"] = millis();
docInput["Device"] = "Temperature Sensor";
docInput["OpCode"] = "Read";
docInput["Temperature"] = tempF;
docInput["Unit"] = "°F";
serializeJsonPretty(docInput, payload);

// ..... Next code lines go here
```

Listing 33.2: JSON Document for Thermometer.

Upload the final sketch to the board and notice the output on the Serial Monitor as shown below.

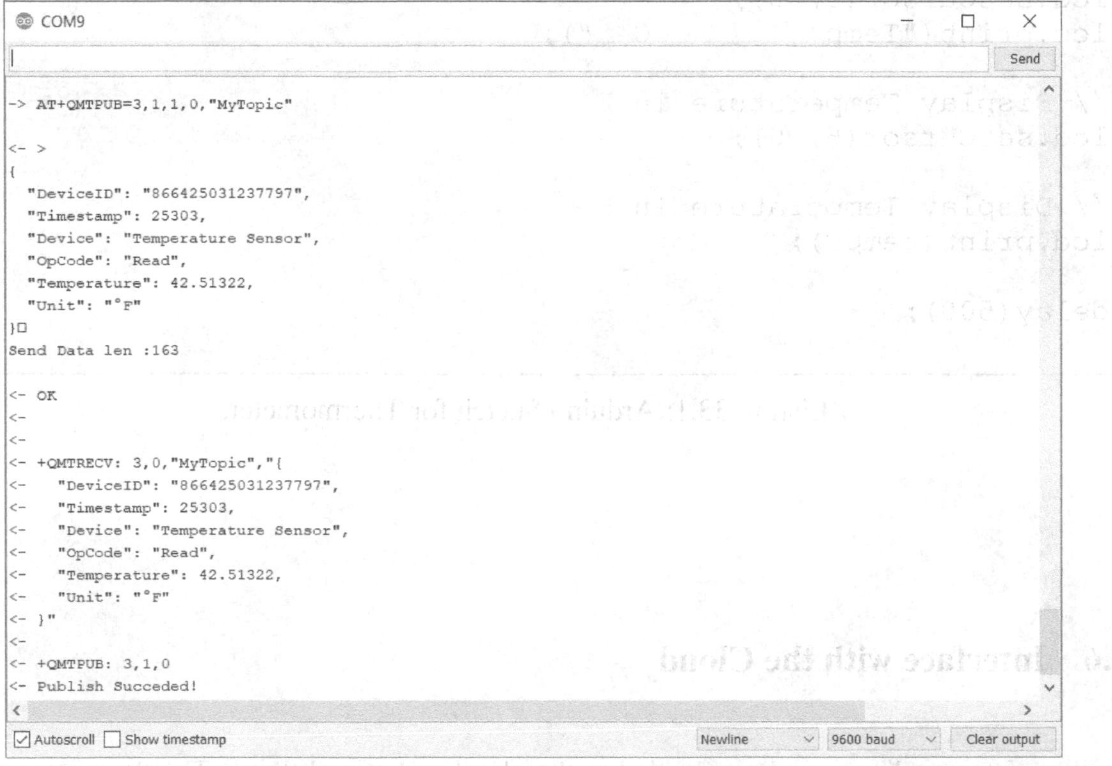

Figure 33.4: Serial Monitor Output for JSON Data Published by the Thermometer.

Go to the AWS IoT, and the JSON data received at the cloud are displayed on AWS dashboard. The received data on the cloud can be stored in a database and analyzed.

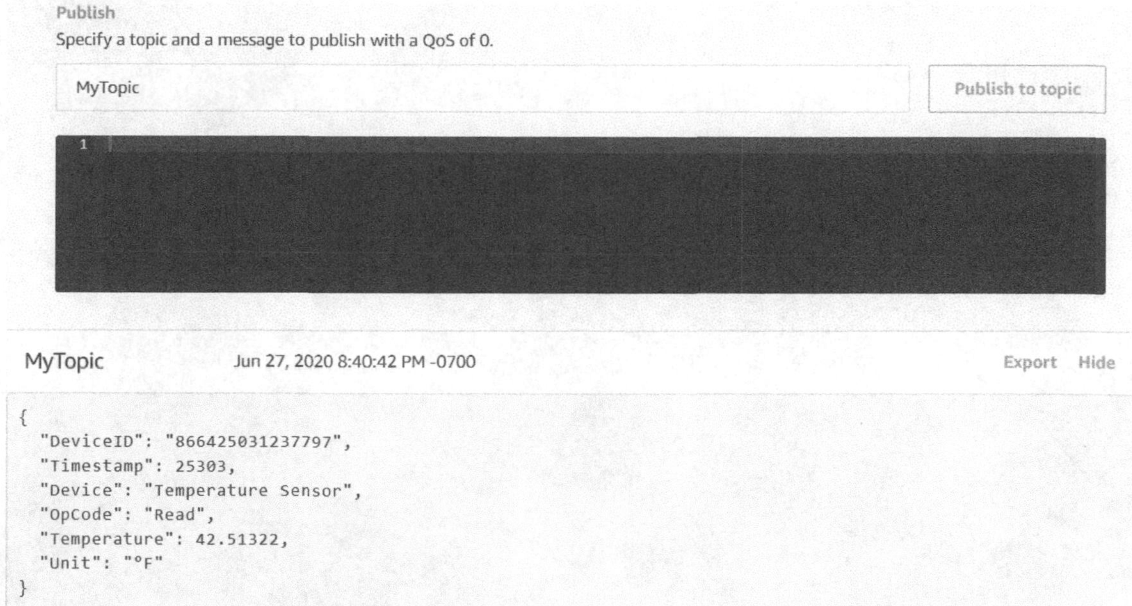
Publish
Specify a topic and a message to publish with a QoS of 0.
MyTopic
Publish to topic
MyTopic
Jun 27, 2020 8:40:42 PM -0700
Export
Hide
{
"DeviceID": "866425031237797",
"Timestamp": 25303,
"Device": "Temperature Sensor",
"OpCode": "Read",
"Temperature": 42.51322,
"Unit": "°F"
}

Figure 33.5: JSON Data on AWS IoT for the Thermometer.

Chapter 34

Gyroscope Sensor

In this chapter, you will use gyroscope and accelerometer. Gyroscope are used for angular velocity while accelerometer is used to measure acceleration. You will use the GY-521 module which is a breakout board for the MPU-6050 chipset Micro-Electro-Mechanical Systems (MEMS). MEMS is a system that combines both mechanical and electrical component. MPU-6050 features a 3-axis gyroscope, a 3-axis accelerometer, a digital motion processor (DMP), and a temperature sensor. MEMS sensors have many applications such as balancing robots, Motion-enabled games, smart phone.

34.1 Hardware Component Required

- 1 x NB-IoT hardware board
- 1 x Micro USB cable
- 1 x GY-521 module
- 1 x F-M wires

34.2 Circuit Operation

A gyroscope is a device that measure or maintain rotational motion or angular velocity. The units of angular velocity are measured in degree per second (°/s) or Revolution Per Second (RPS). Angular velocity is simply a measurement of speed of rotation. A 3-axis gyroscope can measure rotation around three axes: X, Y, and Z.

Accelerometers are devices that measure acceleration, which is the rate of change of the velocity of an object. The unit of measurement are in meter per second squared (m/s^2) or in G-forces (g). Accelerometers are useful for sensing vibrations in systems or for orientation applications.

The GY-521 sensor contains a MEMS accelerometer, a MEMS gyro, and processor in a single chip. It contains 16-bits analog to digital conversion hardware for each channel. Therefore, it captures the X, Y, and Z channel at the same time. The sensor uses the I^2C bus to interface with the hardware board.

An accelerometer works on the principle of the piezoelectric effect. If there is a cuboidal box with a small ball inside it as in the figure below, acceleration can be detected. The walls of this box are made with piezoelectric crystals. Whenever the box is tilted, the ball moves in the direction of the inclination due to gravity. The wall where the ball collides with creates tiny piezoelectric currents. There are three pairs of opposite walls in a cuboid. Each pair corresponds to an axis in 3D space: X, Y, and Z axes. Depending on the current produced from the piezoelectric walls, we can determine the direction of inclination and its magnitude.

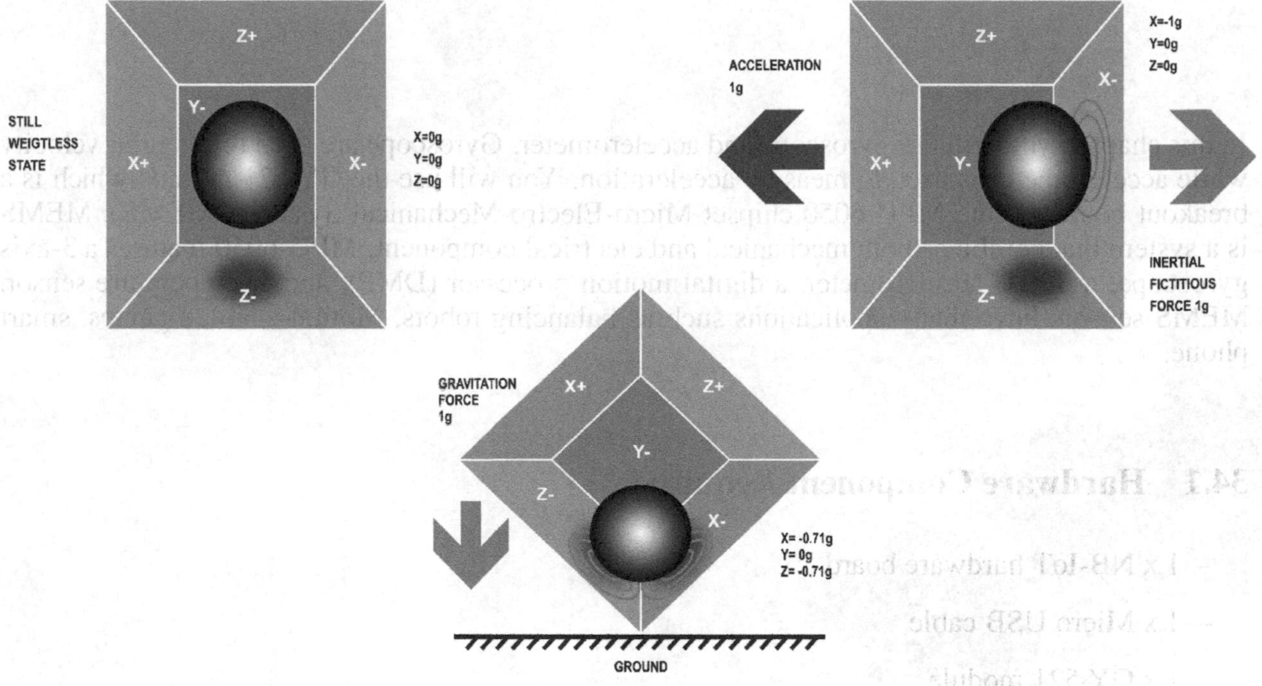

Figure 34.1: Cuboidal Box with a Small Ball Inside.

Gyroscope, in the most basic form, is a spinning wheel on an axle. When the wheel is not spinning, the gyroscope will fall over, obviously because of the gravity. However, if the wheel is spinning, the gyroscope will defy gravity. The main reason that a gyroscope defy gravity is due to phenomenon known as the angular momentum which will be in angular direction from gravity force and thus enable the gyroscope to defy gravity. The effect of the angular momentum on the spinning wheel causes the rational axis to deflect. This results in the rational axis to find a middle ground between the influence of the gravity and angular momentum.

34.3 Schematic Diagram

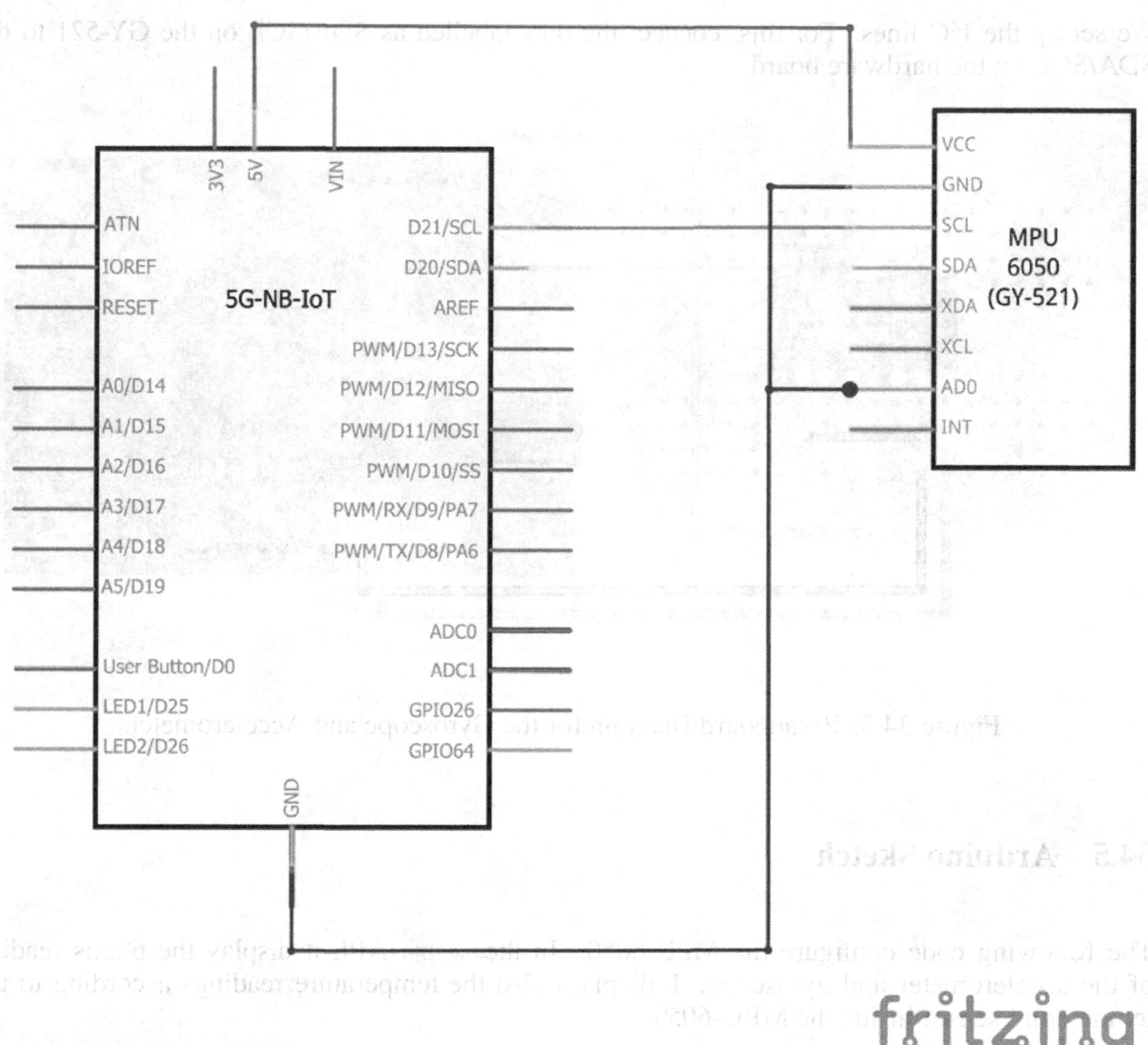

Figure 34.2: Schematic Diagram of the Gyroscope and Accelerometer.

34.4 Breadboard Diagram

We set up the I^{2}C lines. For this, connect the pins labelled as SDA/SCL on the GY-521 to the SDA/SCL on the hardware board.

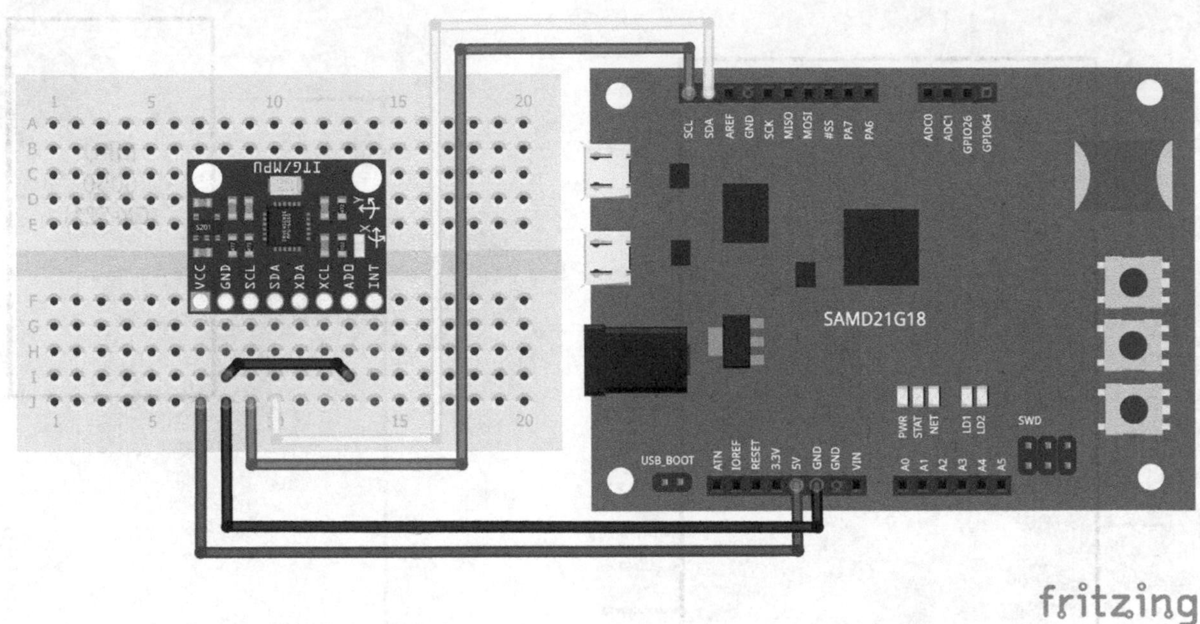

Figure 34.3: Breadboard Diagram for the Gyroscope and Accelerometer.

34.5 Arduino Sketch

The following code configure the MPU-6050. In the loop() API, it display the 6-axis reading of the accelerometer and gyroscope. It displays also the temperature readings according to the temperature sensor inside the MPU-6050.

```
#include<Wire.h>

#define DSerial SerialUSB

const int MPU_addr = 0x68; // I2C address of the MPU-6050
int16_t AcX, AcY, AcZ, Tmp, GyX, GyY, GyZ;
void setup()
{
  DSerial.begin(115200);
  while (DSerial.read() >= 0);
  DSerial.println("This is the _5GNBIoT Debug Serial!");
```

```
  Wire.begin();
  Wire.beginTransmission(MPU_addr);
  Wire.write(0x6B);  // PWR_MGMT_1 register
  Wire.write(0);     // Set to zero (wakes up the MPU-6050)
  Wire.endTransmission(true);
}

void loop()
{
  Wire.beginTransmission(MPU_addr);
    // Starting with register 0x3B (ACCEL_XOUT_H)
    Wire.write(0x3B);
  Wire.endTransmission(false);
  Wire.requestFrom(MPU_addr, 14, true); // Request a total of 14
   registers
  AcX = Wire.read() << 8 | Wire.read(); // 0x3B (ACCEL_XOUT_H) &
   0x3C (ACCEL_XOUT_L)
  AcY = Wire.read() << 8 | Wire.read(); // 0x3D (ACCEL_YOUT_H) &
   0x3E (ACCEL_YOUT_L)
  AcZ = Wire.read() << 8 | Wire.read(); // 0x3F (ACCEL_ZOUT_H) &
   0x40 (ACCEL_ZOUT_L)
  Tmp = Wire.read() << 8 | Wire.read(); // 0x41 (TEMP_OUT_H) & 0
   x42 (TEMP_OUT_L)
  GyX = Wire.read() << 8 | Wire.read(); // 0x43 (GYRO_XOUT_H) & 0
   x44 (GYRO_XOUT_L)
  GyY = Wire.read() << 8 | Wire.read(); // 0x45 (GYRO_YOUT_H) & 0
   x46 (GYRO_YOUT_L)
  GyZ = Wire.read() << 8 | Wire.read(); // 0x47 (GYRO_ZOUT_H) & 0
   x48 (GYRO_ZOUT_L)
  DSerial.print("AcX = "); DSerial.print(AcX);
  DSerial.print(" | AcY = "); DSerial.print(AcY);
  DSerial.print(" | AcZ = "); DSerial.print(AcZ);
  DSerial.print(" | Tmp = "); DSerial.print(Tmp / 340.00 + 36.53)
   ;
  // Equation for temperature in degrees C from datasheet
  DSerial.print(" | GyX = "); DSerial.print(GyX);
  DSerial.print(" | GyY = "); DSerial.print(GyY);
  DSerial.print(" | GyZ = "); DSerial.println(GyZ);
  delay(333);
}
```

Listing 34.1: Arduino Sketch for Gyroscope.

The Serial Monitor shows up the accelerometer, temperature, and gyroscope readings.

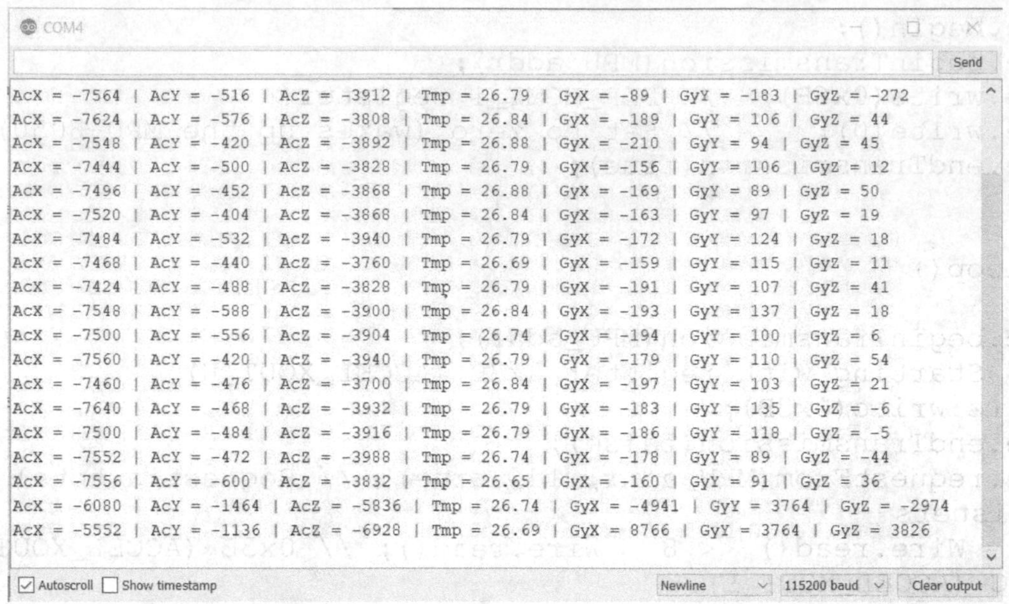

Figure 34.4: Serial Monitor Output for the Gyroscope and Accelerometer.

34.6 Interface with the Cloud

The gyroscope and accelerometer readings can be uploaded to the cloud and stored there. To make the Arduino sketch uploads the readings to the AWS cloud, add the following Arduino lines of codes to the above sketch and use the MQTT codes as explained in Listing 7.1 and Listing 7.2. Use the following JSON format to upload the accelerometer, temperature, and gyroscope readings to the cloud.

```
// ...... Previous code lines go here

docInput["DeviceID"] = IMEI;
docInput["Timestamp"] = millis();
docInput["Device"] = "Gyroscope";
docInput["OpCode"] = "Read";
docInput["AcX"] = AcX;
docInput["AcY"] = AcY;
docInput["AcZ"] = AcZ;
docInput["Tmp"] = Tmp;
docInput["GyX"] = GyX;
docInput["GyY"] = GyY;
docInput["GyZ"] = GyZ;
docInput["TmpUnit"] = "°F";
serializeJsonPretty(docInput, payload);

// ..... Next code lines go here
```

Listing 34.2: JSON Document for Gyroscope.

Upload the final sketch to the board and notice the output on the Serial Monitor as shown below.

Figure 34.5: Serial Monitor Output for JSON Data Published by the Gyroscope.

Go to the AWS IoT, and the JSON data received at the cloud are displayed on AWS dashboard. The received data readings on the cloud can be stored in a database, analyzed, processed. This application can be used for remote sensing and control, motion sensing, camera-shake detection systems in digital cameras, radio-controlled helicopters, and robotic systems.

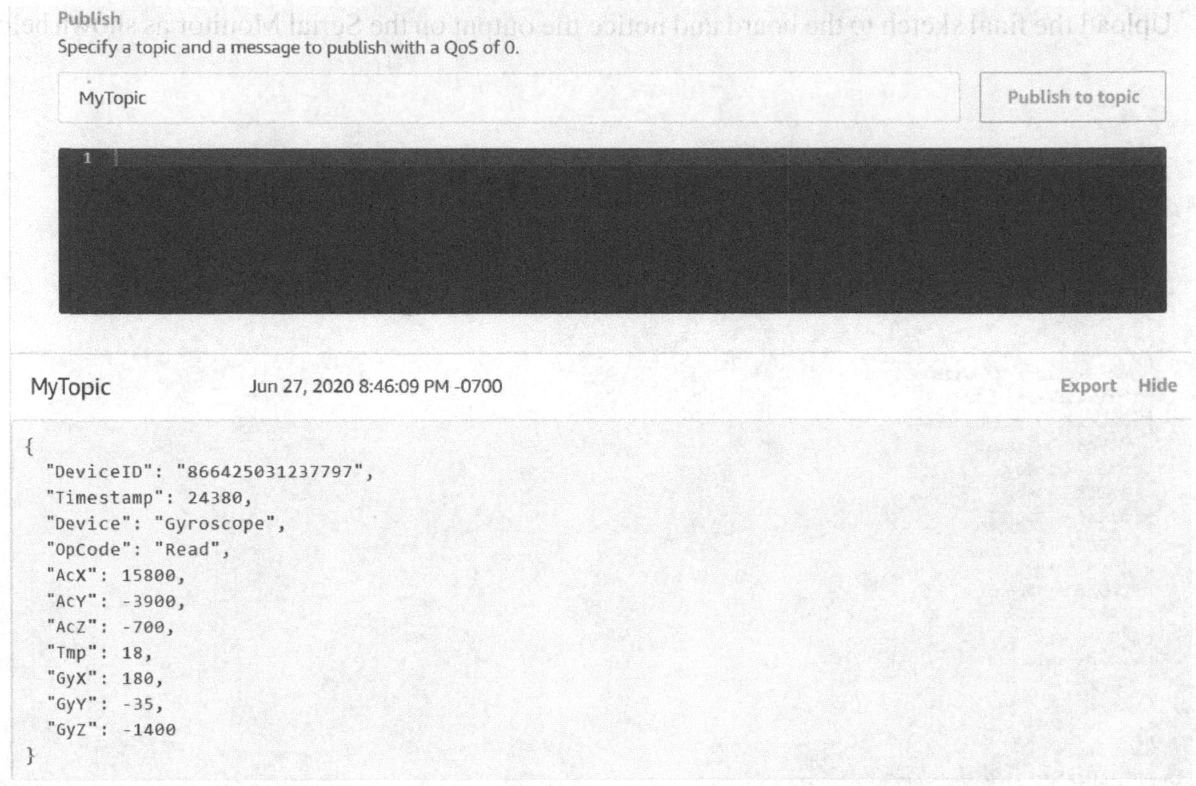

Figure 34.6: JSON Data on AWS IoT for the Gyroscope.

Part IV

Actuators

Chapter 35

Servo Motor

Servo motor is a type of motors that is geared and can rotate in an angular degrees (i.e., 30, 60, 90, or 180 angle). It is controlled by sending electrical pulses from hardware board. The electrical pulses make the servo moves to a specific position. They are used in robotics and toys.

35.1 Hardware Component Required

- 1 x NB-IoT hardware board
- 1 x Micro USB cable
- 1 x Servo (SG90)
- 1 x F-M wires

35.2 Schematic Diagram

Servo motors have three wires: power, ground, and signal. The power wire is typically red and should be connected to the 5V pin on the NB board. The ground wire is brown and is connected to a ground pin. The signal pin is orange and should be connected to a digital pin on the NB board. Servo motors draw a considerable amount of power, so if you need to drive more than one or two, you need to power them from a separate supply (i.e. not the +5V pin on the NB board). Always connect the grounds of the board and external power supply together.

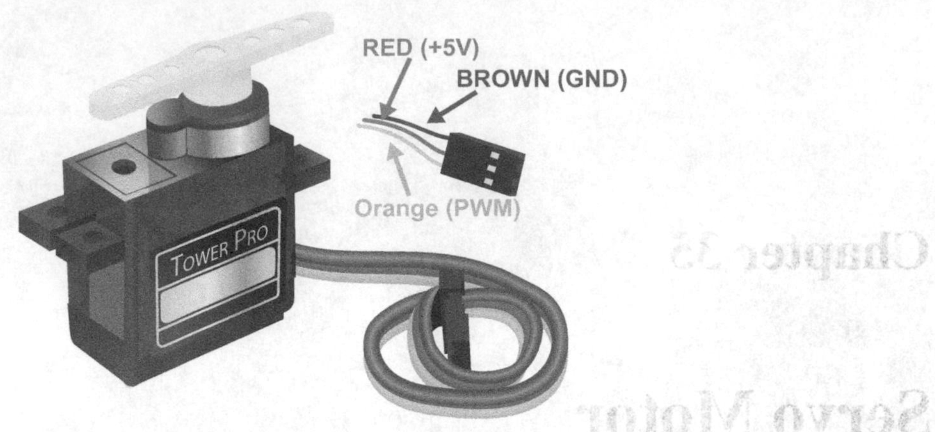

Figure 35.1: Servo Motor.

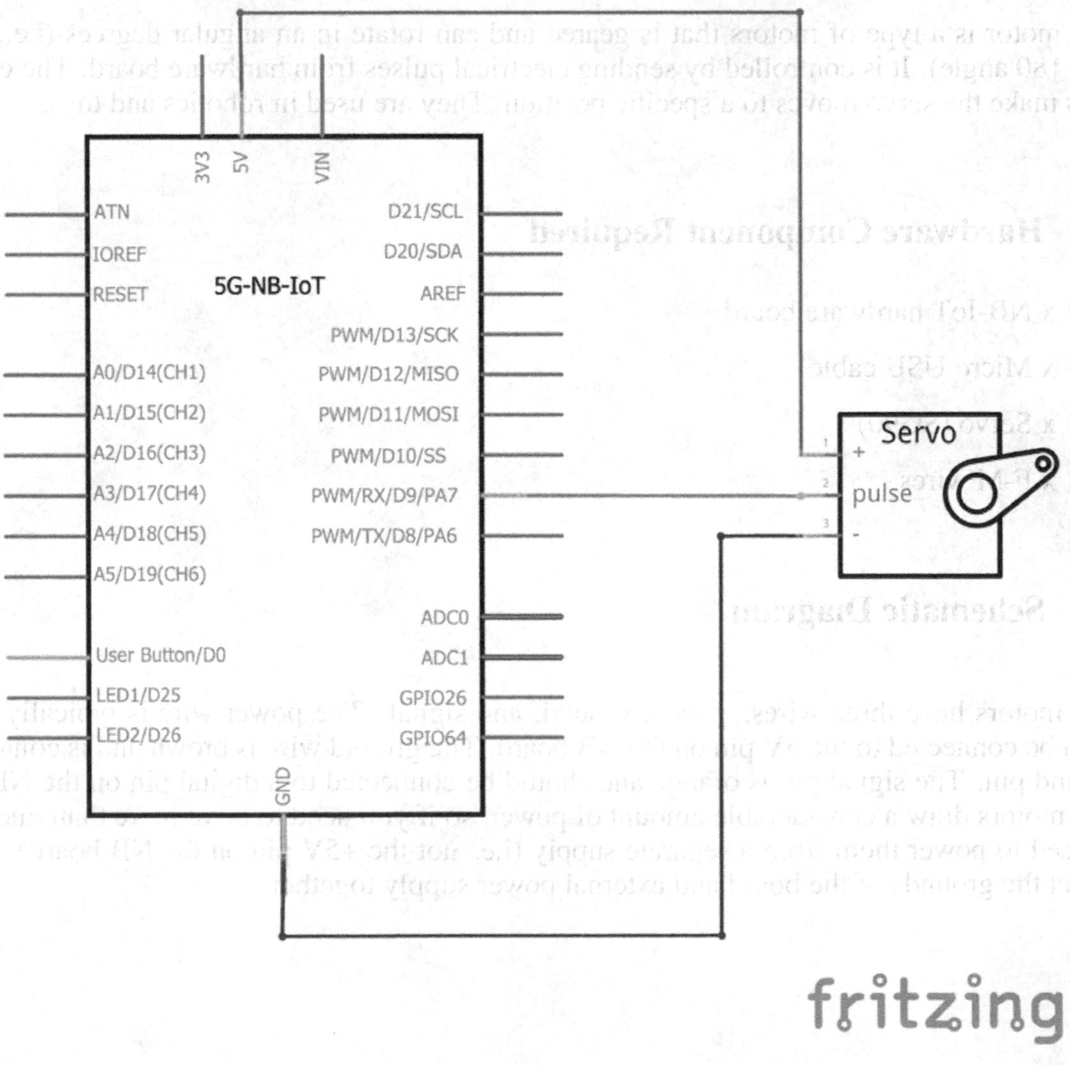

Figure 35.2: Schematic Diagram of the Servo Motor.

35.3 Breadboard Diagram

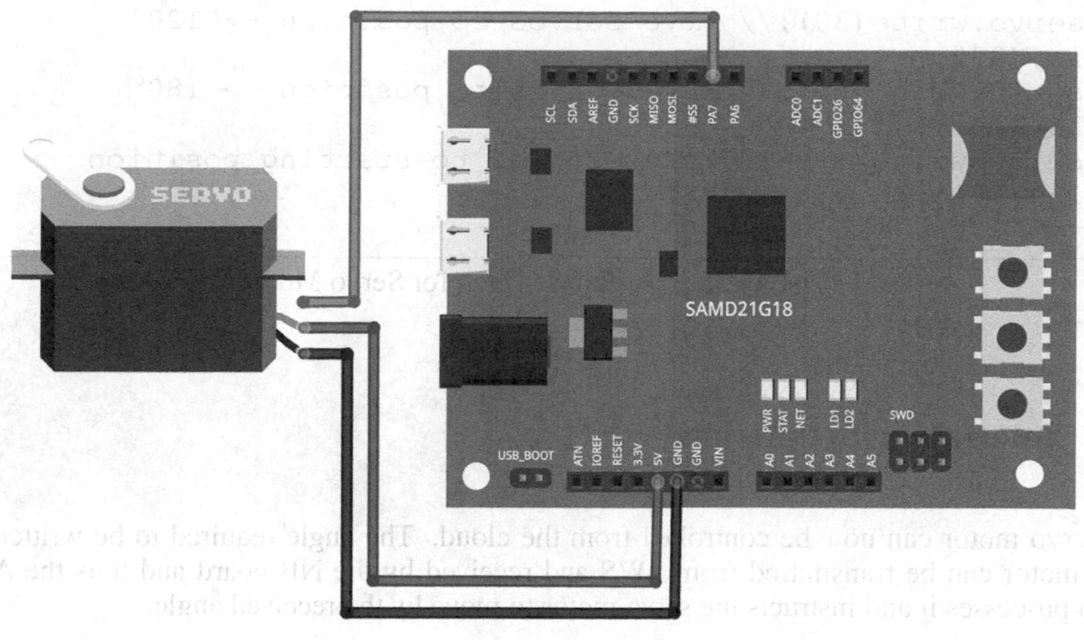

Figure 35.3: Breadboard Diagram of the Servo Motor.

35.4 Arduino Sketch

The Arduino sketch is shown in Listing 35.1. The signal wire of the servo motor is attached to pin PA7 on the NB board and then rotates the motor 90 degree.

When the Arduino sketch is uploaded and starts running, the servo motor will rotate slowly from 0 degrees to 90 degrees. It then increments by 30° (at position 120°) then increments by 60° (at position 180°) and finally increments by additional 180° which brings the motor to the initial and starting position.

```
#include <board.h>
#include <Servo.h>
Servo myservo;

void setup()
{
  myservo.attach(PA7);
  myservo.write(90);// move servos to center position -> 90°
}

void loop()
```

```
{
  myservo.write(90);// move servos to position -> 90°
  delay(500);
  myservo.write(30);// move servos to position -> 120°
  delay(500);
  myservo.write(60);// move servos to position -> 180°
  delay(500);
  myservo.write(180);// move servos to starting position -> 0°
  delay(500);
}
```

Listing 35.1: Arduino Sketch for Servo Motor.

35.5 Interface with the Cloud

The servo motor can now be controlled from the cloud. The angle required to be written to the servo motor can be transmitted from AWS and received by the NB board and thus the Arduino sketch processes it and instructs the servo motor to move by the received angle.

To make the Arduino sketch receive the servo motor movements from the cloud, the following Arduino lines of codes are added to the above sketch and the MQTT codes explained in Listing 7.1 and Listing 7.2 are also used.

```
// ...... Previous code lines go here

case MQTT_RECV_DATA_EVENT:
error = deserializeJson(docOutput, payload);

if (error == DeserializationError::Ok)
{
  if (docOutput["Device"] == "Servo")
   {
    DSerial.println("Device is a Servo motor!");

    DSerial.println(docOutput["DeviceID"].as<String>());
    DSerial.println(docOutput["Timestamp"].as<double>(), 6);
    DSerial.println(docOutput["Device"].as<String>());
    DSerial.println(docOutput["OpCode"].as<String>());
    DSerial.println(docOutput["Angle"].as<int>());
    DSerial.println(docOutput["Unit"].as<String>());

    if (docOutput["OpCode"] == "Write")
    {
      myservo.write(docOutput["Angle"]);
      DSerial.print("\r\nAngle written to servo motor:");
      DSerial.println(docOutput["Angle"].as<int>());
```

```
    }
  }
  else
  {
    DSerial.println("Device is not a Servo motor!");
  }
}
else
{
  DSerial.println("\r\n Error in  Deserialization!");
  DSerial.println(error.c_str());
}
break;

// ..... Next code lines go here
```

Listing 35.2: JSON Document for Servo Motor.

To control the servo motor from the AWS IoT cloud, a JSON-formatted message is transmitted from AWS IoT. The JSON message contains the 15-digit IMEI so that only message designated to the device can be processed. Timestamp which includes the date and/or time of the day, the device name, set to "Servo", and OpCode (set to "Write" indicating a write operation), and the angle to be written to the servo motor, and finally the unit of the angle which is in degree.


```
{
  "DeviceID": "866425031237797",
  "Timestamp": 122219,
  "Device": "Servo",
  "OpCode": "Write",
  "Angle": 30,
  "Unit": "Degree"
}
```


Listing 35.3: JSON Data for Servo Motor.

Go to the AWS IoT, writes the JSON data to be transmitted to the NB board, and click **Publish to topic**. The JSON message is transmitted to the device.

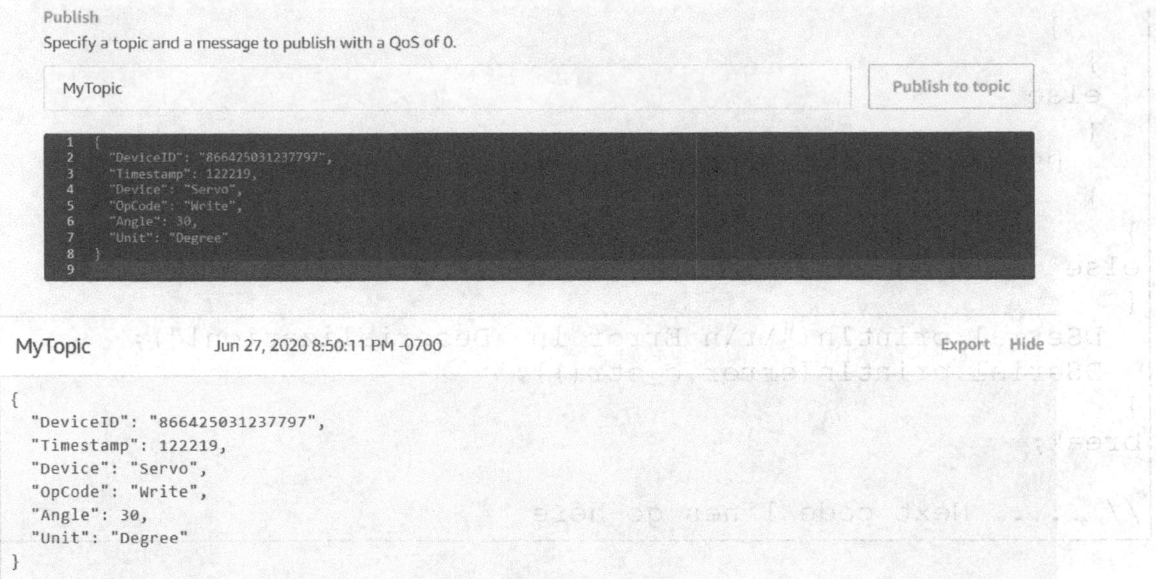

Figure 35.4: JSON Data Published on AWS IoT for the Servo Motor.

In the Serial Monitor, the JSON data is received by the NB board, deserialized, and finally the servo motor is moved by the angle included in the JSON message.

Upon deserialization of the JSON message, more processing can be done such as discarding those messages if the IMEI is different than that of the current device or if the OpCode is not supported by the device, or any other condition as seems appropriate.

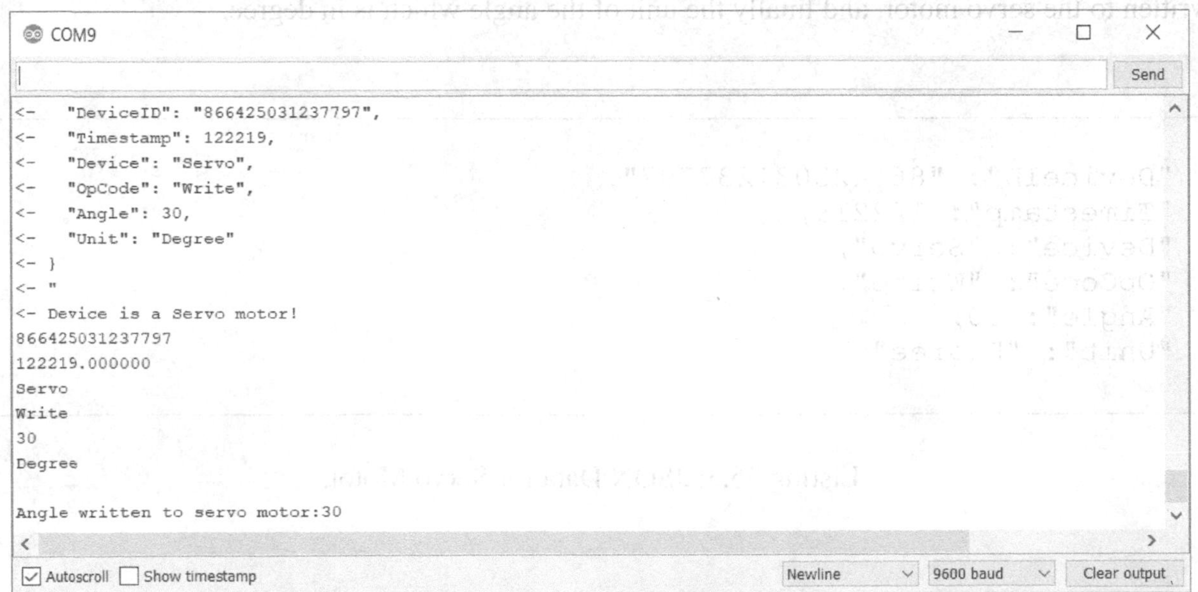

Figure 35.5: JSON Data Received by the Servo Motor.

Chapter 36

Stepper Motor

In this chapter, you will use and drive a stepper motor. A stepper motor is a DC motor that moves in discrete steps. It has multiple coils that are organized in groups called "phases". By energizing each phase in sequence, the motor rotates, one step at a time. You can control the stepper motor to achieve very precise positioning and/or speed control. stepper motors are used in many precision motion control applications such as hard disk drives, robotics, antennas, telescopes, and toys. The stepper motor has its own driver hardware board to make it easy to connect to the NB board.

36.1 Hardware Component Required

- 1 x NB-IoT hardware board
  - 1 x Micro USB cable
  - 1 x IR receiver module
  - 1 x IR remote
  - 1 x ULN2003 stepper motor driver module
  - 1 x 28BYJ-48 stepper motor
  - 1 x 9V1A adapter
  - 1 x Power supply module
  - 1 x F-M wires
  - 1 x M-M wire

36.2 Circuit Operation

A stepper motor is an electromechanical device which converts electrical pulses into discrete mechanical movements. The shaft or spindle of a stepper motor rotates in discrete and precise step increments when electrical pulses are applied to it in the proper sequence. The motors rotation has several direct relationships to these applied input pulses. The sequence of the applied pulses is directly related to the direction of motor shafts rotation. The speed of the motor shafts rotation is directly related to the frequency of the input pulses and the length of rotation is directly related to the number of input pulses applied. One of the most significant advantages of a stepper motor is its ability to be accurately controlled in an open loop system. Open loop control means no feedback information about position is needed. This type of control eliminates the need for expensive sensing and feedback devices such as optical encoders. The stepper motor position is known simply by keeping track of the input step pulses. The stepper motor position is known simply by keeping track of the input step pulses.

A stepper motor can be unipolar or bipolar. A unipolar stepper motor can be used as unipolar or a bipolar stepper motor. A bipolar stepper motor can only be used as a bipolar. The unipolar stepper motor usually has five wires coming out of it including one wire for common center connection. It has two independent sets of coils as shown in the figure below. The common coil wires are tied together internally and brought out as a fifth wire.

The simplest way of interfacing a unipolar stepper to the NB board is to use a ULN2003 transistor array chip (transistor arrays are also called Darlington configuration). A stepper motor consumes high current and a driver IC, such as ULN2003, is needed in order to control the motor from the hardware kit. ULN2003 driver is known by its high current and high voltage capacity, the ULN2003 gives a higher current gain than a single transistor and enables the low voltage and low current output of a hardware board to drive a higher current stepper motor. The ULN2003 contains seven Darlington transistor drivers all in one package. The ULN2003 can pass up to 500 mA per channel and has an internal voltage drop of about 1V when on. It also contains internal clamp diodes to dissipate voltage spikes when driving inductive loads.

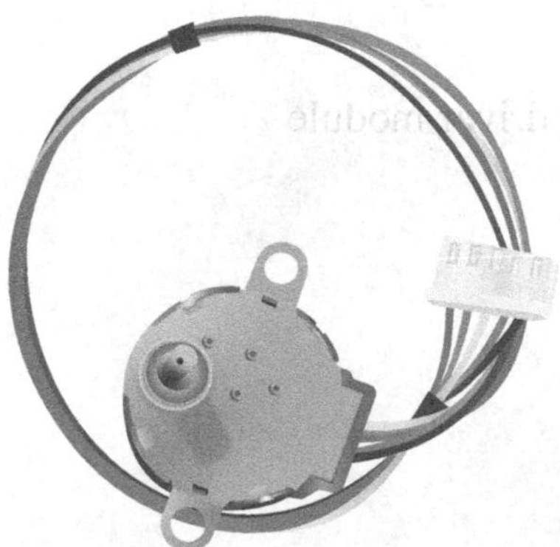

Figure 36.1: Stepper Motor.

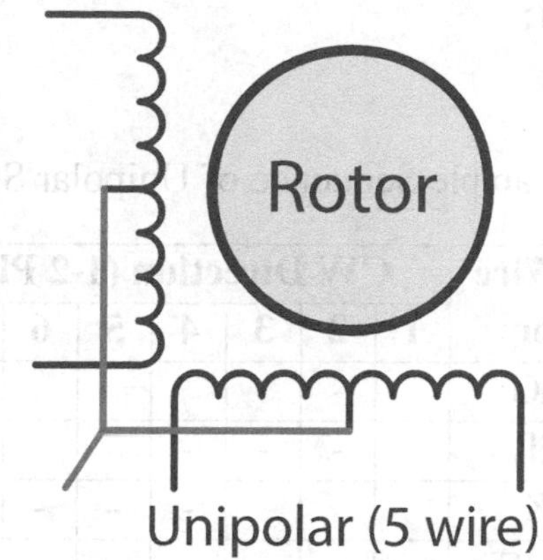

Figure 36.2: Unipolar Stepper Motor with Two Independent Coils.

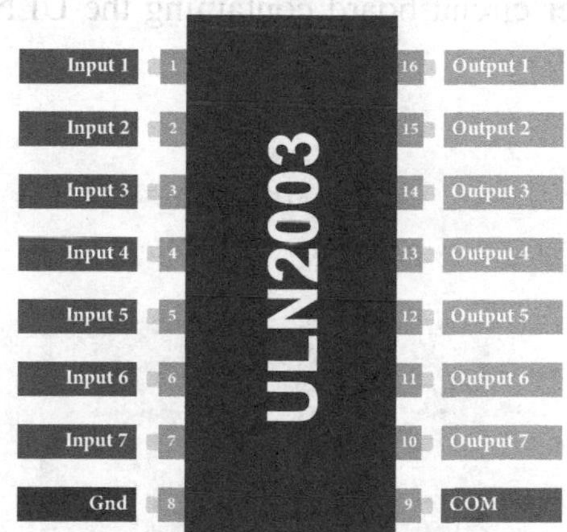

Figure 36.3: ULN2003 Driver chip.

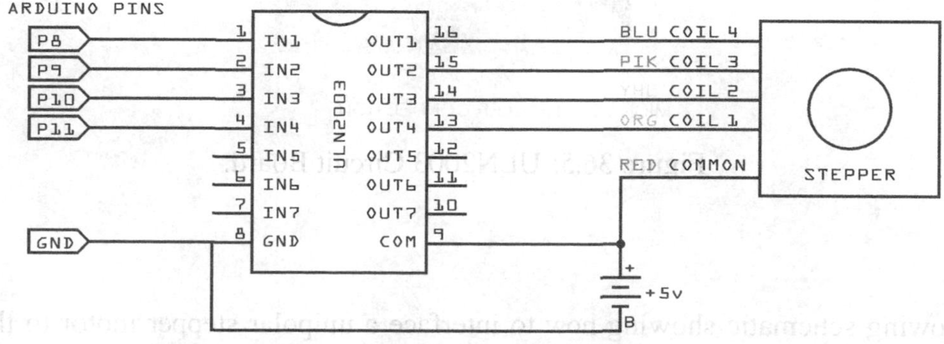

Figure 36.4: Stepper Motor with ULN2003 Driver Interface.

To control the stepper motor, apply a voltage to each of the coils in a specific sequence. An example sequence is in Table 36.1:

Table 36.1: Example Sequence of Unipolar Stepper Motor.

Lead Wire Color	CW Direction (1-2 Phase)							
	1	2	3	4	5	6	7	8
4 ORG	-	-						-
3 YEL		-	-	-				
2 PIK				-	-	-		
1 BLUE						-	-	-

The following is a controller circuit board containing the ULN2003 and is used to drive and interface with the stepper motor.

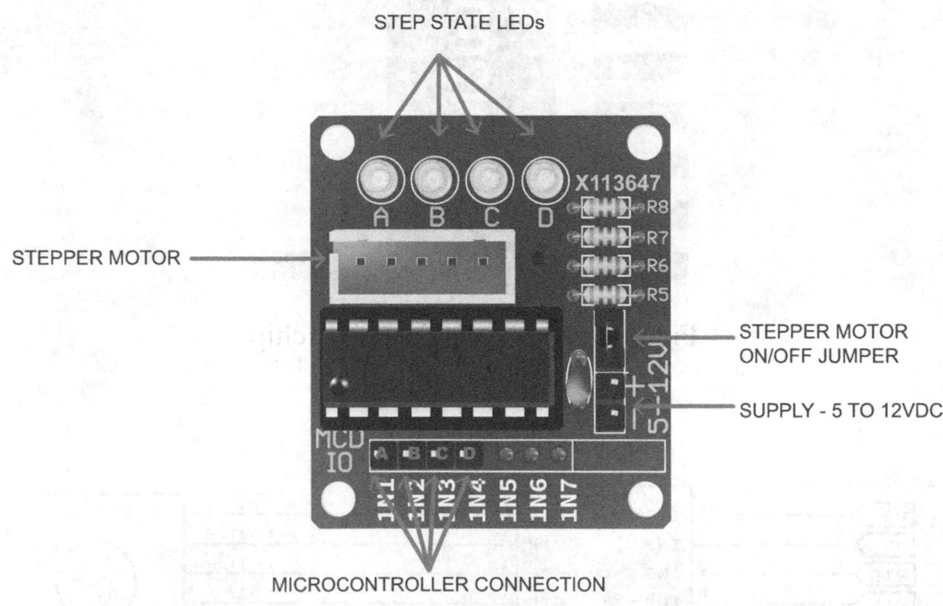

Figure 36.5: ULN2003 Circuit Board.

The following schematic showing how to interface a unipolar stepper motor to the controller pins using an ULN2003 driver and showing how to interface to the NB board using four pin which controls the stepper motor through the ULN2003 driver. The ground is connected to the stepper motor.

36.3 Schematic Diagram

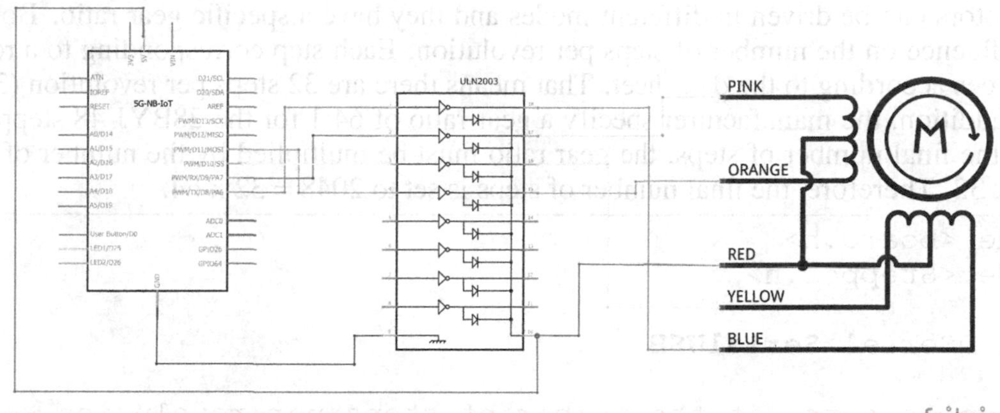

Figure 36.6: Schematic Diagram of the Stepper Motor.

36.4 Breadboard Diagram

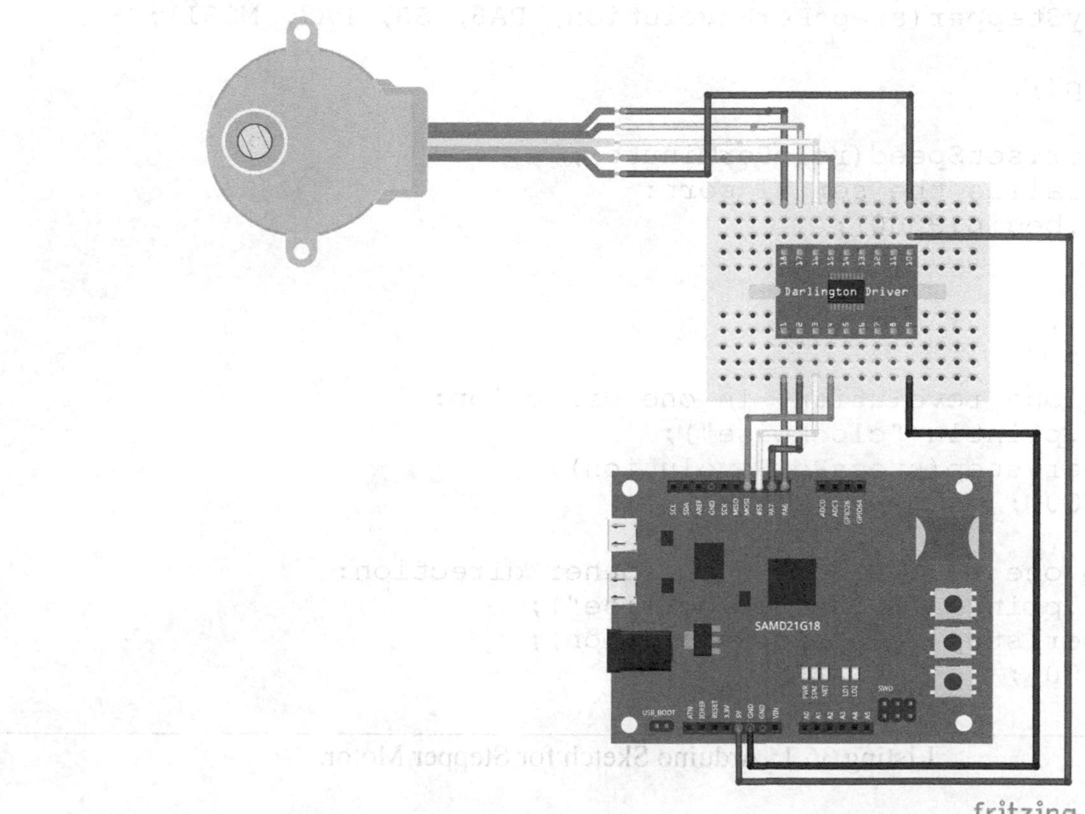

Figure 36.7: Breadboard Diagram of the Stepper Motor.

36.5 Arduino Sketch

Stepper motors can be driven in different modes and they have a specific gear ratio. Both factors have an influence on the number of steps per revolution. Each step corresponding to a rotation of 11.25 degrees according to the datasheet. That means there are 32 steps per revolution (360/11.25 = 32). In addition, the manufacturer specify a gear ratio of 64:1 for the 28BYJ-48 stepper motor. To obtain the final number of steps, the gear ratio must be multiplied by the number of steps per revolution, 32. Therefore, the final number of steps is set to 2048 = 32 x 64.

```
#include <board.h>
#include <Stepper.h>

#define DSerial SerialUSB

// Change this to fit the number of steps per revolution
const int stepsPerRevolution = 2048;

// Adjustable range of 28BYJ-48 stepper is 0~17 rpm
const int rolePerMinute = 15;

// IN1 - PA6, IN2 - PA7, IN3 - SS, IN4 - MOSI
// Initialize the stepper library on pins PA6, SS, PA7, MOSI
Stepper myStepper(stepsPerRevolution, PA6, SS, PA7, MOSI);

void setup()
{
  myStepper.setSpeed(rolePerMinute);
  // Initialize the serial port:
  DSerial.begin(9600);
}

void loop()
{
  // Step one revolution  in one direction:
  DSerial.println("clockwise");
  myStepper.step(stepsPerRevolution);
  delay(500);

  // Step one revolution in the other direction:
  DSerial.println("counterclockwise");
  myStepper.step(-stepsPerRevolution);
  delay(500);
}
```

Listing 36.1: Arduino Sketch for Stepper Motor.

After uploading the sketch, the stepper motor starts to rotate in a number of steps and the Serial Monitor shows up the direction of movement.

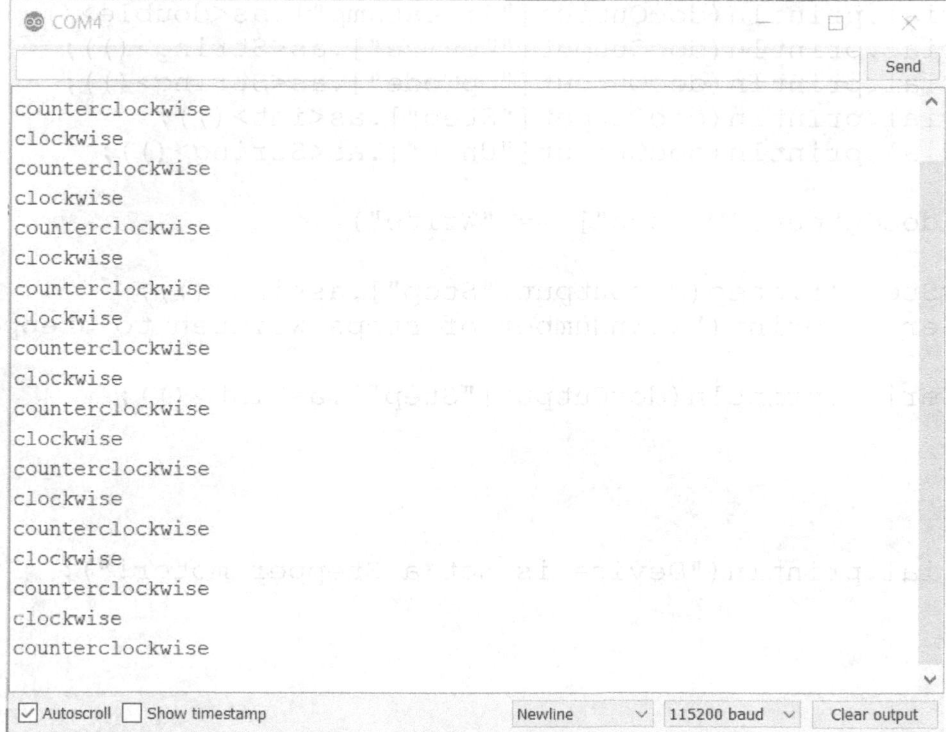

Figure 36.8: Serial Monitor Output for the Stepper Motor.

36.6 Interface with the Cloud

The stepper motor can be controlled from the cloud. The number of steps required to be written to the stepper motor can be transmitted from AWS IoT and received by the NB board and thus the Arduino sketch processes it and instructs the stepper motor to move by the received number of steps. Stepper motor can move clockwise or anti-clockwise through specifying positive or negative number of steps to move the stepper motor clockwise or anti-clockwise respectively.

To make the NB board receives the steps for the stepper motor and be control the stepper motor from the cloud, the following Arduino lines of codes are added to the above sketch and the MQTT codes explained in Listing 7.1 and Listing 7.2 are also used.

```
case MQTT_RECV_DATA_EVENT:
error = deserializeJson(docOutput, payload);

if (error == DeserializationError::Ok)
{
  if (docOutput["Device"] == "StepperMotor")
  {
    DSerial.println("Device is a Stepper motor!");
    DSerial.println(docOutput["DeviceID"].as<String>());
```

```
    DSerial.println(docOutput["Timestamp"].as<double>(), 6);
    DSerial.println(docOutput["Device"].as<String>());
    DSerial.println(docOutput["OpCode"].as<String>());
    DSerial.println(docOutput["Step"].as<int>());
    DSerial.println(docOutput["Unit"].as<String>());

    if (docOutput["OpCode"] == "Write")
    {
      myStepper.step(docOutput["Step"].as<int>());
      DSerial.print("\r\nNumber of steps written to stepper motor
   :");
      DSerial.println(docOutput["Step"].as<int>());
    }
  }
  else
  {
    DSerial.println("Device is not a Stepper motor!");
  }
}
else
{
  DSerial.println("\r\n Error in  Deserialization!");
  DSerial.println(error.c_str());
}
break;
```

Listing 36.2: JSON Document for Stepper Motor.

To control the stepper motor from the AWS IoT cloud, a JSON-formatted message is transmitted from AWS IoT. The JSON message contains the 15-digit IMEI so that only message designated to the device can be processed, Timestamp which includes the date and/or time of the day, the device name (set to "StepperMotor"), and OpCode (set to "Write" indicating a write operation), and the number of steps to be written to the stepper motor, and finally the unit of the rotation which is in step.


```
{
  "DeviceID": "866425031237797",
  "Timestamp": 122219,
  "Device": "StepperMotor",
  "OpCode": "Write",
  "Step": 5,
  "Unit": "Step"
}
```


Listing 36.3: JSON Data for Stepper Motor.

Go to the AWS IoT, writes the JSON data to be transmitted to the hardware board, and click **Publish to topic**. The JSON message is published to the device.

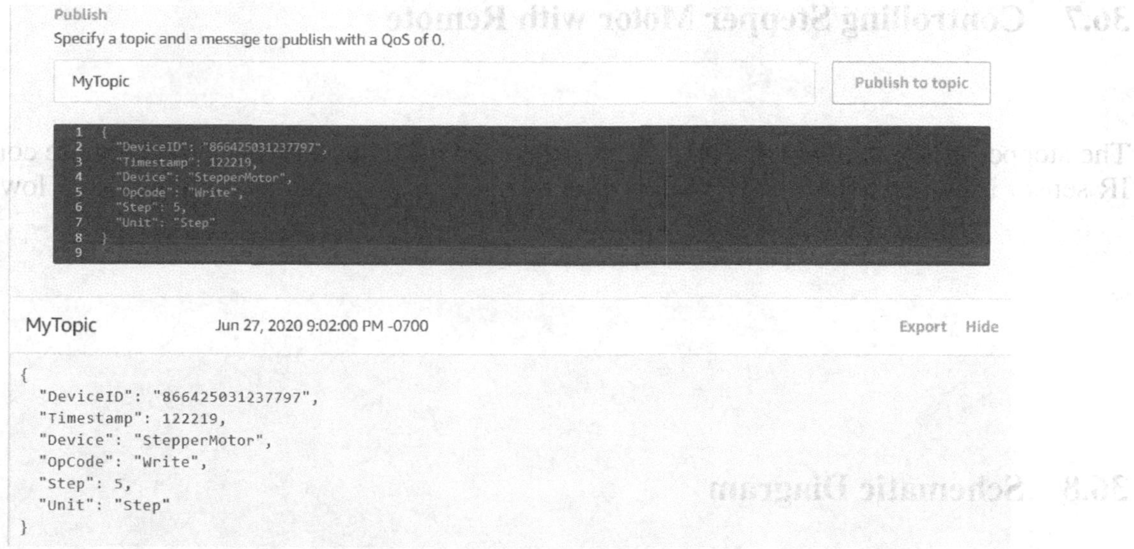
Publish
Specify a topic and a message to publish with a QoS of 0.
MyTopic
Publish to topic
MyTopic
Jun 27, 2020 9:02:00 PM -0700
Export
Hide
{
"DeviceID": "866425031237797",
"Timestamp": 122219,
"Device": "StepperMotor",
"OpCode": "Write",
"Step": 5,
"Unit": "Step"
}

Figure 36.9: JSON Data Published on AWS IoT for the Stepper Motor.

In the Serial Monitor, the JSON data is received by the NB board, deserialized, and finally the stepper motor is moved by the number of steps included in the JSON message. Upon deserialization of the JSON message, more processing can be done such as discarding those messages if the IMEI is different than that of the current device or if the OpCode is not supported by the device, or any other condition as seems appropriate.

```
COM9
<-    "DeviceID": "866425031237797",
<-    "Timestamp": 122219,
<-    "Device": "StepperMotor",
<-    "OpCode": "Write",
<-    "Step": 5,
<-    "Unit": "Step"
<- }
<- "
<- Device is a Stepper motor!
866425031237797
122219.000000
StepperMotor
Write
5
Step
Number of steps written to stepper motor:5
Autoscroll  Show timestamp    Newline    9600 baud    Clear output
```

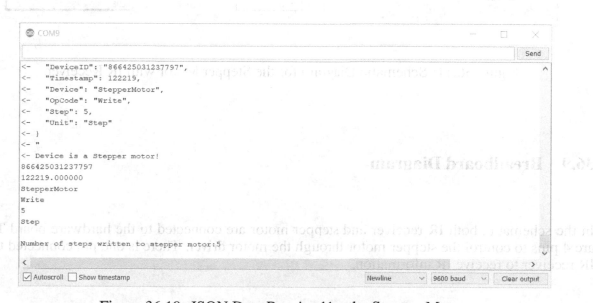

Figure 36.10: JSON Data Received by the Stepper Motor.

36.7 Controlling Stepper Motor with Remote

The stepper motor can be controlled from a distance using an Infra-Red (IR) remote control. The IR sensor is connected to the NB board directly since its power consumption is very low.

36.8 Schematic Diagram

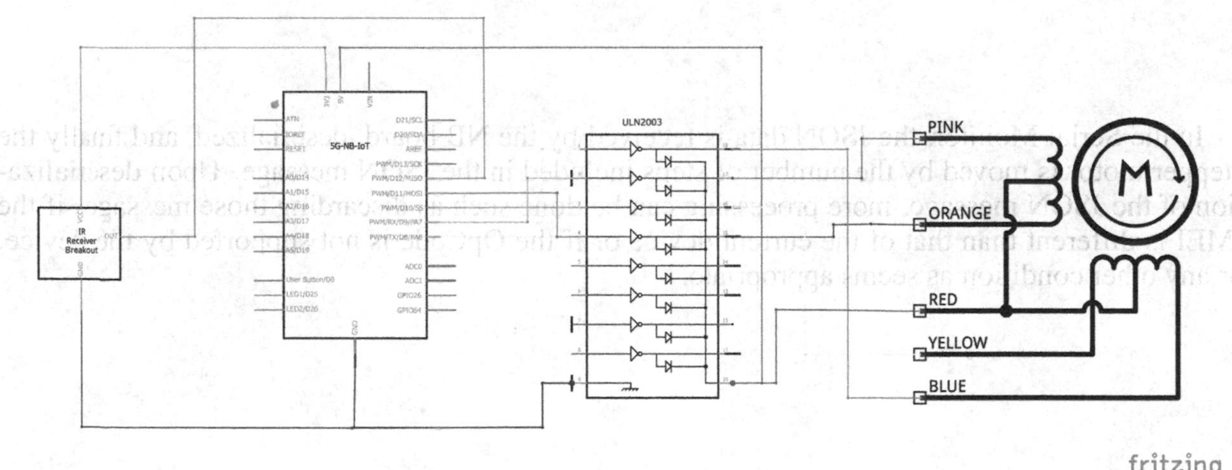

Figure 36.11: Schematic Diagram for the Stepper Motor with IR Receiver.

36.9 Breadboard Diagram

In the schematic, both IR receiver and stepper motor are connected to the hardware board There are 4 pins to control the stepper motor through the motor driver. There is one pin connected to the IR receiver to receive IR information.

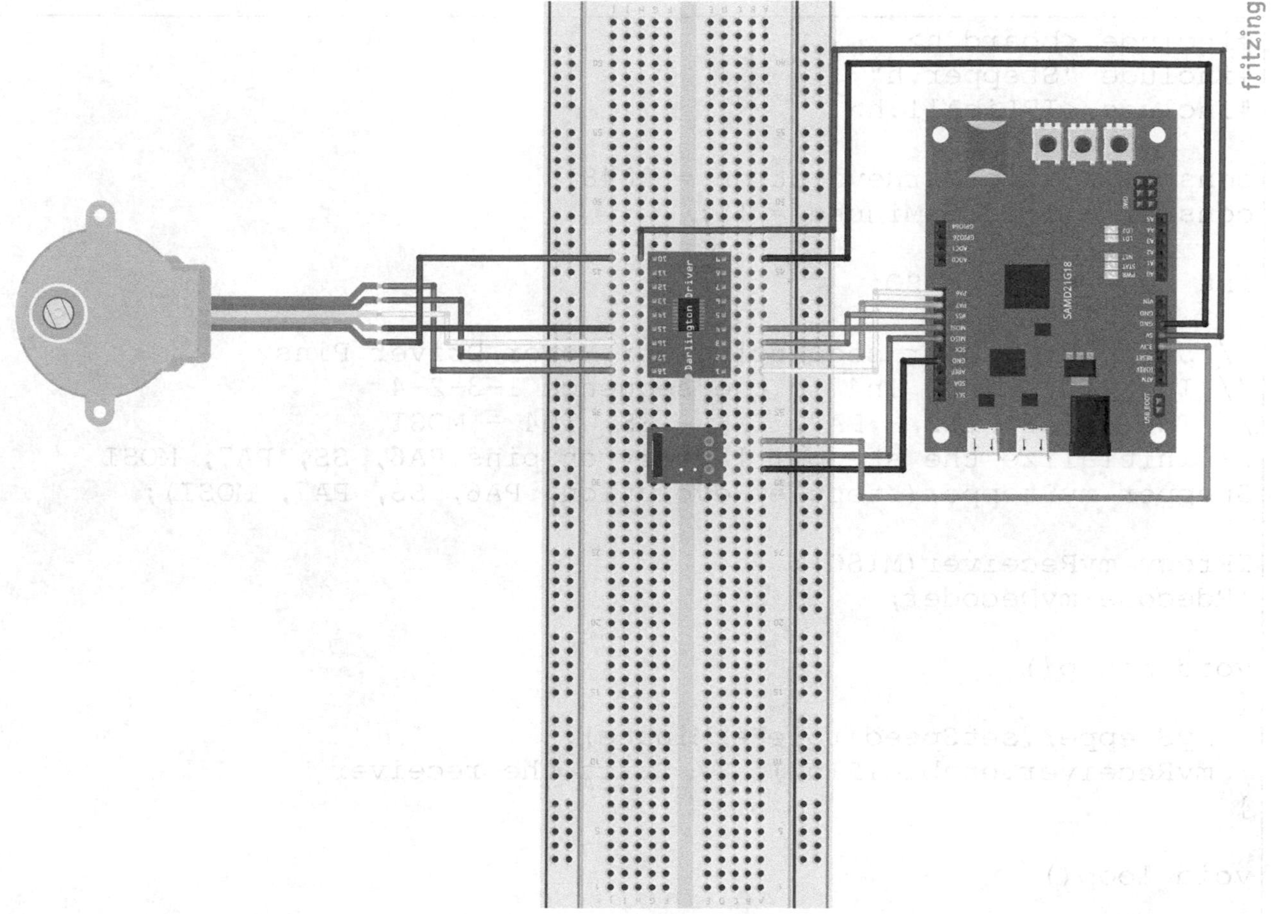

Figure 36.12: Breadboard Diagram for the Stepper Motor with IR Receiver.

36.10 Arduino Sketch

The following Arduino sketch starts by configuring the stepper motor. Using the IR remote, the stepper motor movement can be controlled using the VOL+ and VOL- buttons on the IR remote. Pressing VOL+, moves the stepper motor clockwise while pressing VOL- moves the stepper motor anti-clockwise.

```
#include <board.h>
#include "Stepper.h"
#include <IRLibAll.h>

const int stepsPerRevolution = 2048;
const int rolePerMinute = 15;

int receiver = MISO;

// Setup of proper sequencing for Motor Driver Pins
// In1, In2, In3, In4 in the sequence 1-3-2-4
// IN1 - PA6, IN2 - PA7, IN3 - SS, IN4 - MOSI
// initialize the stepper library on pins PA6, SS, PA7, MOSI
Stepper myStepper(stepsPerRevolution, PA6, SS, PA7, MOSI);

IRrecv myReceiver(MISO);
IRdecode myDecoder;

void setup()
{
  myStepper.setSpeed(rolePerMinute);
  myReceiver.enableIRIn(); // Start the receiver
}

void loop()
{
  if (myReceiver.getResults())
  {
    myDecoder.decode();
    if (myDecoder.protocolNum == NEC)
    {
      switch (myDecoder.value)
      {
        case 0xFFA857: // VOL+ button pressed
        myStepper.step(stepsPerRevolution);
        break;

        case 0xFFE01F: // VOL- button pressed
        myStepper.step(-stepsPerRevolution);
        break;
      }
      delay(500); // Do not get immediate repeat
      myReceiver.enableIRIn(); //Restart the receiver
    }
  }
}
```

Listing 36.4: Arduino Sketch for Stepper Motor.

Chapter 37

Relay

In this chapter, you will learn how to control high voltage devices using the NB board. The Relay can be used to turn on/off light bulbs, home appliances, or other high-voltage devices in home, office, or industrial location.

37.1 Hardware Component Required

- 1 x NB-IoT hardware board
- 1 x Micro USB cable
- 1 x 3-6V DC motor
- 1 x KY-019 5V Relay
- 1 x Power Supply Module
- 1 x External 5V DC power supply
- 1 x F-M wires

37.2 Circuit Operation

A Relay is a switch which is electrically operated by an electromagnet. The electromagnet is activated with a low voltage. For example, a low voltage of 5V from a microcontroller pulls a contact to make or break a high voltage circuit such as a 220V light bulb, stove, fridge, electrical appliance, or a DC motor. Relay can be used to control high voltage electronic devices and appliances.

Using the KY-019 5V relay module, which has a rating of 10A @ 250V and 125V AC and 10A @ 30V and 28V DC. The high voltage output connector has 3 pins, the middle one is the common

Figure 37.1: Relay.

pin and one of the two other pins is for normally open connection and the other one for normally closed connection.

On the other side of the module we have three pins. One pin for the ground, another pin for the VCC, and third pin for signal. Connecting these three pins from the NB board, the relay is directly powered from the board and controlled from the board.

37.3 Schematic Diagram

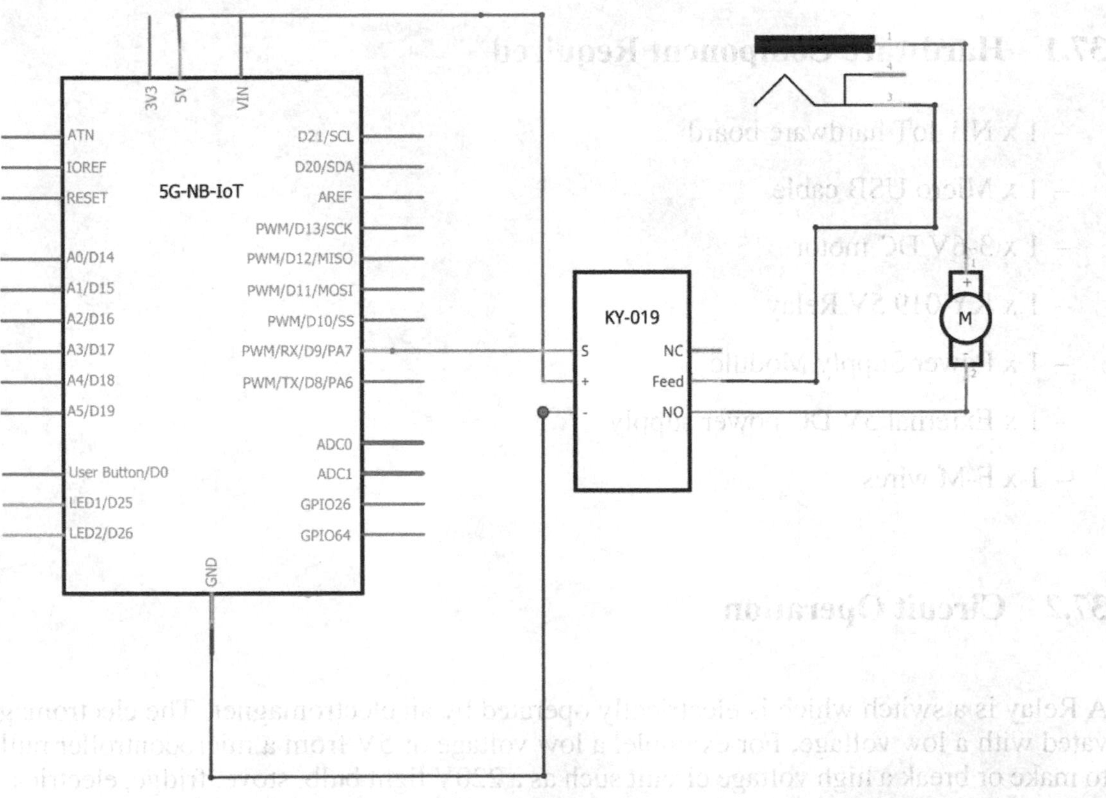

Figure 37.2: Schematic Diagram for the Relay.

37.4 Breadboard Diagram

The NB board 5V and GND pins are connected to the VCC and GND pins of the relay. The relay is used to control a DC motor. The DC motor is powered from external 5V DC power supply. The DC motor has two wires, one wire is connected to the positive of the external DC power supply while the second wire of the DC motor is connected to the normally open pin of the relay. With this configuration, when the relay is activated, the DC motor circuit is closed and as a result the motor starts to rotate.

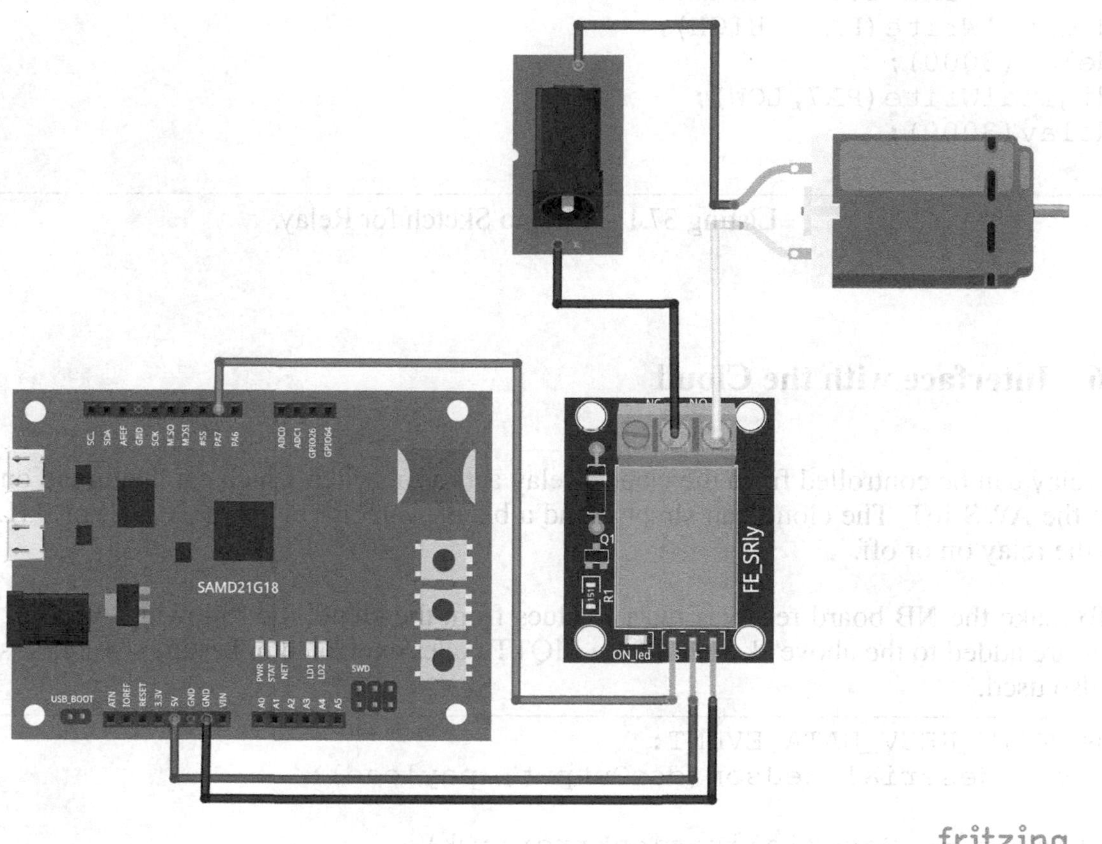

Figure 37.3: Breadboard Diagram for the Relay.

37.5 Arduino Sketch

The Arduino sketch is shown below. In the setup, it configures PA7 as the output signal to the relay. In the loop, it sends a high and low signal which closes the motor circuits making it starts to rotate and stops rotating alternatively.

```
#include <board.h>

void setup()
{
  pinMode(PA7, OUTPUT);
}

void loop()
{
  // Back and forth example
  digitalWrite(PA7, HIGH);
  delay(3000);
  digitalWrite(PA7,LOW);
  delay(3000);
}
```

Listing 37.1: Arduino Sketch for Relay.

37.6 Interface with the Cloud

The relay can be controlled from the cloud. Relay acts as a switch which can be turned on and off from the AWS IoT. The cloud can simply send a binary value or either 1 (HIGH) or 0 (LOW) to turn the relay on or off.

To make the NB board receives binary values from the cloud, the following Arduino lines of codes are added to the above sketch and the MQTT codes explained in Listing 7.1 and Listing 7.2 are also used.

```
case MQTT_RECV_DATA_EVENT:
error = deserializeJson(docOutput, payload);

if (error == DeserializationError::Ok)
{
  if (docOutput["Device"] == "Relay")
  {
    DSerial.println("Device is a Relay!");

    DSerial.println(docOutput["DeviceID"].as<String>());
    DSerial.println(docOutput["Timestamp"].as<double>(), 6);
    DSerial.println(docOutput["Device"].as<String>());
    DSerial.println(docOutput["OpCode"].as<String>());
    DSerial.println(docOutput["Relay"].as<int>());
    DSerial.println(docOutput["Unit"].as<String>());

    if (docOutput["OpCode"] == "Write")
```

```
        {
          digitalWrite(PA7, docOutput["Relay"].as<int>());
          DSerial.print("\r\nNumber of steps written to Relay:");
          DSerial.println(docOutput["Relay"].as<int>());
        }
      }
      else
      {
        DSerial.println("Device is not a Relay!");
      }
    }
    else
    {
      DSerial.println("\r\n Error in Deserialization!");
      DSerial.println(error.c_str());
    }
    break;
```

Listing 37.2: JSON Document for Relay.

To turn the relay on or off, a JSON-formatted message is transmitted from AWS IoT. The JSON message contains the 15-digit IMEI, Timestamp, the device name, set to "Relay", and OpCode (set to "Write" indicating a write operation), and a binary value of either 1 or 0, and finally the unit of control which is binary.

```
{
  "DeviceID": "866425031237797",
  "Timestamp": 122219,
  "Device": "Relay",
  "OpCode": "Write",
  "Relay": 1,
  "Unit": "Binary"
}
```

Listing 37.3: JSON Data for Relay.

Go to the AWS IoT, writes the JSON data to be published to the device, and click **Publish to topic**. The JSON message will be transmitted to the device.

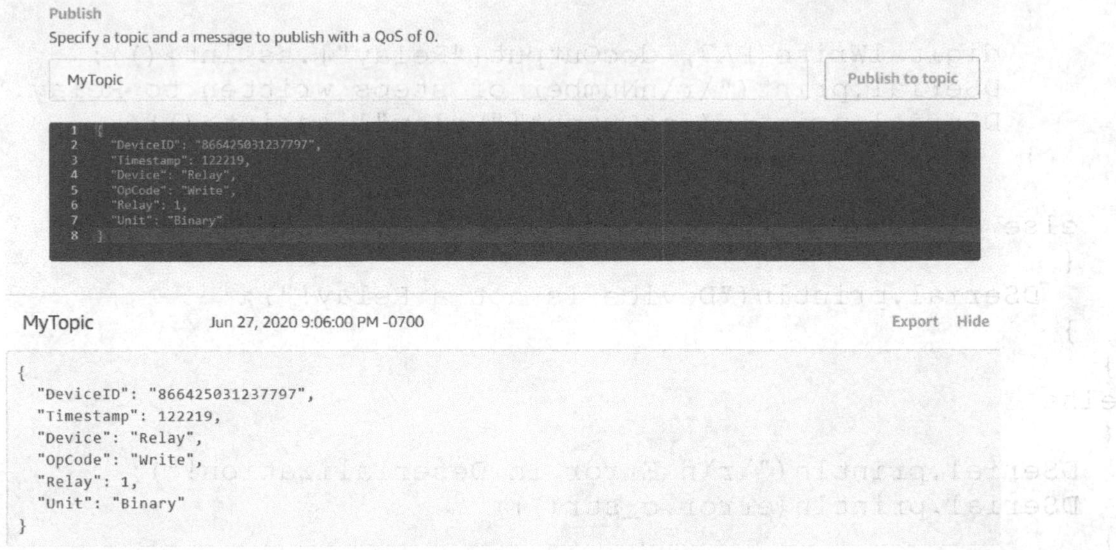

Figure 37.4: JSON Data Published on AWS IoT for the Relay.

In the Serial Monitor, the JSON data is received by the NB board, deserialized, and finally the relay is either turned on or off according to the value in the JSON message. More JSON messages can be transmitted from the AWS IoT in order to toggle the relay. Upon deserialization of the JSON message, more processing can be done such as discarding those message if the IMEI is different than that of the current device or if the OpCode is not supported by the device, or any other condition as seems appropriate for the relay actions.

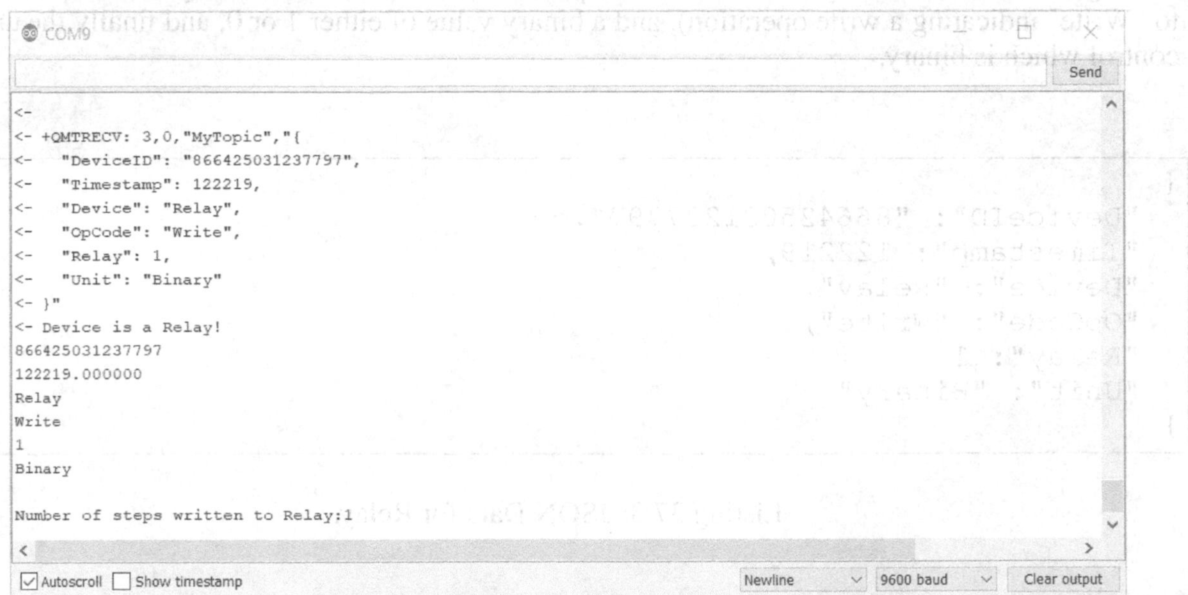

Figure 37.5: JSON Data Received by the Relay.

Chapter 38

Hardware Parts

Table 38.1: Hardware Parts Used in the Book.

Lesson	Hardware Part
NB-IoT Hardware Board	https://www.arduino.cc/en/main/software
JSON Serialization	https://arduinojson.org/
Breadboard	https://www.amazon.com/dp/B07DL13RZH/ref=cm_sw_em_r_mt_dp_U_o8caFbBJ14B40
Resistors	https://www.amazon.com/dp/B072BL2VX1/ref=cm_sw_em_r_mt_dp_U_J5caFbEG3TB3B
Wires	https://www.amazon.com/dp/B01EV70C78/ref=cm_sw_em_r_mt_dp_U_66caFbGKVZX5M
RGB LED	https://www.amazon.com/dp/B077XGF3YR/ref=cm_sw_em_r_mt_dp_U_RYcaFb7CJ1BRM https://www.amazon.com/dp/B07FKKN2TC/ref=cm_sw_em_r_mt_dp_U_5ZcaFbAWSNJZ3
Making Sound Using Active Buzzer	https://www.amazon.com/dp/B01N7NHSY6/ref=cm_sw_em_r_mt_dp_U_B2caFbJMPS7TN
Making Sound Using Passive Buzzer	https://www.amazon.com/dp/B01GJLE5BS/ref=cm_sw_em_r_mt_dp_U_l3caFb6BC5Z33
Keypad	https://www.amazon.com/dp/B07RB47RM1/ref=cm_sw_em_r_mt_dp_U_g1caFbD9KZBKY
Push Button	https://www.amazon.com/dp/B073PY9FNH/ref=cm_sw_em_r_mt_dp_U_ZmcaFb8J1GAWR

Table 38.1 – Continued from Previous Page

Lesson	Hardware Part
Analog Joystick	https://www.amazon.com/dp/B07YZT5NSW/ref=cm_sw_em_r_mt_dp_U_hpcaFbGPDTM0G https://components101.com/sites/default/files/component_datasheet/Joystick%20Module.pdf
Infra-Red (IR) Receiver	https://www.amazon.com/dp/B01EE4VXS0/ref=cm_sw_em_r_mt_dp_U_L39bFb5JZTXV1 https://www.amazon.com/dp/B07MY2SWRZ/ref=cm_sw_em_r_mt_dp_U_zscaFbNB0XJP2 https://www.amazon.com/dp/B07ZP1QMM4/ref=cm_sw_em_r_mt_dp_U_lxcaFb2FDGXZE
RFID	https://www.amazon.com/HiLetgo-RFID-Kit-Arduino-Raspberry/dp/B01CSTW0IA https://www.nxp.com/docs/en/data-sheet/MFRC522.pdf http://www.handsontec.com/dataspecs/RC522.pdf
Eight LED and Shift Register & Seven-Segment Display	https://www.amazon.com/dp/B00EZBGUMC/ref=cm_sw_em_r_mt_dp_U_P-aaFb3KPNXVM http://www.ti.com/lit/ds/symlink/sn74hc595.pdf
Real Time Clock	https://www.amazon.com/dp/B082LTHR28/ref=cm_sw_em_r_mt_dp_U_uycaFbG2C1BST https://datasheets.maximintegrated.com/en/ds/DS1307.pdf
Tilt Sensor Switch	https://www.amazon.com/dp/B00RGN0KY0/ref=cm_sw_em_r_mt_dp_U_fAcaFbA6R0HZ7
Photocell	https://www.amazon.com/dp/B01N7V536K/ref=cm_sw_em_r_mt_dp_U_DBcaFbRBXV9DC
Ultrasonic Sensor	https://www.amazon.com/dp/B07RGB4W8V/ref=cm_sw_em_r_mt_dp_U_UCcaFb7TP9QPH
Temperature and Humidity Sensor	https://www.amazon.com/dp/B01DKC2GQ0/ref=cm_sw_em_r_mt_dp_U_YDcaFbA2T2E3D https://www.mouser.com/datasheet/2/758/DHT11-Technical-Data-Sheet-Translated-Version-1143054.pdf
Water Level Detection Sensor	https://www.amazon.com/dp/B07BGVCCR6/ref=cm_sw_em_r_mt_dp_U_3bbaFbJPEHFAM
Microphone Sound Sensor	https://www.amazon.com/dp/B0173OAWE4/ref=cm_sw_em_r_mt_dp_U_o-9bFbEMAFZ8F

Table 38.1 – Continued from Previous Page

Lesson	Hardware Part
Thermometer & LCD	https://www.amazon.com/dp/B07P5QC26X/ref=cm_sw_em_r_mt_dp_U_hFcaFbZNQ6TD0 https://www.amazon.com/dp/B07S7PJYM6/ref=cm_sw_em_r_mt_dp_U_Na-bFb2WB73SK
Gyroscope Sensor	https://www.amazon.com/GY-521-MPU-6050-Module-Sensors-Accelerometer/dp/B08184X254 https://www.invensense.com/wp-content/uploads/2015/02/MPU-6000-Datasheet1.pdf
Servo Motor	https://www.amazon.com/Micro-Helicopter-Airplane-Remote-Control/dp/B072V529YD http://www.ee.ic.ac.uk/pcheung/teaching/DE1_EE/stores/sg90_datasheet.pdf
Stepper Motor	https://www.amazon.com/dp/B01CP18J4A/ref=cm_sw_em_r_mt_dp_U_AfbaFb8PYRRZS https://www.amazon.com/dp/B00LPK0E5A/ref=cm_sw_em_r_mt_dp_U_pHcaFbRTPETCD https://datasheet.octopart.com/STEP-MOTOR-5V-%2828BYJ-48-5V%29-mikroElektronika-datasheet-17563577.pdf https://www.ti.com/lit/ds/symlink/uln2003a.pdf
Relay	https://www.amazon.com/dp/B07L6J6FHH/ref=cm_sw_em_r_mt_dp_U_Ae-bFbZQ5ZKHS

References

[1] H. Fattah, *5G LTE Narrowband Internet of Things (NB-IoT).* CRC, 2019. [Online]. Available: https://www.routledge.com/5G-LTE-Narrowband-Internet-of-Things-NB-IoT/Fattah/p/book/9781138317604

[2] *Architecture description*, 3GPP™ Std. 36.401, Dec. 2017, v15.0.0.

[3] Recommendation ITU-R M.2083-0. [Online]. Available: https://www.itu.int/rec/R-REC-M.2083-0-201509-I/en

[4] *User Equipment (UE) radio access capabilities*, 3GPP™ Std. 36.306, Jul. 2020, v15.9.0.

[5] *User Equipment (UE) radio access capabilities*, 3GPP™ Std. 36.306, Sep. 2016, v13.3.0.

[6] "3GPP low power wide area," White Paper, GSMA, Oct. 2016.

[7] IoT for smart city. [Online]. Available: https://www.microsoft.com/en-us/internet-of-things/smart-city

[8] MQTT. [Online]. Available: http://MQTT.ORG

[9] "3GPP." [Online]. Available: https://www.3gpp.org/

[10] Coral gables smart city hub. [Online]. Available: https://www.coralgables.com/smartcity

[11] Information technology. [Online]. Available: https://www.coralgables.com/departments/InformationTechnology

[12] "Mobile IoT developer." [Online]. Available: https://www.gsma.com/iot/mobile-iot-modules/

[13] *BG96 Hardware Design*, Quectel, v1.3.

[14] *AT Command Set for User Equipment (UE)*, 3GPP™ Std. 27.007, Dec. 2017, v15.0.0.

[15] *BG96 AT Commands Manual*, Quectel, v2.3.

[16] *BG96 TCP(IP) AT Commands Manual*, Quectel, v1.0.

[17] *BG96 SSL AT Commands Manual*, Quectel, v1.0.

[18] *BG96 MQTT Application Note*, Quectel, v1.1.

[19] *BG96 HTTP(S) AT Commands Manual*, Quectel, v1.0.

[20] *BG96 FILE AT Commands Manual*, Quectel, v1.0.

[21] *BG96 GNSS AT Commands Manual*, Quectel, v1.0.

[22] *BG96 DFOTA User Guide*, Quectel, v1.0.

[23] E. T. Bray, "The javascript object notation (JSON) data interchange format," IETF, RFC 8259, 12 2017. [Online]. Available: https://tools.ietf.org/html/rfc8259

[24] C. Bormann and P. Hoffman, "Concise binary object representation (CBOR)," IETF, RFC 7049, 10 2013. [Online]. Available: https://tools.ietf.org/html/rfc7049

[25] "CBOR." [Online]. Available: https://cbor.io/

[26] B. Petersen, H. Bindner, S. You, and B. Poulsen, "Smart grid serialization comparison: Comparision of serialization for distributed control in the context of the internet of things," in *2017 Computing Conference*, 2017, pp. 1339–1346.

[27] "YACL: Yet another CBOR library." [Online]. Available: https://github.com/telecombretagne/YACL
[28] Javascript tutorial. [Online]. Available: https://www.w3schools.com/js/
[29] Google cloud platform console. [Online]. Available: https://console.cloud.google.com/google/maps-apis/overview
[30] Javascript charting. [Online]. Available: https://www.chartjs.org/

Index

9780367690144